TO PAT

☆ ☆ ☆ ☆ ☆

Contents

☆ ☆ ☆ ☆ ☆

Preface

"POLITICAL SCIENCE with-
out biography," Harold D. Lasswell once remarked, "is a
form of taxidermy." Even *with* biography political science,
history, and the other social sciences and humanities can be
taxidermic; a great deal depends on the definition of biography and the skills, insights, and approach of the biographer.
As John A. Garraty has observed:

> Every biographer, as he settles down at his desk, must make cer-
> tain basic decisions before he begins to write. Shall he do a long
> "definitive" study or a brief study? Shall he simply delineate his
> subject's actions, or strike out boldly and try to explain the signifi-
> cance of these actions? Shall he emphasize his hero's career, or
> stress his personality and the intimacies of his private life?[1]

Presumably the decisions made by biographers have more and
more favored a psychoanalytical and psychological approach.
"The time is coming," Garraty quotes one 1927 critic of this
approach, "when the biographers ain't going to the records
but to the neighbors."

The present study is based both on records and on "neighbors." The former include the Forrestal papers housed in the

---

1. In *The New York Times Book Review*, July 5, 1959. See also John A.
Garraty, *The Nature of Biography* (New York: Alfred A. Knopf, 1957).

Princeton University Library, *The Forrestal Diaries,* edited
by Walter Millis and published by Viking in 1951, letters to
and from Forrestal made available by his friends, and a variety
of other documents. "Neighbors" in this context should refer
to Forrestal's friends, associates, and colleagues in Beacon,
New York, Princeton, Washington, London, Rome, and elsewhere. I interviewed or corresponded with more than fifty
"neighbors," and talked with several psychiatrists who were
involved, directly or indirectly, in Forrestal's illness. My effort
to map the physical route he had traveled in life began with
a visit to the house in Beacon where he was born, and ended
one overcast afternoon when I stood before his grave in
Arlington National Cemetery. Notwithstanding this research,
the pages that follow do not constitute a full-length biography. I set out to produce a psychological portrait of James
Forrestal that would focus on the complex interplay between
his personality, the policy process of which he was a part, and
the political arena in which he was a central figure. When I
began work I suspected there was no clear line between Forrestal the man, Forrestal the Navy Secretary and Secretary of
Defense, and Forrestal the politician and sometime presidential aspirant. I finished my research convinced that these roles
continually merged with one another during most of his
career, with results both good and ill for the world, the nation, and James Forrestal.

My interest in Forrestal, in other words, relates less to the
fact that he was a distinguished American public servant—he
was certainly that—than to his significance in any study of the
relationship between personality, especially personality disorders, and politics. Forrestal was not the first high official to
become mentally ill, but he is the highest-ranking American
official to have committed suicide. The tragedy that ended
his life in May, 1949, underscores the observation that we
need to know much more about the tensions and frustrations
of high office. And if it be doubted that the Forrestal case
proves the point, perhaps it is enough to refer briefly to some

other officials whose medical histories reflect stress and strain in high office.

Since 1900 two American Presidents (excluding McKinley) have died in office, one was incapacitated before the expiration of his term, and one was forced to curtail seriously his activities as a result of heart illness. There is a body of opinion which holds that illness and exhaustion affected decisions made by Presidents Woodrow Wilson and Franklin D. Roosevelt during their last years in the White House.[2] More recently ulcers, hypertension, coronary disease, and "exhaustion" have affected or terminated the political careers of Generals George C. Marshall and Walter Bedell Smith, former Secretaries of State Hull, Stettinius, Byrnes, and Acheson, Under Secretary of State Sumner Welles and Deputy Secretary of Defense Robert A. Lovett.

Needless to say, the "tension diseases" are not exclusively American. The British list of those who have suffered incapacitating physical or mental illness while in office includes Anthony Eden, Ernest Bevin, Stafford Cripps, Neville Chamberlain, Stanley Baldwin, Ramsay MacDonald, and Andrew Bonar Law.[3] Russian victims of stress are hardly less numerous; perhaps the best known are Joseph Stalin (hypertension and paranoia), Andrei Y. Vishinsky (duodenal ulcer), and Nikita Khrushchev (hypertension).

"Is the fate of the world—*our* fate," Burnet Hershey asked in June, 1949, "in the hands of sick men?"[4] One month after Forrestal's death the question was timely, and also timely was a congressman's remark that "The secret malady of

2. The medical histories of Wilson and Roosevelt are given chapter-length treatment in Noah D. Fabricant, M.D., *13 Famous Patients* (Philadelphia: Chilton Company, 1960).

3. In two articles in *The Practitioner,* Dr. Hugh L'Etang has dealt with illness of senior British and French military officers in both world wars, and with the medical histories of Wilson, Roosevelt, Harry Hopkins, Forrestal, MacDonald, Bevin, Cripps, and others. See his "The Health of Statesmen and the Affairs of Nations," *The Practitioner,* January, 1958; and "Ill Health in Senior Officers," *The Practitioner,* April, 1961. I am indebted to these articles and to their author for many valuable insights and suggestions.

4. *The Nation,* June 18, 1949.

a statesman can be as disastrous as his secret diplomacy." In the light of what we know now about the behavior of Hitler and Stalin,[5] it may be permissible to suggest that a statesman's "secret malady" can be more disastrous than secret diplomacy. In the 1960's, when the survival of civilization may depend upon sanity in high places, the question is especially urgent and the remark well worth pondering.

Unfortunately, in Washington, and no doubt in London, Paris, Bonn, and Moscow as well, there is a mental-health mythology that turns aside such a question or at least regards it with suspicion. The mythology, which is discussed at length in the last chapter, holds in essence that Very Important Persons do not become mentally ill, or at any rate not while they are in office. Thus the invariable rule is that VIP's never experience anything more than "exhaustion," and the exhaustion, of course, reflects the fact that they overworked themselves in the nation's service. Only many years later— and sometimes not then—is it discovered that the "exhaustion" was an incapacitating psychosis. This does not deny the reality of a physical and mental fatigue that may precede or accompany a psychosis and require an extended rest or change of job. It remains true, however, that there is no psychosis clinically known as "exhaustion."

Nevertheless, the official mythology remains hostile to the question "Is our fate in the hands of sick men?" and even if it welcomed such a question there would still be difficulties. Understandably, no living government official wishes to be regarded as a psychotic or neurotic, and few want the public to know that they suffer from ulcers, heart disease, hypertension, and other ailments. The families of those who are

---

5. Of a number of books concerned with Hitler's behavior and personality development, one of the most important is Alan Bullock, *Hitler: A Study in Tyranny* (New York: Harper & Brothers, 1953). Less has been published about Stalin, but Khrushchev's report to the 20th Congress of the Soviet Communist Party may be read with profit. His report was published in the United States as *The Crimes of the Stalin Era: A Special Report to the 20th Congress of the Soviet Union,* February 24–25, 1956, supplement to *The New Leader,* July 16, 1956.

dead are hardly more willing to have the physical or mental decline of the deceased made a matter of common knowledge. Where Very Important Persons are concerned, it is almost as if a confession of illness were a confession of weakness, and a confession of weakness a confession of failure.

The popular suspicion of psychiatry as an occult science, the tendency to regard the "headshrinker" as a modern version of the witch doctor, also play a role. If in some circles it is fashionable to discuss one's analysis, in Washington circles it is awkward and may even be costly to admit that one is making regular visits to a psychiatrist. Far from agreeing that public officials would benefit from psychoanalysis or psychotherapy, the public is more apt to conclude that those who require a psychic massage at any time in their lives are unfit to hold office. In effect, a known psychiatric patient has as much chance of being elected President as a known homosexual or alcoholic.

This does not deny the very real problems involved in diagnosing, treating, and curing personality disorders. Differences among psychiatrists regarding theory and therapy are sharp and frequently acrimonious; the outsider, listening to psychiatrists and psychoanalysts argue a case, is sometimes tempted to exclaim "Physician, heal thyself!" And even if there is agreement, can any psychiatrist be certain that a depressed and suicidal patient is cured, able to return to the family and job, capable of resuming a normal life? If the job is a political position of the highest importance, if the patient has responsibility for decisions that affect the course of history, the psychiatrist must be courageous indeed to recommend resumption of appointive or elective office. And even more courage is required on the part of appointing officials or voters who have some knowledge of the situation if his recommendation is to be accepted.

The widespread feeling that exploration of the psyche may be more art than science is reflected in the relative paucity of biographies that base themselves on psychoanalytic insights and formulations. Despite pleas that historians and social scientists make more use of psychoanalytic concepts, pleas similar to that issued by Harvard historian William L. Langer in 1957, few biographies and biographical studies cast even a glance in Freud's direction.[6]

While it is true that not all great men require a psychiatric biography, anymore than all men require a psychiatrist, there are many distinguished heroes and villains in history whose biographies—to paraphrase the expression quoted earlier—lacking psychiatric insights, tend to be taxidermic. One thinks immediately of Alexander Hamilton and Aaron Burr, of John Stuart Mill and William Gladstone, of Elizabeth I and Catherine de Medici. In certain instances, the most suggestive treatment of an important personage has appeared in the form of a novel, for example, the novels that were inspired by the careers of Ramsay MacDonald and Huey Long.

But despite the difficulties that arise in efforts to analyze motives and probe the unconscious, such efforts must continue to be made if there is ever to be any reliable answer to the question "Is our fate in the hands of sick men?" The question will never be a welcome one, but it would be foolhardy to pretend that it does not exist. The illnesses of Wilson and Roosevelt, the suicides of James Forrestal and John Winant, draw attention to the question, and so do the recent novels and films that concern themselves with the possibility of annihilation as a consequence of illness or error. The film *Dr. Strangelove*, reads a full-page advertisement in *The New York Times*, is

A Nightmare Comedy in which a psychotic Air Force General triggers an ingenious, foolproof and irrevocable scheme, unleashing his Wing of B-52 H-Bombers to attack Russia.

6. The outstanding exceptions in recent years have been Alexander and Juliette George, *Woodrow Wilson and Colonel House: A Personality Study* (New York: John Day, 1956); Erik Erikson, *Young Man Luther: A Study in Psychoanalysis and History* (New York: W. W. Norton, 1958); Alex Gottfried, *Boss Cermak of Chicago* (Seattle: University of Washington Press, 1962).

The President of the United States, unable to recall the aircraft, is forced to cooperate with the Soviet Premier in a bizarre attempt to save the world.[7]

Such books and films do not establish the existence of "psychotic" Air Force generals, much less demonstrate that our fate is being decided by "sick men." But their popularity—many of the books have been best-sellers—tends to confirm the impression that there is a good deal of anxiety about the physical and mental condition of our leaders.

The following pages assume that this anxiety is both unhealthy and unnecessary. Forrestal's illness and suicide were not inevitable; the illnesses and suicides of other world leaders are not inevitable; and it is not inevitable that the world community become ill and commit suicide. But there will be other Forrestals and other wars if attempts are not made to prevent, detect, treat, and cure those illnesses that affect rational mental processes in decision-making environments. The Forrestal case, in and of itself, does not indicate with certainty what steps need to be taken, although certain proposals are advanced in the last chapter. More knowledge, more discussion, and more case studies are necessary if citizens everywhere are to have some assurance that the policy process does not suffer from the contamination of illnesses that affect the mind.

In the meantime, the question "Is our fate in the hands of sick men?" becomes ever more relevant, and anxiety about the answer becomes ever more widespread. Perhaps it is well to remember that certain sicknesses, whether physical or mental, personal or national, are contagious. Some of them can also be fatal.

---

7. *The New York Times,* Western Edition, February 18, 1963. See also Eugene Burdick and Harvey Wheeler, *Fail-Safe* (New York: McGraw-Hill, 1962) and Fletcher Knebel and Charles W. Bailey, *Seven Days in May* (New York: Harper & Brothers, 1962).

I

☆ ☆ ☆ ☆ ☆

Death of a Hero

INITIALLY THERE was no reason to suppose that the resignation as Secretary of Defense of James Forrestal would differ markedly from the resignations of other high officials of the Truman Administration. As was customary in such cases, Forrestal, on March 28, 1949, was present at the Pentagon when his successor, Louis Johnson, lawyer, former American Legion Commander, and principal fund-raiser for the Truman-Barkley ticket in 1948, formally replaced him in the nation's second-ranking Cabinet post. Following the ceremony, and also in accordance with custom, Forrestal proceeded to the White House for a final word with President Harry S Truman. Much to his surprise, Forrestal found the President assembled with a large number of Cabinet members, military officers (including the Joint Chiefs of Staff), and other government dignitaries. Truman read a citation honoring Forrestal for "meritorious and distinguished service," added his own personal congratulations, and pinned on Forrestal's coat lapel the Distinguished Service Medal. The retiring Secretary of Defense was visibly flustered, and he was totally unable to respond to the President's action. But speeches on such occasions are not called for, whereas emotional reactions, at the expense of speech, are hardly out of order. The depth and intensity of Forrestal's feelings, the exact nature of the emotions that prevented him from making an appropriate response to the citation, few at the time, apparently, were able to gauge. Most of those among his friends and associates who were aware that Forrestal was suffering from extreme physical and nervous exhaustion, that he had lost a good deal of weight during the preceding months, and that he more and more frequently was experiencing moods of deep depression, were convinced that he required nothing more than a long period of rest and relaxation.

The day following the White House ceremony Forrestal was further honored by the Committee on Armed Services of the House of Representatives. At a special meeting on March 29 of the Committee, which was also attended by Secretary Johnson, Chairman Carl Vinson paid tribute to Forrestal's "long and brilliant career." Much of that career, Vinson noted, had been devoted to finance and industry. "But it is in the service of your country," he continued, "as a high official of our Government, that you have most singularly distinguished yourself among your fellow citizens." After reviewing Forrestal's achievements as Under Secretary of the Navy, Secretary of the Navy, and Secretary of Defense, Vinson declared that the members of the Committee "want it long remembered and permanently recorded here that your outstanding talents and accomplishments on the highest levels of our Government have been appreciated and valued highly by this committee and the Congress." Vinson then presented to Forrestal a silver bowl, upon which, he told the retiring Secretary, you will find engraved "our names in testimony of our regard. That regard is also indelibly inscribed in our hearts."

Similar sentiments were expressed by Representative Dewey Short. "As you leave us, Mr. Secretary," he concluded his remarks, "we want to wish you continued success, which we know your clean and clear mind, your stout and honest heart, and your ready and able hands will achieve. We hope most of all that you will get just a little well-earned and well-deserved rest. We wish you the best of health and God-speed in all your undertakings."

Secretary Johnson testified that he subscribed "to everything that has been said about Jim Forrestal's record." He added that he and Forrestal had worked closely together during the preceding sixty days, in the course of which "I came to value Jim Forrestal's friendship. I came to value, too, a keen, incisive mind, one of the best analytical minds I have ever come to know. . . . I know I can do a little better job from this sixty days of intensive effort on Jim Forrestal's part to indoctrinate me." Referring to his affection for Forrestal and his appreciation of Forrestal's work as Secretary of Defense, Johnson emphasized "that never knowingly will there be a word come out of the Pentagon against the great record of Jim Forrestal."

In contrast to his performance at the White House the day before, Forrestal made three brief but gracious speeches during the Committee's special session. He commended the Committee and its Chairman for their work in building the defense forces, expressed confidence in Secretary Johnson, and called attention to the contributions of the three Service Secretaries, especially Secretary of the Army Royall "who has given the most devoted and loyal service," and Secretary of the Air Force Symington "whose zeal and high devotion to his beliefs will be a lasting tribute to his record."[1]

Although it was not known at the time, Forrestal's attendance at the special session of the House Armed Services Committee was his last public appearance. Following the ceremony at the old House Office Building, Symington expressed a desire to accompany Forrestal on the ride back to

---

1. *Congressional Record*, House of Representatives, Appendix A, 1953–1955, March 30, 1949.

the Pentagon. "There is something," he told Forrestal, "I would like to talk to you about." When they reached the Pentagon, Forrestal went to a small office that had been assigned to him for the purpose of dictating replies to the many persons who had written or wired him deploring his departure from public life.

A short time later, one of his aides entered the office and immediately became aware that Forrestal was sitting in an extremely rigid position. He was still wearing his hat, the bowl was in front of him on the desk, and he was staring at the bare wall directly opposite. Forrestal appeared not to know that someone had entered the room. His assistant, disturbed by Forrestal's manner and appearance, asked, "Is something the matter?" Forrestal did not at first reply, but after the question was repeated he responded, "You are a loyal fellow." He was to repeat that statement several times during the next few hours.

When Forrestal left the Pentagon for his home in Georgetown, he was bewildered to find that he no longer enjoyed the use of an official government limousine. He appeared to be dazed by that knowledge, and his aide, who was now greatly alarmed by his behavior, arranged for the two of them to be driven to Forrestal's Georgetown house by Dr. Vannevar Bush's chauffeur. Finding no one at home when they arrived, and sensing that Forrestal should not be left alone, the aide got in touch with Ferdinand Eberstadt, a New York investment banker and one of Forrestal's closest personal friends. The aide suggested that Eberstadt persuade Forrestal to fly to Hobe Sound, Florida, where his wife, Robert Lovett, and other friends were vacationing at the time. Eberstadt was to follow this advice, but first he proceeded to the house to make his own judgment of his friend's physical and mental condition.

He was shocked to discover that Forrestal was extremely agitated and depressed. In the privacy of his home Forrestal confessed to Eberstadt that he was a complete failure and that he was considering suicide. He also expressed the conviction that a number of individuals—Communists, Jews, and certain persons in the White House—had formed a conspiracy to "get" him, and had finally succeeded. He insisted that some of "them" were probably in his home at that very moment, and he proceeded to search closets and other areas of the house where they might be hiding.

Shocked by his behavior, Eberstadt telephoned Secretary Johnson to report that Forrestal was a very sick man in need of immediate medical attention. Johnson agreed that Forrestal undoubtedly would be helped by a long rest in Hobe Sound, where Robert Lovett and some of Forrestal's other close friends maintained residences. An Air Force Constellation was made immediately ready for the trip to Florida, and on March 29, in the early evening of the same day that Forrestal had been honored by the House Armed Services Committee, the Air Force plane with Forrestal aboard put down at a small field near Hobe Sound.

The Forrestal party was met by Mrs. Forrestal, Lovett, and a small circle of friends. Lovett recalls that Forrestal, when he debarked from the plane, was so changed in appearance that it was not at all easy to recognize him. In addition to looking haggard and much older than his years (he was fifty-seven), Forrestal's always thin mouth was so tightly drawn that neither the upper nor the lower lip could be seen. His eyes, which appeared sunken in an ashen face, searched suspiciously among the small group of friends that had gathered to meet him. At one point, when it seemed that he would fall off the ladder from the plane (there was no landing ramp available), Lovett reached up to catch him. In an effort to be jocular, Lovett said, "Jim, I hope you've brought your golf clubs, because the weather here has been perfect for golf."

Forrestal's only reply was, "Bob, they're after me."

During the next several days Forrestal made at least one suicide attempt. As a result, all implements that can be, and have been, used in suicide efforts—such as knives, razor blades, belts, and so on—were hidden or kept under surveillance. Forrestal was at no time left alone; when he was taking a shower or shaving himself, swimming in the surf or strolling on the beach, one or more friends was always in his company. Since proximity to the ocean presented special risks, Forrestal was always accompanied in the water by a friend who was an especially strong swimmer.

There were occasions during the few days in Hobe Sound when it appeared that Forrestal's mental and physical state was improving. At times he seemed to be enjoying himself, and once or twice he was even able to joke about the fact that his friends found it necessary, as a precaution against his committing suicide, to join him in the bathroom. But such occasions were rare; Forrestal's general mood was one of depression and despondency. Even when he was relatively relaxed, the conviction expressed to Lovett, that "they're after me," was never entirely absent. One afternoon, for example, while walking along the beach, Forrestal pointed to a row of metal sockets fixed in the sand for holding beach umbrellas, and remarked: "We had better not discuss anything here. Those things are wired, and everything we say is being recorded." There were also frequent indications that Forrestal was profoundly disturbed by real or imagined threats to the nation's security. He was certain that the Communists were planning an imminent invasion of the United States. Indeed, at various times he talked as if the invasion had already taken place. He expressed anxiety about the presence of Communists, or communist influence, in the White House, the Defense Establishment, and other agencies of the government. Convinced that the American people had been duped by Communists and communist sympathizers, Forrestal believed that he had been chosen as their Number

One target for liquidation as a consequence of his efforts to alert Americans to the communist menace.

Clearly Forrestal was a very ill man, but he was not too ill to be aware that he required an immediate psychiatric examination. The evening of his arrival at Hobe Sound he indicated that he would be willing to talk with Dr. William Menninger of the famous Menninger Foundation in Topeka, who was consultant to the Surgeon General of the Army. Menninger, then in New York, was reached by Dr. Howard A. Rusk, medical editor of *The New York Times*. Menninger had met Forrestal during the war, had served as a consultant to the Navy's Research and Development Board, and had talked with Forrestal on several occasions about personnel problems in the Armed Forces. As a consequence, Forrestal and Menninger had become casual acquaintances, and it is doubtful that Forrestal at that time knew any other psychiatrist.

Menninger and Eberstadt flew to Florida in a private plane, and Menninger had several lengthy talks with Forrestal on the evening of his arrival. The following day, March 31, he was joined by Captain George N. Raines, chief psychiatrist at the United States Naval Hospital at Bethesda, Maryland. Upon his arrival, Dr. Raines was informed that Forrestal had indicated a desire to talk with Menninger, and Raines therefore did not interview Forrestal until the latter had returned to Washington. "On ethical grounds," Raines subsequently stated,

I felt it improper to see Mr. Forrestal since he had designated a physician of his own choice. . . . After Dr. Menninger had interviewed Mr. Forrestal, he and Mr. Eberstadt, acting for the family, and I met in consultation. It was Dr. Menninger's opinion, based on his examination of Mr. Forrestal, that the patient was suffering with a severe depression of the type seen in operational fatigue during the war."[2]

---

2. Quoted in the *New York Herald Tribune*, May 24, 1949.

After some discussion among the two psychiatrists and Eberstadt, it was determined that Forrestal's condition required his immediate admission to a hospital. Although the medical services, including hospital facilities, of the Menninger Foundation were available for the purpose, the Bethesda Naval Hospital was deemed more appropriate for the treatment of Forrestal's illness. One argument in favor of Bethesda was that it was a general hospital, whereas the Menninger organization was solely concerned with mental illness. It was assumed, or at least hoped, that with Forrestal at Bethesda, the specific nature of Forrestal's condition could be kept secret from the public at large. For one thing, security arrangements, the screening of visitors, and the isolation of Forrestal from inquiring newspapermen could be more easily arranged than would be the case in Topeka. It was also thought that Forrestal himself would benefit, in a variety of ways, from confinement at the Naval Hospital. As a patient in a general hospital, Forrestal would be less inclined, perhaps, to regard himself as hopelessly and incurably ill. Furthermore, Washington (of which Bethesda is essentially a suburb) was "home," and his being there might be supportive of recovery. As recovery proceeded, he would be able to see relatives, friends, and associates, most of whom lived convenient distances from the hospital. Finally, there was no question that the treatment he would receive at Bethesda was among the best available in the United States.

For these reasons, Forrestal, accompanied by Menninger and a few friends, was flown to Washington on April 2 and formally admitted to the Naval Hospital that evening. The plane in which they traveled taxied to a remote corner of the airfield, to escape the attention of the press and those who, given the opportunity, would have been merely curious.

Forrestal, although he had been given sedation, was in a state of extreme agitation during the flight from Florida. Again he talked of those "trying to get me," and of suicide.

At one point he raised the question whether he was being "punished" for having been a "bad Catholic"—"bad" referring to the fact that he had not practiced his faith for more than thirty years, and had married a divorced woman. Although he was repeatedly reassured that he was not being "punished" and that no one wished him ill, much less wanted to destroy him, Forrestal's agitation increased during the trip in a private car from the airfield to the hospital. He made several attempts to leave the car while it was in motion, and had to be forcibly restrained. Arriving at Bethesda he declared that he did not expect to leave the hospital alive. It was not clear whether he was referring to suicide or to a conviction that he would be murdered.

Forrestal was visited the following day, April 3, and again on April 6, by Menninger. Menninger did not see the patient after that date, and although there were occasional consultations between Raines and Menninger in the course of the following weeks, Raines was officially in charge of the case.

Raines diagnosed Forrestal's illness as involutional melancholia, a depressive condition sometimes seen in persons who have reached middle age. In most cases of involutional melancholia,

mental faculties in general become less acute. There is a tendency to bewail the past, and to feel that the future has nothing in store. The mind is occupied with the "might-have-beens," and in consequence doubt, indecision, fear and anxiety readily show themselves. The glands of internal secretion begin to fail in their functioning, and the bodily health is lowered.[3]

Although some psychiatrists regard involutional melancho-

---

3. Sir David Henderson and R. D. Gillespie, *A Text-Book of Psychiatry*, Seventh Edition (New York: Oxford University Press, 1950), p. 272. See also Norman Cameron, *The Psychology of Behavior Disorders* (Boston: Houghton Mifflin Company, 1947), pp. 521–523; Oscar J. Kaplan, *Mental Disorders in Later Life*, Second Edition (Stanford, Calif.: Stanford University Press, 1956), pp. 246–259; and *American Handbook of Psychiatry*, Silvano Arieti, Ed. (New York: Basic Books, 1959), 2 vols. I, pp. 508–546.

lia psychosis as one of the mixed states of manic-depression, and others feel that it is a form of schizophrenia, there is broad agreement that the symptoms include anxiety, self-doubt, depression, and nihilistic tendencies.

The underlying personality characteristics of a typical involutional melancholic, according to one authoritative source, include a devotion to hard work and pride in work. Many of those who develop the illness are "sensitive, meticulous, over-conscientious, over-scrupulous, busy, active people. . . ."[4] They have also been described as showing "a narrow range of interests, poor facility for readjustment, asocial trends, inability to maintain friendships, intolerance and poor adult sexual adjustment, also a pronounced and rigid ethical code and a proclivity to reticence. . . ."[5] In the treatment of involutional melancholics, suicide is always a great risk, and therefore the average patient "is best treated in a mental hospital."[6]

A percentage of involutional melancholics experience paranoid ideation; in Forrestal's case such ideation was particulary apparent. The belief that he was a victim of "plots" and "conspiracies" antedated his visit to Hobe Sound, and despite the treatment prescribed by Raines in Bethesda, this delusion was never fully displaced in his mind.

When it was reported that Forrestal was a patient at Bethesda, there was a sense, the *Washington Post* (now the *Washington Post & Times Herald*) commented editorially, of "continuing shock" in Washington circles. "It had long been known," ran the *Post* editorial of April 9, "that the former Secretary of Defense was worn out." But the general public, the *Post* stated,

little realizes the onerousness of the burden that is imposed upon its public servants in these harassing days . . . [who] have to live and work under the white glare of criticism.

---

4. Henderson and Gillespie, p. 274.
5. *Ibid.*
6. *Ibid.* p. 292.

In Forrestal's case, added the *Post*, the burden was particularly difficult because the Department of Defense was not adequately organized to accomplish the purpose for which it was created. The editorial expressed the hope that Forrestal's illness—"the revelation of the nervous exhaustion that he was reduced to—should expedite legislative action." Referring to a current proposal to give the Secretary of Defense greater administrative authority, the *Post* urged Congress to provide

a framework of organization adequate to the tasks expected of our administrators. In the meantime Mr. Forrestal will have the good wishes of everybody who observed him day after day and sometimes night after night trying to carry out a Sisyphean assignment without wincing and without losing the modesty and naturalness which high office ruins in most men.

A *New York Times* editorial of April 13 quoted Forrestal's "physician" as saying that the former Defense Secretary was suffering from "operational fatigue." The term "operational fatigue," the *Times* informed its readers, was coined during the Second World War "to describe the physical and emotional reaction that came from fighting too long without respite." Some soldiers, the editorial continued,

developed the symptoms after a short time at the front; others fought for months without breaking. . . . However, one fact was established: every man has a breaking point, and when this point comes he must rest.

For Forrestal, the *Times* remarked, there was no respite after V-E Day or V-J Day:

He continued in the "front lines" seven days a week for eight years, first fighting the war, and then struggling with the problems of reorganization and unification. Fortunately, with rest and proper treatment, the outlook for recovery from operational fatigue is excellent. For this we can all be grateful, for if ever a man gave his strength and his energy to his country, James Forrestal has done so.

His "untiring efforts and self-sacrifice," the editorial concluded, "have earned for him the gratitude and respect of
his fellow-citizens, and the rest he so richly deserves."

On April 14 the *Washington Post* published a further
and more extended comment on Forrestal's illness under the
title "Job Fatigue." The illness has become "familiar," the
Post commented, "since the United States has become a
world power and assumed Atlas-like responsibilities." Once
more the *Post* admonished Congress that the reorganization
of the Defense Department was a pressing need. Forrestal,
the editorial pointed out, "was compelled to work day and
night on details that ought to have been done by an Under-
secretary and Assistant Secretaries of Defense."

But there is "another lesson," continued the *Post,* to be
drawn from Forrestal's illness:

Job fatigue is apt most generally to develop as soon as an administrator quits his job. All keyed up for years, he finds no rest
when he stops, only a nervous tension which brings on a crackup.
In England, cabinet members and under-cabinet members still
have their seats in Parliament even after resignation, and the
problem is not so acute there.

Nevertheless, the editorial added, the problem is not unknown in England, and to make its point the editorial quoted
a lengthy statement by Winston Churchill referring to his
personal experience following his departure from the Admiralty in late May, 1915. "The change," it quoted Churchill,
"left me gasping."

Like a sea beast flushed up from the depths, or a diver too
suddenly hoisted, my veins threatened to burst from the fall in
pressure. I had great anxiety and no means of relieving it; I had
vehement convictions and small power to give effect to them. . . .
At a moment when every fiber of my being was inflamed to
action, I was forced to remain a spectator of the tragedy, placed
cruelly in a front seat.

Noting that "the muse of painting" came to Churchill's

rescue, and "saved him from job fatigue," the *Post* concluded that the problem

is remediable not only by Government provision of a proper framework of organization, but also by the officials themselves—and all of us—developing interests, as Churchill did with his painting, that would not leave them high and dry on retirement.

In his syndicated column of May 5, Marquis Childs commented critically on one of the more "sensational" descriptions of Forrestal's illness and the symptoms alleged to have accompanied it. Drew Pearson, Childs reported, had declared on the radio that Forrestal was "out of his mind," that in Florida he had rushed out in the street screaming that "the Russians are attacking." Pearson "implied," Childs continued,

that Forrestal had been mentally unbalanced prior to his resignation and suggested that the decisions he took in his last months in office be reviewed. That broadcast, giving what Forrestal's friends and family say was a false picture of his illness, has become the base of a wide-spread Communist propaganda campaign.

Behind the Iron Curtain, Childs further wrote, "millions are being led to believe that Forrestal's 'insanity' is the explanation for the Marshall Plan and the Atlantic Pact. It is hinted that while Forrestal's condition is acute, all American policy makers suffer from the same phobia." The true facts of the case, Childs urged, should be revealed. Withholding news "the public should legitimately have opens the way for sensationalism and exaggeration." Hinting that Pearson's statements fell wholly or partly in such categories, Childs emphasized that Secretary of Defense Johnson "recently visited Forrestal and reported him as recovering rapidly with the prospect that within a few weeks he would be able to make a survey trip around the world as requested by Johnson."

Despite Childs's plea for the release of those facts to which the public legitimately was entitled, the nature of Forrestal's illness was not disclosed until after his death.

While he was alive, those who discounted Pearson's reporting—and with few exceptions almost all newspapers, news
magazines, reporters, and columnists refused to publish
"sensational" accounts of Forrestal's illness—could believe
either that Forrestal was suffering from no more than
"fatigue" and "exhaustion," or that he had experienced
something that was identical with, or similar to, a "nervous
breakdown." The government officials and newspapermen
who were familiar with the details of the case were unable,
or unwilling, to provide the public with an accurate report.
Throughout Forrestal's seven weeks in Bethesda, there was,
of course, a good deal of unauthorized gossip and speculation
about his condition. But despite the fact that he was suffering from a severe psychosis, the public was repeatedly assured by government spokesmen and the news media that
Forrestal was not seriously ill and that his complete recovery
was probable, even certain.

Meanwhile, the treatment prescribed for Forrestal at
Bethesda proceeded in accordance with Raines's diagnosis of
the illness as a case of involutional melancholia. Forrestal's
response was encouraging to the narcosis employed during
the first week of treatment, and the following four weeks
were devoted to subshock insulin therapy accompanied by
daily sessions of psychotherapy. The results of the insulin
therapy, however, were less successful than had been hoped.
Nevertheless, by the beginning of May, Raines and other
members of the Bethesda psychiatric staff observed a marked
improvement in the patient's condition, although the improvement, in Raines's words, "as is usual in such cases, was
not steadily upward, but gradually upward in a wavelike
advance. A tendency to increased depression toward the end
of the week was early noted."[7]

Since there were clear signs that Forrestal was recovering,
signs that included a weight gain of approximately five
pounds, the close watch over Forrestal's movements that was

7. Quoted in *New York Herald Tribune*, May 24, 1949.

maintained at all times was somewhat relaxed in the early part of May. While a trained resident of the hospital, or a Navy Medical Corpsman, was stationed each night in a room adjoining his suite on the sixteenth floor, Forrestal in May was permitted certain liberties that had been denied him in April. For example, he was encouraged by Raines to leave his room occasionally and visit other patients on the floor. He was also allowed to use the telephone at the nurses' desk down the hall from his room. The flow of visitors increased; he was seen frequently by his only surviving brother, Henry L. A. Forrestal, and on separate occasions in May by President Truman and Defense Secretary Johnson, among others. Other "liberties" included access to a small diet kitchen, or pantry, which was directly across the corridor from his suite, although the use of the diet kitchen was customarily denied patients.[8] The window screen in the diet kitchen, unlike the heavy metal screens in his bedroom that were kept locked, was fastened only by small hooks, and Forrestal was permitted to go alone to the kitchen to make himself a snack or a cup of coffee.

In view of Forrestal's suicidal tendencies, the relaxation of restrictions involved a "calculated risk," but one justified, in Raines's opinion, by his continuing improvement and also the need to restore, as far as possible, his confidence in himself. Forrestal bitterly resented these restrictions, and it was hoped that their relaxation would be therapeutic in the sense that he would regard his greater freedom of movement as evidence that he was recovering, that, in a word, he could be trusted *not* to take his own life. Moreover, in frank discussions with Raines of his depressions and suicidal tendencies, he had repeatedly declared that if he committed suicide it would be by hanging himself and not by jumping from the window.

---

8. A typed notice over the work space in the diet kitchen read, "Mr. Forrestal's diet: regular diet with large portions, extra feeding at 1500 and 2100 (3 P.M. and 9 P.M.) to be taken in by nurse."

By May 14 Forrestal's apparent improvement was such that Raines discontinued the daily psychotherapy sessions, and made plans to leave Washington on or about May 18 for a combined vacation and trip to Montreal to attend the forthcoming meeting of the American Psychiatric Association. He also had previously advised Mrs. Forrestal that she could depart for Europe, as originally planned, on May 12, and Forrestal's elder son, Michael, that he could return to his post with the Economic Cooperation Administration in Paris on May 13. In both instances his advice was accepted. The younger of Forrestal's two sons, Peter, was working in Washington at the time and was living at the family home in Georgetown.

Raines's last interview with Forrestal took place on the morning of May 18. "I found him somewhat better than on the corresponding day of the preceding week," he subsequently stated,

and felt that barring any unforeseen incident he would be able to carry along during my absence from the city. I also felt at that time that he was nearing the end of his illness and that the next thirty days should see him ready to leave the hospital.

I further recognized the well-known psychiatric fact that the next thirty days would constitute the most dangerous period of the illness as far as suicide was concerned, inasmuch as suicidal preoccupations had to be present and at the same time privileges had to be extended to the patient to allow his full recovery.[9]

As previously noted, Raines had early observed in Forrestal "a tendency to increased depression toward the end of the week." On Friday, May 20, however, two days after Raines's departure, there was no visible sign that Forrestal was depressed; indeed, he appeared to one visitor to be in high spirits. Rear Admiral Morton D. Willcutts, commanding officer of the Naval Medical Center, which includes the

---

9. Quoted in the *New York Herald Tribune*, May 24, 1949.

Bethesda facility, visited Forrestal at noon, and watched him consume a large steak lunch. Forrestal had arisen that morning, Admiral Willcutts later reported, with a sparkle in his eye. He was "meticulously shaven," and eager to greet his visitors.

So far as is known, the remainder of that day and Saturday, May 21, passed without incident and without anyone observing any marked change in Forrestal's frame of mind. Late on the evening of May 21 Forrestal informed the Naval Corpsman on duty that he did not want a sedative or sleeping pill and that he was planning to stay up rather late and read. When the Corpsman looked in at approximately 1:45 on the morning of Sunday, May 22, Forrestal was copying onto several sheets of paper Sophocles's brooding "Chorus from Ajax," as translated by William Mackworth Praed in Mark Van Doren's *Anthology of World Poetry*. The Corpsman went on a brief errand while Forrestal transcribed:

> Fair Salamis, the billows' roar
>   Wanders around thee yet,
> And sailors gaze upon thy shore
>   Firm in the Ocean set.
> Thy son is in a foreign clime
>   Where Ida feeds her countless flocks,
>   Far from thy dear, remembered rocks,
> Worn by the waste of time—
> Comfortless, nameless, hopeless save
> In the dark prospect of the yawning grave. . . .
>
> Woe to the mother in her close of day,
> Woe to her desolate heart and temples gray,
>   When she shall hear
> Her loved one's story whispered in her ear!
>   "Woe, woe!" will be the cry—
> No quiet murmur like the tremulous wail
> Of the lone bird, the querulous nightingale—[10]

---

10. The "Chorus from Ajax" continued:
        "But shrieks that fly
    Piercing, and wild, and loud, shall mourn the tale;

When Forrestal had written "night" of the word "nightingale," he ceased his copying, inserted the sheets into the back of the book, and placed the open book on his night table. He then walked across the corridor into the diet kitchen. Tying one end of his dressing-gown sash to the radiator just below the window, and the other end around his neck, he removed the screen, and jumped or hung from the window. When the diet kitchen was inspected later, it was found that the windowsill and the cement work immediately outside were scratched, suggesting but not establishing that Forrestal had hung suspended for a brief time and had tried to climb back through the window. But no one will ever know with certainty what transpired in those final moments. Seconds after Forrestal entered the diet kitchen a nurse on the seventh floor of the hospital heard a loud crash. Forrestal's broken body, his watch still running, was found on the roof of a third-floor passageway connecting two wings of the hospital. The dressing-gown sash was still tied around his neck. According to Rank Brochart, coroner of Montgomery County, Maryland, who arrived on the scene shortly thereafter, death was instantaneous.

Raines, notified in Montreal of Forrestal's death, immediately flew back to Washington. That evening he issued a statement which said, in part, that responsibility for the

---

And she will beat her breast, and rend her hair
Scattering the silver locks that Time hath left her there.
Oh! when the pride of Graecia's noblest race
Wanders, as now, in darkness and disgrace,
              When Reason's day
Sets rayless—joyless—quenched in cold decay,
              better to die, and sleep
The never-waking sleep, than linger on,
And dare to live, when the soul's life is gone;
              but thou shalt weep,
Thou wretched father, for thy dearest son,
Thy best beloved, by inward Furies torn,
The deepest, bitterest curse thine ancient house hath borne!"

suicide rested with him and not with Forrestal's family or with other naval authorities. Noting that the details were being investigated by "a special board,"[11] Raines stated:

Psychiatrically, it is my opinion that Mr. Forrestal was seized with a sudden fit of despondence in the evening and early morning of May 22. This is extremely common in all depressions of the severity of which he suffered.

Suicide is the mortality rate of therapeutic psychiatry. The Navy has not and does not subscribe to the view that psychiatric patients should be thrown in a dungeon. It is our belief that calculated risks must be accepted for the practice of modern psychiatry. . . .

It is needless to add that I am deeply regretful of the unfortunate outcome in Mr. Forrestal's case.[12]

Three days after his fatal plunge from the sixteenth floor of Bethesda Naval Hospital, James Forrestal was buried with full military honors in Arlington National Cemetery. The ceremonies on Wednesday morning, May 25, began with a nineteen-gun salute, the howitzers booming at three-minute intervals as the caisson bearing Forrestal's casket made its way toward the central amphitheater. The caisson was preceded by soldiers from the three military services, each of which also supplied a band. The Naval Academy Band, the most prominent, played Beethoven's "March of the Hero," Chopin's "Funeral March," and Handel's March from *Saul*.

When the caisson, drawn by seven gray horses, arrived at the amphitheater, the casket was taken up by eight Service men, representing the Army, Navy, Marine Corps, and Air Force. Awaiting the casket in the chapel of the amphitheater were President Truman, Vice President Alben W. Barkley,

---

11. Both the Surgeon General of the United States and the Navy conducted official inquiries. The results of these investigations have never been made public.

12. Quoted in the *New York Herald Tribune*, May 24, 1949.

and a group of honorary pallbearers that included former President Herbert Hoover. The funeral service was performed by the Right Reverend Wallace E. Conkling, Episcopal Church Bishop of Chicago and a friend of the Forrestal family. Bishop Conkling read from the 46th and 130th psalms, from the Episcopal Book of Common Prayer, and from I Corinthians.

As the procession moved to the graveside, the Army Band played "Onward Christian Soldiers." At the request of the family, the group at the site of burial was confined to members of the family and a few close friends or associates of the former Defense Secretary, including Bishop Conkling, Rear Admiral William N. Thomas, Navy Chief of Chaplains; Admiral John E. Gingrich, and Raines. Following the Episcopal Committal Service, read by Bishop Conkling, the howitzers boomed their second nineteen-gun salute, this time in rapid fire. There were three volleys of rifle fire, and as "Taps" was sounded, Forrestal's casket was lowered into the grave.

One of those present in the amphitheater was Senator Arthur H. Vandenberg, Republican of Michigan, who confided to his diary on May 25:

It was a beautiful clear day—but sharp and cold (and I all but froze in the Memorial Amphitheatre at Arlington). I was in a box next to the President. The papers say that there were 6,000 present. It was a full military funeral. Of course Jimmy wasn't very big—but the casket looked *so small!* There were four of the most famous bands in the country. The Marine Band played "Nearer My God to Thee" with infinite pathos. The Navy Band played Handel's "Largo"—and of course that put me wholly out of commission. The Air Force Band played "Lead Kindly Light"—!!!

And then as they slowly marched from the Amphitheatre to the high hillside where Jimmy finds his peace at last, the big Army Band played "Onward Christian Soldiers"—and I thought I would expire. There was something about it all which was so intimately tragic and yet so spiritually exalted. I am sure Jimmy did not die in vain. Mrs. F. did not come to the Amphitheatre; but, of course she was with a rather small group of us at the grave. So be it. And amen.[13]

Reporters present estimated that more than 6,500 persons, of whom 2,500 were former friends and associates of Forrestal, attended the funeral ceremonies. "Observers of the service today," ran a *New York Times* account of May 25, "said it had not been surpassed by the ceremonies for any of the nation's great heroes buried here. The last such funeral was that of General of the armies [*sic*] John J. Pershing. . . .[14]

At the time of his burial Forrestal's grave was headed by a small wooden marker that read:

JAMES FORRESTAL
Lot 674
Lt. U.S.N.

"Lt. U.S.N." was a reference to Forrestal's Navy rank in World War I. Mrs. Forrestal had been requested to propose a permanent inscription for the tombstone, and she suggested the following:

JAMES FORRESTAL
Navy Lieutenant
World War I
First Navy Under Secretary
Secretary of the Navy
First Secretary of Defense
World War II
Born 1892—Died 1949
In the Great Cause of Good
Government so that Others Might
Live in Peace and Prosperity.

---

13. Arthur H. Vandenberg, Jr., with the collaboration of Joe Alex Morris, *The Private Papers of Senator Vandenberg* (Boston, 1952), pp. 486–487.
14. Walter H. Waggoner in *The New York Times*, May 26, 1949.

The inscription finally engraved reads:

JAMES FORRESTAL
Lieutenant, U.S.N.R.F.
World War I
Under-Secretary of the Navy
Secretary of the Navy
First Secretary of Defense
World War II
Born 1892—Died 1949
In the Great Cause of Good Government.

The nation's capital contains one other visible memorial to James Forrestal. On the right-hand side of the entrance to the Pentagon, there is a bust of Forrestal with the inscription:

JAMES FORRESTAL
First Secretary of Defense
1947—1949

Attached to the left side of the column supporting the bust is the following plaque:

This memorial to James Forrestal, as a spontaneous tribute to his lasting accomplishments in providing for National Security and his selfless devotion to duty, was erected by thousands of his friends and co-workers of all ranks and stations.

Forrestal's other memorials include one of the nation's most formidable aircraft carriers, a research center in Princeton, New Jersey, and a school in Beacon, New York, where Forrestal was born and spent the early years of his life. All of them bear his name, and testify, at least in part, to the esteem in which he was held by a very large number of his fellow Americans.

That esteem was first reflected in initial reactions to Forrestal's death. The news of his suicide was, of course, a profound shock to official and unofficial Washington, the nation, and a large part of the world. President Truman declared that he was "inexpressibly shocked and grieved," and added,

"This able and devoted public servant was as truly a casualty of the war as if he had died on the firing line."

In her column "Society" that appeared in the *Washington Times Herald* of May 23, Achsah Dorsey Smith reported that the

tragic news of the death of former Secretary of Defense James V. Forrestal came as such a shock that festivities at the reception which the president of the Gridiron Club and Mrs. Richard L. Wilson gave yesterday from 5 until 7 P.M. at the Statler were much subdued. At noon Presidential Secretary Charles G. Ross telephoned Mr. Wilson that out of respect for his former Cabinet minister [*sic*] and friend, President Truman and his family would be unable to attend. . . .

The President ordered a period of national mourning which was to last until after Forrestal's funeral, during which all government flags, at home and abroad, were to fly at half-mast. He also placed his personal airplane, the *Independence,* at the disposal of Mrs. Forrestal and her son Michael, both of whom were flying home from Paris to attend the funeral.

Secretary of State Dean Acheson, who was in Paris to attend a meeting of the Big Four Foreign Ministers, returned to Washington immediately. Forrestal's death, he said in a formal statement, "was a heavy shock to me and to other members of this American delegation." Referring to Forrestal's "long, devoted and invaluable service to his country," the "weight of responsibilities he had carried and the steady self-sacrifice he had contributed," Acheson concluded:

I had hoped and expected that rest would restore his reservoirs of strength and that his great capabilities would again be at the call of his country. . . . My own sadness at the loss of a friend and colleague is very deep, indeed.[15]

Secretary of Defense Louis Johnson told reporters that when he had last seen Forrestal at Bethesda he had found him "like his old self and in good health," with plans to leave

---

15. Quoted in the *New York Herald Tribune*, May 23, 1949.

the hospital in a few weeks. "The shock of Mr. Forrestal's death," he confessed, "touches me deeply."[16]

Similar sentiments were expressed by former President Herbert Hoover, FBI chief J. Edgar Hoover, and other high government officials. In London the First Lord of the British Admiralty, A. V. Alexander, described Forrestal as "a great servant of his country, and its fighting forces, and the cause of democracy as a whole."[17] President Enrico Dutra of Brazil referred to Forrestal as a "victim of duty . . . [who] did so much for the cause of democracy."[18]

When informed of Forrestal's death, Representative Leslie C. Arends, Republican whip in the House of Representatives, exclaimed: "Oh, dear God! I'm sorry to hear that. I had great admiration for Mr. Forrestal. I think he did a terrifically good job, and he was under so terrible a strain for so many years."[19] Representative Joseph W. Martin, minority House leader, told reporters that Forrestal's death was a great loss to our country; "Mr. Forrestal was a notable patriot and his sad death is directly the result of overwork in a time of great crisis."[20] Senator Millard Tydings, Democrat of Maryland, and Chairman of the Senate Armed Services Committee, commented that Forrestal had served his country with "intelligence, comprehension, tenacity and patriotism." He referred to Forrestal's traits of patience and kindness, and declared that he was a man devoid of bitterness. Forrestal, he concluded his characterization, was "part poet and part warrior."[21] Senator Scott Lucas, Democrat of Illinois and majority leader in the Senate, said that the late Defense Secretary had given "every ounce of his energy, every thought of his brilliant mind to the service of his country."[22]

---

16. Quoted in *ibid.*
17. Quoted in the *Washington Star*, May 23, 1949.
18. Quoted in *ibid.*
19. Quoted in the *Washington Post*, May 23, 1949.
20. Quoted in *ibid.*
21. Quoted in *The New York Times*, May 23, 1949.
22. Quoted in *ibid.*

On Monday, May 23, the day following his suicide, Forrestal was eulogized in the House of Representatives by a large number of congressmen. Most of the tributes to Forrestal did not deal directly with his suicide, but there were two efforts to account for the fact that he had taken his own life.

Representative Paul Shafer, pondering "the manner in which he suddenly became ill, and, at last, ended his career with a tragic act," instructed his House colleagues that Forrestal's suicide carried

a great lesson to the people of the United States. I mean the dangerous threat which the efficient, methodical, blood-thirsty rulers of the Kremlin pose to the free world as we know it.

James V. Forrestal hated the Communists. He hated the thoughts of their undermining this land of ours, in which he had been able to work himself up from a poor man to one of wealth and high position. He hated the thoughts of allowing the Communists to overrun Poland, Estonia, Latvia, Lithuania, Rumania, Hungary, Bulgaria, Czechoslovakia, and China. There is every reason to believe that the dangers of communism and the manner in which so many of our citizens overlook those dangers preyed on his mind, until, finding a weak spot, the pressure caused his collapse which ended in his tragic demise.

"Let us pray," Shafer concluded, "that all of us fight as good and as long a fight as did Jim Forrestal."[23]

Representative Thomas Hale Boggs, Democrat of Louisiana, "noting the tragic manner in which he died," thought it noteworthy to mention that

this public official, probably more than any man of our time, was subjected to a campaign of abuse and vilification the like of which I have never heard. It would seem to me that this should give pause to the irresponsible elements both in the press and on the radio who abuse the privileges of liberty of expression . . . in attacking men of character and honor. . . . In this Capital of the United States the most devastating weapons used—more devastating than machine guns or mortars or the other weapons

---

23. *Congressional Record*, House of Representatives, May 23, 1949, 6773.

of battle—are the cruel weapons of distorted words, and they were
used against this great man in a most unfair, uncharitable, and
unthinkable manner.[24]

The "campaign of abuse and vilification" to which Boggs
referred was the subject of much comment in the days and
weeks that followed Forrestal's suicide. But even before Forrestal's resignation the columns and radio broadcasts of
Drew Pearson, Walter Winchell, and others, which had been
critical of Forrestal ever since he had become Secretary of
Defense, aroused widespread resentment in government circles and in the newspaper world. On August 22, 1948, Robert
S. Allen, substituting for Pearson while the latter was on
vacation, reported that Forrestal, disturbed by the "bad
press" he had, was "surrounded" by twice as many press advisers as any other Cabinet member. In his column of September 3, 1948, Pearson stated that Forrestal had been meeting secretly with Republican presidential candidate Thomas
E. Dewey. "It's an open secret," Pearson told his readers,
"that Forrestal would like to hold on to his job regardless of
the outcome of the November election. Governor Dewey,"
he added, "did not commit himself." On November 23, 1948,
Pearson described Forrestal, along with John Foster Dulles,
W. Averell Harriman, and William H. Draper, Jr., as "gentlemen [who] loaned the money to build up the [German]
Ruhr between World Wars I and II. These are also the
gentlemen who have now decided that the Ruhr shall go
back to the big German cartels." A large number of other
Pearson columns in late 1948 reported that Forrestal's relations with President Truman had been deteriorating and
that Forrestal's resignation would be one of the first requested by the President after his inauguration.

Forrestal's connections with Wall Street and Big Business
were topics particularly favored by Pearson. "Ever since
election day," he wrote on December 15, 1948, "Secretary of

---

24. *Ibid.*, 6772.

Defense Forrestal has been frantically painting himself a true and loyal Democrat. But here is an off-the-record talk indicating the kind of men Forrestal puts in high position." The remainder of the column was devoted to a conversation alleged to have taken place between Donald Carpenter, "Forrestal's newly hand picked chairman of the Munitions Board," and William Bourne of the State Department. Carpenter, according to Pearson, quoted Forrestal as saying that "we want to be sure not to get one of these New Dealers in this job," and Carpenter himself was reported by Pearson as saying, "In making war we have to depend on big business. Only big business can turn out the materials we need in the volume we need." Carpenter "thinks that way," Pearson informed his readers, because: "He is a member of the same du Pont-Carpenter family which contributed a cool $186,780 to the 1940 campaign to defeat Roosevelt, which organized the Liberty League in 1936, and which in the last election poured still uncounted thousands into the battle against Truman." Admitting that "it is hard to understand why Forrestal hires a member of the du Pont tribe," Pearson suggested that "this may be one explanation":

Back in the 1920's, Secretary Forrestal's Wall Street firm loaned 20 million dollars to Bolivia, used to buy arms to wage war against Paraguay . . . some time after Forrestal loaned this money to Bolivia, the Remington Arms Co., of which Donald Carpenter is now vice president, stepped in to profit by it. Remington got a contract for 7.65 mm. and 9 mm. cartridges. Carpenter had just joined the firm when this sale was made.

So Forrestal and Carpenter, once operators in indirectly fomenting war in Latin America, are now together in running American defense.

In late 1948 and early 1949, Pearson and Walter Winchell devoted several columns and radio broadcasts to allegations that Forrestal had been unethical, or worse, in establishing in 1929 a dummy Canadian corporation in order to realize

an income-tax savings, although Forrestal had long since
cleared himself of such a charge in testimony before a Senate
Committee. They also suggested that Forrestal's opposition
to the establishment of the State of Israel was connected with
his former partnership in the investment banking concern
of Dillon, Read, since Dillon, Read had financed a number
of oil companies with major holdings in the Arab world.
On the program "Author Meets the Critics," broadcast over
WNBC the afternoon of January 23, 1949, Ira A. Hirschmann stated that the I.G. Farben works in Frankfurt had not
been bombed during the war because Forrestal owned I.G.
Farben stock. Hirschmann added that Draper, a former partner of Forrestal's, was currently "right-hand man" to General
Clay, head of United States Forces in Germany.

Even Forrestal's personal courage was not left unquestioned. In early January, 1949, both Pearson and Winchell
devoted column space to an alleged demonstration of cowardice by Forrestal on an occasion in July, 1937, when Mrs.
Forrestal was robbed of $48,000 in jewels. The jewel thieves,
according to Pearson and Winchell, accosted Mrs. Forrestal
in front of the Forrestal home at 27 Beekman Place in New
York City. Instead of doing something about the holdup
men, Forrestal, they suggested, had left the house through
the back door.

There can be no question that Forrestal was bitterly hurt
by these attacks upon his honor, integrity, and courage. He
made numerous efforts to answer or refute them, by having
his aides prepare factual memoranda on the subjects discussed by Pearson, Winchell, and others, and by supplying
corrective information to newspapermen who were friendly
to him. The Pearson column dealing with Carpenter, for
example, was summarized for Forrestal in a memo drawn up
by one of his staff assistants. Forrestal wrote on the memo:
"How many du Pont men have we [in the Department of
Defense]?" and he also obtained a letter from Carpenter,
dated January 24, 1949, stating that only one member of the

Munitions Board had any du Pont connections, and that he, Carpenter, had never discussed Munitions Board business with anyone from du Pont. On January 25 Forrestal had his assistant, Marx Leva, write to a New York attorney for information regarding (1) the tax savings Forrestal realized through his investment in the Canadian corporation that he had organized in 1929; (2) German companies financed by Dillon, Read after World War I; (3) oil-company securities underwritten by Dillon, Read while Forrestal was associated with the firm; and (4) oil-company securities underwritten by Dillon, Read after Forrestal had left the firm.[25]

At 11:00 P.M. on the evening of the Hirschmann broadcast, WNBC issued a formal retraction of the Hirschmann charges. Forrestal, the announcer said, had informed the station that the charges were not true.

In an effort to answer those who were critical of Forrestal's business background, Marquis Childs devoted two columns in January, 1949, to the "Attacks on Forrestal." Forrestal, wrote Childs on January 14, "in depressed moods . . . says that perhaps there is no place for the Wall Street man in Government, since the public seems to find it hard to believe a businessman can divorce himself from his private interests." He insists, the Childs column continued, "that he has little influence on German policy. And when the charge of military domination is made, he points out that the State Department, under James Byrnes, declined to take responsibility for administering occupied Germany."

Returning to this theme and related themes on January

25. On January 28, 1948, Forrestal had testified before a Senate committee that he had severed all connections with Dillon, Read in 1940, when he was appointed an administrative assistant to President Franklin D. Roosevelt. He also furnished the committee with a list of oil securities which Dillon, Read had underwritten between 1915 and 1940 (Forrestal had become a partner in Dillon, Read in 1923). His testimony was read into the *Congressional Record* by Senator Claude Pepper, Democrat of Florida, on March 31, 1948. On October 13, 1933, Forrestal testified at length on the tax situation that resulted from his organizing the Canadian corporation in 1929. See below, pp. 82–88.

15, Childs observed that Forrestal had been under greater attack than anyone else in the Truman Administration ever since the November, 1948, election. Childs noted:

In most of these attacks, he is represented as the spokesman of big business . . . who is seeking to restore private ownership and the old cartel system in Germany's Ruhr. He is also accused of being imperialistic and anti-Zionist because of his public insistence that oil from the Middle East is essential to American security and the success of the Marshall Plan.

Since Forrestal "had said nothing," Childs had decided to interview him, and the remainder of the column appeared in question-and-answer form. Once again, as Childs reported, Forrestal stated "I do not have, and have not had since 1940, any interest in Dillon, Read & Co." And "I see no likelihood of any American investment participation in the industry of the Ruhr." To the question: "Are you in favor of restoring industry in the Ruhr to the German corporations that held ownership prior to 1940?" Forrestal replied: "This question has not come to me before and I have no opinion." Asked whether he believed that "war with communism, as represented in the Soviet Union and the satellite countries, is almost certain to come, within, say, a decade," Forrestal answered: "No one in a free democracy can accept war as inevitable. Any concept of war initiated by the United States would be unthinkable."

The stories adverting to Forrestal's lack of personal courage in the jewel-theft incident were particularly offensive to Forrestal, his friends, and an overwhelming majority of newspaper columnists. Forrestal, wrote Tris Coffin in his column, "The Daybook," of January 26, 1949, is no "glowing Sir Galahad," but he does not deserve the stories being circulated about him. "One of them," Coffin remarked, "is hitting below the belt." According to Coffin, Mrs. Forrestal, on the night of the robbery, had been attending a party with Richard Hall, a friend of the Forrestals. Forrestal, Coffin added, was not fond of parties, and when Mrs. Forrestal arrived home accompanied by Hall, he was asleep in bed. He remained asleep while the thieves stuck a knife in Hall's ribs and relieved Mrs. Forrestal of the jewels. The next day, Coffin reported, when Forrestal opened the front door he saw a crowd of reporters and photographers. In an attempt to escape them, he left the house through the back door.[26]

In his column "Fair Enough," of May 24, 1949, two days after Forrestal's suicide, Westbrook Pegler again referred to the jewel-theft story. In a column that was largely devoted to criticizing Drew Pearson, Pegler reported that Mrs. Forrestal had told him that "instead of the chauffeur opening the door [of the automobile] a man jumped in back with us. He said, 'This is no joke; it's a stickup.' I told him it was a silly way to make a living." Pegler added: "The Forrestal house is on the east side of Beekman Place. There is no alley through which Forrestal could have fled if he had been the coward that Pearson said he was."[27] On January 18, 1949, Arthur Krock, chief of *The New York Times* Washington bureau and a long-time friend of Forrestal's, wired Pearson urging him to correct the numerous errors in his column account of the jewel theft.[28]

---

26. *Washington Times-Herald*, January 26, 1949.
27. *Washington Times-Herald*, May 24, 1949. In January, Pegler had written Forrestal with reference to the jewel theft: "I feel challenged as a newspaperman by the viciousness of this and similar slanders from the same source [Pearson] and from Winchell. If our press is worth a damn it ought to destroy these bastards. . . . I am telling you, you ought to have terminated Winchell's [Naval officer] commission a long time ago. You know damned well he was a coward afraid to take sea duty in the war and you are guilty to a serious degree yourself in permitting this coward to retain his commission." Forrestal dictated a reply, but his letter to Pegler, which was short and which dealt only with the details of the theft, was never sent.
28. On July 3, 1937, *The New York Times* reported that Mrs. Forrestal had been robbed of $48,000 worth of jewels. According to the *Times*, Mrs. Forrestal had been attending a party at the Plaza Hotel with Hall, Mrs. George Atwell, Jr., and Count Lichtenstein. When she returned home accompanied by Hall at 2:10 A.M., in a car driven by his chauffeur, she was robbed of four pieces of jewelry. On July 16, 1937, the *Times* further reported that a reward of $5,000 had been offered for the capture of the thieves and the

As previously noted, Pearson had broadcast a number of "sensational" statements about Forrestal's mental collapse while the former Defense Secretary was a patient in Bethesda.[29] He returned to this subject at various times after Forrestal's death, and by so doing kept very much alive the controversy that raged about his own alleged role in contributing to Forrestal's illness and suicide. In his broadcast on the evening of the suicide, Pearson stated that Forrestal had tried four times to take his own life, and the fourth attempt "was frustrated" only two weeks before by Bethesda

---

return of the jewelry. Almost three years later, on March 3, 1940, the *Times* announced that one Michael Lamours, a union official, had been arrested in connection with the robbery. Assistant District Attorney of New York, Abraham M. Portez, declared that the theft involved not $48,000, as originally reported, but $78,000. A member of the Lamours family told the *Times* reporter that the arrest of Lamours "looks like a frame-up to me to get him out of the labor movement." Lamours's union was not identified. In a story of May 13, 1941, the *Times* revealed that a Mrs. Dorothy Stirrat had been convicted of having "put the finger" on Mrs. Forrestal the night of the robbery.

29. One such broadcast provoked the following letter to Forrestal, dated April 12, from an unidentified journalist who wrote from the National Press Club in Washington. Forrestal, of course, was never shown the letter. The full text of the letter is as follows:

"Ex-Secretary of National Defense:
Honorable James Forrestal
U.S. Naval Hospital—Bethesda, Maryland.

"DEAR MR. SECRETARY:
"The teletype this noon speaks of your being in 'for a general check-up'—and refers to your condition as one of 'occupational fatigue'—all of which is natural & proper.
"BUT YOU SHOULD TAKE SOME COGNIZANCE OF DREW PEARSON'S (last) SUNDAY NIGHT'S BROADCAST, in which he stated you had run out at Key West, when planes went overhead, shouting: THE RUSSIANS ARE ATTACKING US, etc—asserting you'd been out of your right senses for many months—that President Truman knew all that—and carried you along—and that BECAUSE OF YOUR (indicated) INSANITY, ALL YOUR RECENT DECISIONS AND REGULATIONS SHOULD BE REVIEWED & INSPECTED & DETERMINED ALL OVER AGAIN.
"THIS—has caused more talk than ever before about you. ALL THIS has again focused the American Mind on the 'possibility' of your knowing more serious things than ever hinted about—
"IN MOSCOW, the newspapers ALL PLAYED UP THIS PEARSON REPORT. Radio Moscow last night 3 times re-broadcast the fantastic story.

employees. (Rear Admiral L. O. Stone, commanding officer of the hospital, when informed of Pearson's report, denied that there was any truth in the story.) Pearson further announced that Forrestal had tried to hang himself, had slashed his wrists, and had taken an overdose of sleeping pills while in Florida. He concluded his reference to Forrestal by saying that his death was a "great tragedy" and that the "entire nation will mourn."

Broadcasting the same evening over the Mutual Network, William Hillman told his listeners that the "tragedy of James Forrestal is an American tragedy. . . . It should be an

---

"SO—NOT ONLY YOURSELF HAS SUFFERED FROM D.P'S MALICE & LIES BUT THE AMERICAN PEOPLE ARE NOW BEING GIVEN 'THE JITTERS' also.

" (It's commonplace for OVERWORKED MEN to suffer from strain—even from delusions. There's nothing undignified or un-natural. (BUT IT IS EXCEPTIONAL WHEN A CHRONIC LIAR LIKE PEARSON WHIPS UP THE WHOLE WORLD—WITH SUCH EXAGGERATED GOSSIP.))

"I HEARD YOU ADDRESS PRESS CLUB LUNCHEON 30 days back—and I WAS SPECIALLY IMPRESSED (as were all of us) WITH YOUR WISDOM & CALM SURVEY & BALANCED ANSWERS TO ALL TOUGH QUESTIONS. YOU SHOWED CONTROL & BALANCE & INTELLIGENCE & MANLINESS THAT MADE EVERY PRESS CLUB MEMBER OF DECENCY VERY VERY PROUD OF YOU AND YOUR VERY FINE RECORD IN THE OFFICE AT THE PENTAGON.

"2nd hand, a friend hears also of YOUR PLAYING GOLF IN A VERY NORMAL NATURAL WAY in Georgia or Florida, just 2 days before your alleged breakdown—so, knowing PEARSON'S GOSSIP RACKET—

"I would simply urge you to:

"DEFEND YOURSELF AND YOUR COUNTRY FROM SUCH LIARS & INTRIGUES & SMEARS, by some simple appearances—by some clear statement in public—

"I'M MERELY WARNING YOU OF INDIANS IN AMBUSH AGAINST YOU. YOU WILL KNOW BEST WHAT TO DO—AND WHEN—AND HOW.

"We Pray God in behalf of your Health & Sanity & Happiness. Our Nation owes you a Great Debt of Thankfulness.

"So let not your heart be troubled—Believe in God—Stand Steadfast—unmoved—by liars and tricksters—falsities.

"BELIEVE IN GOD & KEEP WELL & STRONG

KEEP OUTDOORS—

Walk 8–10 hours daily—across country

Swing an ax or pickax in a dirt ditch

Work on a Farm—

THAT'S A SURE CURE FOR NERVOUS PROSTRATION OR OVERSTRAIN—such as I've OFTEN HEALED MY WEAKENED CONSTITUTION with—no drugs, no doctors, no confinements, no "cures" needed—

"GOD BLESS YOU & HELP YOU

"A Newspaper Friend."

hour of deep soul searching by Americans—of questioning
how far we can go in pillorying and crucifying men in public
office. It is one thing to say that Forrestal made a mistake—
if mistake he did make . . . let me say this—nothing was done
by Mr. Forrestal as Secretary of Defense that has not been
thoroughly reviewed for any errors that might have arisen
in moments of stress."

From Montreal the American Psychiatric Association
issued a statement describing Forrestal's suicide as "a familiar
reaction to excessive stresses and strains." Noting that "there
is a breaking point for every one of us, if the pressures are
great enough," the Association commented that while Forrestal was "being given the finest kind of medical care he
was subjected to the destructive influence of unenlightened
attacks."[30]

On May 26 and 27, the *Washington Post* published a
number of letters to the editor dealing with Forrestal's suicide. Howard C. Petersen, former Assistant Secretary of War,
wrote to the *Post* on May 26 praising Forrestal's work as
Under Secretary of the Navy, Secretary of the Navy, and
Secretary of Defense. "He, as much as anyone in the Government," Petersen's letter continued, "kept this Nation alive to
the possibility of Russian aggression, and it is in large measure through his insistence on a tough and realistic policy
that we have witnessed the recent turn in our favor in the
cold war." Petersen suggested that Pearson's column be
dropped from the paper.

A woman who signed herself "Wife of a public servant,"
asked:

What kind of a country is ours that a foremost public official
should choose death rather than a life in retirement? What kind
of a public office is it whose duties are so strenuous that they
bring nervous exhaustion? . . . Is death the reward our democracy
holds out for its loyal servants? These are some of the essential
questions which this tragic event raises.

_____
30. Quoted in the *New York Herald Tribune*, May 23, 1949.

"I wonder how Drew Pearson feels," wrote John Nealon of Washington.

In the editorial section of the *Post* on May 30, headed "Pearson Replies: A Communication," Pearson declared that he was "greatly disturbed that some people seem to believe that my reporting of the illness of the late James Forrestal should have contributed to his death." The "facts," according to Pearson, were that he had made "little other reference" to Forrestal "after I reported on [his] mental illness." In fact, he had complimented Forrestal for cooperating with Secretary of Defense Johnson, "and I also suggested that he be given a long vacation at Government expense." While in the hospital "under sedatives," he added, Forrestal had not been permitted to listen to any radio programs or read any newspapers. And if the Navy "had taken proper precautions instead of minimizing the facts Jim Forrestal would be alive today." The lack of "precautions," Pearson argued, included the placing of Forrestal on the sixteenth floor instead of the ground floor of Bethesda. He also criticized Raines for his departure to Canada at a time that constituted "the most dangerous period" of Forrestal's illness. Pearson's reply continued:

In the end, it may be found that Mr. Forrestal's friends had more to do with his death than his critics. For those close to him now admit privately that he had been sick for some time, suffered embarrassing lapses too painful to be mentioned here. . . .

Yet during the most of last winter, when Jim Forrestal was under heavy responsibilities and definitely not a well man, the little coterie of newspapermen who now insinuate Jim was killed by his critics, encouraged him to stay on. This got to be almost an obsession, both on their part and on his, until Mr. Truman's final request for his resignation undoubtedly worsened the illness.

The real fact is that Jim Forrestal had a relatively good press. All one need do is examine the newspaper files to see that his press was far better than that of some of his old associates.

Noting that Secretary of Labor Frances Perkins, Winston Churchill, and Herbert Hoover had been bitterly criticized in their time, and that the suicide of Laurence Duggan[31] and the death of Harry Dexter White[32] were in some measure traceable to congressional investigations and "a free press," Pearson urged that

the above cases pose a difficult question for both newspapermen and congressional investigations. Are public officials to be immune from criticism or investigation for fear of impairing their health? . . . if we are to withhold the check of congressional investigation or newspaper criticism from any public official, no matter how mild, because of health, then the Government of checks and balances created by the Founding Fathers is thrown out of gear.

It was not criticism which caused Jim Forrestal to conclude that his life was no longer worth living. There were other factors in his life that made him unhappy.

Pearson's lengthy rejoinder to his critics did not settle the matter of his alleged responsibility, in whole or in part, for Forrestal's suicide. A column by Westbrook Pegler, syndicated in Hearst papers, stated in May that Forrestal had been "hounded" by Pearson and Winchell "with dirty aspersions [and] insinuations, until . . . one of the finest servants that the Republic ever had died by suicide. . . ." Pearson promptly announced that he was suing Pegler for $250,000 for libel. Winchell, in an obvious reference to Pegler, wrote, "It is typical of one presstitute [that when he] condemned critics of Forrestal [he also attacked] Roosevelt." The *Hartford Courant* commented editorially that Americans "are sick at the stomach over the cur-pack that long yelped at the heels of [Forrestal]," and the *New York Herald Tribune* lamented the "juvenile savagery" of Forrestal's press critics.[33]

---

31. Duggan, a former State Department official, jumped to his death from a New York office building late in 1948 shortly after being questioned by the FBI and the House Un-American Activities Committee.

32. White, former Treasury Assistant Secretary, died, apparently of a heart attack, a few days following testimony before the Un-American Activities Committee.

33. Quoted in *Time*, June 6, 1949.

In an editorial of June 18, 1949, entitled "Don't News-paper Ethics Apply to Columnists?" the *Saturday Evening Post* remarked that it

is an interesting speculation as to what extent [Forrestal's] des-peration was deepened by a group of ill-assorted columnists and ideological libertarians. During his whole Government service it was implied in a continuous stream of billingsgate that Forrestal was in the Government to serve his former partners in the invest-ment-banking business, that he was a "cartelist" and a truckler to facism, . . . It is a little late to go into all that, but it is not too late to make the obvious comment that the responsibility for this abuse of a free press goes beyond the malice of gossip columnists and rests firmly on the heads of publishers who permit their news-papers to take from syndicated columnists libelous and half-baked abuse which they would not print if it were written by their own reporters. . . . It is not necessary to have agreed with everything James Forrestal believed or did, but it is reasonable to insist that news and opinion regarding the acts of public men or private citizens for that matter, be held to ordinary standards of accuracy, fairness and decency.

"There is an important lesson to be learned," wrote Childs in his column of May 25, "from the tragedy of James Forrestal. It gets down to the real meaning of that tragedy. . . ." Forrestal "came to believe that he was being persecuted. This took such an exaggerated form as to be a major symptom of his mental illness." Noting that Forrestal's last months in office were spent "under an attack that amounted to persecution," that certain press and radio com-mentators were "out to 'get Forrestal,' " Childs observed that the "campaign" against David E. Lilienthal was taking on some similar characteristics. He expressed the hope that the attacks on Lilienthal would not reach "the degree of per-sonal innuendo and vilification" that marked the treatment accorded Forrestal.[34]

---

34. More than ten years after Forrestal's death, Drew Pearson's animus toward Forrestal was apparently still very much alive. In reply to a letter from the present writer requesting certain information pertaining to his

Not all commentators and editorial writers, of course, in paying tribute to Forrestal or in attempting to account for his collapse and suicide, chose to emphasize the alleged irresponsibility of certain sections of the press and radio media. In his "Today and Tomorrow" column of May 24, 1949, Walter Lippmann recalled that since Forrestal's breakdown he had been

remembering how for years, no matter what else we talked about, Forrestal would bring up somewhere and somehow a variant of the same theme: how this Government, which he knew was almost unmanageable, could be made to work, how men could be found who were competent to administer it, how methods and situations could be devised to make it possible for competent men to be wise.

In the end, Lippmann observed, the problem which had long preoccupied Forrestal became

his own insoluble and unendurable personal problem. He was like a doctor who had studied a disease and then contracts it himself. He saw with an awful clarity his own mistakes and his failures . . . so sharply that the affection of his friends could not console him, that public tributes could not deceive him. He saw them with such terrible conscientiousness and scruple, so out of proportion in the record of his achievements, that he was exhausted—not so much by the long hours he worked as by the realization that he would never have a chance to repair his mistakes and to achieve what he had been appointed to achieve.

I cannot help feeling [Lippmann added], that whatever the doctors may say, there is a public factor in this tragedy, and that it lies in the destructive and soul-destroying political custom of casting public men aside in the middle of their careers. Of all the wastes in the American system of government, our practice of retiring public men is the most expensive. . . . I shall always believe

---

columns and radio broadcasts about Forrestal, he wrote on July 2, 1959, that while he was very busy he was "interested in knowing just what kind of book you plan to write about Forrestal. There have been various laudatory treatises on him which haven't even skimmed the surface, and I am not particularly interested in cooperating with another such venture." Although he was assured that the book would endeavor to be objective and impartial, he was not heard from again.

that if Forrestal had known before he left the Pentagon that he was really wanted somewhere else, as indeed in all justice and common sense he should have been, he would have had a reason for living, and the fatigue the doctors talk about would not have overcome his will to live.

Forrestal's "exhaustion," the *Washington Post* commented editorially on May 23,

had been the subject of private comment long before he resigned. He was inconsecutive in conversation, indecisive in conclusion. But there were mental and spiritual complications which dogged the body and harassed it in its efforts to recuperate. An inner conviction seems to have seized James Forrestal that his career had been a failure.

Noting that Forrestal felt "impotent" in the task of re-organizing the Defense Establishment, the *Post* went on to observe that Forrestal had made a number of "major mis-takes" in rendering advice on foreign policy:

For instance, he miscalculated the equation in the Middle East—the result of relying upon oil magnates and missionary educators, all of them advisors who were unrealistic, though on different grounds. . . . Another mistake lay in his overestimate of the mili-tary needs for this Nation. In this respect he succumbed partly to military badgering for all that the traffic would bear, partly to an obsession that the Cold War was the prelude to a shooting war. This obsession become an *idée fixe* as time went on.

Nevertheless, the *Post* editorial concluded, Forrestal was an honest and sincere man, one who was "never swelled" by conceit and feelings of self-importance. In a more personal appraisal, the *Post* remarked that Forrestal

had a passion for intellectual truth which he sought in voracious reading. Whether he digested what he read is another matter . . . his reading made him a full man, but it never gave him a work-ing philosophy of life or determined his actions. He looked tough, with his stocky little figure and broken nose, but he belied his looks. He gave a curious impression of a man everybody and nobody knew. He combined a solitary soul with a gregarious disposition, and his lack of serenity was betrayed by the spasmodic restlessness with which he sought the society that diverts but does not satisfy. . . .

Measured by sincerity, James Forrestal was a great man, and probably no one who has appeared on the Washington scene in a post of authority was more likeable, or evoked more affection.

A *Washington Times-Herald* editorial of May 24 began:

James V. Forrestal is the only public man of his rank in American affairs to commit suicide. No President ever has, nor has any Cabinet officer, governor, senator or important general, admiral or administrator, that we have been able to recall, and only one ambassador, John G. Winant.

Suicide, the editorial continued, "is usually associated with failure." But Forrestal was not a failure; on the contrary:

His life in many ways sums up the American ideal. He started as a poor boy with the fortunate gift of great intelligence and industry and even more fortunate, high character.

In the usual American way he first concentrated on making his stake, so as to be independent. Then he began giving back to the country that had made him rich, the talents that had also made him famous.

"We have been reading and listening," the editorial comment ended,

to the eulogies that have followed. A good 90 per cent, we should say, are the routine samples of usual unadulterated Washington hypocrisy tossed off by people who never gave Forrestal an honest thought while he was alive.

Unfortunately, he was not the political type. But he was very much a man . . . we hope he doesn't have to read some of the blubber in print that has been pouring out of these last 36 hours.

Writing in the *New Republic* of June 13, 1949, Harold L. Ickes informed his readers that while he "was never an intimate of James Forrestal's . . . for a number of years we were good friends and I greatly respected his personal and official integrity."[35] Although he had no "predilection" for "Wall Street," Ickes wrote,

I soon discovered that [Forrestal] had ideas that soared far beyond the acquisition of money for its own sake. He told me one day with a smile that, in going back over the Navy files to discover what they might contain with respect to himself when he volunteered for service during the First World War [see below, pages 67–68] he discovered that he had been suspected of being a socialist. I was both surprised and interested on another occasion when he told me he read the *New Republic,* to which he had been a subscriber for many years. And I well remember the time I asked him whether he would go back to Wall Street when he was through with his government service. His answer was no. He thought he might publish a liberal magazine.

Noting that Forrestal had been opposed, "on principle," to the unification of the Armed Services, Ickes gave his opinion that Forrestal should have resigned rather than have attempted "a unification which never could have been more than a patchwork because his heart was not in it. . . . My own belief is that if Mr. Forrestal had done this, he would be alive today, with as much peace of mind as might have been possible considering other worries he might have had." No one, Ickes thought, could blame newspaper and radio comments for Forrestal's suicide. Ickes asked:

Who of his own knowledge could possibly know that Mr. Forrestal ever read or heard any criticism of him that had the effect

35. It is doubtful that Forrestal would have described himself as Ickes's "good friend." His private papers include frequent reports of controversies with Ickes, and generally adverse references to Ickes's character and personality. In December, 1946, when Ickes, a former Secretary of Interior, had written an article critical of the Navy's interest in the Pacific islands that had been seized from Japan, Forrestal, then Secretary of the Navy, referred to Ickes in a memorandum as "bathed in the serene light of his own self-approval, emanating the ectoplasm of conscious virtue, [and viewing] the motives of most men as mean and vulgar, with, of course, one notable exception. . . . Mr. Ickes, among other things, is an expert on yes-men. He has taken pains to have a satisfactory number around him. . . ." A fuller account of this memorandum appears in Walter Millis, ed., *The Forrestal Diaries* (New York: Viking, 1951) , p. 232, hereafter referred to as *Diaries.* Ickes and Forrestal were also frequently at odds over oil policy in the Middle East.

of pushing him beyond his self-control? Lacking such sure knowledge, he is an unscrupulous person indeed who would recklessly seize upon this tragic affair to display his own ill-will against those who, if they criticized Mr. Forrestal, doubtless did so in good faith.

Although he could name officials of both the Roosevelt and Truman administrations with respect to whom "the newspapers, the columnists and the commentators have been actually sadistic," Ickes urged that those who were blaming the press for Forrestal's suicide, "perhaps without realizing it, are indirectly encouraging suppression of the freedom of opinion that is essential to our institutions. . . . God save the mark," he continued, "when a Pegler presumes to pronounce judgment upon fellow craftsmen! . . . only history, in its own good time, can weigh the life and deeds of James Forrestal and set the golden nuggets of his patriotic devotion to duty over against the dross that he shared with all of the rest of us."[36]

On Sunday, May 29th, one week after Forrestal's death, the Reverend A. Powell Davies preached a sermon titled "Mr. Forrestal Left a Warning," at Washington's All Souls' Church. The Reverend Mr. Davies, who knew Forrestal, observed that Forrestal had sought, and succeeded in finding, wealth and power but that neither had seemed to him "a satisfying aim." He had then turned to wisdom, endeavoring to become "a modern philosopher-statesman, judicious, free from partiality, superior to the lower motives, zealous in the public interest. . . ." But Forrestal had found, according to the Reverend Mr. Davies, that, in the words of the Welsh proverb, "All wisdom must be paid for with pain." Instead of increasing

both his self-respect and the esteem in which his fellow-man would hold him, [Forrestal] found . . . that his reward was opprobrium, misrepresentation and ill repute, which forced him after a while to doubt himself so severely that at last he was un-

---

36. *The New Republic*, June 13, 1949, pp. 15–16.

willing to continue so unsatisfactory a life, and thus like a true and typical philosopher-statesman, he followed the tradition of what Confucious called "the superior man"—the superior man discredited—and took his own life. [Forrestal's "quest for wisdom," continued Davies], perhaps was also deepened by his loss of personal happiness. I am not going into this, today, but I wish to indicate that I am not unaware of it. Very few tragedies indeed do not have a personal and intimate side to them and it is not often that a man takes his own life if the inner fortress of his personal happiness is still secure. For this gives him a place of refuge: a life within a life, from the joy of which his strength is renewed and he finds fortitude. But in the case we are considering, devotion to the public service had been substituted for the forlorn hope of personal happiness. Undoubtedly, the drive towards achievement was powerfully reinforced by the need to forget frustrations. But this was consciously understood, I think, by Mr. Forrestal—at least as well so as anyone ever does understand such matters when one's own situation is concerned.

[The "warning" left by Forrestal, Davies told his congregation, was] a silent one, but one, nevertheless, that America in these evil days should heed.

For if Mr. Forrestal died by his own hand he had first of all been destroyed by the hands of his fellow citizens . . . Some of them by conspicuous onslaughts . . . [some of them] were not really onslaughts; what they amounted to was the passive side of what the active tormentors were doing. For American democracy has this unhappy distinction among all the democracies of the world—this distinction and this threatening flaw—that American democracy resents natural superiority and loves levelers and detractors: loves, that is to say, whatever drags superiority down towards the level of mediocrity. Or considerable elements in America do so. And since anyone in public life who consciously tries to be worthy of public trust is certain to develop superior qualities, he will be suspected and distrusted and even hated. In this way the people of the United States . . . make sure that as many of their public servants as possible will be mediocrities, and that any who show promise of greatness will be discredited and destroyed.

Much of our leadership at the present time, the Reverend Mr. Davies concluded, is neither capable nor devoted. "James Forrestal knew this. It was part of his anxiety. He did not see how the United States would survive—in a world of enemies—without leadership that was adequate. That is a further reason why his death is a warning."

The "warning" discussed by the Reverend Mr. Davies, the lessons to be learned from Forrestal's life and death, continued to be discussed and debated long after the first Secretary of Defense had been laid to rest in Arlington National Cemetery. Immediately after his death, in two columns that appeared in the (now defunct) *Daily Compass,* reporting from the American Psychiatric Association convention in Montreal, Albert Deutsch argued that the "most serious aspect" of Forrestal's suicide "lies in the fact that the Brass Hats not only told the public that Forrestal had no psychosis but that they really believed what they said. It is no secret that Navy medicine is hostile to psychiatry." The frequent references to "nervous exhaustion," "battle fatigue," and "excessive fatigue," with reference to Forrestal's illness, Deutsch urged, were based on "two myths": (1) that "it is a disgrace for anybody to experience a mental illness"; and (2) that "no Very Important Person, under any circumstances, can possibly suffer from a psychosis and that it is unpatriotic to admit or even to suggest such a possibility." Who was responsible, Deutsch asked,

for placing Forrestal, in a profound state of depression, with suspected suicidal tendencies, in an insufficiently protected suite on the 16th floor? That suite was first built for the late President Roosevelt. It was not intended to house a psychiatric patient.[37]

In an article in the *New American Mercury* in December, 1950, entitled "Untold Facts in the Forrestal Case," William Bradford Huie informed his readers, "In the twenty months since the destruction of James Vincent Forrestal, there has been a creeping realization in this country that what happened was much more than a poignant personal tragedy— that it was an historic national disaster in which a patriot

---

37. *Daily Compass,* May 23 and 29, 1949.

with vision was allowed to be done to death by lesser men." Asserting that "Much of the truth has thus far been suppressed," Huie asked:

Why was the attack on Forrestal so reckless and sadistically savage? Why have his papers been held secret? Where is the report of those who investigated his death? Why was the deposed Defense Secretary held a virtual prisoner at Bethesda Naval Hospital—a prisoner who could not be visited by his own priest?

According to Huie, Forrestal's brother, Henry L. A. Forrestal, who was worried about the confinement at Bethesda, had told Raines in April:

What my brother needs is not to be cooped up there on the 16th floor. He needs to be on an estate somewhere, among friends, where he can walk around in the sun. He has been an exceedingly active man.

Raines, of course, did not release Forrestal, but he told his brother, Huie reported, that Forrestal was "fundamentally okay."

Henry Forrestal also informed Raines that his brother wished to speak with Monsignor Maurice S. Sheehy, former Naval Chaplain and at the time a faculty member of Catholic University. Father Sheehy subsequently stated that he had tried to see Forrestal on six occasions during the week before his death; each time, he told reporters, he was turned away by Raines because Raines did not believe that such a visit "would be in the patient's best interest." Finally, Father Sheehy appealed to Secretary of the Navy John L. Sullivan, who assured him that he would be able to see Forrestal. But it was then, according to Father Sheehy, too late; Forrestal's suicide occurred two days later.[38]

38. William Bradford Huie, "Untold Facts in the Forrestal Case," *New American Mercury*, December, 1950, pp. 643–652. Huie quotes Henry Forrestal as saying to Raines in May: "How long do you want to wait, doctor [before Forrestal was permitted to talk with Father Sheehy]? We have waited five weeks. Delays in such cases can be dangerous. Have you ever heard of a case where being visited by a clergyman has hurt a man?" Huie also reports

In addition to those who believed, with Huie, that Forrestal had been "destroyed" by persons inside and outside the government, there were those who were convinced—and who remain convinced—that Forrestal did not, in fact, commit suicide. Forrestal's widow, in early June, 1949, in a preliminary application for payment of a $10,000 accident insurance policy held by Forrestal, claimed that her husband had met "accidental death." A letter to the Commercial Travelers Mutual Accident Association of America, sent in her behalf by the firm of Wyllys Terry and James Terry, Inc., of New York, stated that since Forrestal's death did not involve suicide, the policy, which was payable in the case of accidental death, should be paid in full.[39]

If one element of mystery, with respect to his death, was supplied by his widow, another, with respect to his life, emerged from the handling of his personal files and papers. One of Huie's questions, "Why have his papers been held secret?" was partly answered in 1951 by the publication of *The Forrestal Diaries,* edited by Walter Millis. But the *Diaries* were incomplete; between the time of Forrestal's

---

Father Sheehy's statement that "Had I been allowed to see my friend, Jim Forrestal, receive him back in the Church, and put his mind at ease with the oldest and most reliable medicine known to mankind, he would be alive today. His blood is on the heads of those who kept me from seeing him." On November 18, 1949, however, Father Sheehy issued a more temperate statement to a United Press reporter who interviewed him in Washington. In its story headed "New Argument Stirred Over Forrestal Death," the UP reported that while Raines had declined to comment on Father Sheehy's statement that he had been "turned away" on six occasions when he tried to see Forrestal, a "Navy spokesman" had said that the hospital had never "refused permission" for a priest to talk to Forrestal. Father Sheehy, the UP story continued, "agreed that the Navy attitude was not one of outright refusal but of believing that Mr. Forrestal's condition did not warrant calling in a priest."

39. It is not known whether or to what extent Mrs. Forrestal's claim was contested by the insurance company. Apart from the $10,000 insurance policy in question, Forrestal held large amounts of insurance and securities. His gross estate was appraised at $1,338,754, of which net assets totaled $1,201,019. Securities alone were valued at $739,401. The principal beneficiaries of his will, which was drawn up in 1936, were his widow and his two sons, Michael and Peter. There was also legacies to his brother, Henry, of $25,000, $10,000 to his financial assistant, Paul M. Strieffler, and $5,000 to his Dillon, Read secretary, Mary McGirr.

death and the beginning of Millis's research (sponsored by the *New York Herald Tribune*), on White House orders a number of papers and documents were removed from Forrestal's files, either for "security" reasons or other reasons. Although evidence is not conclusive, it is probable that certain individuals, for a variety of reasons, were reluctant to make Forrestal's private papers available until they had been properly "screened." Two such individuals, apparently, were President Truman and Secretary of Defense Johnson. In a memorandum to the President of August 27, 1949, Johnson wrote:

I am glad to be able to advise you that the individuals who were in the best possible position to know the truth or falsity of the rumors about the Forrestal "diary," the Forrestal "recordings" of telephone conversations with you, etc. have assured me that there is absolutely no truth whatever to the stories which you and I have heard.

Specifically, I have received categoric assurances to the following effect:
(1) There was never a recording device on Forrestal's White House 'phone.
(2) No conversation between you and Forrestal was ever recorded, either by machine or otherwise.
(3) There was never an occasion when a secretary or anyone else was permitted to pick up the extension 'phone and "listen in" on conversations between you and Forrestal.
(4) There was never a volume that could accurately be described as a Forrestal "diary."[40]

Despite the "categoric assurances" referred to by Johnson, many of Forrestal's telephone conversations were recorded or transcribed, and Forrestal, of course, did keep notes dealing with his thoughts and activities. His papers, however, do not contain any transcripts of telephone or other conversations with President Truman.

The years since Forrestal's suicide have not settled the

---

40. In 1959, in a letter to the present writer, Johnson declared that he had no recollection of this memorandum, and therefore could not comment on its significance or discuss the context in which it was written.

controversies and mysteries in which he was involved during his life, and which continued, and even increased, after his death. More than fourteen years after his funeral, James Forrestal remains a complex, almost enigmatic, figure. Much of this complexity relates to his role in the government, especially after 1945, to his attitude toward a variety of foreign-policy issues, to his views about national security and the organization of defense, and to his relations with President Truman and other high government officials. But even if his government career were less controversial, the complexities of his life and personality would still pose a formidable challenge, not merely to biographers, but to his friends, acquaintances, and associates. Among those who knew him best, there is little agreement as to the facts of his life or the true circumstances of his death. To those who admired him Forrestal was a dedicated public servant; to those who disliked him, he was an intellectual *poseur* and front-man for Wall Street and Big Business. In the circle of his friends he is regarded as a victim of political chicanery and an irresponsible press; in the circle of his enemies his death is attributed to the frustrations of ruthless ambition and megalomaniacal obsessions. Officially, of course, Forrestal committed suicide on May 22, 1949. But among those close to him there are some who believe that his death was accidental, and there are even a few who are certain that he was murdered, or if not murdered, that his death was very much desired by individuals and groups who, in 1949, held great power in the United States. A hero to some and a villain to others, there is no more agreement about the death of Forrestal than there is about the Forrestal who was very much a part of the Washington scene in the late 1940's.

In essence, the questions about James Forrestal resolve themselves into the question: *Who* was James Forrestal?

The following pages are devoted to an effort to tentatively answer that question.

II

☆ ☆ ☆ ☆ ☆

A Career in the Making

JAMES FORRESTAL, like many another American who has influenced our history, began life in a small town on the banks of a great river. The village of Matteawan, New York, where Forrestal was born in 1892, was hardly more than a crossroads on the east bank of the Hudson between New York City and Poughkeepsie.[1] Directly across the Hudson from the larger town of Newburgh, sixty-one miles from New York City, Matteawan in those days was a sparsely settled community largely made up of first-generation Irish, Scandinavian, German, and Italian immigrants. The Matteawan gentry, a small proportion of the citizenry, built their mansions on the profits derived from lumbering, quarrying, and farming. Most rank-and-file citizens worked in these trades, or were employed by the New York Central, or made their living by taking in each other's laundry. A number of men, unable to find work in their home community, commuted to jobs in Newburgh.

The third child and third son of James and Mary Toohey

---

1. In 1913 Matteawan was merged with another adjoining community and renamed Beacon. The name Beacon was chosen, apparently, to commemorate the fact that fires were burned on neighboring hilltops during the Revolutionary War to warn colonists of the approach of British troops.

Forrestal, the future Secretary of Defense, was born on February 15, 1892, and christened James Vincent Forrestal.[2] His maternal grandfather, Mathias Toohey, had settled in Matteawan as early as 1840, and by the time his daughter Mary, Forrestal's mother, was five years old, Mathias Toohey had prospered to the extent of owning a large farm and a considerable amount of land.[3] The first Catholic service in the community was held at his home, and he also was instrumental in establishing St. Joachim's Parish with its own church and parochial school. Mary was educated in Catholic schools, and at the time of her marriage in 1880 was a schoolteacher in Matteawan.

Forrestal's father, James, was a boy of nine when he arrived alone in New York from County Cork, Ireland, in 1857. Taking a train to what was then called Fishkill Landing, he joined his mother, Anastasia, who was employed in the domestic service of the Hart family, one of Matteawan's wealthier families. Anastasia's first husband, the boy's father, had died in Ireland when James was two, and she had since married Patrick Kennedy who was also employed on the Hart estate.

Not long after joining his mother and stepfather, James became an apprentice carpenter. He spent several years traveling around the country, learning a good deal about the construction business and saving as much money as possible. By 1875, when he was twenty-seven, he had saved enough to organize his own construction and woodworking business,

---

2. Forrestal answered to a variety of names and nicknames during his life. In Matteawan, he was commonly addressed as "Vince," at Princeton as "Vince," "Vint," "Jim," or "Runt," and at Dillon, Read he was referred to as "J.V." He usually signed his letters and other documents "James V. Forrestal," but he dropped both the "V." and "Vincent" shortly after arriving in Washington in 1940. Nevertheless, in the press and elsewhere, he continued to be known as "James V. Forrestal."

3. The James V. Forrestal School in Beacon, named in honor of Forrestal at a ceremony on June 5, 1954, was built on land once owned by the elder Toohey.

and in 1880 he was able to build a substantial house for himself and his young wife. Owning the choice acreage around the house, he established an office and shop on the property behind it.[4] It was also in 1880 that James was appointed a major in the 21st Regiment of the New York National Guard. Business continued good, and by 1892 the Forrestals owned extensive properties in and around Beacon, the monthly rental income from which was the substantial sum for those days of more than $250. In addition to building and renting houses, the James Forrestal Construction Company erected a hospital and several commercial buildings during the decade of the nineties.

The senior Forrestal, a Cleveland Democrat, was also active in politics. In 1894 he was appointed postmaster of Matteawan by President Grover Cleveland, and he served in that capacity for four years. A Democratic committeeman and occasional delegate to Democratic national conventions, James Forrestal met and became an acquaintance of Franklin Delano Roosevelt very early in the latter's career. At various times he visited Roosevelt at his Hyde Park home, and in 1910, when Roosevelt was a candidate for the state Senate, he actively campaigned for him. His efforts in Roosevelt's behalf were partly intended to allay rumors that Roosevelt was anti-Catholic, or at least harbored some prejudice against Catholics.[5]

Apart from business and politics, James Forrestal's other major interest was military affairs. He was extremely proud

---

4. The house at 62 Fishkill Avenue in Beacon, in which Forrestal was born, is today occupied by his only surviving brother, Henry.

5. In return for his support James Forrestal in 1913 was given a framed photograph of FDR inscribed

"To Major Forrestal
With my very warm regards
Franklin D. Roosevelt
July 1913."

of his position in the New York National Guard, and he took a prominent part in military parades that were a feature of patriotic celebrations in Matteawan. He was a fervent supporter of the Spanish-American War, and his office wall held maps on which were pinpointed the dispositions of American and Spanish forces.

Some Matteawan oldtimers remember an occasion, during or shortly after the Spanish-American War, when Major Forrestal was in command of a National Guard contingent that was proceeding to Albany. The train on which they were to travel was crowded on that particular day, and the conductor would not initially permit the soldiers to enter the cars. When Major Forrestal ordered his men onto the train, the conductor announced that he would uncouple the cars occupied by the soldiers. The major thereupon posted a guard with fixed bayonet at each coupling with orders to use bayonets on anyone who attempted to carry out the conductor's instructions. As a result, the train proceeded to Albany with the soldiers aboard.

Although the senior Forrestal's public demeanor reflected forcefulness, stubbornness, and strength of character, the Forrestal home was dominated by his wife. Mrs. Forrestal was a large, heavily built woman who possessed, according to a contemporary, a "commanding physical presence." She was a strict disciplinarian who exercised close supervision over the education and training of her three sons. When the boys violated her rules, which were numerous and rigidly enforced, it was she who punished them either with a strapping or by sending them off to bed without supper. A close friend of the senior Forrestals remembers Mrs. Forrestal as someone who believed that disciplinary actions "spoke louder than words." Mr. Forrestal, on the other hand, tried to be a "buddy" to his sons. When they were involved in mischief, he would "talk to them and try to find out what had happened and why it had happened. Mrs. Forrestal, in other ways an admirable woman, didn't believe in wasting that much time."

An illustrative story, told by Henry Forrestal, concerns a time when he and his brother, James, at play in the backyard, found themselves in an argument about how sand should be loaded in their toy trucks. Henry insisted that the sand should be smoothed off in the bin of the trucks, while James maintained that the trucks should be filled until the sand formed a cone-shaped pile towering above the sides of the bin. Finally, James in a fit of temper hit his brother with a toy wooden tool, and knowing that he would be punished, ran off and hid in one of the sheds on the property. "He was afraid," Henry remembers, "that Mother would really lace him." James did not emerge from the shed until after dark, and then only because his father, the more permissive of the parents, came calling him.

A staunch Catholic, Mary Forrestal insisted that her husband and sons attend Mass regularly, and in all other ways conduct themselves as devout Catholics. She did not tolerate swearing or jokes, or permit the boys to bring home pulp magazines. And even when they had reached adolescence and were going to dances and related social affairs, they were required to be home no later than eleven o'clock. One of James Forrestal's childhood friends, who was present with him at a dance, recalls an evening when, promptly at eleven, Major Forrestal came for James and Henry and took them home.

In addition to her family and religion, Mary Toohey Forrestal's other major interest was music. Under her tutelage Will Forrestal, the oldest and also the favorite of her sons, became an accomplished musician. Rather sensitive and introspective by nature, Will was regarded by contemporaries as a "mother's boy." Devoted to music, books, and the more aesthetic pleasures of life, Will did not mix much with other boys and girls while he was growing up, and he never mar-

ried. Unlike his two younger brothers, Will did not play
football, box, or engage in other "manly" sports, and
throughout his life, which ended some years before his
brother's suicide, he remained attached to his mother and
to the way of life of which she was the center and guiding
spirit.

Henry Forrestal, the middle brother, was a star football
player in his youth, and even today, although he is partly
crippled by arthritis, retains something of the robust physique of his younger days. All his life—he was born on April
11, 1889—he proudly tells visitors, he has "studied hard,
worked hard, and played hard." The only university he ever
attended, he adds, was "the university of experience." Of
his accomplishments in life, the two that give him the most
retrospective satisfaction are his capacity for oration, and his
business acumen. Until his retirement, he traveled widely
around the country addressing business and labor organizations, Kiwanis and Rotary clubs, and branches of the Knights
of Columbus. A frequent speaker at commencements, he
considers himself, with some justice, an authority on the art
of speechmaking. "A good speech," he declares, "should not
be too long, because if it is you lose your audience. Make
your points brief and concise, and when you have said what
you have to say, stop. Then you'll be invited back."

In contrast to his brothers Will and James, Henry entered the family contracting business as a young man, and
became head of it when his father died in 1923. Although
he is proud of the fact that he "put the spark in the business,"
he quickly adds that the Forrestal Construction Company
was already a substantial concern when his younger brother,
James, was growing up. A "few years" after James left for
college, he points out, "we were doing a million dollars a
year worth of business." He also remembers, with evident
pleasure, that in 1932, when Roosevelt was campaigning for
the presidency, he served as a presidential elector, and that

in 1933 he and James went to Washington for the inaugural ceremonies.

Will Forrestal was a little more than nine years old, and Henry almost three, when James was born in February, 1892. Forrestal in his early years was what was termed in those days a "sickly" child. In addition to the usual childhood diseases, he contracted pneumonia while still an infant, and for a time it was by no means certain that he would recover. But while he did recover, he remained through childhood and into adolescence rather susceptible to illness, and, as a consequence, somewhat frail in appearance. In an effort to build himself up physically, Forrestal engaged in a variety of body-building sports, including weight lifting, wrestling, boxing, tennis, swimming, and golf. Later, in New York and Washington, no matter how busy he was he always found time for exercise, and when he boxed, wrestled, played tennis or golf, a friend remarks, "he had a grim determination, and you knew it wasn't just for fun." During the early years of his Dillon, Read career Forrestal would spend an hour or two each afternoon boxing at a gym at the corner of Forty-second Street and Broadway. Forrestal continued to box even when he was making a reputation for himself in New York financial circles. It was in 1923 or 1924, while he was boxing a few rounds at one of New York's athletic clubs, that he had his nose broken, giving his face thereafter a tougher and somewhat puglike cast. According to a contemporary, the broken nose was Forrestal's "reward" for hitting the "pro" with whom he was boxing "a little too hard."

Frequently he and a business associate would run around Gramercy Park, and in the thirties, when the Forrestals owned a house on Long Island, Forrestal would rise early in the morning and trot around a polo field that adjoined the house. Nevertheless, despite such activities, Forrestal never achieved a rugged physique, or succeeded in creating the impression of great physical strength. In 1917, when he was twenty-five years old, he was five feet nine and one-half inches tall, and he weighed one hundred and fifty pounds.[6]

As a youth in Matteawan, Forrestal attended St. Joachim's Parochial School and the local public high school. His contemporaries report that he read widely and generally among books that were well beyond his age level. Certainly his high school grades reflect a higher-than-average intelligence and application. At the end of his first year he received a grade of 100 in United States history, 95 in English, 93 in physiology and hygiene, 90 in Latin, and 81 in algebra. His grades continued good during his second year, although he apparently was having some trouble with Greek history, earning in that subject a grade of only 79. His third year in high school, which ended with his graduation in June, 1908, was hardly less distinguished than the others. His final examination grades were as follows:

Advanced German	87
Advanced English	83
Cicero	80
Physics	90
Advanced drawing	83
American history	98
Solid geometry	80
Latin prose at sight	93

Following graduation—he was sixteen years old at the time—Forrestal decided that he was interested in a newspaper

6. Later in life, Forrestal was inclined to emphasize the importance of certain sports activities for military purposes. Writing to his brother Henry on January 1, 1948, Forrestal thanked him for a résumé of the season's football games played by Beacon High School, and added: "The more I have seen of war, the more I believe in the value of so-called contact games as a training for military life. I hope, therefore, that football will continue at Beacon next year." In a 1944 letter to Peter, who was attending Culver Military Academy, Forrestal wrote, "I am glad you are going in the boxing match, because you will learn everytime you go into this sort of competition—one thing in particular, that even if you get popped in the nose it is better not to lose your head but to keep cool enough to wait for your own opening."

career, although it had long been his mother's foremost wish that he become a priest. Through the efforts of his father, who was a friend of the editor, he initially obtained a job on the *Matteawan Journal* as a "cub" reporter. The *Journal* connection also afforded him an opportunity to learn editing, and to become familiar with the business side of running a newspaper. In the summer of 1909 he obtained a position with the *Mount Vernon Argus,* and a year later, in 1910, he went to the *Poughkeepsie News Press* as city editor, holding that position until September, 1911. By that time he had decided that his career would necessarily be limited unless he acquired more formal education, and early in September of that year he returned home and announced, somewhat to his family's surprise, that he had applied and been admitted to Dartmouth College.

Forrestal remained at Dartmouth for one year, where his chief interests appear to have been Latin, and, in terms of extracurricular activity, skiing. In the spring of 1912 he decided against remaining at Dartmouth, and he applied to Princeton University for admission as a transfer student. Early in Forrestal's first year at Princeton, Dean Charles F. Emerson of Dartmouth wrote to Professor C. W. McAlpin of Princeton, that

Mr. Forrestal, I am happy to say, was a good student, somewhat above the average in standing, gave us no trouble and we were very sorry to have him withdraw, but we desire every man to get his education where he wishes and he was given a letter of honorable dismissal without any question.[7]

The reasons for Forrestal's transfer to Princeton remain obscure. According to some of his friends, he entered Dartmouth in the first instance only because he knew that he would not be admitted to Princeton direct from the Matteawan high school. He had calculated, they report, that a year in Hanover would facilitate his chances. But in view of his

7. October 7, 1912.

high school record it is doubtful that this assumption is correct. Moreover, Forrestal subsequently told a number of his friends that since Princeton's standing was considerably above that of Dartmouth, he had concluded that his career would be helped much more by attending Princeton.[8] To one friend, for example, he confided that one was much more likely to meet worthwhile people—his phrase was "people who counted for something"—at Princeton than at Dartmouth.[9] No one can say, of course, what Forrestal's career might have been had he remained at Dartmouth. There can be no doubt, however, that Forrestal did meet "people who counted for something" during his three years at Princeton and that as a result of this period doors were opened for him in the future that might otherwise, had he gone to Dartmouth or somewhere else, have remained closed.

On his application for Princeton, Forrestal described his father's occupation as "contractor." In the blank headed "occupation in view," Forrestal wrote "newspaper work."

Although his brother reports that the family supplied him with an estimated $6,000 during the three years at Princeton, Forrestal, for reasons not clear, was almost continually in financial distress. On one occasion, as a result of his entreaty, his board costs were reduced from $5.50 per week to $4.50. In return for this reduction Forrestal was re-

---

8. One of these friends writes, with reference to the Dartmouth-Princeton transfer: "As you know, Princeton had become the scene of great national interest in 1912. Woodrow Wilson, who had been a storm center in educational circles during his Presidency of Princeton University and in the world of politics during his term as Governor of New Jersey, was nominated as the Democratic Presidential candidate in the summer of 1912. So when we entered the University in September, 1912, Princeton was probably the most discussed college in the country and it was certainly an exciting place to be as an undergraduate. Although Forrestal never mentioned why he had transferred to Princeton, it seems safe to assume from my acquaintance with him that the national interest in Princeton made it more attractive to him at the time than the remote and possibly limited atmosphere he found at Dartmouth. Furthermore, the opportunities for advancing toward the goals of his ambitions would seem to have been more plentiful then from his point of view at Princeton."—Communication to the author, June 17, 1960.

9. The friend added that "after all, he was only being practical."

quired to render "monitor services." Not long after he was admitted he applied to the university for remission of tuition on the grounds of "Lack of funds for current year. Owing to business troubles parents are handicapped in furnishing of funds."

Most of his friends believed that Forrestal, or "Vint" as he was frequently called in those days, came from a poor or even impoverished family; indeed, that belief is still widely held with regard to Forrestal's origins and early years. The Wall Street Forrestal, from this point of view, was a "poor boy who had made good."[10]

The legend of Forrestal's early poverty, however, would appear to be somewhat exaggerated. To begin with, his family did supply him with a substantial amount of money. And if Forrestal was poor, why did he choose, first Dartmouth, and then Princeton, both of which, in 1911-1912, charged above-average fees, and catered to the sons of the wealthy? Why, further, if Forrestal could not depend upon his family for financial aid, did he join one of Princeton's more exclusive "eating" clubs, Cottage Club, early in 1913? Finally, assuming poverty, how can one account for the fact that Forrestal, although he worked at a variety of jobs, was inclined to reject those which were, in the words of a Princeton contemporary, "dull, tiresome, and unimaginative"?[11]

The probable explanation for the disparity of fact and legend reveals a good deal about Forrestal's sense of himself and his relations with his family. There is evidence to suggest that while Forrestal's parents could and did help him

---

10. In a memoir of Forrestal after his death, one of his Princeton contemporaries wrote: "Jim had to work. College was his own idea, no help from anyone." Frank P. Leslie, *James Forrestal/Princeton Class of 1915.* (Maplewoods, Wayzata, Minnesota, Christmas, 1951). The memoir was first published in the *Minneapolis Star* of November 5, 1951.

11. In a revealing anecdote, the contemporary reports that one day in September, 1912, he and Forrestal applied for jobs at the Princeton Bureau of Self-Help. They were assigned to work at the university's farm (an area now occupied by the Stadium). The farm overseer, he continues, "gave us hoes and told us that the job that day was 'hilling beans.' This meant hoeing and piling soil around the base of the beanstalks to make them grow stronger

financially, Forrestal did not want their assistance, indeed, felt guilty about accepting it. Although circumstances forced him to accept family help he was extremely reluctant to do so, and in fact wrote his father on several occasions telling him not to send any more money, that he, Forrestal, did not want to be a "drain" on his father and his brother Henry, or the business.

But it was not the "drain" aspect of the matter that gave him the most serious concern. Sometime, or perhaps somewhere between St. Joachim's Parochial School and Princeton University, Forrestal underwent a psychological experience that is often referred to as "adolescent rebellion." Such "rebellion" is typically characterized by a rejection of one's parents and the values they represent. Although the rejection may not be overt—it does not require, for example, that the youngster leave home or that the parents be "told off" on numerous occasions—the adolescent's feeling is very real that his parents do not want to understand him, or even try to understand him, and that they are trying to impose upon him a way of life that is alien to his nature. If, in addition, the parents are restrictive rather than permissive in their attitudes toward his self-expression, including sexual expression, the adolescent himself may develop a rigid and tense personality structure that will limit his own growth and future maturity. A homelife during childhood in which love and affection are rarely manifested, either between the parents or between parents and offspring, is likely to produce an adult who is severely handicapped in establishing warm relationships with others. Deprived as a child of love and

---

and more deeply rooted. It was a dull, tiresome and unimaginative chore. I could see that 'Vint' did not relish the job and after two hours, he threw down his hoe and said, 'There must be better ways of making money than hilling beans.' With that firm ultimatum, he left the farm and did not return again." Communication to the author, May 25, 1960. It is not known whether Forrestal immediately obtained another job, but according to the informant, "Job opportunities for needy students were scarce at Princeton in those days."

understanding, he may as an adult be unable to offer them even to those who stand closest to him.

Without, for the moment, suggesting that Forrestal was such an adult, it is appropriate to point out that there were elements in Forrestal's Matteawan experience that promoted estrangement from his family, and contributed to the formation of the moody, taciturn, and withdrawn figure he was later to become. Despite his father's hope, the young Forrestal took no interest whatever in the family business. And despite the earnest wishes of his mother, who was the more significant figure in his early life, Forrestal refused to enter a seminary and become a priest. As he grew older, he also found himself less and less in sympathy with the narrow, rigid mores of Matteawan and its rather parochial attitudes. First the newspaper world, then Hanover, and finally Princeton marked the end, for Forrestal, of early curfews, of forbidden ideas and books, of attendance at Mass, and of much else that he disliked or from which he increasingly felt estranged.

His alienation from home and community revealed itself in a variety of ways. Beginning in 1912, when he transferred from Dartmouth to Princeton, his visits to Matteawan became less and less frequent, and practically ceased altogether after he was established in Wall Street. Although Forrestal occasionally wrote to his parents and to his brothers Will and Henry, he did not confide in them, much less discuss with them his personal problems. He rarely spoke to any of his friends about his childhood and adolescent years; indeed, some of them had the impression that Forrestal was an orphan. Those who inquired about his background quickly discovered that he was extremely reluctant to discuss it, and many of them, as a consequence, did not know until after his death that he had spent the early years in Matteawan. His two sons did not even meet their Matteawan relatives until 1949.

His self-exile from the family circle, however, was accompanied by a burden of guilt which was not relieved by the passage of years. In the early twenties Forrestal made several efforts to compensate his parents, his mother particularly, for the disappointments he had caused them. Early in 1925 he rented an apartment for his widowed mother in New York, specifying that the apartment should contain a wood-burning fireplace because, in her view, no home was complete without one. He also bought her a fur coat. But she neither wore the coat nor lived in the apartment before her death in October, 1925. The shower of gifts, in any case, could not entirely alleviate a conscience made guilty by a choice of life and career to which both parents were opposed. To the end of their days, neither parent, and again the mother especially, could forgive their youngest son for having rejected not merely the priesthood but the Church itself. Their son, for his part, carried that rejection as a scar on his conscience, and it was one of many scars that did not disappear.

Forrestal's estrangement from his family made it difficult for him to accept their financial support during the Princeton years and the period that followed. Although it would have been easier for him to pretend that the estrangement did not exist, neither then nor later was Forrestal skilled in the arts of pretense and self-deception. Aware of the great gulf between his own values and those of his parent, and determined at the same time to make his own way in the world, he nevertheless was forced by circumstances to accept his father's money while at Princeton. But he did so with remorse, and when he left Princeton in 1915 he preferred to borrow money from friends rather than request additional assistance from his family.[12]

---

12. Shortly after leaving Princeton, Forrestal borrowed $500 from Donald Douglas who was associated with the Quaker Oats Company in Chicago. He told Douglas at the time, "I don't know when I'll be able to pay it back, but I will." A few years later Douglas received a check for the $500 plus 6 percent compound interest.

Of this early conflict that raged in Forrestal's mind his Princeton fellow students knew little or nothing. The Forrestal they saw for almost three years was ambitious, introspective, sports-minded, and witty in a dry sort of way. Proud of the fact that as a "Mick" or Irish-Catholic of middle-class background he had been admitted to a university that, at that time, accepted very few students who were not both Protestant and rich, Forrestal, like F. Scott Fitzgerald, another undergraduate "Mick," enjoyed the company of those who came from many of America's wealthiest and most powerful families. But while he joined one of the fashionable clubs, drank Martinis rather than beer, and bought his clothes at the more expensive haberdashery stores on Nassau Street, he was not a snob and he had no great liking for snobs.[13] His identification with Princeton was intense and lifelong,[14] but it did not preclude a genuine sympathy for a variety of campus underdogs, including students who were poor and who failed to "make" a club.

While Forrestal was not the type of Princeton undergraduate who could be described as a "big man on campus," he was popular enough, and "big" enough, to become, in his senior year, editor of the *Daily Princetonian,* and to be voted by his class the "man most likely to succeed."[15] Popularity brought with it other, more significant, advantages. It promoted contacts with "people who counted for something," and it also provided Forrestal with a glimpse of that world into which he was to move later with such conspicuous success. Indeed, he was already a part of that world, in which

13. As one of his friends who knew him at Princeton remarks, Forrestal "had a great respect for character and merit wherever he saw it and little respect for the spoiled boys who come from some homes of wealth. But he also had a special admiration for strong character bred in the atmosphere of the temptations of wealth."—Letter to the Author, November 27, 1959.

14. In addition to raising money for the university and serving, toward the end of his life, as one of its trustees, Forrestal was an active participant in alumni affairs. When he became Navy Secretary and Secretary of Defense, he spoke frequently at Princeton gatherings, and occasionally spent weekends and holidays with friends who lived there.

15. Editorship of the *Princetonian* paid him approximately $1,200.

a number of his friends moved comfortably and confidently, when he reached his senior year in 1915. Park Avenue and Sutton Place were almost more familiar to him than any street in Matteawan, and, it need hardly be added, far more appealing.

To the bewilderment of his family and friends, approximately six weeks before graduation Forrestal withdraw from Princeton, and as a result never received his bachelor's degree. Although the reasons for his action are not entirely clear, it is probable that financial problems and course difficulties were important contributing factors. According to some accounts, he found himself in a serious financial crisis when the paying editorship of the *Daily Princetonian* rotated to another student in midyear. Of greater significance, perhaps, was the fact that he had flunked an English course and refused to take it again. Many years later Forrestal confided to a close associate that a certain Professor of English had not liked him, with the result that Forrestal ceased to attend any of his lectures (which were optional). Just before midterm examinations, Forrestal recalled, the professor had called him in and said that because he had missed the lectures he would not pass the course no matter how well he did in the examinations. Despite the warning, Forrestal still refused to attend the lectures, and he left Princeton when he was officially notified that he would have to repeat the course the following year in order to graduate.

It was also during his last year at Princeton that Forrestal's gradual withdrawal from the Catholic faith became final and complete. A classmate of his at the time reports that late in 1914 Forrestal engaged in a quarrel with the Catholic chaplain at Princeton, a quarrel involving a Church doctrine in which Forrestal did not believe and which he regarded as ridiculous. The recollection of other friends, however, is that Forrestal's church attendance was always sporadic, and the belief of one of them is that Forrestal ceased to be religious after he began to read the works of Karl Marx. But whichever is the more correct account, it is certain that when Forrestal left Princeton he had ceased altogether to think of himself as a practicing Catholic, and so far as is known, he rarely thereafter attended a Catholic Church service.

It was clearly necessary, when Forrestal departed from Princeton in 1915, that he obtain a job immediately, and he initially found employment with the New Jersey Zinc Company. His connection with that firm, however, was a short one. Through the father of Robert Christie, a close Princeton friend, Forrestal was offered, and accepted, a position with the American Tobacco Company. Although the job paid well, and held a good deal of future promise, Forrestal quickly tired of it; one of Forrestal's friends reports him saying at the time that "he had not come all that way, and worked all that hard, to spend the rest of his life selling cigarettes." His third employer was the New York *World,* and in his later years Forrestal was to regard the period he spent as a *World* reporter as one of the most satisfying of his life. His reporting for the *World,* in addition to reviving his old interest in newspaper work, brought him into contact with Wall Street society and its intoxicating atmosphere of money and power. He especially admired those Wall Streeters he met who were bright, tough, and successful, and he resolved to make his career among them at the first opportunity.

Fortunately, the opportunity was at hand in the person of William A. Phillips, then in charge of the sales organization of William A. Read and Company. In 1915, while Forrestal was still at Princeton, Phillips had sent Dean Mathey, later a vice-president of Dillon, Read, to Princeton to recruit bond salesmen in the graduating class. Mathey, himself a Princeton graduate of 1912, "asked one question," according to a Dillon, Read informant. The question was "Who is editor of the *Daily Princetonian?"* He was told, the informant continues,

it was a fellow named Forrestal, and he then said, "Tell me about him." He was informed that Forrestal was working his way through college, and was a member of the Cottage Club. Mathey met him but his impression was based solely on his record. That was the only thing he cared about at the time.

Mathey talked to Forrestal about coming to Read, and Forrestal was interested because he was about to face a career and he was interested in anything. But he did not commit himself then. He wanted to make money and get underway. Mathey suggested he come to New York and talk to Phillips. Forrestal eventually did, and it was really Phillips who persuaded him to go to work for Read.

Not long after Forrestal joined the firm as a bond salesman, William A. Read died, and his widow (whose only son was killed in World War I) sold her interest in the company to one of its senior partners, Clarence Dillon. The firm then became Dillon, Read and Company, and during the years that Forrestal was associated with it, which began in 1916 and did not end until 1940, the company established itself as one of New York's best-known and most influential investment banking houses.

Forrestal's career at Dillon, Read was meteoric. He began at Read as a bond salesman in the Albany area, which, at the time, was a one-man operation. His territory included Buffalo, Rochester, and other cities in upper New York State, and within a short time the business had expanded sufficiently to require additional salesmen. Appointed manager of the Albany office, he recruited an able sales force, which had never existed before, and proceeded to make the Albany branch one of Read's most successful selling organizations. He did so well, in fact, that in less than three years he was called back to New York and appointed head of Dillon, Read's sales department. By 1923 he was a partner in the firm, by 1926 a vice-president, and in 1938, when he was forty-six years old, he became its president.

Forrestal's Dillon, Read career, covering a span of almost twenty-five years, was interrupted briefly by World War I. When the United States entered the war, Forrestal and his friend Ed Shea (who was later to become an Ethyl Corporation executive) made several efforts to join one of the services together. Finding that they were too late to receive commissions in the Army and Air Force, they tried the Marine Corps. At the Marine recruiting station, Forrestal engaged in a rather heated quarrel with the sergeant on duty who did not share Forrestal's assumption that he and Shea were entitled to commissions. "I see," the sergeant is supposed to have said, "that you're another one of those goddamn leaders. Well, we got enough of them, and we don't need any more." Forrestal's response to the sergeant's statement was to step out of the recruiting line. He and Shea then enlisted in the Naval Reserve at the New York Navy Yard.

Deciding that they needed some training in order to qualify for a commission, Forrestal and Shea spent several weeks at Princeton as members of an informal ROTC group. The mother of one of the students, a Mrs. Warberton, offered to finance flight instruction for twelve of the ROTC members, and from Princeton Forrestal and Shea went to East Greenwich, Rhode Island, for private flying lessons. They never received their licenses, however, because the Naval Reserve had other plans for Forrestal, Shea, and some of the others.

Called into active service on July 5, 1917, Forrestal was sent to Toronto, Canada, for flight training with the Royal Flying Corps.[16] In November he was promoted to ensign and

---

16. Many years later, when he was Secretary of the Navy, Forrestal had the Navy Department archives searched for information pertaining to his training with the Royal Flying Corps. In the files of the Bureau of Aeronautics at the National Archives, one of his aides found a report made on Forrestal in 1917 by Ensign F. S. Allen, commander of the Naval Aviation Detachment in which Forrestal served. The full text of Ensign Allen's report read: "J. V. Forrestal. Good flyer. Not a technical mind. Used to write for magazines. Has helped me with official paper work. Dependable worker, but lacks practical push. With a little experience will make good officer. Needs

assigned to the First Naval District with headquarters in Boston, Massachusetts. Early in January, 1918, he was transferred to the Aviation Division of the Office of the Chief of Naval Operations, Admiral William S. Benson. By March, Forrestal had completed flight tests at the Naval Air Station, Hampton Roads, Virginia, and he was then designated a Naval Aviator. In June he was promoted to Lieutenant (junior grade). Released from active duty in December, 1918, he was promoted to Lieutenant the following June. He resigned from the Service in December, 1919, and shortly thereafter rejoined Dillon, Read and Company.

The early twenties found Forrestal sharing an apartment with three other bachelors at 660 Madison Avenue in New York. The original group consisted of Kenneth R. Smith, Allen Ames, and Artemus Gates, in addition to Forrestal, but there were changes from time to time as a consequence of moves, business transfers, and marriages. Replacements included Ed Shea, John Vincent (later a partner in the law firm of Lord, Day and Lord), and Manning Barr, of Barr Brothers. And there were also other apartments, in one of which, on upper Fifth Avenue, Forrestal lived for several years before his marriage. In 1920 Forrestal and his bachelor friends acquired a summer place at Glen Cove, Long Island, where they spent weekends and vacations.

The Forrestal of those days was similar in many respects to the Forrestal who later achieved fame as the nation's first Secretary of Defense. In New York, as earlier in Princeton and later in Washington, Forrestal's behavior reflected ambition, drive, and dedication to work. In the words of one of his roommates of the period, Forrestal

was a serious and hard worker. He had a sense of humor but he was always dedicated to what he was doing. If he was working

---

toning down from a radical socialistic attitude with men, & worrying about whether it is right to be a soldier." Forrestal was greatly amused by the reference to his "radical socialistic outlook," but pleased to find that Ensign Allen had rated him second in the class of twenty-one cadets.

hard, he had no time to be humorous. If something didn't fit into his plan, it exasperated him.

In those early days he would work until 1 or 2 A.M. and all through the weekends. He thought he could work beyond anyone else's limit. He was driving for superiority. I knew that if it were humanly possible he would be at the top of the heap someday. We all thought he'd go beyond us.

At that time he had hardly any social life whatsoever. However his fast rise in business gave him a broad social acquaintance.

But while he found it difficult to relax, Forrestal could be, recalls another friend, "a delightful companion [and] always popular because he was such good company." Apparently, however, Forrestal in his bachelor days was not precisely a ladies' man, much less a Don Juan. Although he was "socially very attractive," a Wall Street acquaintance reports,

he didn't see much of women in those days. He was too busy and a little shy of them but that wore off in time. I would often go to some of the Junior League dances, but he rarely went. He was really quite shy with women until he got married.

He was a damned good boxer and loved music. He had seats for the Philharmonic and he went all the time. That was his pastime.

Introspective, reserved, and even secretive by nature, Forrestal, reminisces a former roommate,

never opened up, even though I shared a bedroom with him at 660 Madison. We both went our own ways. And yet he was a very good friend. We had business relations together, and he was very generous. You could go to him and ask his advice and you knew he would give you an honest and worthwhile decision.

He was all right if you didn't bother him. If you did, he'd move out of the apartment or have you moved out. He had a temper, but most of the time it was very well controlled. He'd seethe and boil and finally break out with what was wrong.

In another appraisal, someone who knew Forrestal well in the twenties remembers him

as a peculiar fellow. He had a strange, complex personality. There was a socialistic streak in him right from the start. He was always a little contemptuous of wealth, and yet he would always strive for it. He was cynical about wealthy people and yet he loved to spend time with people like Jock Whitney.

There was a real split which was quite obvious. He liked to be with prominent people but I don't think he was really socially ambitious. He was never disloyal to them. He liked the best things and the glamour of having them, but he wasn't socially competitive.

Despite the "socialistic streak," Forrestal is remembered by his friends as someone who liked to live well and did so with a certain flair. A "meticulous dresser," as one of the New York friends puts it, he had all of his clothes "from the skin out" custom-made. He wore Peale shoes, for example, and purchased his suits, jackets, and slacks either from Brooks Brothers or Anderson and Shepherd in London. After his marriage he employed a chauffeur and valet, and there were always several servants attached to the Forrestal household. He traveled first-class to Europe almost every year, usually in the spring or summer, and while there customarily hired a car and chauffeur for touring purposes. He was especially fond of the British Isles.

By the mid-twenties he was well-to-do, successful, and although he was past his thirtieth birthday, still single. He had had at least one love affair, and not long after it was ended, by the girl rather than by him, he met at one of the Long Island parties an attractive, intelligent, and sophisticated *Vogue* editor who almost immediately fell in love with him. At the time of their meeting Miss Josephine Ogden, the divorced wife of Adam Stovall and daughter of the Howard Newton Ogdens of Huntington, West Virginia, was dating one of his friends, but it was not long after that she and Forrestal established a close relationship.

Forrestal's rather unconventional ideas about marriage inclined some of his friends to believe that no woman, no matter how romantically attached, would make the mistake of marrying him on his own terms. One of his convictions, for example, was that husbands and wives were entitled to lead separate private lives if they so desired. He was opposed to having children on the grounds that they interfered with such privacy and with career interests. He also frequently observed that most people he knew were failures as parents, and he doubted that he himself could ever be a satisfactory father. If and when he found himself married, he told friends, he would refuse to be "bothered" by children or try to be a "fulltime father." The average wife, he thought, was an aggressive and demanding creature who was more apt to impede her husband's career than advance it. "If you asked me to sum up Forrestal's attitude toward women," one of his friends comments, "I would quote the character from Shaw's *Man and Superman* who says: 'I know all your tricks. Don't try and fool me.' "

Consequently many of his associates were genuinely surprised on Thursday, October 12, 1926, when Josephine Ogden became Mrs. James Forrestal following a ceremony at New York's Municipal Building. On the day of his marriage Forrestal left a note on the desk of a Dillon, Read colleague which read: "I'm committing the mistake called matrimony. Unfortunate woman is Josephine Ogden. See you Monday. J.V." Another Dillon, Read colleague at that time, who "had never met nor heard of Mrs. Forrestal before they were married," recalls that Forrestal

went out to lunch one day and a City Hall reporter whom I knew called me and said: "What's all this about?" I didn't know what he was talking about, but it turns out Forrestal had just gotten married. He came back to the office the same day.

For a brief time the marriage appeared to be a success, but within a few years the Forrestals began to lead lives that were more often apart than together. Given the differences between them of taste and temperament, it was inevitable that the marriage would prove to be a difficult one, although no one foresaw in 1926 that ultimately it would have tragic consequences for both Forrestals. Josephine Forrestal, everyone who knew her in the early days agrees, was gay, witty, and amusing. A charming hostess who loved to entertain frequently, she particularly enjoyed the gaiety of large dinner gatherings, cocktail parties, dances, and other social affairs. She was at home in the company of the "smart" people who comprised New York's café society, and she initially made a number of efforts to persuade her husband that there was more to life than the daily "Wall Street grind."

Forrestal, on the other hand, as he became more immersed in business and, later, political affairs, found it increasingly difficult to relax in the company of those his wife regarded as her friends. Therefore, as the years passed, he spent less and less time in the social circle of which his wife was so much a part. Much more by preference than by necessity, he often worked late at night and on weekends, occasionally to avoid social engagements to which his wife had committed them, and when he was not working he preferred to spend his time with his own friends who themselves were largely occupied with business or politics. Apart from some mutual friends and the requirements of official entertaining, the Forrestals were infrequently seen together during the last fifteen years of their marriage, and when they were in each other's company, a friend recalls, "they never acted like a husband and wife together. I rarely saw them out, and when I did see them they were awfully cold."

Living increasingly apart and even taking their vacations separately, Forrestal's life, especially in Washington, was essentially that of a bachelor. Although in Washington as in New York he frequently worked evenings and weekends, he found time for female companionship, and was an intimate friend of a number of women in New York, Washington, and Europe. Several of these women, who were also unhappily married, were in love with him, and at least one of them strongly urged him to obtain a divorce. There is no evidence, however, that either he or his wife ever seriously considered dissolving their marriage.

Indeed, both of them continued to be fond of each other long after they had gone their separate ways. None of Forrestal's friends can recall ever hearing him quarrel with Josephine or comment adversely on her behavior. Although he "did his best in a weird Irish way to appear hard-boiled," a Washington colleague of his remembers, "he was as soft as butter when his heart was involved. He was completely patient with Josephine through their whole marriage. I never heard him complain about her or speak harshly to her. The real problem was his fierce independence and desire not to have any strings attached to him, and I think he was always surprised to find himself married."

Josephine, meanwhile, aware that she was relatively unimportant in her husband's life, made frequent visits to Europe where she would occasionally remain for months at a time. In marrying her, she believed, Forrestal had been seeking a mistress and companion rather than a wife and a mother for his children, and when she discovered she was gradually becoming "a Germanic chattel," she began to absent herself from New York and Washington as much as possible. Forrestal was not always happy about her extended European trips, and in 1949, following his illness and suicide, Josephine was to feel somewhat guilty about them. But considering Forrestal's attitude toward marriage, and especially his reluctance "to have strings attached to him," it is rather doubtful that her absences contributed significantly to the later tragedy.

Despite Forrestal's views about marriage and children, by 1931 he had become the father of two sons, Michael Vincent, born on November 26, 1927, and Peter Ogden, born on August 2, 1930. The two boys saw relatively little of their father during childhood and adolescence, partly because Forrestal was away a good deal of the time and partly because his ideas about raising children, like his ideas about marriage, were rather unconventional. To begin with, he had great difficulty in communicating with children. You could not deal rationally with them, he once complained, until they were sixteen or seventeen, and in the interim they could not be "held off" as others could be "held off" who were capable of reasoning. Perhaps for this reason Forrestal believed that children should be brought up in an environment separate from the home. An admirer of the English system of raising children outside the family, he sent both boys to boarding schools in the United States and abroad.

He was not a strict disciplinarian, however, preferring to make suggestions, sometimes of a teasing nature, rather than give orders or issue direct commands. "Our relationship," one of his sons recalls,

was that of Victorian son to Victorian parent. When we lived on Long Island before the war, we rarely saw much of him except on Friday nights when we were ushered into the dark library and would report to him on our week's activities. There was always a feeling of inadequacy on our parts, and it was a problem for us to think of what to report to him. We were always somewhat nervous about how to face him in the next conference. He did this to satisfy his feeling that he wasn't paying enough attention to us. but I'm sure he was as uncomfortable as we were.

We never exchanged letters until the latter part of my prep school years. It was then that he began to develop a real interest in my studies and in what I was going to do.

When he did discipline the boys, it was not by spanking them but by letting them know that they had done something wrong or improper. Disciplinary efforts, moreover, were usually based on the complaints of the servants, some of whom were much less tolerant of misconduct, and it also appears that Josephine was inclined to punish the boys when they misbehaved far more often than her husband.

Placing a strong emphasis on the need to learn self-reliance early in life, Forrestal particularly feared that his sons would grow into manhood severely handicapped by the fact that they had had wealthy parents and that too much had been given to them. He therefore made it a rule of never doing anything for them that they could do themselves. He was especially parsimonious where money was concerned, to such an extent that some of his friends, who were also fathers, regarded him as rather "stingy" with his children. One of these friends recalls that he once argued with Forrestal about the living standards he should provide for his two sons. The friend's attitude was that the sons of the rich would not be spoiled by too much money provided they learned to shop for bargains, and, in other ways, came to know the value of money. As an example he cited a recent purchase of a boat by his own son. The friend, subsequently investigating and discovering that cheaper boats of the same quality were available, continually reminded his son that he had been "taken." Instead of depriving his sons of money, he suggested, Forrestal should give them as much as they wanted, but see to it that they were "humiliated" if they did not spend the money wisely. Forrestal "shrugged," the friend remembers, and said that he had known too many "spoiled rich kids" at Princeton to risk making the same mistakes their parents had made.

As young children the Forrestal boys spent most of their time at the Long Island house where they saw more of their servants than of their parents. In addition to a Mr. and Mrs. Duffy, who served as gardener and cook, Forrestal's valet Stanley Campbell (who was employed by him from 1936 to 1946), and chauffeur Patrick O'Toole, there was a succession of nurses, none of whom stayed with the family as long as the other servants. Both boys remember two French nurses known as "Thundercloud 1 and 2," a Swiss nurse, and a Mrs. Bond who was from Scotland. It was the latter who decided on the name Peter when the Forrestal's second son was born. Both parents had been considering "Jonathan" but were persuaded by her to reject it.

Except for family celebrations of birthdays, Thanksgiving,

and Christmas, there was little "togetherness" in the home.
The boys recollect that their parents did a great deal of
entertaining, and on such occasions they were usually
trundled out to meet the guests. They also recall being taken
to the 1939 World's Fair in New York, the Broadway hit
"Hell'sapoppin'," and the Blue Mountains in the summer
of 1935 or 1936. Frequently during the summer they would
accompany their father to the Creek Club where they were
deposited by the swimming pool while Forrestal played golf.

In certain respects, the childhoods of the boys were not
very different from those of other children whose parents
owned homes on Long Island's fashionable North Shore.
They attended the Episcopal Sunday school (neither son was
raised as a Catholic), learned to swim and play tennis, and
traveled in Europe. Although their father had no interest in
horses, Michael had his own horse, and Peter his own pony,
for several years. There was also a garden house on the place
which the two brothers converted into a play area containing
their electric trains and other prized possessions.

Unlike many other fathers, however, Forrestal maintained an emotional as well as physical distance from his
sons. He was not, one son reports,

a physically demonstrative man. He showed us affection more
with words and by being fair and understanding when my
brother and I battled with each other, which was frequently, than
any other way. I can't remember being bounced on his knee. He
wasn't that type of man.

Once when I had the mumps, for example, he paid me very
little attention. He simply was not a solicitous kind of person.

The other son recalls that

during a golf game once, I was hit in the face with a club. It was
about the only time Dad showed that he was nervous and upset
over something which had happened to me. He was terrified that
it was serious.

Choosing to be remote and aloof from his children, Forrestal
appeared to them almost totally indifferent to their welfare,

but it is probable that this indifference was to some extent feigned. Many years later, when Michael was ill in the Navy, he discovered that his father "found out from the doctors all there was to know about what was wrong with me, and not until then did he relax about it."[17] When they were children, however, neither son was able to penetrate the father's emotional reserve. The son who had the mumps recalls that as a child "I don't think I had any feeling about Dad."

Forrestal's stress on the early development in children of self-reliance affected the choice of schools to which the boys were sent. Michael, who attended the preparatory Aiken School, in Aiken, South Carolina, and later Exeter, recalls that

Mother's influence prevailed in the choice of Aiken. Dad didn't like the idea, as Aiken is rather horsey. (Ma loved horses.) But he didn't object too violently as long as he thought the school was rough. He had a slight feeling against Aiken because it was a resort town and, he thought, full of useless people.

Exeter was also Ma's idea. I think she had met Louis Perry and watched him play tennis or something. In the summer of 1941 we made a tour of prep schools and chose Exeter. Dad approved of it because he had been told that it was hard.

When the boys were nine and seven, respectively, they embarked by themselves on the *Champlain* to attend the La Châtaigneraie School in Coppet, Switzerland. Again, it was "Ma's idea to send us abroad at an early age so that we could learn a foreign language," but for Forrestal the major attraction was that the boys would learn self-reliance by traveling abroad alone.

During the summer of 1937, Michael and Peter underwent an experience in self-reliance, the details of which they were never to forget. They had been staying with their parents in a house at Biarritz, and after a time they were sent to the Isle of Wight to visit family friends. Leaving Biarritz

---

17. When some of the doctors informed him that Michael would receive special attention, it was characteristic of Forrestal that he insisted his son be given the same care as that given other patients.

with a Basque chauffeur who, in Michael's words, "was quite nuts," they crashed into a farmhouse on the way to Le Havre, backed up, and continued the trip. They arrived in Le Havre with just enough time to put themselves and their baggage on board the *De Grasse* before it sailed. As the ship was leaving the harbor, they were paged by loudspeakers and shortly after taken off by a police boat which carried them back to Le Havre. Their mother had forgotten to give them their passports, and the boys were told they would be placed under "protective custody," that is, sent to jail.

The American consul in Le Havre located Forrestal at the Ritz bar in Paris, and Michael talked to his father on the telephone. "He asked me," Michael remembers,

> what had happened. I explained, almost in tears, and said that he should come down and do something. He replied, "As soon as you get it all straightened out, meet me in the bar at Claridge's in London." That was all. We didn't speak to Ma, but I assumed Dad had contacted her.
>
> I was worried because we had very little money. We spent one night in jail and were then moved to a nearby hotel where we were under guard for two days. It was just before the war, and I think the French were suspicious. I'm sure they thought we were carrying something from Germany out of the country.

Although they did not hear from their father for three days, he or their mother sent them the passports, and after purchasing a new set of tickets they set out again on another ship. There was no one to meet them at Southampton, and Michael, who "didn't have a dime left," paid for their passage to the Isle of Wight by giving the boat's captain his watch. Arriving at the Isle of Wight, they were met by the family friends who reimbursed the captain, thereby reclaiming Michael's watch. "Dad," Michael continues,

> had evidently talked to them, told them what had happened, and asked them to meet all boats, which they did for two days before they gave up.
>
> I'm sure that when Dad talked to me from the Ritz, he was

trying to prove to his friends at the bar that he was a tough father and that his children were completely self-reliant. He did everything he could short of coming down.

Believing that travel and self-reliance were closely related, Forrestal also felt that self-reliance had its physical side, and he encouraged both his sons to engage in sports activities, including football and boxing. One of the boys recalls that when they attended St. Bernard's School in New York, February—June, 1939,

we used to get beaten up regularly as we walked to school. We lived at 17 Beekman Place (at the corner of 50th Street) and had to walk to 54th and Park to pick up the school bus. We wore blue coats and blue caps and looked like the kind of kids you instinctively wanted to kick. On a couple of occasions I really got trounced. I told Dad that I couldn't take it anymore. So he arranged for me to take boxing lessons at St. Bernard's. That was his answer to the problem.

When it was time to plan his sons' college or university education, Forrestal was Navy Secretary, and he made some effort to interest them in the Naval Academy at Annapolis. When one of them refused to attend the Academy, on the grounds that it lacked "good standards" and "graduated fools," Forrestal, according to the son's recollection,

became quite exercised about it. I think it was all part of the science "kick" he was on, and then he was very impressed with the Navy and thought the country would have need of men with military training. He had come to know [Admiral] Radford and had great respect for him.

In any case, he asked me to look it over. I went down there during spring vacation and came back with the same impression I had had. He told me "the chances are that if a man is a horse's ass when he goes in, he will be one when he gets out—it's not the fault of the institution."

Eventually Michael and Peter attended Princeton, where, apart from suggesting that they take more science and mathematics and fewer literature courses, Forrestal intruded as little as possible on their curricular and extracurricular activities.[18]

By the time they entered Princeton, his relations with both boys were a good deal closer. It was during his last year at Exeter, in 1944—1945, Michael remembers, that his father began to take more interest in what he was doing and thinking. One of Michael's warmer memories of that year concerns a time when he had become involved

in campus politics. We had a mock convention and the most popular candidate was Minnesota's Senator Joseph Ball, primarily because of his name. I had written Dad and told him all about it. Suddenly, out of the blue, he wrote that he was arriving at Exeter on the eve of the convention with the Senator.

It was the first magnificent thing he had done for his kids. It was a great coup. There was a dinner and then they both spoke. Ball ran away with the vote and Dad really enjoyed himself. It was the beginning of communication between us because now we had a subject for conversation.

He also came to my graduation at Exeter which is something I would not have expected him to do. He even spoke at the ceremony, but typically he made sure he was covered. As the father of a student he didn't want to make *the* speech. So he brought [Arthur] Compton with him and Compton made the longer speech.

Later, when Michael was attached to Roving Ambassador W. Averell Harriman's staff in Moscow, he sent his father long letters about his experiences and impressions, letters which Forrestal had copied and sent to numerous friends and col-

---

18. In a letter to Michael of October 4, 1947, Forrestal urged his son to take courses in logic, mathematics, natural sciences, and history because these fields constituted "grand areas of intellectual preparation." They also have relevance, he added, to making practical decisions based on scientific methods, and he observed that "in my own experience, a great many decisions—both in business and government—have been reached more on emotional than on intellectual levels." On another occasion he urged Michael, who was studying Russian, to read the plays and stories of Chekov. "Gogol, Turgenev and Dostoevski," he commented, "are another matter. I never got very much out of them myself, although if you like morbid and psychoanalytical stuff, you will find plenty of it in Dostoevski."—Letter to Michael, February 4, 1946.

leagues in Washington. Although he was proud of these letters, it was characteristic of Forrestal that he did not share his pride with his son, Michael, who did not discover until sometime later that his letters had been widely circulated. It was also typical of Forrestal that he rarely discussed his children with his friends and business associates. One of those who shared an apartment with him in the twenties and frequently saw him during the thirties "never heard him mention his children. As a matter of fact," he adds, "for a long time I didn't even know he had any."

However much or little his friends knew about his personal life, all of them were well aware that his domestic affairs were not permitted to intrude upon his career or detract from the energies he devoted to it. When he was transferred from Albany to Dillon, Read's New York office, a Wall Street colleague observes,

Forrestal was very aggressive and built up the sales department very quickly. To be honest about it, I always felt that he had over-expanded the department. He went too fast. But he was very much respected in the organization, although he didn't have much time for small things and chitchat. He was too busy building.

His secretary at the time recalls that after working a full day Forrestal

would write sales letters. He'd start dictating them about four in the afternoon, and he always paced while he dictated. Many is the night I'd be there until nine or ten typing those letters.

Already a Dillon, Read vice-president by the time of his marriage, Forrestal in the following years achieved an impressive number of business and financial successes. In the late twenties and early thirties Forrestal engineered a number of Wall Street coups that were the talk of the investment banking world. One of them, in particular, marked him out as the probable successor to Clarence Dillon as president of

Dillon, Read. Another which ultimately netted him a gross
profit of almost $900,000, helped assure his own and his
family's financial security. The latter venture, however, did
not redound entirely to his personal credit. In 1933 it brought
him to the attention of the Pecora Committee investigation
of "Stock Exchange Practices," and years later, when he was
Secretary of Defense, it was used against him by Drew Pearson and others who were opposed to Forrestal's continuance
in high government office.

The transaction that firmly established Forrestal's Wall
Street reputation and Dillon, Read's future involved the
Dodge and Chrysler automobile empires. Following the
deaths in 1920 of the two Dodge brothers, their heirs operated the Dodge company for approximately five years before
selling control of it to Dillon, Read for $146,000,000. For-
restal had played a major role in the negotiations, and in
1928 he was again involved when Dillon, Read approached
Walter Chrysler and suggested that he combine his own
business with the Dodge enterprise. Chrysler, cautious and
deliberate, insisted that the terms of the merger, which involved the purchase by him of Dillon, Read's interest, be
acceptable to holders of 90 percent of every class of Dodge
stock. As a consequence of his position, influential opinion in
Wall Street was that the merger would never take place.

Forrestal and other Dillon, Read executives, however,
refused to concede that the difficulties were insurmountable.
On July 30, 1928, Wall Street was taken by surprise when
Dillon, Read went into the open market and bought up
enough Dodge shares to satisfy Chrysler's 90 percent requirement. Forrestal personally was given a good deal of credit for
the success of the negotiations. The merger netted Dillon,
Read a substantial profit, and thereafter Forrestal was regarded by many as the "boy wonder" of Wall Street.

Forrestal's other venture, which brought with it unwanted
publicity, involved his participation in a common-stock dis-

tribution of the United States and Foreign Securities Corporation. The corporation, an investors' holding company, was established by Dillon, Read in 1924 to handle a large number of stock and bond flotations, many of them concerned with the financing of industry, transportation, and the exploitation of mineral resources in foreign countries. Of the common stock of the corporation, 500,000 shares were transferred to Dillon, Read for the total price of $100,000. Dillon, Read partners shared in the distribution of the 500,-000 shares, and ultimately Forrestal acquired some 37,000 shares in his own name.

On October 13, 1933, Forrestal appeared before the Senate Banking and Currency Committee to testify about the disposal of these shares and certain related transactions.[19] Cross-examined by committee counsel Ferdinand Pecora, Forrestal revealed that in July and August, 1929, he had transferred 20,000 of his shares to the Beekman Company, Ltd., a Canadian corporation which he had organized. The stock of the Beekman Company, Ltd., was in turn owned by the Beekman Corporation of Delaware, which had also been established by Forrestal. Of Beekman Corporation stock, Forrestal owned 70 percent, and his wife 30 percent. The president of Beekman, Ltd., Forrestal told Pecora, was Paul Strieffler, an employee of Dillon, Read who was also Forrestal's assistant, handling his financial transactions and tax matters. For his services as president, Strieffler received a salary of $100 per month. John Vincent, whom Forrestal described as his personal friend and legal counsel, served without salary as vice-president and secretary of Beekman Company, Ltd. Both Strieffler and Vincent were also officers of the Beekman Corporation of Delaware.

---

19. Forrestal's testimony was reproduced in *Hearings Before the Committee on Banking and Currency*, United States Senate, Seventy-third Congress, Second Session, Part 4, "Dillon, Read & Co," October 3 to 13, 1933, pp. 2053–2076.

Asked what purpose he had had in causing the two Beekman organizations to be incorporated, Forrestal replied:

As I recall it, either I, myself, had heard of the incorporation of companies in Canada with some advantages in the handling of taxes, or Mr. Strieffler had mentioned it to me. Which of these two is correct I do not recall. . . . I frankly only—I knew nothing about the details of taxes. I knew that my counsel, Mr. Vincent, who acted not only as counsel, but with whom I had a personal relationship—I had complete confidence in him, and when this suggestion was made to me, whether it was made by my assistant or by somebody else, I instructed him to go to Mr. Vincent, lay the whole matter before him, and to follow exactly and specifically whatever suggestions or whatever advice of any kind my counsel gave.[20]

As testimony developed, it became clear that both corporations had been organized to reduce income taxes that would ordinarily have been paid on the sale of all or part of the original 37,000 United States and Foreign Securities Corporation shares that Forrestal owned. Immediately following the incorporation of the two Beekman organizations, Forrestal revealed, Beekman, Ltd., had sold 16,788 United States and Foreign shares for a total aggregate price of $892,-000, or approximately $53 per share.[21] Despite this transaction, Beekman, Ltd., had filed no income-tax return for 1929, 1930, or 1931, although it did file a return on June 16, 1933, covering the preceding years. Asked by Pecora to explain the "circumstances" that led Beekman, Ltd., to file in 1933, Forrestal replied:

Mr. Strieffler, I think came to me some time in April or May [1933] and said that—I am not certain; I may have raised the question with him, but I am not certain whether it was at my instance or his—but in any event he said that he thought there

---

20. *Op. cit.*, pp. 2058–2059.
21. It was also brought out that each of the first 7,500 shares acquired by Forrestal had cost him $0.20, each of the next 17,000 shares $0.75, and each of the remaining shares of the total of 37,000, $10.00.

were certain transactions which he had overlooked and made a mistake in returns of 1932 or 1929, I have forgotten which. . . .[22]

Pecora, not entirely convinced by Forrestal's statement, pursued the matter further by asking:

As a matter of fact, Mr. Forrestal, weren't you and Mr. Strieffler prompted to do these things . . . because shortly previously to that date [June 16, 1933] you had heard or read of certain testimony introduced before this committee during the months of May and June with respect to income-tax returns filed in behalf of members of another banking firm?[23]

Forrestal's reply was straightforward. "Undoubtedly," he told Pecora, "I am sure that was the case. I mean that was undoubtedly the reason for surveying all of the transactions that had taken place."[24]

Forrestal, however, could give no reason for the failure of the Beekman Company, Ltd., to file an income tax return for 1929. Subsequent questioning by Pecora elicited the information that the money received by Beekman, Ltd.—almost $900,000—was invested in other securities. But it was also revealed that during 1929 Forrestal had borrowed some $589,331.89 from Beekman, Ltd., and another $185,000 during 1930. These loans were repaid, Forrestal testified, by his selling certain securities to Beekman, Ltd. Beekman was also lending money to the Beekman Corporation of Delaware: $50,000 in 1929; $155,000 during 1930; $127,000 during 1931; and $94,000 during 1932. Beekman, Ltd., however, while it was an active buyer and seller of securities and lender of money, did not pay any income taxes in either the United States or Canada, or declare any dividends.

In sum, Pecora reminded Forrestal, instead of receiving dividends which would have been taxable as income, Forrestal instead had borrowed almost $800,000 from Beekman,

22. *Op. cit.*, p. 2065.
23. *Ibid.*
24. *Ibid.*

Ltd. While most of this had been repaid in the form of securities, chiefly in the form of shares in Dillon, Read, the net effect of the various transactions was a substantial reduction in Forrestal's income tax for the years 1929—1932. The cross-examination on this point, in which Senator James Couzens (Republican, Michigan) briefly participated, proceeded as follows:

COUZENS: So, in effect, all these transactions were really between yourselves, because you owned all [of the corporations]; and all these transactions, no matter how the bookkeeping entries may have been made, were really, in effect, between yourselves?

FORRESTAL: Certainly for myself, Senator.

COUZENS: In other words, leaving out all legal technicalities and legal entities, the fact was that you were just switching money back and forth between one pocket and another?

PECORA: Money and securities.

COUZENS: Yes, money and securities.

FORRESTAL: Well, I had not thought of it in that fashion.

PECORA: As I understand your testimony, Mr. Forrestal, the net sum for your 16,788 shares . . . was $892,936.01, and that the stock originally cost you an aggregate of $28,539.60, resulting in a difference of $864,396.41?

FORRESTAL: Yes.

PECORA: And if sales of those 16,788 shares . . . had been made . . . by you . . . it would have resulted in a profit to you of the sum of $864,396.41, would it not?

FORRESTAL: Yes. That is the difference between the two figures.

COUZENS: What would have been the taxable income on that had it been reported directly by you?

FORRESTAL: I think it was a figure of $95,000.

PECORA: That figure of $95,000 would have represented the tax on that profit if it had stood alone, if it had represented your entire taxable income for that year, would it not?

FORRESTAL: Yes.

PECORA: But you had other profits; you individually derived other profits from your business or securities transactions for the year 1929, did you not?

FORRESTAL: Yes.

PECORA: Those profits were of a size or magnitude that required

your paying individually to both the Federal Government and
the State of New York sums approximating $300,000?

FORRESTAL: Yes, Sir.

PECORA: So if this profit of $864,000 and odd had been included
for the taxable year 1929 in your taxable income for that year,
it would have placed your taxable income into still higher
brackets for that year, would it not?

FORRESTAL: Yes.

PECORA: And the tax which you would have been required to pay,
by virtue of this additional profit of $864,000 and odd, would
have greatly exceeded $95,000 additional, would it not?

FORRESTAL: Yes.[25]

The remainder of Forrestal's testimony, and subsequent
testimony by Strieffler and others who were involved in the
complex affairs of the two Beekman corporations, did not
alter the fact that while Forrestal had done nothing illegal, he
had engaged in transactions that raised certain questions
from an ethical point of view. Forrestal could not honestly
deny that, in Senator Couzens's words, he had been "switching money back and forth between one pocket and another";
he could only say, somewhat defensively, that he "had not
thought of it in that fashion." Nor could he disagree with
Committee Counsel Pecora that his entire purpose in establishing the two Beekman organizations had been to avoid
paying income taxes on the profits derived from the sale of
the United States and Foreign Securities Corporation shares.
Clearly, in the minds of Pecora and committee members,
the line separating avoidance of taxes from evasion of taxes
was a thin boundary, and one which Forrestal had come very
close to crossing, or at least straddling.

It is possible, of course, that in establishing the two Beekman organizations Forrestal was badly advised by some of
his associates, but characteristically he made no effort to
transfer responsibility from himself to others. Not long after
his appearance before the Pecora Committee he dissolved

---

25. *Ibid.*, pp. 2071, 2072.

both Beekman corporations, and arranged an income-tax settlement with the Internal Revenue Division of the Treasury Department. Forrestal was never again called upon to testify regarding his stock-market operations, and so far as is known his income-tax returns were not subsequently investigated by government tax officials.

But perhaps the most significant consequence of the entire episode related to its effect upon Forrestal's future political career. Unlike most of his Wall Street colleagues, Forrestal supported the most important New Deal banking and financial reforms. Although he was not a New Dealer and, in fact, had no great respect or affection for Franklin D. Roosevelt,[26] Forrestal welcomed the Securities Exchange Act of 1934, establishing the Securities and Exchange Commission.[27] Perhaps his support of this and other Roosevelt measures was, in part, a penance related to his personal involvement in those transactions that had been investigated by the Pecora Committee; perhaps, once again, Forrestal was motivated by the necessity to repair a conscience that had been made to feel guilty by another type of "rebellion." But whatever his motivation, his support of the Securities and Exchange Act commanded favorable attention from Harry Hopkins, Thomas Corcoran, and other high-ranking New Dealers. As a result, in 1940 when Roosevelt was seeking as one of his "anonymous" assistants someone with a background in finance and banking, Forrestal appeared to be a natural choice.

---

26. See below, pp. 91, 252, 273.

27. The 1934 Act provided for "the regulation of securities exchanges and of over-the-counter markets operating in interstate and foreign commerce and through the mails to prevent inequitable and unfair practices on such exchanges and markets." The Act included provisions dealing with margin requirements; borrowing by stock-exchange members, brokers, and dealers; manipulation of securities' prices; and the functions of brokers, dealers, and others connected with the buying and selling of securities.

III

☆ ☆ ☆ ☆ ☆

Introduction to Politics

EARLY IN 1940 Forrestal spent a weekend in New York with Harry Hopkins, one of Franklin D. Roosevelt's key advisers and a confidant of the President. Although Hopkins, a committed New Dealer and *bon vivant,* appeared to have little in common with Forrestal, he was friendly toward him and had a high regard for his abilities. Moreover, Hopkins's suspicion of Wall Streeters, while not shared by Forrestal, was occasionally appeased by Forrestal's shrewd and acidulous comments about Wall Street in general and some of his colleagues in particular. On one occasion, for example, Forrestal remarked that it was not difficult to succeed in Wall Street provided one had slightly above-average intelligence and was willing to work hard. These qualities, he observed, were not widely distributed along "the Street." As a matter of fact, Forrestal confided to Hopkins, he was both surprised and depressed by the number of people he had met in the investment banking business who were of less than average intelligence, or lazy, or both.

At the time of the weekend meeting in New York the prospects of an Allied victory in Europe were exceedingly dim. It was Hopkins's opinion that there could be no victory without United States military intervention and that inevitably we would be drawn into the conflict. He also believed that the coming war effort would require the services of the most capable citizens in business and elsewhere. Forrestal did not disagree with these views. Indeed, he told Hopkins, and subsequently Thomas Corcoran and others who were close to Roosevelt, that he was eager to leave Wall Street and would welcome an opportunity to serve the government in some capacity. Despite the loss of income that a government position would entail, he informed Hopkins and other Administration officials that he was available "for the duration."

Rumors that Forrestal would be offered an important post in Washington were confirmed on June 22, 1940. The White House announced that Forrestal had been appointed one of six $10,000-a-year administrative assistants to the President.[1] Forrestal was to begin work on June 26. In keeping with the principle that White House assistants would, or should, share "a passion for anonymity," the White House announcement did not specify the exact nature of Forrestal's duties. *The New York Times* reported that Forrestal was "expected to serve in some capacity as a liaison man for the President in handling the national defense program. . . . It was pointed out," the *Times* story continued,

that the rearmament program would require considerable financing either by government, private sources or both. It was believed Mr. Forrestal would advise the President when such financing should be undertaken, the form it should take and other details, as well as act as liaison officer between Mr. Roosevelt, the Treasury Department and other governmental financial agencies, including the Securities and Exchange Commission.[2]

---

1. At the time of Forrestal's appointment, the other administrative assistants were Lauchlin Currie, William McReynolds, and James Rover. Roosevelt told press representatives that a fifth assistant would be appointed shortly and that the sixth post would be left vacant until an emergency.

2. *The New York Times*, June 23, 1940. In identifying Forrestal for its readers, the *Times* reported that Forrestal had worked his way through Princeton, graduating from the university in 1915.

Six days later, on June 29, the *Times* cited a presidential statement describing Forrestal's duties as the "coordination of efforts of the special Cabinet committee working on plans of a Pan American union."[3]

Forrestal served as an administrative assistant to President Roosevelt less than two months. For a variety of reasons he was not particularly happy in the position. He did not find some of his duties, especially those in which his role was essentially that of "errand-boy" between officials and agencies of the government, very challenging or rewarding, and he disliked the Roosevelt custom of assigning responsibility for a job to two or even three individuals, each of whom was led to assume that his recommendations would be accepted. He found it difficult to communicate with the President and some of his principal advisers, and he objected to Roosevelt's free-wheeling and casual approach to certain problems.[4] It was also true that Forrestal did not like, or easily associate with, some of the other presidential assistants. Finally, he was not persuaded that everything was being done that should be done to prepare for the coming involvement in World War II. Within a few weeks of his appointment, he intimated to Hopkins and others that his talents and abilities were not being fully utilized and that, as a result, he did not plan to continue as an administrative assistant beyond the end of 1940.

Meanwhile, on June 20, 1940, Congress had approved legislation creating the wholly new post of Under Secretary of the Navy. Three weeks later, Frank Knox, publisher of

---

3. *The New York Times,* June 29, 1940.

4. Forrestal, like Secretary of War Henry L. Stimson, often found it difficult to engage Roosevelt in serious discussion. In late 1940, Stimson confided to his diary: "Conferences with the President are difficult matters. His mind does not follow easily a consecutive train of thought but he is full of stories and incidents and hops about in his discussions from suggestion to suggestion and it is very much like chasing a vagrant beam of sunshine around a vacant room." Quoted in Elting E. Morison, *Turmoil and Tradition: A Study of the Life and Times of Henry L. Stimson* (Boston, Mass.: Houghton Mifflin Company, 1960), p. 510.

the *Chicago Daily News* and Republican vice-presidential candidate in 1936, was appointed Secretary of the Navy.[5] Under terms of the June 20 Act of Congress, the Secretary of the Navy was authorized to define the duties and responsibilities of the Under Secretary. Since the legislation creating the position had linked it with the national emergency, it was widely—and as events showed wrongly—assumed that the office of Under Secretary was a temporary one.[6]

Forrestal informed a number of Roosevelt's advisers that he was willing and even eager to serve as Navy Under Secretary. Acceptable to Knox and to others high in the Administration, his nomination for the post was sent to the Senate on August 6. Two weeks later he was officially sworn in as Under Secretary, and he was to serve in that position until the death of Knox almost four years later.[7]

Although the public was never fully informed about the exact nature of Forrestal's duties,[8] Knox intrusted to him a wide range of responsibilities. Forrestal was placed in charge of procurement and contract negotiations, tax and other legal matters affecting the Navy, and liaison with a large number of government agencies. Throughout his government career, Forrestal was inclined to take a broad rather than a narrow view of his duties and responsibilities, and his conception of the role of Navy Under Secretary was hardly an exception. Knox's directive assigning him his duties could

5. Also in July, another Republican, Henry L. Stimson, was appointed Secretary of War.

6. *The New York Times* of August 6 made this point in reporting Forrestal's nomination to be Under Secretary.

7. Forrestal's role as Under Secretary is discussed at length in Robert H. Connery, *The Navy and the Industrial Mobilization in World War II* (Princeton, N.J.: Princeton University Press, 1951). I have relied upon this indispensable work for information pertaining to Forrestal's career in the Navy Department. See also Robert Greenhalgh Albion and R. Connery, *Forrestal and the Navy* (New York: Columbia University Press, 1962).

8. In its story of August 6, *The New York Times* stated that " (w)hile no specific duties have been assigned Mr. Forrestal, he will assist with the national defense program and possibly serve also in connection with economic matters that impinge on defense in the Western Hemisphere."

mean much or little, and characteristically Forrestal chose to interpret it in a comprehensive fashion. In the course of time, although this was not specified in the directive, his office "was to develop as the chief material coordinating agency of the Navy Department."[9]

It was not long before Forrestal began to demonstrate capabilities that were to assure him a distinguished career in the government service. Within a relatively short period he had established his previously unknown office upon a firm footing, making it in the process one of the key agencies in the entire Defense Establishment. A man of intense loyalty to those he liked or admired, Forrestal quickly gathered around him men (and women) who were equally devoted to him and whose capacities for sustained hard work were hardly less than his own. The group included Commander (later Admiral) John E. Gingrich, USN, his naval aide, who was an astute guide to the manners and mores of the professional Navy.[10] Charles F. Detmar, Jr., served as legal assistant,[11] and in December, 1940, Forrestal appointed H. Struve Hensel[12] and W. John Kenney[13] to advise him on contract provisions. In dealing with problems involving the

9. Connery, *op. cit.*, p. 56.

10. Gingrich remained attached to Forrestal's office until late in the war when, at his own request, he was transferred to active duty in the Pacific theater of operations. After the war Gingrich served as an Assistant Chief of Naval Operations, and as Director of Intelligence and Security for the Atomic Energy Commission. A personal friend of Forrestal's, he was one of those present in Florida when Forrestal suffered his mental collapse. At the time of his death in May, 1960, Gingrich was a vice-president of International Telephone and Telegraph Corporation.

11. Detmar, a member of the law firm that served as legal counsel to Dillon, Read, and Co., was personally known to Forrestal.

12. Hensel was highly recommended to Forrestal by a number of New York attorneys who specialized in corporate law and finance. At the time of his appointment Hensel was a partner in the law firm of Milbank, Tweed, and Hope.

13. Kenney, a Los Angeles attorney, had been attached to the Securities and Exchange Commission, and was recommended to Forrestal by Justice William O. Douglas, previously Chairman of the SEC. Kenney subsequently served as Assistant Secretary of the Navy, and in September, 1947, he was appointed Under Secretary of the Navy.

organization of the Navy Department, Forrestal frequently turned for advice to Ferdinand Eberstadt, a longtime friend and former Wall Street colleague.[14] His public-relations adviser was Eugene Duffield,[15] and Miss Katherine Foley served as his personal secretary. Some of these individuals expected to be with Forrestal only a short time; in the end most of them were with him for the remainder of the war, and there were even a few who remained attached to his staff until his retirement as Secretary of Defense.[16]

Of the problems confronting Forrestal when he took office as Under Secretary, the most pressing involved the organization of the Navy Department. To begin with, there was no overall organization within the Department responsible for coordinating the procurement activities of the various Bureaus. Moreover, the Bureaus lacked sufficient men trained to handle the complex problems that developed in connection with research, design, purchasing, production, and transportation. There was no centralized general counsel's office staffed by lawyers competent to deal with the legal and commercial aspects of procurement contracts. Clearly, if the Navy was to fight and win the production battle, a battle that ultimately was to transform the limited peacetime Navy into the world's most formidable armada of combat

---

14. Forrestal's relations with Eberstadt, a former partner of Dillon, Read, and founder of the investment banking firm of F. Eberstadt and Company, were extremely close during the entire period that Forrestal served in the government. Indeed, many of the policies associated with Forrestal as Under Secretary and Secretary of the Navy, and Secretary of Defense, owed a good deal to Eberstadt's influence and point of view. Although Eberstadt's role in the war effort and, later, in the organization of the Department of Defense has never been adequately treated, certain relevant information pertaining to the war years may be found in Connery, *op. cit.*, pp. 143–145, 157–159, and 163–174.

15. Duffield, whose career had been mainly in journalism and public relations, later collaborated with Walter Millis in editing *The Forrestal Diaries* (Viking, 1951).

16. The services of Hensel and Kenney did not come to an end until long after the war was over. Miss Foley remained with Forrestal through the entire period of his government service.

ships,[17] steps would have to be taken to remove the bottle-necks and confusion of responsibilities that characterized the Navy Department itself.

One of Forrestal's first actions was to investigate the procedures related to the granting of amortization certificates for the construction of defense-related plants and facilities. The second Revenue Act of 1940 had provided that the cost of privately built industrial facilities necessary for the national defense could be amortized, that is, charged against net income, over a period of five years instead of the usual twenty.[18] The Act authorized the War and Navy Departments to certify which facilities financed by private investment were necessary to the war effort and, hence, eligible for rapid amortization. The Departments were also required

---

17. On July 1, 1940, the United States Navy consisted of 1,058 vessels of all types, 383 of which were combat vessels. Uniformed personnel totaled 189,000 men. By November 1, 1944, the number of ships had increased to more than 40,000. The additions included 9 battleships, over 70 aircraft carriers, 34,500 planes, 20 cruisers, more than 500 destroyers and destroyer escorts, and over 100 submarines. Altogether there were more than 1,500 combat vessels, and the total of personnel was 3,600,000, of whom 100,000 were women.

18. To the manufacturer who qualified, the principal benefit of rapid amortization was a substantial reduction in income-tax liability. Indeed, as two students of the subject have pointed out, if the five-year period "coincides with high net earnings, high corporate tax rates, and an excess-profits tax, the privilege (of accelerated amortization) is very lucrative indeed. For example, assume that a large steel company undertakes a $100 million expansion and is certified for a 60 percent rapid write-off, i.e., $60 million written off at the rate of $12 million per year for five years. This is predicated on the very questionable assumption that only 40 per cent of the total new investment, or $40 million, will have any post-emergency usefulness or earning capacity. Now, at normal rates of depreciation, assuming a 25-year productive life expectancy, the company would be entitled to charge against income for tax purposes only 4 percent or $2,400,000 per year on this portion of its investment. But, under accelerated amortization, it can charge off against income $12 million, thus reducing its net taxable income by $9,600,000—the amount of the excess amortization. If the corporate tax rate is 52 percent, the saving in taxes would be $4,992,000—i.e., 52 percent of the excess amortization. If the company is subject to an excess-profits tax, the tax saving would be much greater; in fact, the excess amortization may suffice to offset excess profits entirely."—Walter Adams and Horace M. Gray, *Monopoly in America: The Government as Promoter* (New York: The Macmillan Company, 1955), pp. 84–85.

to make certain that the owners of such facilities were not being reimbursed elsewhere in the government.[19]

Within the Navy Department applications for amortization certificates were processed by a Certification Unit in the Office of the Judge Advocate General (OJAG). Forrestal quickly discovered, however, that the Certification Unit was not adequately staffed to process these applications, and it was not long before he became aware that the OJAG itself was ill equipped for the performance of other functions in the procurement field. The Bureau officers who dealt with amortization certificates were often not familiar with the statute requirements or the procedures that had been established for handling the applications. Frequently the applications had not been properly filled out by those submitting them. There was also a large number of applications awaiting action. Similar problems existed in the contracting area, and it was obvious that drastic changes were required.

In December, 1940, at Forrestal's request, Hensel and Kenney undertook a special study of amortization procedures. Forrestal indicated to both men that the situation was urgent, especially with regard to the substantial backlog of applications awaiting action, and he made it clear that he wanted their recommendations as soon as possible. The study proceeded mainly under Hensel's direction, and he gave to it something of the drive and dedication that characterized Forrestal's own approach to the responsibilities of government service. Working evenings and weekends,[20] Hensel in

---

19. The justification for rapid amortization during both world wars and the Korean War has been that facilities necessary for war production would not be financed by private capital without such an incentive. It is estimated that amortization allowances during World War I totaled approximately $650 million. Between 1940 and 1947 the value of amortization certificates reached $7.3 billion, of which about $5.7 billion was actually used and reported for tax purposes. By March 3, 1954, the total cost of projects subject to rapid amortization was slightly more than $29 billion.—Adams and Gray, *ibid.*, pp. 84–87.

20. It was at this time that Forrestal initiated the practice of having his special aides and assistants join him at breakfast conferences. Since these

January, 1941, submitted a report the major features of which Forrestal quickly approved. A Certification Supervisory Unit (CSU) was created in Forrestal's office, and it was charged with the function of reviewing applications for certificates. The CSU was also authorized to coordinate the work of the various bureaus involved in amortization clearance. Other procedural changes recommended by Hensel were put into effect, and as a result there was a substantial improvement in the overall processing of amortization applications.

Dissatisfied with the Navy's procurement contracting procedures in general, Forrestal once again turned to Hensel for a detailed investigation of the methods by which procurement contracts were made and signed in the Navy Department. It was typical of Forrestal that he "was not content to accept the traditional passive position of a Secretary of the Navy and sign whatever was put before him. He wanted to know what he was signing, and why he was signing it, and why he was not signing something else."[21] Hensel's study revealed that the Navy Department was legally authorized to procure needed matériel under so-called negotiated contracts. Negotiated contracts had first made their appearance under an Act of April 25, 1939, and authority to draft such contracts had been extended by a subsequent Act of June 28, 1940. In essence, the 1940 Act provided that whenever the President deemed it to be in the best interests of national defense, the Secretary of the Navy was authorized to negotiate contracts for the acquisition, construction, repair or alteration of naval vessels and aircraft. Unlike some other forms of contract, negotiated contracts did not require com-

conferences frequently began at eight o'clock in the morning, or even earlier, there was a certain amount of grumbling about them, especially by those persons on his staff who were inclined to work until late in the evening, or who led active social lives. But Forrestal was not easily put off; and it should be noted that Forrestal demanded no more of his staff than he demanded of himself.

21. Connery, *op. cit.*, p. 61.

petitive bidding. The price, however, had to be fair and reasonable, and bonds were still required from the contractor. Although the cost-plus-a-percentage-of-cost contract was prohibited, cost-plus-fixed-fee contracts were authorized when necessary.[22]

Hensel's report and his own long experience in the business world led Forrestal to prefer the negotiated contract with certain modifications. He successfully urged the Bureau of Ships to substitute for the usual cost-plus-fixed-fee arrangement a contract under which a portion of the fee was fixed, with the remainder paid as a bonus for cost economies. In effect, such a contract provided that a contractor who economized on costs would be permitted to "pocket" some portion of the savings to the government. Later in the war, the Navy Department developed a more extended form of incentive contract, the purpose of which was to encourage economies by giving the contractor a substantial share of any savings he might effect.[23]

Hensel also recommended that the legal aspects of procurement be handled by a staff of lawyers attached to Forrestal's office. Under regulations in effect when Forrestal

---

22. Summarized from Connery, *op. cit.*, pp. 58–75.

23. Forrestal argued that the incentive contract "gives the company a definite incentive to cut its costs. In fact, the heart of the contract is the conviction that American business can perform miracles of low-cost production if it is given a profit incentive for doing so. The Navy Department by giving business this incentive stands to save millions of dollars through lower costs of munitions. You will perceive, however, that the *sine qua non* for an incentive contract is a contract price which is based on actual cost experience and which is very close to the current cost line. Without a firm, close contract price, the incentive contract would be open to abuses; the contractor would achieve a saving by merely squeezing the water out of an inflated contract price." Letter to Albert Bradley, executive Vice-President of General Motors Corporation, August 26, 1943, quoted in Connery, *op. cit.*, p. 218.

While there can be no doubt that the incentive contract was moderately successful in terms of promoting both efficiency and economy, successive government reports since World War II have stressed the desirability of letting contracts on the basis of competitive bids rather than negotiated bids. See, for example, Attorney General, *Report Prepared Pursuant to Section 708(e) of the Defense Production Act of 1950*, December, 1950.

became Navy Under Secretary, the Office of Judge Advocate General had cognizance of all legal questions, civil and military, involving the Navy Department.[24] Hensel's report stressed the fact that the OJAG had difficulty acquiring competent civilian lawyers and that it was not skilled in utilizing the abilities and talents of its legal staff, especially with reference to procurement matters. He therefore recommended that a Procurement Legal Division, headed by a civilian lawyer, be created in the office of the Under Secretary.

Forrestal accepted his recommendation, and with Knox's approval submitted it for comment to the JAG at the time, Rear Admiral Walter B. Woodson. Forrestal did not expect that Woodson would be willing to surrender any of his authority, and in this he was hardly disappointed. Flatly rejecting Hensel's recommendation and the clear implication that the OJAG was deficient in discharging certain of its responsibilities, Woodson argued forcefully that under the laws and regulations in effect the Navy's legal business was wholly entrusted to the JAG. And for good measure he made it evident that he would oppose, in Congress and elsewhere, any effort to create a legal authority separate from and independent of his own office.

Forrestal, meanwhile, had employed a number of attorneys, including Hensel, as his special assistants, and he was determined, despite Woodson's opposition, to assign some of these assistants to procurement. But initially both he and Knox attempted to persuade Congress to create a separate legal division, staffed by fifteen attorneys, in Forrestal's office. Ultimately, however, the House Naval Affairs Committee rejected their proposal on grounds of "economy." The bill

24. At the time of Forrestal's appointment as Under Secretary the legal staff of the OJAG was made up of regular Navy officers and civilian attorneys. Navy officers without legal training who were attached to the OJAG were permitted to attend a law school. Legal experience as such was acquired on-the-job, and it was from this group of officer-lawyers that the Judge Advocate General was chosen for a four-year term, and given the rank of Rear Admiral.

that was finally reported by the Committee, and subsequently passed, appropriated funds for the employment of one additional attorney in the office of Under Secretary.

Ostensibly defeated in his efforts to reorganize the legal aspects of procurement, Forrestal found other means of accomplishing his objective. Although Woodson continued in opposition, on July 10, 1941, Forrestal announced that he was establishing a Procurement Legal Division to advise him on contract negotiation, preparation, and performance. The PLD would also have the function of sending prepared contracts to the JAG for his examination. Two months later, on September 10, the PLD was formally created, with Hensel at its head. Since Hensel served as the one additional attorney authorized by Congress, the PLD legal staff depended for its existence on a variety of makeshift arrangements. Some of Forrestal's special assistants, twelve of whom were lawyers, were assigned to the PLD, and a number of attorneys on its staff were employed on a *per diem* basis. Nevertheless, the PLD functioned effectively as a key agency in the Navy Department. With representatives in most of the contracting bureaus, the PLD enabled Forrestal to exercise supervision over the entire area of Navy procurement.

The PLD, however, did not solve all problems that arose in connection with procurement. Forrestal continued to feel that the Navy's material program was suffering from the lack of overall coordination, and in December, 1941, a few weeks after Pearl Harbor, he recommended to Knox the establishment of a new coordinating agency subsequently known as the Office of Procurement and Material.[25] Organized early in

---

25. Despite its title, the OP&M did not function as a procurement agency. As Connery observes, "[i]t did not buy anything; it merely coordinated the purchasing activities of the material bureaus. The actual contracting was done by the Bureau of Supplies and Accounts for all standard stock items and generally for items common to two or more bureaus . . . in the Navy Department, there were five major agencies buying naval material and supplies. They dealt in different types of material but they had the same business and contracting problems. The functions [of the OP&M] were to keep

1942, the OP&M, which was responsible to Forrestal, dealt with planning and statistics, procurement, production, and resources. In May, 1942, a fifth branch, concerned with inspections, became part of the OP&M as a result of recommendations submitted to Forrestal by Lieutenant Commander, later Rear Admiral, Lewis L. Strauss.[26]

Despite the establishment of the OP&M and attendant procedural changes in the various contracting bureaus, Forrestal was never convinced that the problem of coordinating the Navy's complex material activities had been satisfactorily resolved. Nor was evidence lacking to support his view. While the situation had significantly improved by the middle of 1942, largely owing to Forrestal's efforts, it always appeared to him that much remained to be done. In addition to material coordination problems within the Navy Department—and they did not cease to be formidable even after 1942—the task of relating the Navy's requirements to those of other government agencies and departments was difficult, challenging, and on more than one occasion frustrating, throughout the entire war period. Indeed, the whole problem of Navy Department organization, of which procurement and related matters formed only one aspect, occupied an increasing amount of Forrestal's time from 1942 until V-J Day.

Within the Navy Department, Forrestal was never able to achieve a smooth working relationship with Fleet Commander in Chief and Chief of Naval Operations Admiral

---

the procurement policies, forms of contracts, and procurement procedures of the different Navy procurement agencies in line with each other and with the other government procurement agencies, assist in solving common production problems, and facilitate planning and the collection of material statistics."—Connery, *op. cit.*, pp. 148-149.

26. Strauss, senior partner of Kuhn, Loeb and Company and a commissioned officer in the Naval Reserve, was assigned in 1941 to the recruitment of inspectors for the Bureau of Ordinance. Encountering difficulty in recruiting qualified personnel, Strauss made a study of the Navy's material inspection problems. The establishment of the Inspections Administration of the OP&M was based on his report.

Ernest J. King.[27] Admiral King, who in his capacity as a member of the Joint Chiefs of Staff was responsible to the President and not to the Secretary of the Navy, consistently took the position that logistics, which included procurement, was properly a concern of Naval Operations. Despite the objections of Knox and Forrestal to military control of logistics, objections supported by Roosevelt, King again and again advanced proposals that, if adopted, would have increased his own authority at the expense of the civilian heads. One proposal envisaged the appointment of two Assistant Chiefs of Naval Operations, one concerned with material and the other with personnel. In 1943 King advanced a reorganization plan for the Navy Department that would have confined the Under Secretary to overall administrative supervision of the Department's bureaus and offices, including those involved in procurement and material. Under this plan the Office of Naval Operations would have been charged with the key function of directing and coordinating the activities of bureaus and offices, and for this reason, among others, the plan was strenuously opposed by Knox, Forrestal, and their subordinates. Once again they were supported by the President. Subsequent reorganization plans put forward by King, all of which were designed to enhance the power of the Chief of Naval Operations, were based on the premise that military and logistics functions could and should be combined in one office.[28]

---

27. Admiral King became Chief of Naval Operations in March, 1942.

28. King was strongly of the view that there was a good deal of unnecessary duplication and overlapping of functions between the OP&M and the Office of Naval Operations. Ultimately the problem was resolved, to the extent resolved at all, by the creation of an Organization Control Board under Forrestal's chairmanship. Membership on the board fluctuated, but it always included Forrestal, King, and key personnel attached to the Office of Naval Operations, the Commander in Chief of the Fleet, and the OP&M. The Organization Control Board stemmed from a recommendation submitted by T. P. Archer, vice-president of General Motors, and George W. Wolf, president of United States Steel Export Company. Archer and Wolf in April, 1944, had been requested by Knox to make a study of King's proposals, and

Despite King's position, military procurement remained a separate operation under the control of the Under Secretary and the Assistant Secretary.[29] Policy matters involving industrial mobilization in general continued to be the responsibility of the Under Secretary; in effect, the principle of civilian control was sustained. In Forrestal, it was clear, King, no less than Admiral Woodson, had found no ordinary antagonist, much less someone who could be easily intimidated by military rank and especially Navy "brass."

Unfortunately, however, King never forgave Forrestal for his determined opposition to the successive reorganization plans. As Fleet Commander in Chief, King rarely confided in Forrestal even after the latter became Navy Secretary, and he made a point of not discussing naval operations with Forrestal unless the situation required such discussion. As a result, Forrestal's association with King never approximated the relationship between Secretary of War Stimson and Army Chief of Staff General George C. Marshall. Frequently Forrestal first learned of developments involving the Navy from persons outside his own Department.[30]

King's dislike for Forrestal was not based only on their differences over Navy reorganization. In the latter part of 1945, when the question of responsibility for Pearl Harbor was very actively debated, Forrestal had declared that Admiral Harold R. Stark was at least as much to blame as

---

their final report, the so-called Archer-Wolf Report, backed Knox and Forrestal in maintaining that there was a clear demarcation line between military operations and logistics.

29. Ralph A. Bard served as Assistant Secretary from February, 1941, to June, 1944. He was succeeded by Hensel, who held the post between January, 1945, and March, 1946; and Kenney, who was in office March, 1946, to July, 1947.

30. "James Forrestal . . . obtained in part his understanding of the many things Admiral King never told him by inviting [Assistant Secretary of War] John McCloy frequently for lunch."—Morison, *op. cit.*, p. 499. It was also true that Stimson's influence in the military area was far greater than that of Knox and Forrestal, partly because, unlike them, he enjoyed the full confidence of Roosevelt.—Morison, *ibid.*, p. 508.

Admiral Husband E. Kimmel. Following the report of a
Naval Court of Inquiry, Forrestal as Navy Secretary relieved
Stark of his duties as Commander of Naval Forces in Europe,
a post which he had held since 1942. He made it clear that
he fully endorsed the Court's statement that neither Stark
nor Kimmel should hold posts requiring the "exercise of
superior judgment."[31]

King was outraged by Forrestal's action, and for more
than three years he insisted that Stark's services in Europe
merited his being awarded the Distinguished Service Medal.
Forrestal was difficult to persuade, however, and it was not
until September, 1948, that Admiral Stark was decorated
by Secretary of the Navy John L. Sullivan. There were also
occasions when Forrestal disapproved of Flag Officers Selection Board recommendations, although the Board had traditionally enjoyed the rights of selecting those captains who
were to be promoted to rear-admiral rank. On some of these
occasions, King was sufficiently provoked to appeal over Forrestal's head to the White House.[32]

King was well known in the Navy for his stubbornness
and arrogance, and it was these qualities rather than his
many virtues of which Forrestal was most aware. But in
addition, Forrestal's relations with King, like his relations
with Truman (see below, pages 266-281) were affected by
the difficulties Forrestal had in confronting authority and
authority figures. His ambivalence toward authority was
especially apparent in his relations not only with King but
with all admirals (and Army and Air Force generals) with
whom he had official contacts. As Ladislas Farago later observed, Forrestal often attempted to relieve the tension and

<hr />

31. *The New York Times,* August 30, 1945.
32. The Forrestal-King relationship is discussed in some detail in Ernest J.
King and Walter Muir Whitehill, *Fleet Admiral King: A Naval Record*
(New York: W. W. Norton and Co., 1952). As may be expected from the
authorship, the book is somewhat partial to the positions taken by Admiral
King.

stiffness he felt in the company of admirals by a labored camaraderie that failed to achieve its purpose. Writing in July, 1949, when he was Research and Planning Chief of the Navy's Special Warfare Branch, Farago noted that Forrestal sometimes alarmed or alienated civilians by his obsequious treatment of Navy brass. He would, for example, address them by their Academy nicknames in an effort to establish intimacy, and substitute their "hazy, stultified lingo" for his own "highly articulate vocabulary." He also allowed himself to be drawn into those Navy ceremonies and pageantry which most civilians regard with a mixture of amusement and embarrassment. Forrestal's innate democratic instincts, Farago suggests, clashed with the Navy's authoritarianism, and perhaps Forrestal was never able to resolve the conflict between the two worlds.[33]

But whatever the explanation of the Forrestal-King relationship—and King was hardly less complex a figure than Forrestal—King's intransigence immensely complicated the perennial problem of Navy Department reorganization. Reorganization, however, was only one of Forrestal's concerns.

The Office of Production Management (OPM), which fixed the quantities of vital commodities that were allocated to the military and civilian economies, Lend-Lease, and economic warfare, often reached decisions to which Knox and Forrestal were strongly opposed. They objected, in particular, to the allocation of scarce recources to the Soviet Union except in those cases where the Russians could demonstrate that the resources requested would make a significant contribution to the Russian war effort. Both Knox and Forrestal protested bitterly that the shipments of machine tools, aluminum, and other commodities would have an adverse effect on our own military program and that at the very least the Russians should supply detailed information

---

33. Ladislas Farago, "Death of a Statesman," *United Nations World*, July 18, 1949.

pertaining to their military needs. Forrestal complained, on more than one occasion, that it was easier for the Russians to obtain needed material than it was for either the Army or the Navy. Despite their protests the OPM, frequently under direct or indirect orders from the White House, usually took a favorable view of the Russian requests. Nor did the Soviet Union ever supply much information relating to its war production.[34]

The whole problem of production and resource allocation was further complicated by the regulations created for the purpose of controlling prices and excess profits. Forrestal's position was always that the material needs of the Armed Forces should not be allowed to suffer because of concern over price and profit levels—and in his own circle of friends and associates he made no secret of the fact that he distrusted the motivations of a number of officials who were administering and enforcing price controls. He could not agree with some of these officials, he confided, that most businessmen were dishonest and eager to derive monetary advantage from the national emergency. After Pearl Harbor, when Congress was considering enactment of the Emergency Price Control Act, Forrestal and Under Secretary of War Robert P. Patterson wrote to Senator Robert F. Wagner, Chairman of the Senate Banking and Currency Committee, requesting that the Services receive broad exemptions from controls established under the Act. Asked for his opinion by Senator Wagner, price administrator Leon Henderson took the position that price controls of military end products, such as tanks, ships, and weapons, were a proper function of the War and Navy Departments, but that the prices of other commodities and materials should not be exempted from the proposed legislation. Despite a further appeal by Forrestal and Patterson, the Wagner Committee supported Henderson. Nor were the two Under Secretaries more successful in ap-

---

34. Connery, *op. cit.*, pp. 99–107.

proaching the White House. Consequently, the Price Control Act as passed on January 30, 1942, contained no exemption for war materials.

Rebuffed by the President, Congress, and Price Administrator Henderson, Forrestal and Patterson nevertheless believed that while they had lost a battle they had not necessarily lost the war. As Forrestal viewed the situation—and the view was to become a firm doctrine with him—no governmental decision was ever really final or irreversible. In the spring of 1942, he and Patterson attempted to persuade Henderson not to establish price ceilings on certain types of military combat equipment. They argued that prices and profits could be effectively controlled through improved purchasing and procurement techniques. Although Henderson was not convinced, he granted certain exemptions on the condition that the War and Navy Departments made every effort to control both prices and profits.

In the fall of 1942, after a series of conferences, an agreement was reached under which the Office of Price Administration (OPA) would refrain from placing price ceilings on certain combat articles and their component parts, but reserve the right to impose ceilings on parts and assemblies when sold immediately after the first stage of their production. The OPA also agreed to furnish the Departments with information pertaining to their procurement programs, prior to any action related to procurement that the price agency proposed to take. In effect, the agreement, which became known as the Henderson-Patterson-Forrestal agreement, provided for consultation between the OPA and the military Departments in advance of any OPA policy decision affecting the Army and Navy.[35]

Once again Forrestal, powerfully assisted by Patterson, had scored a significant victory. But the victory was a partial one, and Forrestal was never convinced that the agreement

35. Connery, *ibid.*, pp. 225–231.

with the OPA was the best that could be obtained. The suspicion never left him that the OPA, or at least some of its top officials, harbored an antibusiness "philosophy," that is, a view that the business community was determined to extract the maximum possible profit from the war effort. Noting that certain OPA officers had been fervent New Dealers before the war and that some had been associated with antitrust policies, Forrestal frequently remarked on the irony that many of the businessmen who had been harassed by government in the thirties were those upon whom, in the forties, the nation most depended for production-line miracles. He was also critical of the attitude he attributed to "radicals" in the Administration, namely, that any big business was necessarily a "bad business" in the sense that it had been built not by hard work but by collusion and other monopolistic practices. Without big busines, he commented more than once, "the nation would be in one hell of a shape."

Nevertheless, Forrestal took issue with certain policies advocated by important sections of the business community. Although he favored the recapture of excess profits through contract renegotiation rather than taxation—which in effect meant that a large measure of responsibility for determining profits would be transferred from Congress to the War and Navy Departments—he opposed business-supported amendments to the Renegotiation Act designed to raise profit levels. His opposition was based partly on his own sense of what was fair and equitable and partly on his fear that if war profits became too inflated, postwar public opinion would swing violently against business.[36] Forrestal was always sensitive to the possibility that charges of business misconduct during the war could generate a postwar return to the radical politics and policies exemplified in the New Deal.

---

36. Arthur Krock, in his *New York Times* column of December 16, 1943, reported that this fear was shared by a number of Forrestal's colleagues whose backgrounds were similar to his.

In testimony before Senate and House committees and in a number of speeches, Forrestal repeatedly argued that business would deal honestly with the government in contract negotiation and that the government, for its part, should try to understand the problems involved in industry efforts to increase production. Urgent war-production needs, he told the House Rules Committee in January, 1943, often made it impossible to apply accurate yardsticks to profit levels. Denying that greed and other selfish motives were responsible for the high costs of some defense contracts, Forrestal defended the contracting system, adding, for good measure, that he "would rather have a warship than a simon-pure record."[37] At meetings of industrialists Forrestal called for even greater efforts to achieve production goals. He assured the businessmen that the War and Navy Departments would give industry just treatment in the renegotiation of contracts. The power to recapture excessive profits, he told his audiences, would be exercised "within the limits of reason and not on a punitive basis."[38]

Forrestal's position on renegotiation of contracts was broadly acceptable to the business community, but renegotiation was an issue only for businessmen who held defense contracts. The majority of businessmen were not defense contractors, and their role in the production effort was the subject of almost continuous debate in the Navy Department and elsewhere in the government. When it became clear that a large number of businesses would be forced to close unless they obtained raw materials for civilian-goods production or defense contracts, the businessmen affected appealed to their congressmen for assistance in obtaining Navy and/or War Department contracts. Not all of these businessmen, of course, were engaged in small business enterprise, but with the release early in the war of figures revealing that more

---

37. Quoted in *The New York Times,* January 20, 1943.
38. See, for example, his speech to the War Congress of American Industry at the Waldorf-Astoria Hotel in New York, December 4, 1942.

than half of all contracts had been awarded to the largest corporations,[39] the issue of Big Business versus Small Business was joined. Forrestal was never allowed to forget that such an issue was politically explosive and that regardless of economic or even military considerations, the Administration, Congress, and the nation insisted that small business receive its share of war contracts.

Characteristically, Forrestal was impatient with the intrusion into military areas of what he regarded as political and, in a sense, ideological considerations. In this instance, however, pressures favoring contract dispersal were too powerful to be resisted, much less disregarded. Although he continued to insist that defense needs were far more important than civilian morale in general and small-business morale in particular, he authorized several investigations of the extent to which Navy procurement could be handled through subcontracting. These investigations, however reluctantly begun in 1941, produced one conclusion to which Forrestal could give his wholehearted support.

For eight months [he noted on September 18, 1941] the Navy, in collaboration with the Defense Contract Service, has been trying to spread work. Limited statutory authority has circumscribed the Navy's complete freedom of action in this regard to a comparatively narrow orbit.[40]

In accordance with this analysis, Forrestal urged that the Navy be given greater freedom to negotiate contracts, and in

---

39. Between June, 1940, and September, 1944, according to the War Production Board (WPB), prime military contracts worth a total of $175 billion were awarded to 18,539 corporations. The largest one hundred corporations received two-thirds, or $117 billion worth, of the total; the top thirty-three received more than one-half; and the top ten 30 percent. An essentially similar pattern of concentration characterized military procurement during the Korean War. For details see Adams and Gray, *op. cit.*, pp. 101–116.

40. Letter to Floyd B. Odlum, head of the Division of Contract Distribution of the Office of Production Management (OPM), quoted in Connery, *op. cit.*, p. 121.

due course his freedom in this area was extended by an Executive Order.[41] Following the presidential directive, the Navy's procurement bureaus made an even greater effort to achieve a broader distribution of contracts or, in Forrestal's words, to "spread work."

The small-business share of Navy contracts, however, did not substantially increase, and as a result the suspicion developed in certain quarters that the Navy preferred to deal in matters of procurement with the larger corporations. Some part of this suspicion fell on Forrestal personally, partly because of his Wall Street background and partly because of his expressed doubts about the extent to which the "spread work" philosophy could or should be applied in industrial mobilization. Forrestal attempted to counter his critics by emphasizing, in a number of speeches and in his testimony before congressional committees, that the Navy had undertaken a variety of steps to promote subcontracting and, in general, a larger role for small business in Navy procurement. Criticism, nevertheless, continued throughout the war, and in the end Forrestal concluded that the problem was mainly one of public relations. The Navy was misunderstood, he finally decided, because it was handicapped in explaining its position, and he therefore gave greater attention to the Navy's need for adequate staffing in publicity and public-relations areas. Two years after the war, when the issue of defense reorganization was before Congress and the nation, he again was to feel that the Navy was not adequately equipped to tell its story to those who most needed to hear it.[42]

There were other occasions during the time that Forrestal was Under Secretary when the Navy failed to tell its

---

41. On October 7, 1941, the President authorized the Secretary of the Navy to negotiate certain types of contracts without competitive bidding or any advertising to the effect that such contracts were about to be let.

42. See below, pp. 214ff.

story or to explain its position adequately. Forrestal was hardly in office, in December, 1940, when he and certain others in the government were charged with wanting to establish "a complete military dictatorship."

On December 19, 1940, *The New York Times* reported that President Roosevelt, Secretaries Stimson and Knox, Assistant Secretary of War Patterson and Forrestal had "agreed in principle" on a defense reorganization plan designed to increase production of vital war materials. The plan called for the establishment of a defense council composed of Secretaries Stimson and Knox, and William S. Knudsen, industrial member of the Defense Advisory Commission. Asked for his opinion, Representative Woodruff, according to the *Times* story, commented: "There are those in Washington who believe, and not without reason, that the administration was waiting for what at least appeared to be a public demand for the enactment by Congress of the industrial mobilization plan, which means the setting up in peacetime of a complete military dictatorship. . . . That demand . . . has come."

In September, 1941, when the War and Navy Departments announced plans for military censorship of communications to and from the United States in the event of war, Forrestal was again accused of seeking dictatorial powers. Although he and Patterson stressed that such censorship would not involve the press, newspaper editors were generally critical of the proposed action.[43] Of a more trivial nature, although Forrestal was hardly less irritated, were adverse remarks directed at Mrs. Forrestal's role in the war effort. A number of newspaper columnists objected to her appointment as an unpaid civilian adviser to the Waves, and it was popular in certain quarters to comment sarcas-

---

43. Despite the reaction the War and Navy Departments, in September, 1941, sharply curtailed the flow of information from Navy bases, Navy yards, and Army arsenals.

tically on the Wave uniform which she had designed in collaboration with Mainbocher.[44]

As Navy Under Secretary Forrestal was often in contact with representatives of organized labor, some of whom served in Washington during the war, and he was frequently involved, directly or indirectly, in union-related issues connected with the Navy's industrial procurement program. While Forrestal was not in principle opposed to unions,[45] he drew a firm line between what he regarded as legitimate and illegitimate union demands. Specifically, he did not welcome production interruptions occasioned by strikes, jurisdictional disputes, and union demands for minimum wage guarantees and other types of job security. He felt strongly that some unions in their wage negotiations were attempting to take advantage of labor shortages and that others were using their bargaining power less for the benefit of their members than as a means of consolidating their position vis-à-vis other labor organizations. He also believed, as a result of confidential reports from the Federal Bureau of Investigation (FBI) and Naval Intelligence, that certain industrial unions were under strong communist influence.[46]

---

44. Mrs. Forrestal during the war also made a number of trips to London "on government business." In April, 1943, for example, she traveled to the British capital for the purpose, according to *The New York Times,* of studying the "practical experience" of the Wrens with a view to applying it to the Waves. There were those who believed, not without reason, that these trips made little or no contribution to the war effort; and Forrestal, privately, was not inclined to defend them.

45. For Forrestal's attitude toward the controversial Taft-Hartley Act of 1947, see below, pp. 270–272.

46. Forrestal was convinced that a number of strikes between September, 1939, and June, 1941, were instigated by Communists under orders from the Communist Party and/or Soviet agents in the United States. With the involvement of the Soviet Union in the war on June 22, 1941, the problem of communist infiltration of unions became less urgent. Forrestal, however, kept a file of reports dealing with such infiltration, and he referred to it frequently during and after the war. He also had his aides compile dossiers concerned with individuals, organizations, and publications, here and abroad, suspected of being under communist influence. See below, pp. 125–133.

As a result of these views, he frequently took positions on labor questions that aroused enmity in union circles and charges by some labor leaders that he was antiunion.

In December, 1940, for example, Forrestal was accused of exerting influence in favor of big unions and discriminating against small, independent labor organizations. The National Council of Marine Draftsmen, an unaffiliated union of 2,500 members concentrated in Atlantic- and Gulf-coast shipbuilding yards, charged in December that the union had been denied membership on the government's Shipbuilding Stabilization Committee because it was not affiliated with either the AFL or CIO. E. E. Benzenger, president of the union, in addition to demanding union representation on the Stabilization Committee, proposed that minimum pay scales be established for marine draftsmen as a means of reducing labor turnover.

In replying to the union proposals, Forrestal on December 7 expressed doubt that the fixing of minimum pay rates would prevent labor turnover or reduce dissatisfaction with working conditions in the shipbuilding yards. He insisted, however, that the National Defense Commission was aware of the need for stabilization, and was consequently planning to establish uniformity in wages and working conditions. Rejecting the demand for union representation, Forrestal argued that the large number of unions made full representation on government boards impossible. He suggested, instead, that unions not represented, such as the National Council of Marine Draftsmen, designate one or two of the major labor organizations to represent them.[47]

Six months later, in May, 1941, Forrestal actively intervened in a labor dispute that had sharply curtailed construction in eleven San Francisco Bay Area shipyards. The strike, involving machinists' demands for higher pay scales, had pre-

---

47. *The New York Times,* December 29, 1940.

viously brought forth a request for early settlement from Governor Culbert L. Olson of California. On May 16th Forrestal telegraphed John P. Frey, president of the metal-trades division of the AFL, that the senior officers of the Twelfth Naval District had been ordered to give him "every assistance in his endeavor to settle the strike." The telegram, which was similar in content to one sent to Frey by Admiral Land of the Maritime Commission, was interpreted by the striking machinists as a "go back to work or else dictum."[48] Long after the dispute was settled the machinists remained suspicious of Forrestal's use of the phrase "every assistance," and they also continued resentful that pressure to end the work stoppage was exerted on the strikers and not on the employers involved.

In September, 1941, Forrestal drew fire from a number of maritime unions for supporting a bill empowering the government to deny or suspend the licenses of ship radio operators suspected of being subversives. Forrestal's letter to the Senate Commerce Subcommittee that was holding hearings on the measure, previously passed by the House, stated that unless the bill was quickly approved it would be necessary to place Navy radio operators aboard all merchant ships. "There is," he informed the subcommittee, "an appreciable number of [radio] operators who are suspected of being members of subversive groups."[49] This allegation was bitterly resented by the principal union involved and other maritime unions. Nevertheless, the bill was approved by the Senate and signed by the President.

Forrestal also lent his support to a legislative enactment that was opposed by almost all sections of organized labor.

---

48. *The New York Times,* May 18, 1941. The *Times* story commented that "[s]ince the 11 yards are building only for the Navy and the [Maritime Commission] the two telegrams would seem to preclude any possibility of a compromise between the terms of the master agreement and the demands of the strikers."

49. *The New York Times,* September 20, 1941.

In November, 1941, he joined Patterson in urging Congress
to pass the War Labor Disputes bill, a measure authorizing
the government to take over and operate strike-bound defense plants, mines, and other facilities in time of emergency.
Testifying before a Senate Judiciary Subcommittee, Forrestal told the subcommittee that while the Navy Department, in principle, did not favor government intervention
in labor-management relations, it had a clear and urgent
interest in ensuring the orderly production of goods needed
by sailors manning our ships on the high seas. Expressing the
hope that the power to seize defense plants and other facilities would seldom need to be exercised, Forrestal insisted
that the passage of the bill was of vital importance. Had such
legislation been in effect in late 1940, he informed the senators, there would have been a quick settlement of a strike at
the Allis-Chalmers plant in Milwaukee, one effect of which
was to delay destroyer construction for periods ranging from
two to six months.[50] "We cannot, as in normal times," *The
New York Times* quoted Forrestal, "sit and wait for the
composition of differences between employer and labor by
any method that rests solely on tests of strength. France tried
that and failed."[51] Backed by Forrestal, Patterson, and other
high-ranking government officials, the War Labor Dispute
bill was enacted by Congress, vetoed by the President, and re-

---

50. There is evidence that the Allis-Chalmers strike in 1940–1941 was
Communist-inspired. A report on the strike prepared for Forrestal by one
of his naval aides, Lt. R. L. Gridley, USNR, dated October 3, 1944, stated that
the strike had been led by Communists as part of an effort to disrupt the
defense program. Although Lt. Gridley described the strike as "principally
inter-union (CIO v. AFL) and intra-union (CIO-UAW)," his report identified Harold Christoffel, president of UAW Local 248, as a Communist.
Attached to his report were seventeen pages of photostated clippings from
the *West Allis Guide* and other Local 248 publications prior and subsequent
to the German invasion of the USSR on June 22, 1941. The clippings established that the *West Allis Guide* had opposed the war until the involvement
of the Soviet Union.

51. *The New York Times,* November 22, 1941.

enacted in 1943 with sufficient votes to overcome the presidential veto.[52]

By April of 1944, Forrestal had served as Navy Under Secretary for a period of almost four years. Although his relations with other officials, with high-ranking naval officers, and with certain congressional committees were not always harmonious, his friends and admirers within the government were far more numerous than his enemies and critics. And among the latter there were few who could entertain any serious doubt as to his sincerity, and none at all who could question his seemingly unlimited capacity for sustained hard work. Even those who actively disliked Forrestal, on personality or policy grounds, were unable to deny that he possessed considerable gifts and that these gifts were dedicated to the advancement of the national interest as Forrestal conceived it.

As a result, in part, of the marriage of ability and energy that was reflected in Forrestal's role as Under Secretary, the Navy Department in 1944 bore little resemblance to the organization of which Forrestal had become the second-ranking official in August, 1940. The ships and planes that Forrestal, in a sense, had bought, were winning major battles against the Japanese in the Pacific and the Germans in the North Atlantic. Billions of dollars of weapons and supplies had been delivered to our naval forces deployed on every ocean, and war materials worth billions more were in the pipeline. The production successes that helped make possible the victories at Midway and Guadalcanal could be attributed in no small measure to the substantial reorganization of Navy procurement that Forrestal had effected.[53]

---

52. Under the War Labor Disputes Act and other legislation, a total of forty-seven defense facilities were taken over and operated by the government during World War II.

53. As Connery observes, reorganization achievements owed a good deal to the fact that Forrestal was willing to "buck the system" in his own Department, in Congress, and in the Administration.—Connery, *op. cit.*, p. 75.

Although procurement functions alone made the Office of Under Secretary a vital agency in the military establishment, the responsibilities exercised by Forrestal touched large areas of Navy Department policy. The position to which he was appointed in August, 1940, was newly created, and it therefore lacked the precedents and traditions that, in the case of established agencies, serve to define the roles of successive holders of office. Under different leadership the Under Secretaryship might have become a relatively minor adjunct of the Office of Navy Secretary. Under Forrestal, the Under Secretaryship functioned as the powerful right arm of the Secretary with a reach that extended well beyond the field of industrial mobilization. Had Secretary Knox enjoyed better health, or had he filled his post with more energy and initiative, it is possible that Forrestal would have wielded much less power. But even if Knox had been an energetic administrator, it is all too likely that the Under Secretaryship would have developed in much the same way. Forrestal was always inclined to take a comprehensive view of his powers and responsibilities, but leaving that tendency aside, there were few in the government, however healthy and energetic, who were any match for his vigor and drive. Forrestal, in effect, was "running" the Navy Department by April, 1944, and he was "running" it as least partly because he knew what he wanted to achieve, and worked harder at achieving it than anyone else.

As a consequence, when Secretary Knox suffered a final, fatal heart attack on April 28, 1944,[54] Forrestal's appointment as his successor was, in the words of Admiral William D.

---

54. Knox had previously suffered several heart attacks, and had been in poor health for some time. At a subsequent press conference Forrestal paid tribute to Knox in saying that he "epitomized all that was the finest and best of American life. . . . He never flinched from a responsibility, and his broad shoulders were always ready to take the consequences of bold action. In him, the people of the Navy lost a friend in the broadest sense of that word, and the Nation one of its first citizens."

Leahy, "almost a foregone conclusion."[55] On May 10 President Roosevelt sent Forrestal's nomination to the Senate, where, a few days later, it was approved in accordance with the unanimous recommendation of the Senate Naval Affairs Committee. Press reaction to the appointment was uniformly favorable.[56]

Forrestal was three months past his fifty-second birthday when he was sworn in as Secretary of the Navy. Four of those fifty-two years had been spent in Washington, and the greater part of that four-year period had been devoted to preparing and mobilizing the Navy for war. Forrestal's job had been arduous and demanding, yet the stresses and strains of responsibility, the controversies within the Navy Department and between the Navy and other government agencies, the long hours and hard work, seemed in 1944 to have taken little toll of him. Thirty months earlier, on December 7, 1941, Forrestal had been described in a *New York Times* "Profile" as "pleasant," "easy," and "youthful" in appearance. Then almost fifty, Forrestal was referred to by a *Times* feature writer as a "pipe-smoking man who makes a great point of never being hurried or fussed no matter how pressing the day's duties." Paying tribute to Forrestal's "passion for anonymity," the *Times* article noted that Forrestal thoroughly enjoyed his job and that despite their responsi-

---

55. "Among the first callers after my return to Washington was Representative Carl Vinson, who recommended that I urge the President to appoint the Under Secretary of the Navy, James Forrestal, to the Cabinet post vacated by the death of Secretary Knox. Forrestal had made an excellent record in the No. 2 post and his elevation was almost a foregone conclusion."—William D. Leahy, *I Was There* (New York: McGraw-Hill, 1950), p. 237. *The New York Times* of May 11, 1944, reporting Forrestal's nomination to succeed Knox, noted that his selection had been anticipated.

56. In *The New York Times* of May 12 Arthur Krock, who had known Forrestal since they were together at Princeton, expressed his personal satisfaction with the appointment. Forrestal, Krock commented, had made an outstanding record in the Navy Department. While he was not a favorite of the New Dealers, Krock added, they nevertheless were supporting his promotion.

bilities, no two men in Washington appeared to be "less worried" than Forrestal and Patterson.[57]

The *Times* invoked similar language in an article about Forrestal that appeared on May 11, 1944. The new Navy Secretary, the *Times* revealed, is fifty-two years old but "looks ten years younger." As in the earlier article the *Times* emphasized that Forrestal was a quiet, articulate individual who disliked publicity and made a strenuous effort to "stay out of the limelight." Once again there was reference to Forrestal's "passion for anonymity."[58]

There may have been a good deal of objectivity in these impressions of Forrestal after four years of government service. In another four years, years of successive crises and momentous decisions in many of which he was an active participant, no newspaper could report truthfully that Forrestal "looks ten years younger." On the occasion of his fifty-seventh birthday in February, 1949, he was already a sick man, and he looked much older than his calendar age.

---

57. Charles Hurd, "No. 2 Men with No. 1 Jobs," *The New York Times Magazine*, December 7, 1941. The article also presented a "Portrait" of Patterson. Although accurate in most respects, the article stated that Forrestal had been "pretty much on his own" after finishing high school and that he had graduated from Princeton in 1915. Hurd also reported in error that Forrestal had "never committed himself to a party." While he was not enamoured of the New Deal, Forrestal during his Washington years always referred to himself as a Democrat.

58. An article on Forrestal in the German publication *Das Reich*, of June 11, 1944, also stressed these aspects of Forrestal's personality. *Das Reich* informed its readers that Forrestal "has a great aversion for . . . making himself popular . . . is proud of the fact that even in the midst of the most harassing business he does not lose his calm." Most of the article, however, was an attack on Forrestal as a social climber and front man for Wall Street interests. According to *Das Reich*, Forrestal "had from early years a strong social ambition, equal to his business ambition . . . [at Princeton] he gained admission into the snobbish clubs. . . ." Forrestal probably would have remained president of Dillon, Read, *Das Reich* claimed, "if he had not had an intuition after 1933 that a new era was about to dawn for the financial world, in which big business would join hands with the government and reap enormous profits." It was this intuition, the German organ suggested, that led Forrestal to renew his acquaintance with Roosevelt and make friends with Harry Hopkins.

Only a few months after that birthday, and almost five years to the day that he was sworn in as Secretary of the Navy, his life and career came to an abrupt end.

But in May, 1944, no one could know what the future held. The man who took the oath of office as our forty-ninth Secretary of the Navy was calm, dedicated, and quietly confident. Indeed, some of his friends and admirers, impressed by his past achievements and gratified by the new appointment, were already discussing the possibility that Forrestal's political career, far from having culminated in the Navy Secretaryship, had only just begun.

IV

☆ ☆ ☆ ☆ ☆

Complacency, Communism, and the Cold War

THE NATION's military mood in May, 1944, when Forrestal took the oath of office as Secretary of the Navy, was one of optimism and confidence. Although there were major battles still to be fought in Europe and the Far East—D-Day, for example, was almost a month away, and the Japanese were still in control of vast areas of the Pacific— it was clear to most Americans that an Allied victory was both certain and in sight. Pressures were already developing in favor of partial reconversion of defense industry to civilian production,[1] and many a parent, wife, and sweetheart were happily certain that it would not be very long until Johnny came marching home.[2] There were even rumors that

1. Forrestal became actively involved in the reconversion controversy that was centered in mid-1944 in the persons of Charles E. Wilson and Donald Nelson. Supporting Wilson, who was opposed to the resumption of civilian production, Forrestal confided to his notes on July 4, 1944, that he had "told Senator Truman I thought it [resumption of civilian production] was extremely dangerous, not merely from the standpoint of production itself, but from the indirect psychological results that would flow—namely, the assumption that the war was in the bag." *Diaries*, p. 3.

2. There were even those who questioned the necessity of Johnny's marching away. On March 17, 1945, the Navy Department released an exchange of correspondence between an unidentified woman and Forrestal.

some of the boys (and for that matter girls) would be back in time for Christmas.

Forrestal by temperament was not inclined to be optimistic, and in the spring and summer of 1944 he viewed the general mood not merely with disapproval but with dismay. During the first years of the war he had repeatedly stressed that victory, while inevitable, would not be cheap or easy or soon,[3] and he did not depart from this theme even in the final months of hostilities. World War II might be drawing to a close, but that did not mean, in Forrestal's judgment, that the United States would be able to live in peace or return to "normalcy." Long before V-E Day and the subsequent Japanese surrender to General MacArthur on the deck of the battleship *Missouri*,[4] Forrestal had begun to regard

---

The woman had written Forrestal: "Please, for God's sake, stop sending our finest youth to be murdered on places like Iwo Jima. It is too much for boys to stand, too much for mothers and homes to take. It is driving some mothers crazy. Why can't objectives be accomplished some other way? It is most inhuman and awful—stop, stop." Forrestal in reply stated that on December 7, 1941, "the Axis confronted us with a simple choice: Fight or be overrun. There was then, and is now, no other possibility. Having chosen to fight, we had then, and have now, no final means of winning battles except through the valor of the Marine or Army soldier who, with rifle and grenades, storms enemy positions, takes them and holds them. There is no short cut or easy way out. I wish there were." The exchange was published in the Washington *Evening Star*, March 17, 1945.

3. See, for example, his address to the graduating class of the Coast Guard Academy, June 9, 1943. A report of his speech appeared in *The New York Times* of June 10, 1943.

4. According to James F. Byrnes, the choice of the *Missouri* as the locus of formal surrender originated with Forrestal. "When Secretary Forrestal is really interested in a cause," Byrnes wrote in 1947, "he doesn't sleep, and he doesn't let others sleep. That night the telephone awakened me. It was Secretary Forrestal, suggesting that the surrender ceremonies take place on board the battleship USS *Missouri*. I was sufficiently awake to recognize what the Army would call a 'Navy trick.' Had he said simply, 'a battleship,' it would have remained a debatable question, but when he named the *Missouri*, I knew the case was closed. The President, upon receiving the suggestion, of course, thought it an excellent idea. Thus was averted a great crisis in Army-Navy relations."—*Speaking Frankly* (New York: Harper & Brothers, 1947), p. 213. While the "Navy trick" worked, it is possible that Forrestal's suggestion of the *Missouri* owed less to his desire to "upstage" the Army than to his wish to pay symbolic tribute to the nation's and the State of Missouri's first citizen.

with deep apprehension Soviet postwar intentions in Europe and Asia. The several wartime conferences of chiefs of state, the reports that came to his desk from our ambassadors and emissaries abroad, the frequent conversations with a large number of individuals who were or claimed to be expert analysts of Marxism and Communism, only served to increase his suspicions. Like a good many others, Forrestal was convinced that the Russians were determined to exploit any and all power vacuums that resulted from the defeat of Germany and Japan. He therefore was firmly of the opinion that the United States should retain sufficient military strength to deter Soviet expansionism, and, if deterrence failed, armed Soviet aggression. There would be no peace in the world, no final victory, he believed, until we had demonstrated to the Russians that, as he once put it, "whenever and wherever we say 'no,' we mean business." And we could not "mean business," he insisted, if we demobilized most of the ships, airplanes, tanks, and soldiers that had defeated the Nazi and Japanese militarists.

While this was also the view of others in the Truman Administration when the war ended, Forrestal seems always to have been convinced that what later came to be called the Cold War was inevitable and that it was therefore urgent that the nation maintain a posture of military readiness. As early as September, 1942, in a speech at Princeton University dedicating a service flag to university alumni in the Armed Forces, Forrestal urged the youth of America to see to it "that never again shall the nation be permitted to discard its arms and to rely upon the protocols of good faith and general statements of good will." Postwar plans, he advised the Princeton students, should not be based on the assumption that we will never again need our military strength.[5] In another talk at Princeton, Forrestal once more emphasized that peace would depend on the military capabilities of the

---

5. *The New York Times,* September 21, 1942.

United States and her Allies.[6] A year later, in an address to
the Naval Academy Graduating Class at Annapolis, Maryland, he took a similar position, stressing particularly the
importance of maintaining a strong Navy.[7] "I pray to God,"
he declared in a radio talk over the Columbia Broadcasting
System network on September 2, 1945,

> that we have learned the lesson that peace without power is an
> empty dream, that it is an invitation for evil men to shake the
> very foundations of society. Now more than ever before we must
> make it our business to see that the means to wage war be kept
> in the hands of those who hate war.[8]

Forrestal's advocacy of military preparedness was not confined, of course, to public or semipublic forums. As Secretary
of the Navy and, later, Secretary of Defense his attitude
toward foreign-policy decisions and even toward domestic
political issues was very largely shaped by his estimate of the
probable effect of such decisions on American security. Whatever the issue—the control of the atomic bomb, Palestine,
the occupation of Germany and Japan, the organization of
government, the unification of the Armed Forces, the relations between capital and labor—Forrestal was inclined to
relate it to the Cold War. Nor was this the extent of his
involvement in the overall struggle between Communism
and—to use Forrestal's preferred term—capitalistic democracy.
He made a variety of efforts to investigate and expose communist influence in the government, the labor movement,
the colleges and universities, and the mass media. He also

---

6. *The New York Times,* June 22, 1944.
7. *Ibid.,* June 6, 1945.
8. *Ibid.,* September 3, 1945. References to "peace without power" recur often
in Forrestal's speeches during and after the war. On April 3, 1944, in an address
to the Bond Club, Forrestal warned: "Peace not backed by power remains a
dream. The cornerstone in any plan which undertakes to rid us of the
curse of war must be the armed might of the United States." Forrestal also
advocated on this occasion the maintenance of the Navy at full strength,
compulsory military training, and the fullest exploration of iron and oil
resources.—Washington *Evening Star,* April 3, 1944.

attempted to educate himself and, to a lesser extent, other high government officials in the intricacies and complexities of Marxism-Leninism. All this suggests that Forrestal was a deeply committed man in the foremost controversy of our time—suggests, in fact, that he was more deeply committed than most of his contemporaries. Indeed, it is hardly an exaggeration to say that Forrestal was personally at war with Communism long before the Cold War began, and while in time the two wars were to merge, so to speak, Forrestal was never satisfied that the nation was fighting the Cold War with sufficient enthusiasm, courage, and vigor to achieve a final victory.

The skirmishes and engagements of Forrestal's personal war were fought on many fronts. At least two years before the end of World War II, Forrestal, anticipating that the conclusion of hostilities would generate pressures toward total or almost total demobilization, began to suspect that such pressures would not be entirely innocent in terms of intent and motivation. Some of his aides were assigned the task of collecting information pertaining to certain "peace" movements, magazines, and individuals that had been active in opposing American intervention in both world wars. On August 3, 1943, he instructed the Director of Naval Intelligence to "have someone try to establish a factual confirmation of these statements:

(1) Thomas Mann wrote a defense in 1914 of the German Kaiser, justifying Germany's aggression in World War I.[9]

(2) Donald Ogden Stewart wrote a letter to a left-wing group in either Chile or Peru, early in 1941, stating that our preparations for war were not to be taken

---

9. Forrestal presumably was referring to Mann's 1914 essay *Frederick the Great and the Grand Coalition*. In this and other writings of the World War I era, Mann expressed the view that Germany had been forced into the First World War by the Entente powers, and he defended the Kaiser's action. His *Frederick the Great and the Grand Coalition* featured a number of implied parallels between Prussia in 1756 and Germany in 1914.

seriously, nor were utterances of public officials against Germany.[10]

In September, 1945, Forrestal requested Eugene Duffield to collect articles concerned with preparedness that had appeared during the 1930's in *The Nation, The New Republic,* and *The New Masses,* "particularly articles at the time of the Nye investigation[11] by Rausenbush [*sic*][12] and Charles A. Beard."[13] Although Forrestal was a regular reader of *The Nation* and contributed to its financial support between 1943 and 1946, he distrusted the motivations of its editors, and expressed frequent doubts about the political loyalties of some of its leading contributors.[14]

---

10. Forrestal added: "I should like to speak to whomever you assign before he starts work." This memorandum and other wartime papers and notes suggest that it is not quite correct to say that in September or October, 1945, Forrestal was "suddenly interested in the arguments which in the previous 'aftermath' had led to the decline of American military strength. . . ." (Millis in *Diaries,* p. 100.) Forrestal's examination of these arguments began some time before the end of World War II.

11. Between 1933 and 1935 *The Nation, The New Republic,* and *The New Masses* devoted a large number of articles to the munitions industry and its role during and after World War I. Many of these articles dealt at length with the Senate Committee investigation of the industry headed in 1934 by Senator Gerald P. Nye. The articles in *The Nation* and *The New Republic,* which were extremely critical of the fact that leading industrialists had made a great deal of money from arms contracts during the war, were written by Raymond Gram Swing, George Soule, Jr., and John T. Flynn, among others.

12. Stephen Raushenbush served as chief investigator for the Nye Committee.

13. Memo to Duffield, September 21, 1945. Charles A. Beard was, of course, the distinguished progressive historian who opposed American intervention in the two world wars.

14. Despite such reservations Forrestal wrote *The Nation's* editor, Freda Kirchwey, on April 7, 1943: "At the risk of giving the impression, either as a bureaucrat or as an ex-businessman, of seeking to establish favorable contact with the liberal press, I am enclosing a small check toward the maintenance of *The Nation.* I need scarcely to say that I do not always agree either with the editorial views or the articles that appear in its pages but over a long period of years I have found it entertaining and provocative. We have so few journals of its general character that I should regret seeing it disappear from the scene." Enclosing a check for fifty dollars, Forrestal requested that neither his letter nor his contribution be publicized. His association with the supporting organization of *The Nation,* known as the Nation Associates, extended from April 12, 1943, to June 20, 1946.

The material collected by Duffield and others served, in general, to confirm Forrestal's suspicion that left-wing elements were involved in the opposition to military preparedness, and therefore in part responsible for the nation's "going back to bed at a frightening rate, which is the best way I know to be sure of the coming of World War III.[15] With regard to demobilization, he wrote to a friend in November, 1947: "I did my best to stem the tide—possibly I should have done more—but the demand, stimulated to some extent, I suspect, by our friends to the east, was so overwhelming that I do not believe it could have been deflected."[16]

The statement "possibly I could have done more" haunted Forrestal's thoughts during the early Cold War years, but the record of those years does not reveal what more could have been done by him to alert the nation to the communist threat. Convinced that there was an intimate

---

15. Letter to Ralph A. Bard, October 16, 1945, quoted in *Diaries*, p. 100.

16. Letter to Carl K. Gish, November 7, 1947. In other letters and in conversations during this period Forrestal also lamented the tendency of all nations in peacetime to display ingratitude toward those whose services had been essential in time of war. An admirer of Rudyard Kipling, he had printed and bound for distribution to friends and associates copies of Kipling's "Tommy," a poem that contrasts sharply the differing treatments of the common soldier in peace and war. "Tommy" begins:

> I went into a public-'ouse to get a pint o' beer,
> The publican 'e up an' sez, "We serve no red-coats here."
> The girls be'ind the bar they laughed an' giggled fit to die,
> I outs into the street again an' to myself sez I:
>> O it's Tommy this, an' Tommy that, an' "Tommy, go away";
>> But it's "Thank you, Mister Atkins," when the band begins to play—
>> The band begins to play, my boys, the band begins to play,
>> O it's "Thank you, Mister Atkins," when the band begins to play.

The poem concludes:

> You talk o' better food for us, an' schools, an' fires, an' all:
> We'll wait for extra rations if you treat us rational.
> Don't mess about the cook-room slops, but prove it to our face
> The Widow's Uniform is not the soldier-man's disgrace.
>> For it's Tommy this, an' Tommy that, an' "Chuck him out, the
>>   brute!"
>> But it's "Saviour of 'is country" when the guns begin to shoot;
>> An' it's Tommy this, an' Tommy that, an' anything you please;
>> An' Tommy ain't a bloomin' fool—you bet that Tommy sees!

relationship between domestic and overseas problems and
that policies in both areas were influenced to some extent by
"our friends to the east," Forrestal again and again raised
the question of "the locus in government of any means to
counteract Communist propaganda, not merely throughout
the world but in our own country." Such propaganda, he
informed a Cabinet meeting of February 7, 1947, took a
variety of forms, and he illustrated the point by arguing that

the objectives of the Communist Party as published in the *Daily
Worker* would find support from divers sources (for example,
one of their objectives is drastic reduction in military expenditures, and in this the Republican Party, at the moment, is cooperating). . . .

Harriman, Forrestal confided to his notes,

joined me in emphasizing the need for countermeasures. Marshall stated that he was relying very largely on the development
of the United States Information Service. . . . I said I was not concerned so much with the world as I was with our own opinion
and recalled to his mind that the Nye Committee, headed by a
Republican isolationist, was staffed by Communist attorneys and
that it had much to do with the curtailment of our own arma-
ments industry in the period 1936 to 1939. . . .[17]

Forrestal apparently envisaged the establishment of a domestic counterpart of the later United States Information
Agency. Although an organization of that type was never
created, Forrestal continued to urge its existence, and he also

---

17. *Diaries*, p. 243. At a luncheon that day, attended by Representative
Clarence Brown, Ohio Republican, and Arthur Krock, Forrestal told Brown
that "sometime we would have to look to him for a defense [of activities
designed to increase military capabilities] . . . that at some time in the not-
too-distant future I foresaw the recurrence of attacks such as the Nye investigation, to prove that the Army and Navy and American business were
combining on a neo-fascist program of American imperialism, thought
domination, etc." Forrestal added that Brown "is worth a good deal of
attention not merely for his position in the Republican Party but also because, as a proprietor of a chain of eight newspapers in Ohio, he is a pretty
good reflector of public opinion."—*Diaries*, p. 244. At the time, Brown was
a member of the powerful House Rules Committee.

strongly favored, publicly and privately, "a central organization to coordinate the presently scattered efforts to prevent fifth column activities, sabotage, and other dangers to the 'internal security' of the nation."[18]

As a result of his concern with the problem of communist subversion, Forrestal's office became a kind of clearinghouse for the gathering and dissemination of information relating to communist influence in the United States and elsewhere in the world. From Francis Cardinal Spellman, Forrestal received material relating to communist penetration of the motion-picture industry.[19] Monsignor Fulton J. Sheen supplied bibliographies of books dealing with the theory and practice of Marxism-Leninism.[20] A correspondent in Albany, New York, enclosing clippings concerned with the foreign-policy views of political science Professor Frederick L. Schuman of Williams College, wrote to Forrestal that Professor Schuman "might be of real harm to your program of defense."[21] J. Edgar Hoover sent Forrestal frequent reports of Communist Party activities,[22] and the Office of Naval Intelligence (ONI) furnished Forrestal with a number of

18. Washington *Evening Star,* December 19, 1948. Forrestal added that the proposed organization should be under civilian control rather than a part of the Department of Defense. He did not make clear what relationship, if any, the "central organization" would have with the FBI, and he was always vague about the functions it would perform in addition to those engaged in by the FBI. Presumably he had in mind an active involvement in anticommunist propaganda efforts within the United States.

19. In August, 1945, Cardinal Spellman asked Postmaster General Robert Hannegan, to whom he sent the material, to forward copies of the various documents to Forrestal.

20. One such bibliography, dated September 5, 1945, recommended Charles J. McFadden, *The Philosophy of Communism* (1939); Helen Iswolsky, *The Soul of Russia* (1943); and Nickolas Berdyaev, *The Origin of Russian Communism* (1937).

21. Kenneth G. Reynolds to Forrestal, April 12, 1948. Forrestal sent the letter and clippings to Secretary of State James F. Byrnes.

22. On January 5, 1948, Hoover devoted a letter of three pages to the remarks of a leading Communist Party functionary made before a meeting of the Party's National Committee. The remarks, which dealt with the international communist movement, had reached Hoover "through a reliable confidential source."

memoranda detailing communist infiltration of trade unions, peace groups, and other organizations.[23] Letters from businessman who had encountered communist influence abroad,[24] magazine articles dealing with communist activities,[25] transcriptions of Forrestal's own conversations with government officials who suspected that certain private and public agencies had been infiltrated by Communists[26]—all of these reports became part of a voluminous collection of documents concerned with the communist threat to our internal and external security. The collection also included some literature of doubtful value in understanding and opposing communist influence, literature described by someone who was close to Forrestal at the time as "rather lurid . . . almost crackpot." Among the more lurid examples were pamphlets suggesting that Communists and communist sympathizers existed in large numbers in government, education, and the

23. On July 25, 1947, Forrestal sent his friend John H. Vincent of Center Sandwich, New Hampshire, a two-page ONI report on the "Society for the Prevention of World War III." Noting in an accompanying letter that a mutual friend had become involved in the Society, Forrestal wrote to Vincent: "You might be interested in this—I wonder if [Michael Robertson] realizes what company he is getting into."

24. One letter, in August, 1946, dealt with the activities and objectives of the Venezuelan Communist Party. Signed by fifty-eight American businessmen active in Venezuela, the letter to United States Ambassador Corrigan called on the State Department to take steps to counter communist attacks on the United States and American business firms in Venezuela. Forrestal's copy of the letter originated with Major A. F. Hubbard, AUS, Assistant Military Attaché of the American Embassy, Caracas.

25. Among such articles was a report by Walter Millis, "Communists in a Democracy," *New York Herald Tribune,* February 16, 1948. The article was an analysis of the official Canadian report on Soviet espionage in Canada.

26. On September 28, 1945, Forrestal entered in his notes the opinion of Ambassador Patrick J. Hurley that "many of the American correspondents [in China] . . . were communistically inclined, as well as many of the people in the State Department."—*Diaries,* p. 98. On July 15, 1946, Forrestal quoted Rear Admiral Ellery W. Stone, American chief of the Allied Control Commission for Italy, to the effect that the "general opinion" was that State Department Counselor Benjamin V. Cohen "was the influence on Byrnes' staff which advocated surrendering everything to Russia in order to avoid war."—*Diaries,* p. 181. Although it is not known to what extent, if any, Forrestal was persuaded by these views, he thought them important enough to include in his private papers.

mass media. Some so-called "fact" sheets and "newsletters" argued a connection between the communist movement and "international Jewry."

Although Forrestal was cautious in evaluating certain letters and documents, he became gradually convinced that a number of influential persons here and abroad were either sympathetic to Communism or, if not sympathetic, ignorant of the dynamics of Marxism-Leninism and Soviet foreign policy. At various times he expressed doubts that James F. Byrnes and George C. Marshall "sufficiently understood Soviet ideology,"[27] and for reasons he never made clear he followed the curious practice of sending books exposing the nature of Communism to such avowed anti-Communists as J. Edgar Hoover and William O. Douglas.[28] Copies of a special study of Communism commissioned by Forrestal, "Dialectical Materialism and Russian Objectives," were sent to a variety of individuals in and out of the government, including Henry R. Luce and Senator David I. Walsh.[29]

However naïve Byrnes and Marshall may have been with reference to Soviet ideology, they were, in Forrestal's view, tough-minded realists compared with another of his Cabinet colleagues, Secretary of Commerce Henry A. Wallace. Long before Wallace's involvement with the Progressive Party of 1948, Forrestal had become extremely distrustful of Wallace's views on subjects ranging from the control of the atomic bomb to American relations with the Soviet Union. As early as 1943, Forrestal included among his papers the complete

27. For Byrnes see the reference in *Diaries*, p. 107. On March 10, 1947, Forrestal wrote Paul Smith that "Marshall has the equipment in terms of orderliness of mind and capacity to deal [with world events]. The only areas where I am not sure about his equipment are, first, the economic background, and second, awareness of the nature of Communist philosophy. However, he learns fast." *Diaries*, p. 254. "However, he learns fast" was a penciled insert.

28. Copies of Arthur Koestler's *Darkness at Noon* were sent to Hoover on January 4, 1948, and to Douglas on February 28, 1948.

29. See below, pp. 151–154.

text of a speech delivered by Wallace to the Conference on the Christian Bases of World Order in Delaware, Ohio. In his address to the Conference of March 8, 1943, as reported in *The New York Times,* Wallace stated that there were "three great philosophies" struggling for world supremacy. The first he characterized as "based on the supremacy of might over right" and further belief that "war between nations is inevitable until such time as a single master race dominates the world. . . ." The second, "the Marxian philosophy," insists that "class warfare is inevitable until such time as the proletariat comes out on top, everywhere in the world, and can start building a society without classes." The third philosophy, according to Wallace, "which we in this country know as the democratic Christian philosophy, denies that man was made for war, whether it be war between nations or war between classes, and asserts boldly that ultimate peace is inevitable, that all men are brothers, and that God is their father."

Forrestal would not have summarized the "three great philosophies" in precisely the same way, but he was generally in accord with Wallace's efforts to differentiate between them. The part of the Vice-President's speech that caught Forrestal's attention and aroused his suspicions dealt with what Wallace termed "the seeds of World War No. 3." Toward the end of his speech Wallace argued that a third world war

will be certain if we allow Prussia [*sic*] to rearm either materially or psychologically. That war will be probable in case we double-cross Russia. That war will be probable if we fail to demonstrate that we can furnish full employment after this war comes to an end and Fascist interests, motivated largely by anti-Russian bias, get control of our government.

Unless the Western democracies and Russia come to a satisfactory understanding before the war ends, I very much fear that World War No. 3 will be inevitable. Without a close and trusting understanding between Russia and the United States there is grave probability of Russia and Germany sooner or later making common cause.

Of course, the ground for World War No. 3 can be laid by actions of the other powers, even though we in the United States follow the most constructive course. For example, such a war would be inevitable if Russia should again embrace the Trotsky-ist idea of fomenting world-wide revolution, or if British interests should again be sympathetic to anti-Russian activity in Germany and other countries.[30]

Alarmed by Wallace's views and especially his emphasis on the necessity of a "close and trusting understanding be-tween Russia and the United States," Forrestal in 1944 was determinedly opposed to Wallace's renomination as the Democratic Party's vice-presidential candidate. Like many others in the Roosevelt Administration, Forrestal had grave doubts that the President would live through his fourth term of office. Convinced that Wallace's succession to the Presi-dency would constitute a national disaster, Forrestal in the spring and summer of 1944 urged several high-ranking politi-cal figures actively to seek the vice-presidential nomination. On July 4, 1944, he attempted to persuade Senator Harry S. Truman that it was wrong for him "to resist" efforts of Democratic Party chieftains to promote his candidacy. "I told him," Forrestal noted in his diary,

that it was his duty to take it in view of the fact that the alterna-tive would be Henry Wallace. This alternative he regarded with

---

30. Forrestal also included in his papers excerpts from a *Times* editorial comment on Wallace's remarks. While agreeing with Wallace that postwar plans should be made now (i.e., in 1943), the *Times* observed that Wallace had tended to oversimplify the problems involved in dealing with the Soviet Union. The Russians, commented the *Times*, were capable of double-crossing the United States and other nations. As for Fascism in the United States, the *Times* editorial expressed the view that Americans would not submit "to home-grown Fascists after beating the foreign variety." In con-clusion, the *Times* remarked that "[o]ne of the great privileges of an Ameri-can Vice President derives from his constitutional lack of executive power. He can say what he likes, for the simple reason that he cannot do what he likes. Hence Henry A. Wallace can be the prophet of the Roosevelt Admin-istration without in any way committing that Administration to a course of action."

the same misgivings as myself but still felt he did not want to take the nomination saying that he was happy in the Senate and felt that he was able to exercise as much influence in government as he wished.[31]

Postwar Cabinet discussions of the complex problems of peace and Soviet-American relations only intensified Forrestal's distrust of Wallace and the point of view he represented. After one Cabinet meeting on September 21, 1945, entirely devoted to the question of American policy on the provision of atomic-bomb information to other nations, Forrestal confided to his diary that Wallace "was completely, everlastingly and wholeheartedly in favor of giving it [knowledge of the bomb] to the Russians.[32] Failure to share our information with the Russians, Forrestal quoted Wallace, "would make an embittered and sour people."[33] In a diary

31. *Diaries*, p. 5. In February, 1946, Forrestal was active in encouraging Justice William O. Douglas to accept a Cabinet position as Secretary of the Interior, and again he had occasion to refer to Wallace who was then serving as Secretary of Commerce. Arguing with Douglas that it was his "patriotic duty" to accept, that the Cabinet appointment would provide him with a "forum" for his views, and also the opportunity to serve as "a practical nexus between the liberal and conservative elements of the government," Forrestal added that he found it "very difficult" to talk to Wallace "in practical language, or at least to have any feeling that he understood what I was talking about. . . ." Douglas, on the other hand, while he might "differ" with Forrestal "had a commonsense approach to problems of government. . . ."—*Diaries*, p. 134.

32. The positions of Forrestal and others in the Truman Administration with reference to problems posed by the atomic bomb are dealt with below, pp. 163–175.

33. In 1951, following publication in *The Forrestal Diaries* of these statements, Wallace denied with vehemence that he had ever been "completely, everlastingly and wholeheartedly" in favor of sharing the atomic bomb with the Russians. "This is a lie," he declared in a statement released to newspapers. "I said under oath [before the House Un-American Activities Committee in 1950] that there was a leaking liar in the Cabinet and the President agreed. . . . I do not wish to quarrel with a dead man or his widow and children. Their husband and father wished very much to see me a few months before he died. . . . Undoubtedly at that time he was trying to set his spiritual house in order. May God rest the soul of this curiously tortured man who served his country and the armed services so well in time of war." Quoted in *Time*, October 15, 1951. For another version of Wallace's views see below p. 174.

entry of March 7, 1946, largely given over to a discussion of the shipbuilding industry and—a favorite theme of Forrestal's —the need for a "cementing secretariat" in the government,[34] Forrestal noted that he was sending a recent report on the shipbuilding industry to the Secretary of Commerce [Wallace] "on the assumption that the name of his Department at least implies an interest in such a subject. . . . As I write this it occurs to me that I have never heard the head of the Department of Commerce put forward any views that indicate a desire to help business. I shall look today at the charter and precept of that department."[35]

Wallace, meanwhile, increasingly dissatisfied with the course taken by American-Soviet relations, made a number of statements during the spring and summer of 1946 that were regarded with dismay by Forrestal and other high officials of the Truman Administration. In a letter to the President of March 14, 1946, Wallace recommended a "new approach" to the Soviet Union. The task of newly appointed Ambassador to the Soviet Union Walter Bedell Smith would be made easier, Wallace wrote to Truman, "if we could also at the same time discuss with the Russians in a friendly way their long range economic problems and the future of our cooperation in matters of trade. We know that much of the recent Soviet behavior which has caused us concern has been the result of their dire economic needs and of their disturbed sense of security. The events of the past few months have thrown the Soviets back to their pre-1939 fears of 'capitalist encirclement' and to their erroneous belief that the Western World, including the U.S.A., is invariably and unanimously hostile." Wallace concluded his letter with the suggestion that a "new group"[36] be authorized to visit Moscow for pur-

---

34. See below, pp. 262–267.

35. *Diaries*, p. 142.

36. By "new group" Wallace meant a committee of individuals who were not members of, or identified with, the State Department and/or the Foreign Service.

poses of discussing trade and other economic relations. Should the President concur, he was willing to "make suggestions regarding the composition of this mission."[37]

In March and April, 1946, the Office of the Chief of Naval Operations sent Forrestal memoranda containing excerpts from recent statements and speeches by Wallace and Senator (now Representative) Claude Pepper, Democrat of Florida. Wallace was quoted in one memorandum as insisting that the United States withdraw its troops from Iceland and abandon its efforts to obtain air bases in that country. Senator Pepper, in an address to the Senate intended as a reply to Winston Churchill's speech at Fulton, Missouri,[38] declared himself opposed to any "gang-up" directed at the Soviet Union, and he also demanded that the United States avoid becoming the foremost supporter of "British imperialism." Recommending a Big Three conference on the initiative of the United States, Pepper urged that all atomic bombs and all facilities for making bombs be destroyed before the conference met.

At a subsequent Cabinet meeting of April 19, Forrestal joined Secretary of State Byrnes in protesting these recent statements by Wallace and Pepper. It seemed to him "most inappropriate," he commented with direct reference to Wallace,

for a member of the Cabinet to make independent comments on foreign policy which was being conducted by one of his colleagues. . . . in view of the Secretary's [Byrne's] analysis of the forthcoming conference [of Foreign Ministers], steps should be taken to see that the country is properly informed of the prob-

37. The full text of the latter appears in Harry S Truman, *Memoirs,* Vol. I, "Year of Decisions" (New York: Doubleday and Company, 1955), 555–556. Wallace's letter was "ignored" by him, Truman writes, because "I could see little to be gained from the Wallace proposal."—*op. cit.,* 556.

38. Churchill's now famous speech at Fulton is regarded by some commentators as marking the formal beginning of the Cold War. It was in the Fulton speech that Churchill referred to the Russian-inspired "iron curtain" that had descended upon Europe, and also declared that until the "curtain" was lifted, there could be no certainty of either peace or freedom.

lems that face him, of the attitude of Russia, so that if and when the breakdown occurs he may not be exposed to violent attacks by his own countrymen who follow the "party line."

Forrestal added that he would be glad to make a speech along such lines and "make it as explicit as he [presumably Byrnes] wanted it made."[39]

On July 23 Wallace again wrote to Truman, forcefully advocating a new American approach to the Soviet Union. In a letter of twelve single-spaced typed pages Wallace criticized a variety of programs designed to promote military preparedness, including atomic-bomb tests, the production of heavy bombers, and the establishment of air bases abroad. Such actions, he wrote Truman,

> must make it look to the rest of the world as if we were only paying lip service to peace at the conference table. These facts rather make it appear either (1) that we are preparing ourselves to win the war which we regard as inevitable or (2) that we are trying hard to build up a preponderance of force to intimidate the rest of mankind.

Wallace suggested that the United States make every effort to "allay any reasonable Russian grounds for fear, suspicion and distrust."[40]

Although Wallace was fully aware long before September that his attitudes toward foreign-policy questions had earned him the enmity of Forrestal, Byrnes, and other high-ranking Administration officials, his conversations with the President gave him the impression that while Truman did not support his position he was not opposed to Wallace's making statements on foreign-policy issues. As a consequence of this impression, mistaken or otherwise, Wallace in the late summer

---

39. *Diaries*, p. 155.
40. Quoted in Truman, *op. cit.*, I, 556–557. In his reference to the letter Truman comments that Wallace "had no specific proposals how this might be accomplished without surrendering to them on every count." Notwithstanding this omission and his inability to agree with Wallace's approach, Truman had a copy of the letter sent to Byrnes and "let [Wallace] know that he appreciated the time he had taken to put himself on record."— *Ibid.*, p. 557.

of 1946 accepted an invitation to deliver a foreign-policy address on September 12 to a Democratic Party rally at New York's Madison Square Garden.[41] Two days before the rally Wallace visited the President and showed him a copy of the speech he proposed to deliver. The President read a few pages of the speech, glanced over the rest, and told Wallace that he had no objection to the contents.[42] Wallace left a copy of the speech with Truman, and added to the copies released to the press a sentence stating that his speech had received the President's approval.

At his press conference on the morning of September 12, Truman confirmed Wallace's statement that his forthcoming Madison Square Garden speech had been approved by the White House.[43] One hour before Wallace was to address the New York meeting there was an urgent call to Forrestal's office from Acting Secretary of State Will Clayton. Clayton, extremely disturbed by the tone and contents of Wallace's speech,[44] was calling to request Forrestal's immedi-

---

41. The other principal speaker at the rally, which was sponsored by left-wing Democrats and liberals, was to be Senator Pepper.

42. I believe this account of the Truman-Wallace meeting on September 10 to be accurate, although it differs in one key respect with Truman's own version. According to the former President's *Memoirs*: "Just before he left . . . Wallace mentioned that he would deliver a speech in New York on the twelfth. He said that he intended to say that we ought to look at the world through American eyes rather than through the eyes of a pro-British or rabidly anti-Russian press. I told him that I was glad he was going to help the Democrats in New York by his appearance. There was, of course, no time for me to read the speech, even in part."—Truman, *op. cit.*, I, 557.

43. In his *Memoirs*, Truman in effect takes the position that he erred in saying that Wallace's speech had his approval. "Of course I should have said," he writes, " 'He's told me he is going to make a speech,' because everyone promptly took my answer to mean that I had read the speech and approved every part of its content."—I, 557. Walter Millis, in another version of what transpired at the press conference, states that Truman "gave them [the reporters] to understand both that he had read the whole speech and that he thought it exactly in line with the Byrnes policies."—*Diaries*, p. 207.

44. Apparently no high official in the State Department received a transcript of the speech until the afternoon of September 12. Clayton had not been afforded an opportunity to read the speech until a few minutes before 6:00 P.M., although transcripts had long since been released to newspapers and the wire services.

ate presence at a State Department meeting convened for the purpose of discussing what action, if any, could be taken to prevent delivery of the speech or at least ensure that Wallace made no reference to the fact that Truman had approved it. Wallace's speech, containing criticisms of American foreign policy similar to those he had advanced in his July 23 letter to Truman, was regarded by Clayton as essentially a repudiation of the Truman-Byrnes foreign policy. In the view of Clayton and other State Department officials, including James W. Riddleberger, acting head of the Division of Near and Middle Eastern Affairs, the Wallace speech would be interpreted by the Russians as evidence of weakness and disunity in the Administration. Taking particular exception to such Wallace statements as "we are still armed to the hilt . . . excessive expenses are the chief cause of our un-balanced budget," Clayton, Riddleberger, and Henderson were strongly of the opinion that Wallace's remarks would make it difficult if not impossible for Secretary of State Byrnes, then in Paris, to continue to represent the American position.[45]

In the absence of Forrestal, who was away from Washington at the time, the Navy Department was represented at the State Department meeting by Under Secretary John L. Sullivan and Captain Robert L. Dennison, Assistant Chief of Naval Operations.[46] Sullivan's reaction to the Wallace speech was similar to Clayton's, and he suggested that if the speech were delivered without change Truman "would be obliged to repudiate either Secretary Wallace or Secretary Byrnes." Unfortunately, from the point of view of those gathered at the State Department, Secretary of War Patterson, who was called to the meeting from a dinner party, did not share the general apprehension. Although Patterson thought the

---

45. An account of the State Department meeting and its aftermath appears in *Diaries*, pp. 206–210.

46. Forrestal subsequently received a detailed memorandum reporting the meeting from Sullivan.

speech "pretty bad," and admitted that it "might cause some
stir for six or seven days," he did not "believe the situation
to be as serious," Sullivan later reported to Forrestal, "as
Mr. Clayton and I believed." Despite Patterson's dissent,
Clayton and Sullivan made several approaches to the White
House. Unable to make direct contact with the President,
they urged Press Secretary Charles G. Ross to bring the
matter to the immediate attention of his Chief. Ross initially
committed himself to talking with the President, but shortly
before seven o'clock, after several further conversations with
Ross, Clayton informed the group that Ross "was noncom-
mittal as to whether or not he had discussed the matter with
the President," and it was agreed that "it would be unwise
and useless to press Ross further on this point. . . ."

As Clayton and Sullivan had expected, Wallace's speech
of September 12 was followed by a vigorous protest from
Secretary Byrnes in Paris. Although at a subsequent press
conference Truman reiterated that Wallace's speech did not
foreshadow any change in American foreign policy, high
officials in his Administration, including Forrestal, made no
secret of their view that Wallace's resignation as Secretary
of Commerce was long overdue. Wallace, meanwhile, stated
on several occasions that despite criticism he would continue
to speak out for what he believed to be right. On September
16,[47] following a disclosure that a copy of his letter to
Truman of July 23 had somehow come into the possession
of Drew Pearson, Wallace and Ross agreed on the wisdom of
releasing the letter to the press.[48] On September 17, in an
appearance before the Navy Industrial Association at New
York's Waldorf-Astoria Hotel, Forrestal discarded a prepared

---

47. In a letter of that date, to his friend Palmer Hoyt, editor of the
Denver Post, Forrestal wryly asked, "How would you like a daily column on
foreign affairs from Henry Wallace?"

48. According to former President Truman's *Memoirs*, the release of the
letter "was never approved" by him, and by the time he learned that Wallace
and Ross had agreed on its release, "it was too late to stop it."

address in order to make a blistering attack on Wallace's speech of September 12. Two days later, in response to a request from Truman, Forrestal and Patterson issued a joint statement aimed at Wallace denying that they knew of any responsible Army or Navy officer "who has ever advocated or even suggested a policy or plan of attacking Russia." There was no basis, they indicated, for Wallace's declaration that there was a "school" of military officers who advocated a preventive war against the Soviet Union. On September 20, after Byrnes had made it clear that there was no room in the Cabinet for both him and Wallace, Truman requested, and received, Wallace's resignation.[49]

Although Forrestal always believed that Truman should have terminated Wallace's services much earlier than September 20, 1946, he was gratified by the turn of events, and he made a point of congratulating the President for his "forthright" action. The former Secretary of Commerce, however, while he no longer held any official position in the government, did not cease to be in demand as a speaker on and critic of American foreign policy, and he also did not lose the ability to provoke Forrestal and other Administration officials.[50] In April, 1947, following a report to the

49. "Henry," Truman wrote to his mother and sister on the day of Wallace's resignation, "is the most peculiar fellow I ever came in contact with. I spent two hours and a half with him Wednesday afternoon arguing with him to make no speeches on foreign policy—or to agree to the policy for which I am responsible—but he wouldn't. So I asked him to make no more speeches until Byrnes came home. He agreed to that, and he and Charlie Ross and I came to what we thought was a firm commitment that he'd say nothing beyond the one sentence statement we agreed he should make. Well, he answered questions and told his gang over at Commerce all that had taken place in our interview. It was all in the afternoon *Washington News* yesterday, and I never was so exasperated since Chicago. So—this morning I called Henry and told him he'd better get out, and he was so nice about it I almost backed out!

"Well, now he's out, and the crackpots are having conniption fits. I'm glad they are. It convinces me I'm right. . . . *Memoirs*, I, 560.

50. In speeches following his resignation, Wallace drew attention to the alleged influence of "Wall Street" and "Big Business" in the government and especially the State Department. On October 1, 1947, Wallace charged that

Cabinet by Secretary Acheson concerned with a forthcoming speech of Wallace's in London, Forrestal inquired "why we had not denied Wallace a passport and why we should not do so now." Dissatisfied with Truman's answer that the denial of a passport to a former Vice-President and Cabinet member "would expose us to severe criticism," Forrestal stated that he "would prefer to take the criticism than permit Wallace to interfere with American policy."[51] A year later, following a letter written by Wallace to Soviet Premier Joseph Stalin, Forrestal assigned Marx Leva the task of investigating whether Wallace's letter was in violation of the Logan Act.[52] In a memorandum to Forrestal of May 19, 1948, Leva expressed doubt that the letter was legal under the Act, but added that "[p]olicy-wise, of course, it seems clear that no action should be instituted against Mr. Wallace."[53]

Forrestal, Lovett, and General William Draper were "improper persons" for the positions they held. Citing Forrestal's former connection with Dillon, Read, and Company, Wallace accused Forrestal of having "too intimate a connection with I.G. Farben to satisfy those of us who want that industrial monster laid to rest permanently." Quoted in *The New York Times*, October 2, 1947. Forrestal, in a number of speeches that were, in effect, replies to Wallace, denied that businessmen caused wars, needed wars, or wanted wars. "American business," he stated on one occasion, "has its money invested in peace. . . ."

51. According to Forrestal's notes, Attorney General Tom Clark "suggested that it might even be better to weigh carefully the re-entry of the gentleman in question into the United States."—*Diaries*, p. 261.

52. The Logan Act prohibited, among other things, attempts to trade or communicate with an enemy of the United States.

53. One of Forrestal's friends, a distinguished newspaper publisher, wrote to him with reference to the Stalin-Wallace exchange of letters, that "it is unrealistic not to suppose that the deal was thoroughly rigged by the Commies. Your interest, of course, lay rather in how to counteract the effects of this interchange. It is my belief that the matter has more or less taken care of itself, but I do think the only feasible action on the part of the administration is to keep pointing out that any bilateral talks with Russia at this time would be misunderstood by the entire world. . . . I am also asking [in a forthcoming speech] who is it that really wants war and suggesting that neither the administration, Wall Street, the military nor the newspapers want it, because they all know what the inevitable result would be. This is one of the worst things that the Wallace crowd is doing because everybody wants to believe the worst of the aforementioned categories."—Letter to Forrestal, May 26, 1948.

Wallace's reemergence into politics as the presidential candidate of the Progressive Party in 1948 confirmed Forrestal's worst suspicions not only of the former Vice President but also of the extent to which communist influence had to be reckoned with as a subversive political and ideological force in the United States. A close observer of developments within the Progressive Party, Forrestal in the summer of 1948 was more inclined than others in the government to regard the party as less an immediate electoral threat than as a potential serious challenge to American principles and policies. "I have been looking today," he wrote to Arizona publisher William R. Mathews on July 24, 1948, "at Henry Wallace's convention.[54] It has all the familiar hallmarks of organization under the Moscow dispensation. However, in spite of that, I do not believe it can be entirely disregarded."[55] Even after the 1948 election which saw the Progressive Party decisively rejected at the polls, Forrestal remained convinced that the point of view represented by Wallace and his followers could not be dismissed as insignificant. The Progressive Party, he commented to an associate in late November, 1948, might be dead for all practical purposes, but communist forces in the United States would seek other opportunities to influence public opinion and government policy.

Forrestal was also fearful that sympathizers with Marxism-Leninism would increasingly affect the course of events in Western European countries, especially Italy, France, and Great Britain. Prior to the Italian elections of 1948, he privately raised money to finance the propaganda activities of several anticommunist political movements.[56] On a number

---

54. At the time the Progressive Party was meeting in Philadelphia.

55. On July 29 Forrestal wrote to Palmer Hoyt that "[i]t was a smart thing to get Norman Thomas to report that convention. I wish you would send me the articles."

56. Forrestal was instrumental in raising thousands of dollars to finance anticommunist propaganda and electoral activities in Italy in 1947–48. Much of this money was contributed by friends, but an undisclosed amount, re-

of occasions he discussed with French political leaders, including General Charles de Gaulle, the problems posed by the strength of the French Communist Party, especially among the working class.[57] His attitude toward the British Labour government, in power from 1945 to 1951, was profoundly affected by a deep distrust of certain prominent figures associated with the Labour Party, all of whom Forrestal was inclined to regard as Soviet-line Marxists or quasi-Marxists.

Of these Labour Party personalities, the one toward whom Forrestal was most hostile was the late Harold J. Laski, Professor of Political Science at the London School of Economics and a leading Socialist theoretician. Whether or not it is true, in the words of Walter Millis, that Forrestal "seemed to have a mild obsession with Laski,"[58] there can be no doubt that Forrestal both misunderstood Laski's politics and exaggerated the amount of influence wielded by Laski in Labour Party circles.[59] Whenever he was in London Forrestal was apt to bring up the subject of Laski's role in the Labour Party, and although he was frequently assured that the principal members of the Labour government "had no use for Laski,"[60] Forrestal continued to believe that Laski's writings and activities warranted the closest scrutiny.

portedly in the neighborhood of $12,000, was supplied by Forrestal himself. According to William Bradford Huie, Forrestal was also active in raising $50,000 in December, 1947, in order to bribe communist officials in France to end a general transportation strike. Huie, "Untold Facts in the Forrestal Case," *New American Mercury,* December, 1950, p. 644.

57. See below, pp. 156–158.

58. *Diaries,* p. 80.

59. As a democratic Socialist, Laski was bitterly opposed to Communism, and waged open warfare against communist influences in British intellectual and political life. It was also the case that while Laski was a prominent figure in the Labour Party, he neither held office in the Labour government nor enjoyed the confidence of Attlee, Bevin, Cripps, and other major leaders. For Laski's view of Communism see his *The Secret Battalion: An Examination of the Communist Attitude to the Labour Party* (London: The Labour [Party] Publications Department, April, 1946).

60. This statement is attributed by Forrestal to Ernest Bevin.—*Diaries,* p. 80.

Laski, like Wallace, apparently aroused Forrestal's suspicions even before the end of World War II. In June, 1944, a review of one of Laski's books, *Faith, Reason, and Civilisation,* served to persuade Forrestal that Laski was an apologist for Communism,[61] and thereafter he paid particular attention to Laski's speeches here and abroad. Excerpts from an address delivered by Laski on August 12, 1945, to the International Congress of the French Socialist Party were entered in one of the notebooks,[62] and in December Forrestal again had occasion to refer to Laski in a letter to an English friend. Writing on December 4 to Oliver Lyttleton, Conservative M.P. and member of the Conservative Party's "shadow cabinet," Forrestal suggested that Lyttleton might be "interested in the enclosed clipping from *The [New York Herald] Tribune* this morning on the opening remarks of your distinguished fellow countryman, Mr. Laski. When I get finished with this job," he continued,

I am going to propose to you that you get me invited to some group in England to whom I can make a case for the free and capitalistic society. I remember I was much impressed when some Buddhists sent their priests over to convert America. It seemed to me like a good idea to reverse the process of proselyting, and I think it might be amusing to do so in this instance. . . .

In January, 1946, Forrestal requested a friend who was a Harvard graduate to investigate the "circumstances under which our friend Mr. Laski was invited to separate himself from Harvard.[63] I won't quote you but I would like to have

---

61. The review by Henry Hazlitt appeared in *The New York Times,* June 11, 1944. The review was entitled "Laski's Brief for Communism." In a memorandum to Forrestal, a quotation from another Laski book, *Communism,* was interpreted by an aide as a "presentation of the Marxian concept of the role of trade unions and the labor party. His [Laski's] remarks certainly afford basis for thought when one considers trade union activities in the United States at the present time and also the role of the labor party in England at the present time."

62. The source of the exerpts was Jefferson Caffery, American Ambassador to France.

63. On January 31, 1916, Laski was appointed an instructor and tutor at Harvard. He returned to England during the summer of 1920.

the facts. . . ." The friend subsequently informed Forrestal that Laski's lectures at Harvard had aroused "misgivings" among faculty members and overseers, and had also had an adverse effect on enrollment and the university's endowment. As a result, he wrote Forrestal, Owen Wister, then an over-seer, anonymously wrote a humorous article in the *Lampoon* "spoofing parlor bolsheviks." Laski, according to Forrestal's informant, was "surprised and deeply hurt."[64] The recollection of the friend was that Laski, following publication of the article, which was somewhat anti-Semitic in tone, had resigned, or taught another year and then resigned, or was not asked back.[65]

For Forrestal, Laski also symbolized what Forrestal once termed, in a letter to Raymond Moley, "the subservience of

---

64. Laski owed his appointment at Harvard to Felix Frankfurter, then a professor at the Harvard Law School, who had enthusiastically recommended him to Dean Charles Haskins. While at Harvard, Laski was a regular contributor to *The New Republic*, and he was also active in aiding the Boston Police Force to organize a union. It was this latter interest that provoked certain faculty members and overseers, and led to the publication of an entire issue of the *Lampoon* satirizing Laski's alleged communist sympathies. The *Lampoon's* treatment of Laski, which was not without anti-Semitic overtones, included a bogus autobiography that began: "Born in Kognito, Poland, in 1902 at the age of three. My attention was immediately focussed upon my Constitution, for *Oi Gewalt*! I was delicate . . . my hobby is bombing, and my favorite book is *Childe Harold*!" One of the poetry efforts in the issue featured the verse:

> " 'Twould be greatly to his liking
> If the whole world started striking,
> With himself established at the strikers' head;
> In the parlance of the ghetto,
> He would 'shake a mean stiletto'
> From the firstski to the laski he's a Red!"

According to a biographer, "Laski's first reaction to this immature and libelous attack was to go to President [A. Lawrence] Lowell and ask that no action be taken against its authors."—Kingsley Martin, *Harold Laski: A Biographical Memoir* (London: Victor Gollancz, Ltd., 1953) , p. 41.

65. Asked in 1959 to comment on Forrestal's "mild obsession" with Laski, the friend explained that it seemed to him "natural that [Forrestal] might have distrusted Laski, for it was my impression that he always feared the influence of the radicals in the Democratic party, he himself embodying the genuinely conservative characteristics of a true liberal."—Letter to the writer, June 24, 1959.

American economists to European thought." Writing Moley on February 15, 1946, Forrestal confided:

I have always felt that the start of this veneration for imported theories was the acceptance of German philosophy in the Nineteenth century in most of our universities. After all, Karl Marx was to an extent the spiritual descendant of Fichte, Kant, and Hegel. I believe someone could do an intersting book on the pragmatic evolution of an American social-economic-fiscal system which despite the admiration of some of our best thinkers for Mr. Laski and his associated planners still happens to be, apparently, the chief prop for the rest of the world.[66]

Forrestal did not identify the "best thinkers" he had in mind. It is probable that he was thinking of certain individuals connected with the OPA and other regulatory agencies.

Nevertheless, and despite misgivings, justified or otherwise, about a number of the "best thinkers" and "planners," Forrestal was careful not to identify liberals in general as either Marxists, Communists, or Socialists. Early in 1947, following the appointment by the President of David E. Lilienthal as Chairman of the Atomic Energy Commission, Forrestal on several occasions defended the prospective AEC Chairman against charges in the Senate and elsewhere that he was an extreme radical[67] and/or a communist sympathizer. On February 17, 1947, Forrestal received a letter from a trusted friend inquiring "what's all the 'furse' about Dave Lilienthal?" Writing to Forrestal as a supporter of Lilienthal and as one "who wired the President to appoint him when Conant ran out," Forrestal's confidant was disturbed by certain reports circulating about Lilienthal. "I notice," he wrote Forrestal,

that *Time* took a pretty nasty dig at Dave in their issue of February 17. If you haven't looked at it, do so. It is on the first

---

66. In an earlier draft of this letter, Marx was referred to as a spiritual descendant of Genghis Khan.

67. Lilienthal's alleged radicalism reflected the view of many Republicans that the Tennessee Valley Authority, with which he had been associated, was an outstanding example of "creeping Socialism."

news page and there is a picture of Lilienthal and this Commie. They selected a picture of Lilienthal obviously which would look very much like this man Eisler.

In my conversations with Dave, I thought he had a very enlightened attitude toward Russia, anyway that he understood that it is a police state and not a new kind of democracy.

I will be interested in any lowdown you may have.[68]

In his reply, Forrestal stressed that the criticisms of Lilienthal involved "mostly politics," and he continued:

Although I credit a few of the Republicans with honest misgivings, not that Dave is tinged with Communism but that (*a*) he is a violent public-ownership man and (*b*) that he might fall for some of the Wallace-New Republic-Claude Pepper line of "be gentle with the Russians and they won't screw you."

While I've known Lilienthal only since the time of his appointment I like him and have confidence in him. In fact, after my first meeting I checked with Eberstadt and Lewis Strauss to find out whether I was merely being beguiled by an attractive personality. What I heard from both of them convinced me that my own judgement was correct.

You are on sound ground in supporting him.

Despite the considerable opposition to Lilienthal both before and after his confirmation as AEC Chairman, opposition led in the Senate by Senators Bourke Hickenlooper (Republican of Iowa), William Knowland (Republican of California), Homer Ferguson (Republican of Michigan), and others, Forrestal continued to maintain cordial relations with Lilienthal and express confidence in him. On at least one occasion in 1947, however, he discussed with the President and Lewis Strauss[69] criticisms leveled at Lilienthal by Senator Hickenlooper.[70]

---

68. The letter concluded: "It may interest you to know that Bob Patterson and I . . . decided that you should be the new defense secretary. I think it is a splendid idea, and will protect the interests of the Navy, and at the same time give the Army and Air Corps all they want. Think it over, Bub."

69. Strauss at the time was a member of the Atomic Energy Commission.

70. *Diaries*, p. 255. Hickenlooper, in particular, continued "in later years to wage determined war on Mr. Lilienthal and his administration of the atomic energy operations."—Millis in *Diaries*, p. 255.

The Wallaces, the Laskis, the Schumans, and the Lilienthals to a lesser extent served to convince Forrestal that the theory and practice of Marxism-Leninism were widely misunderstood in the West, misunderstood even by men of unquestioned loyalty to democratic principles. There was need for a comprehensive study, Forrestal wrote Walter Lippmann on January 7, 1946, of " (1) the nature of the Russian state philosophy . . . (2) whether the long-term Lenin-Marxian objectives still hold, and (3) the possibility of accommodation between the democratic and communistic systems." Noting that there was "no place in government where such a study had been made—at least I have been unable to find one—Forrestal emphasized that such a study should be

made as objectively and coldly as possible, because to me the fundamental question in respect to our relations with Russia is whether we are dealing with a nation or a religion—religion after all being merely the practical extension of philosophy.[71]

Forrestal was also doubtful that the nation's colleges and universities were devoting sufficient attention to "the nature of Russian state philosophy." In a letter of June 23, 1947, Forrestal raised with a friend the question "What are we doing to see that a true and objective account of communistic philosophy and practice is taught in American colleges?" He did not have in mind, he continued,

an attack on Communism but rather a scholarly examination of its basic, mystical philosophy, or rather, religion. This requires going back to Hegel, Fichte and Kant and an understanding of the conflict between Bukharin and Bukunin and Lenin. It requires an understanding of dialectical materialism and then of philosophical anarchy, which, as you probably know, is predicated on belief that when man has sufficiently mastered mathematics, physics and chemistry, as well as the social sciences, he can become the master not merely of the globe but of the universe.[72]

71. *Diaries*, p. 128.
72. In referring to "the conflict between Bukharin and Bakunin and Lenin," Forrestal presumably meant the conflict between principles rather

Although it is popularly assumed, Forrestal instructed his friend, that "classic communism" has been abandoned in favor of the "more pragmatic methods of Stalin," the "real essence" of the matter

is this: Lenin and Trotsky broke because Trotsky wanted to proceed immediately with the world revolution. Lenin said it is not time—we must let certain destructive processes first occur within the framework of capitalistic society. Stalin followed this line, but . . . his speech of February 1945 is *fairly* clear evidence that the long-view aims have not been surrendered. . . .

What do you think of the wisdom of trying to give some elementary course along these lines to our Navy recruits? I am definitely against a crusade but I am equally clear that we need to tell the people what the underlying foundations of the Communistic faith are and why its leaders adhere to the belief that for success it requires global application.[73]

Forrestal's deeply felt concern that these "underlying foundations" be thoroughly understood if not by all Americans at least by those who were charged with the making and execution of policy, led him in 1945 to commission a special study of the relationship between Marxist ideology and Soviet foreign policy. The study, which was undertaken by Edward F. Willett of Smith College, was ultimately circulated by Forrestal to a number of persons in and out of the government. Since Willett's paper was intended by Forrestal to serve as a first step toward that comprehensive study of Marxism-Leninism about which he had written Walter Lippmann, Willett's report to Forrestal, entitled "Dialectical

---

than persons. While Bukharin and Lenin were contemporaries, Mikhail Bakunin, Russian anarchist, was an opponent of Karl Marx in the First Communist International. As a consequence of his position, Bakunin, who died in 1876, was expelled from the International in 1872.

73. In 1943–44 Forrestal thought it important to include in the Navy's V-12 program a course dealing with the principles and patterns of international politics. Following discussions with Professors Edward Mead Earle of the Institute for Advanced Study and Harold Sprout of the Department of Politics, Princeton University, a curriculum was developed and tested at six universities. The program eventually produced a syllabus later published in textbook form. See Harold and Margaret Sprout, *The Foundations of National Power* (New York: D. Van Nostrand Co., 1951).

Materialism and Russian Objectives," is worth some examination. Although Forrestal continued to read other articles and books on the subject,[74] he had a high regard for Willett's paper. Indeed, the views expressed in it were very close to his own thinking about Soviet ideology and objectives.

The central thesis of the Willett study, officially submitted to Forrestal on January 14, 1946, was that Soviet ideology, based on dialectical materialism and Marxism-Leninism, "not only is conducive to, but indeed demands, an ultimate conflict between Communism and Capitalistic Democracy . . . unless one or the other is radically modified." Arguing that if "a true Communist could destroy the United States by pushing a button, he would do so," Willett urged that

It is thus quite clear, both from the Communist record of the past and from the records of other fanatical movements, that Capitalistic Democracies can expect no mercy if Communist philosophy prevails; it is equally clear that under these circumstances it is tantamount to suicide to do anything that tends either to strengthen the power of Communism or to weaken our powers to withstand it.

Nevertheless, Willett continued, "[t]here are certain circumstances under which the concept of an inevitable conflict between Russia and the United States, pursuant to the philosophy of Communism, might prove to be a fallacious one." These circumstances included (1) "If Communism is mistaken in its idea that class conflict is inevitable . . ." and (2) "if Communist zealots are not successful in fomenting an aggressive and crusading spirit among the population of those areas that they influence or control. . . ."

---

74. Of all such articles and books, Forrestal was, apparently, most impressed by Charles J. McFadden's *The Philosophy of Communism* (New York: Benziger Brothers, Inc., 1939). His notes on *The Philosophy of Communism* run to five typewritten pages, of which one page is devoted to a summary of Fulton J. Sheen's preface to the book. At the time of publication, McFadden was a faculty member of Villanova University.

Noting that an increase in the material well-being of the proletariat in the capitalist countries would reduce opposition to capitalism, Willett declared:

It should be noted in passing that Communism clearly recognizes this "danger" to the achievement of world revolution and therefore preaches that the function of trade unionism, for example, is not simply to get as much as it can for the worker within a capitalist society, but rather to intentionally make his demands so great that they will necessitate the destruction of that society. One might well raise the question whether the demands of certain elements of labor at the present time do not illustrate this Communist philosophy in action.[75]

Willett also observed that the Russian people were not warlike by nature, that both Russia and the United States were "weary of war," and that Stalin "has a strong sense of what is sometimes referred to as 'Realpolitik'; he is an accurate judge of the Russian people and presumably also of the strength of the United States." Finally, Willett foresaw the possibility that the Soviet Union might move "in the direction of Capitalistic Democracy," and/or that "Capitalistic Democracy might move in the direction of a modified form of Socialism."

In concluding his study of "Dialectical Materialism and Russian Objectives," Willett posed as the fundamental question of Soviet-American relations the extent to which dialectical materialism and Marxism-Leninism govern the actions of the Russian leaders. "The goals of Communism," he wrote,

are a certainty; the extent to which Russian leaders have departed from these goals are [*sic*] an uncertainty; their actions in the past have in no way been inconsistent with such goals. In other words, we have to deal on the one hand with the seeming

---

75. This last sentence was crossed-out by Forrestal who also added a "?" along the margin. Willett commented, in a memorandum to Forrestal: "I think the omission of the deleted material is probably advisable although I think the suggested question is a perfectly legitimate one."

certainty of war if Marxian Communism prevails, and on the other hand with the *possibility* of avoiding war if Communism does not prevail.

Given the fact that no one could predict the degree to which Soviet leaders were and would remain faithful to "Marxian Communism," there were, nevertheless, certain lessons to be drawn from an analysis of Soviet ideology, and in the last two paragraphs of his paper, Willett stated succinctly what these lessons were. "Those persons," he began,

who are unfamiliar with, or willing to overlook, the philosophy of Communism, who ignore the lessons of history in thinking that generous treatment converts potential enemies into friends, and who put their trust in the goodness of human nature, have a heavy responsibility resting on their shoulders.

Efforts to achieve world peace are all of them efforts in the right direction and should be whole-heartedly supported. However, any reliance upon such efforts that involves a weakening of our own purely defensive strength invites only disaster so long as a nation with the apparent principles of Russian Communism and the tremendous power of Russia continues to exist.

With the thought expressed in these paragraphs Forrestal could only agree. If war was a "certainty" under some circumstances and the avoidance of war only a "possibility" under other circumstances, the United States could ill afford either a weak defense posture or a vacillating foreign policy. But what constituted weakness and vacillation in that vast complex of United States military and diplomatic commitments that extended to almost all parts of the world? Forrestal had his own answers to this question, and in the little more than three years of public office that remained to him, he was to insist, again and again, that these answers were the only correct ones.

V

☆ ☆ ☆ ☆ ☆

National Security and Power Politics

IN FORRESTAL's Pentagon office
there was prominently displayed a framed printed card with
the following inscription: "We will never have universal
peace until the strongest army and the strongest navy are in
the hands of the most powerful nation."[1] This sentiment,
reiterated often in his public and private pronouncements,
constituted one central conviction during the war and postwar years.[2] But it was hardly less important than another
closely related conviction that informed his thoughts and
actions during those years. This was the conviction that the

1. The statement was attributed to C. H. Van Tyne. Forrestal in his
speeches and letters also frequently quoted a statement made by George
Washington in 1790: "To be prepared for war is one of the most effectual
means of preserving peace."

2. In a major address to the *New York Herald Tribune* Forum on October
20, 1947, Forrestal asserted that Americans hate war but "believe that war is
preferable to alternatives such as living under a police state." Urging the
need for Universal Military Training (UMT), and the necessity of strengthening the Armed Forces, merchant marine, public education and public
health, Forrestal insisted that "America must be strong to maintain the
balance of power" and that "it is too early to rely upon such formulas as
world government and disarmament, desirable as these goals may be for the
future."—*The New York Times*, October 21, 1947. In other speeches during
1947, he implied that the United States could not rely upon the United Nations
to keep the peace, partly because of Russia's "excessive use" of the veto power.
See, for example, his speech to the Veterans of Foreign Wars convention, as
reported in *The New York Times*, September 5, 1947.

Soviet Union after the war would pose the most formidable threat in history to American interests, and that the question of Russia, in one form or another, would intrude on every major policy decision, including those normally regarded as involving only domestic problems. As a consequence of these views, Forrestal was inclined to raise the question of Russia at every conference in which he was a participant, conferences extending from Cabinet meetings in Washington to private talks with government leaders in cities as far removed as London and Tokyo.

One such talk of more than ordinary interest took place on August 19, 1944, at the private residence of General Charles De Gaulle, then Chief of the French Provisional Government, in Algiers.[3] After some preliminary discussion of the future of Germany and French-American relations,[4] Forrestal queried the General about communist influence in France and the problems raised by what Forrestal termed "The widespread fears in America that a Russian menace

---

3. Apart from De Gaulle and Forrestal, the conference was attended only by a Lieutenant Guy, aide to the General, and Lieutenant Commander John Davis Lodge, USNR, then serving as Forrestal's aide and translator. The account that follows is based on Lodge's notes.

4. De Gaulle's remarks on these subjects largely anticipate the foreign policy he was to pursue when he became President of France in December, 1958. Arguing that "Germany cannot be destroyed," De Gaulle insisted that the Germans "are a strong, vital people and it is not feasible nor desirable to attempt to segregate them into isolated groups or to create separate entities out of Bavaria, Würtemburg, Saxony, etc." The essential thing, he told Forrestal, was that the French people be given "adequate guarantees" against another war with Germany. As regards relations between the United States and France, De Gaulle noted that the United States was the only major power with whom France had never fought a war. He thought it "most fitting" that an *entente* be established between France and the United States. Although there were people who favored an alliance between Great Britain and France, the General expressed the view that the British could not form such an alliance, for three principal reasons. "In the first place," he informed Forrestal, "Great Britain, not being really a continental power, has her attention constantly distracted from Europe by the needs of her empire. In the second place, there are many points at which the interests of France and Great Britain conflict. In the third place, Great Britain and France are too near each other to be able to achieve that solidarity which can be achieved between France and the United States."

would be substituted for a German menace." According to Forrestal's record of the conference, De Gaulle replied:

There were no Communists [in France] in the sense that Lenin and Trotsky were Communists; that is to say, there are no Communists who preach equal division of wealth, the rule of the proletariat, and other familiar Communist preachings. Instead you have a group of individuals who call themselves Communists, who are seeking for disciples and who are talking about the War, the Peace, Justice and Liberty. Indeed, the Russians themselves are no longer Communists in the way that they were at the start of the Russian Revolution. They now have Marshals and an increasing Hierarchy which gives evidence of this change.

Adding that it was impossible at that time to determine the extent of Communism in France, De Gaulle stressed the fact "that the extent to which Communism developed in France would depend on the guarantees given and the help furnished by France's allies."

In his response to Forrestal's question about the "Russian menace," De Gaulle chose to emphasize the importance of Europe in general and France in particular as key factors in the balance of power. Although he conceded that Europe had been "exhausted," "impoverished," "damaged," and "bled," by war, Europe

still has a great capacity for suffering and for work. Europe still has great power of thought. World wars have emanated from Europe and they will continue to emanate from Europe. Consequently, Europe must not be excluded from peace talks and conferences. Great Britain is not, strictly speaking, a European nation. Neither is Russia. But there is no nation in Europe more European than France, and therefore it is of paramount importance to include France in all international conferences. Only in this way will France feel secure. Only in this way can a counterweight to Russian influence be created. France must be made strong and attractive; attractive to the smaller powers, so that, as was the case before the war, the smaller powers will gather around France and not seek to gather around some other powerful nation, such as Russia.

To illustrate his point De Gaulle cited the case of Yugoslavia where, as he put it, "the Serbs followed Mihailovich and the Croats followed Tito. Had France not been defeated, France could have prevented this division and created solidarity in Yugoslavia."

Forrestal did not indicate whether he agreed or disagreed with the General's views, and it remains unknown whether he communicated them to other high-ranking American officials.[5] Forrestal, however, never believed that Europe as a whole, much less France, could serve as effective counter-weights to Soviet expansionism. Soviet ambitions would be thwarted, to the extent thwarted at all, only if the United States made it "clear that whoever tries to impose the products of his own neuroses upon the rest of us will make out second best."[6] And that would never be clear until we had demonstrated beyond any doubt that "the strongest army and the strongest navy are in the hands of the most powerful nation."

If, not long after the Algiers talk, Europe proved to be one area of contention with the Soviet Union, the Far East proved to be another. Indeed, in some respects the initial problems involved in bringing the war against Japan to a close were more complex and involved than those attendant upon the defeat of Nazi Germany. In Europe, the Russians had played a major and perhaps crucial role in the destruction of the Third Reich. On May 8, 1945, subsequently known as V-E Day, the Soviet Army was in control of most of Central Europe east of the Elbe River. The terms of the German surrender were not in dispute, and in fact could not be disputed by the battered and thoroughly beaten *Wehrmacht*. However much Forrestal and almost everyone else on the Western side might have wished that American

5. Before commenting on the "Russian menace," De Gaulle requested that his remarks not be reported "to anyone except the President of the United States or possibly one or two other prominent personages."

6. Letter to W. Douglas Burden, March 25, 1947.

and Russian soldiers had met at the Vistula and not the Elbe, it was clear that the Soviet Army would not withdraw from occupied areas except as a result of hard bargaining. In effect, at the end of World War II in Europe, the United States and her Allies were confronted by a number of Russian *faits accomplis,* the reversal of which would depend, somewhat precariously, on future discussions at conference tables.

In the Far East, on the other hand, there was first of all the problem raised by Soviet participation in the final phase of the war against Japan. At the Yalta Conference of February 3–11, 1945, the Russians had agreed to enter the war after the German surrender, and it was apparent to Forrestal, if not to all others in the Truman Cabinet, that a Soviet contribution, no matter how marginal to victory, would entitle the Russians to demand some influence on postwar decisions affecting Japan. Opposed to the Morgenthau Plan for Germany and other plans that would have precluded Germany's postwar emergence as a foremost industrial and military power,[7] Forrestal was equally opposed to measures designed to render Japan weak and impotent. He was also a strong advocate of the retention by the United States of Japanese bases in the Pacific, on the grounds that these bases would forever preclude the possibility of another Pearl Harbor. Anticipating correctly that the Russians would violently oppose these positions, Forrestal reasoned that the impact of the Russian opposition would vary directly with the impor-

---

7. The so-called Morgenthau Plan, sponsored by Secretary of the Treasury Henry Morgenthau, Jr. (1934–45), proposed that the postwar German economy be organized on an essentially agrarian basis. Submitted to the Roosevelt Cabinet during the summer of 1944, the Plan was predicated upon the assumption that Germany should never again be permitted to create a massive industrial-military complex. Although Assistant Secretary of War John J. McCloy reported to Forrestal on September 18, 1944, that "the President had decided to go along with Morgenthau," the Plan was strongly opposed by Cordell Hull, Byrnes, Stimson, and Forrestal, among others. Whatever Roosevelt's attitude may have been, little was heard of the Plan after Truman succeeded to the Presidency. See *Diaries,* p. 11.

tance of the Soviet Union's military role in the defeat of
Japan. He was therefore desirous, in the late spring of 1945,
that the war against Japan be brought to an early conclusion,
and preferably before the Russians could claim that they
had made any significant contribution to victory.

Forrestal was well aware, however, that there was a dilemma in his position which, no matter how resolved, involved grave risks for the United States. While it was
desirable that the Russian military contribution be minimal,
no one could be certain in the spring of 1945 that Japanese
forces, despite successive defeats in the western Pacific, would
not continue the war in Japan itself and on the Asian main-
land. There were intelligence reports, for example, that
China and Manchuria were held by some two million Japanese soldiers. If these chose to fight on, despite formal surrender by their commanding admirals and generals, final
victory could be substantially delayed and extremely costly
to the United States. Clearly the victory would come sooner
and cost less if the Soviet Union entered the war in a decisive
manner.[8] Alternatively, if the United States, in an effort to
bring the war to an early close, invaded Japan itself, and in
general, pursued a scorched-earth policy, the Japanese would
hardly be in a position to play a role in the postwar balance
of power in Asia. In that event, too, Forrestal believed, the
Russians would gain a strategic advantage, an advantage even
greater if China proved unable or unwilling to contain
Russian expansionism into Manchuria and North China.

---

8. Although there were various views in Washington about the desirability of Russian involvement, there was little doubt in anyone's mind that,
in Forrestal's words, "it would take an army to keep Stalin out. . . ."
Nevertheless, he was critical of the position, which he attributed to Truman
and Byrnes, that the Russians should be urged at Potsdam to enter the war
against Japan at the earliest possible moment after victory in Europe. According to Byrnes, however, Forrestal was told on July 28 that "it was most probable that the President's views had changed; certainly that was not now my
[Byrnes's] view."—James F. Byrnes, *All in One Lifetime* (New York: Harper
& Brothers, 1958), p. 297. *See also* Byrnes, *Speaking Frankly* (New York:
Harper & Brothers, 1947), p. 208; and *Diaries*, p. 78.

At a meeting with top officials of the State Department and War and Navy Departments on May 1, 1945, Forrestal raised a number of questions concerned with the conduct of the war against Japan and the larger issue of American post-war policy in the Far East. These questions, which he regarded as most important, appeared in his notes of the meeting as follows:

1. How far and how thoroughly do we want to beat Japan? In other words, do we want to morgenthau those islands—do we want to destroy the whole industrial potential?
2. Do we want to contemplate their readmission to the society of nations after demilitarization?
3. What is our policy on Russian influence in the Far East? Do we desire a counterweight to that influence? And should it be China or should it be Japan?
4. Have we given careful thought to the question of how far this country will go toward the complete defeat of Japan—the quick, costly assault versus a long, drawn-out siege?

"I said," he added to his notes, "that it was conceivable to me that the people that desired a quick victory might turn out to be the appeasers in the case of Japan."[9]

The questions raised by Forrestal took on special urgency when reports reached Washington, not long after the May 1 meeting, that the Japanese had begun to initiate inquiries through neutral governments about the terms of surrender. When it became clear that the Japanese were insisting on the retention of the Emperor as a condition for surrender, attention focused on the interpretation to be attached to our insistence, enunciated at Yalta, Potsdam,[10] and other wartime

9. *Diaries*, p. 52.
10. The Yalta Conference, February 3–11, 1945, was attended by Roosevelt, Churchill, and Stalin. In return for certain concessions to Russian demands regarding the Soviet sphere of influence in Eastern Europe and the Far East—concessions later attacked as constituting "appeasement"—Stalin agreed to take part in the war against Japan. The Potsdam Conference of Truman, Churchill, and Stalin was held July 7–August 2, 1945. On July 25, following a British general election that was won by the Labour Party, Attlee replaced Churchill.

meetings of heads of state, on unconditional surrender. There were many Americans, Truman declared to a meeting of Byrnes, Leahy, Stimson, and Forrestal on May 10,

who felt that the Emperor was an integral part of that Japanese system which we were pledged to destroy. Could we continue the Emperor and yet expect to eliminate the warlike spirit in Japan? Could we even consider a message [insisting on the retention of the Emperor] with so large a "but" as the kind of unconditional surrender we had fought for?[11]

Discussion of the successive Japanese "peace feelers," a discussion that continued almost until the final moment of surrender on the battleship *Missouri,* established that there were a variety of views on the questions raised by Truman and Forrestal. Stimson, Leahy, Forrestal, Under Secretary of State Joseph C. Grew, Assistant Secretary of War John J. McCloy, and others were of the opinion that the retention of the Emperor was not incompatible with unconditional surrender.[12] Stimson, in fact, went so far as to argue on May 10th that the retention of the Emperor would be advantageous inasmuch as he was "the only symbol of authority which all Japanese acknowledged."[13] Byrnes was inclined to

---

11. Harry S Truman, *Memoirs,* Vol. I, *Year of Decisions* (New York: Doubleday, 1955), p. 428.

12. Another view, put forward by Charles E. Bohlen, among others, was that the United States could not "afford to hold out any clarification of terms to Japan which could be construed as a desire to get the Japanese war over with before Russia has an opportunity to enter."—*Diaries,* p. 74.

13. Truman, *ibid.,* p. 428. This account of Stimson's views should be compared with other authoritative statements summarizing Stimson's position as of May, 1945. For example: "It is possible, in the light of the final surrender, that a clearer and earlier exposition of American willingness to retain the Emperor would have produced an earlier ending to the war: this course was earnestly advocated by Grew and his immediate associates during May, 1945. But in view of Stimson and his military advisors, it was always necessary to bear in mind that at least some of Japan's leaders would seize on any conciliatory offer as an indication of weakness. For this reason they did not support Grew in urging an immediate statement on the Emperor in May. . . . To Stimson, at least, the only road to early victory was to exert maximum force with maximum speed. It was not the American responsibility to throw in the sponge for the Japanese; that was one thing they must

doubt that the submission of the Japanese should be negotiated on any terms other than unconditional surrender,[14] while Forrestal favored a declaration that we would retain the Emperor and "yet define the terms of surrender in such a manner that the intents and purposes of the Potsdam Declaration would be clearly accomplished."[15]

On August 11, after the atomic bombing of Hiroshima and Nagasaki, much of what Forrestal had advocated three months earlier was incorporated in a formal reply to a Japanese note of August 10 accepting the terms of the Potsdam Declaration "with the understanding that the said Declaration does not comprise any demand which prejudices the prerogatives of His Majesty as a Sovereign Ruler." The American statement, drafted by Byrnes and approved by Truman, Stimson, and Forrestal, declared:

> From the moment of surrender, the authority of the Emperor and the Japanese Government to rule the state shall be subject to the Supreme Commander of Allied powers who will take such steps as he deems proper to effectuate the surrender terms.

---

do for themselves." Whatever Stimson's precise views on the question of the Emperor, two years later, in 1947, it "seemed possible" to him that the unwillingness to issue a statement on the subject "had been based on a misreading of the situation . . . history might find that the United States, by its delay in stating its position, had prolonged the war."—Henry L. Stimson and McGeorge Bundy, *On Active Service in Peace and War* (New York: Harper & Brothers, 1947), pp. 628–629.

14. According to Truman, Byrnes on May 10 "was less certain that we should accept anything short of an unequivocal declaration of surrender. He argued that in the present position it should be the United States and not Japan that should state conditions."—Truman, *op. cit.*, p. 428.

15. Truman, *ibid.* Forrestal's papers contain no account of the May 10 meeting at the White House, but there can be no question that he had serious reservations concerning the need for unconditional surrender in the cases of both Germany and Japan. Again and again he raised the question, as on May 29 with reference to Japan, "whether it would not suffice to say that our view of unconditional surrender meant that it was the unconditional surrender of the Japanese military power, that we did not propose to destroy Japan as a nation."—*Diaries*, p. 66. On several occasions in 1944–45 Forrestal urged the issuance of a statement to the effect that while the Allied forces in Europe were determined to eradicate Hitlerism, they had no intention of "morgenthauing" Germany.

The Emperor will be required to authorize and ensure the signature by the Government of Japan and the Japanese Imperial General Headquarters of the surrender terms necessary to carry out the provisions of the Potsdam Declaration. . . .

The ultimate form of government of Japan shall, in accordance with the Potsdam Declaration, be established by the freely expressed will of the people.

Although the statement made no mention of the retention of the Emperor, it did not preclude, and was not intended to preclude, the continuance of the Imperial Dynasty under Hirohito and his successors. To be sure, certain elements of the Japanese military were opposed to surrendering on the terms set forth, but the Emperor himself and most of his advisers, stunned and shocked by the series of defeats culminating in the atomic bomb, accepted the statement in full. At seven in the evening, Washington time, on August 14, Truman announced that the war was over.

The end of World War II, like the end of other wars, did not resolve certain questions about its conduct beginning with Pearl Harbor and ending with the mushroom cloud over Nagasaki. Eighteen years later, as this is being written, the issue of responsibility for Pearl Harbor remains controversial, and the question whether victory would have been achieved without the atomic bomb is still unanswered. Would it have sufficed to drop the bomb on an uninhabited Pacific island rather than on two heavily populated Japanese cities? Given the fact that the invasion of the main Japanese island of Kyushu was not scheduled until November, could the Japanese have been persuaded between August and November, without our use of the bomb, that further fighting was futile? Unlike Stimson, Leahy, and Grew in the years that followed,[16] Forrestal was not deeply troubled by these ques-

16. In 1950 Leahy in effect spoke for all men everywhere who were profoundly disturbed by the implications of Hiroshima and Nagasaki. "It is my opinion," he wrote, "that the use of this barbarous weapon . . . was of no material assistance in our war against Japan. The Japanese were already

tions. While he always believed that the war might have ended sooner had the United States committed itself to the retention of the Emperor, there is no evidence that he had serious misgivings, in 1945 or later, about our employment of the atomic bomb. So far as can be known, any doubts he may have had about the necessity of Hiroshima and Nagasaki he kept to himself.[17]

Even before Hiroshima and Nagasaki, it was clear that the peacetime problems raised by the atomic bomb would be hardly less difficult and controversial than those that arose in connection with its employment during the latter stages of the war. If one major problem area concerned the international control of the atomic bomb, another, although of lesser importance, involved the establishment within the government of an appropriate agency that would supervise all

---

defeated and ready to surrender because of the effective sea blockade and the successful bombing with conventional weapons.

"It was my reaction that the scientists and others wanted to make this test because of the vast sums that had been spent on the project. Truman knew that, and so did the other people involved. However, the Chief Executive made a decision to use the bomb on two cities in Japan . . . but . . . specified that the bombs should be used against military facilities. . . .

" 'Bomb' is the wrong word to use for this new weapon. It is not a bomb. It is not an explosive. It is a poisonous thing that kills people by its deadly radioactive reaction, more than by the explosive force it develops.

"The lethal possibilities of atomic warfare in the future are frightening. My own feeling was that in being the first to use it, we had adopted an ethical standard common to the barbarians of the Dark Ages. I was not taught to make war in that fashion, and wars cannot be won by destroying women and children. We were the first to have this weapon in our possession, and the first to use it. There is a practical certainty that potential enemies will have it in the future and that atomic bombs will sometime be used against us."—William D. Leahy, *I Was There* (New York: McGraw-Hill, 1950), p. 441.

17. The doubts that Forrestal did express related to the question whether the atomic bomb would prove to be the "ultimate" weapon. In contrast to Leahy, Forrestal believed in 1945 that the destructive capabilities of atomic warfare were exaggerated. In a memorandum to Duffield of October 11, 1945, occasioned by a request from a *Life* magazine editor for an article about the limitations of the bomb, Forrestal stressed two points: "*a*. you can't make enough of them; *b*. it is not necessarily a conclusive weapon of attack on a nation."

developments connected with the military and nonmilitary aspects of atomic energy. Although there was general agreement that the principle of civilian control should prevail, there was disagreement over the extent to which military personnel should participate in decisions of such an agency.[18]

As early as 1944 Forrestal was firmly of the opinion that military representatives could not and should not be excluded from membership on any board or commission created for the purpose of conducting atomic-energy research. On the assumption that military applications of atomic power would far exceed peacetime uses for an indefinite period ahead, Forrestal in 1944–1946 supported a variety of proposals designed to strengthen military influence in the atomic energy field. Late in 1944 he endorsed a recommendation of Vannevar Bush for the establishment of a Research Board for National Security, the chief function of which was to conduct research related to military applications of the atomic bomb. The Bush proposal envisaged a Board composed of Army and Navy officers, other representatives of military organizations, and civilian scientists and engineers. Following discussions with Stimson, Forrestal and Stimson early in 1945 created the Board on their own initiative. For a variety of reasons, however, including the refusal of Bureau of Budget Director Harold D. Smith to appropriate any funds for its support, the Board was short-lived. Although Forrestal, never easily balked by what he regarded as "bureaucratic interference," attempted to bypass Smith by having his aides draft a bill

---

18. For a detailed account of the controversy and events leading to the creation of the Atomic Energy Commission, see Richard G. Hewlett and Oscar E. Anderson, Jr., *A History of the United States Atomic Energy Commission*, I, *The New World, 1939–1946* (University Park, Pa.: The Pennsylvania State University Press, 1962). This work is indispensable for an understanding of the complex interplay of scientific, military, and political considerations in the early determination of atomic-energy policy. The history of the Atomic Energy Commission is discussed at length in Morgan Thomas, *Atomic Energy and Congress* (Ann Arbor, Mich.: The University of Michigan Press, 1956).

creating the Board for congressional approval, the bill never received serious consideration.[19]

Subsequent discussion of other atomic-energy legislation, notably the May-Johnson bill which was strongly supported by the War Department,[20] found Forrestal playing a relatively minor role. Anticipating that opposition to the measure from the White House, key senatorial circles, and the scientific community would prove fatal to its passage, Forrestal in the autumn of 1945 began to pay particular attention to the substitute measure introduced by Senator Brien McMahon of Connecticut in December. The McMahon bill, an amended version of which was enacted into law on August 1, 1946, as the Atomic Energy Act of 1946, began by declaring it

to be the policy of the people of the United States that the development and utilization of atomic energy shall be directed toward improving the public welfare, increasing the standard of living, strengthening free competition among private enterprises so far as practicable, and cementing world peace.

Section 2 of the bill established an Atomic Energy Commission (AEC) the five members of which were to be appointed by the President (by and with the advice and consent of the Senate) and to "serve at the pleasure of the President." The President was also empowered to appoint one member of the Commission as Chairman. Section 6, concerned with

---

19. Smith's objections did not relate, apparently, to the composition of the Board, nor was he "just being obstinate, as Stimson and Forrestal seemed to think. . . . The issue was not whether but how the Government would support science. Bush wanted to guarantee the scientists' freedom of research by insulating them from political pressure. Smith believed that large-scale federal support required, if it did not indeed depend upon, effective controls through the regular channels of government."—Hewlett and Anderson, *ibid.*, p. 410.

20. The May-Johnson measure, drafted by a committee consisting of Bush, James Conant, and others, called for a nine-member atomic-energy organization headed by a director. The nine members, essentially a part-time board of directors, would have included one representative of the Army and one of the Navy.

military applications of atomic power, authorized the Commission to conduct experiments in military applications, and to have custody of "all assembled or unassembled atomic bombs, bomb parts, or other atomic military weapons" except those delivered on presidential order to the Armed Forces.

Several of the more controversial provisions of the bill dealt with the relationship of the United States atomic-energy program to the world at large. Section 6 (1) (b) provided:

The commission shall not conduct any research or developmental work in the military application of atomic power if such research or developmental work is contrary to any international agreement of the United States.

Section 9 stated that

Basic scientific information in the field specified in section 3 may be freely disseminated. The term "basic scientific information" shall include, in addition to theoretical knowledge and nuclear and other physics, chemistry, biology, and therapy, all results capable of accomplishment, as distinguished from the processes or techniques of accomplishing them.[21]

Realizing that the McMahon bill, generally supported by scientists[22] and spokesmen for the Administration,[23] would

---

21. Section 3 authorized the Commission "to make contracts, agreements, arrangements, grants-in-aid, and loans— (1) for the conduct of research and developmental activities relating to (a) nuclear processes; (b) the theory and production of atomic energy, including processes and devices related to such production; (c) utilization of fissionable and radioactive materials for medical or health purposes; (d) utilization of fissionable and radioactive materials for all other purposes, including industrial uses; and (e) the protection of health during research and production activities; and (2) for studies of the social, political, and economic effects of the availability and utilization of atomic energy."

22. The drafters of the bill included a number of persons close to the scientific community, such as James R. Newman, a lawyer who was also familiar with mathematics and atomic physics; Thomas I. Emerson, general counsel of the Office of War Mobilization and Reconversion (OWMR) and former general counsel for the OPA; Bryon S. Miller, an assistant to Emerson at the OPA; and Edward H. Levi, special assistant to Attorney General Tom Clark.

23. Administration supporters included Harold Ickes, Henry A. Wallace, John Snyder, and, ultimately, Truman.

constitute the core approach to atomic-energy legislation, Forrestal in the months between January and August, 1946, made a strenuous effort to have the bill amended in favor of the Armed Services position. On January 23, testifying before the Senate Special Committee on Atomic Energy, Forrestal objected to the proposed establishment of a five-member Atomic Energy Commission headed by a chairman. In its stead he recommended the creation of a Commission of four members, each of whom was to be appointed for a six-year term, presided over by a general manager.[24] Arguing that members of the Commission should have a status and salary comparable to those of Supreme Court Justices, Forrestal urged that the President be given no authority to remove AEC commissioners. His own preference, he informed the Special Committee, was that the commissioners be eligible to succeed themselves, and be subject to removal only by impeachment.

Forrestal's main criticism, however, was aimed at the exclusion of the military from AEC decisions. Recommending that the Vice President and Secretaries of State, War, and Navy be included as ex officio members of the Commission, Forrestal declared that " (u)nless the use of atomic weapons is abolished by international agreement, military application should be a joint responsibility of the commission and the War and Navy Departments . . . the Commission and the Joint Chiefs of Staff should determine the broad lines along which atomic weapon development is to proceed."[25]

---

24. Anthony Leviero in *The New York Times,* January 24, 1946. But according to another source, Forrestal "suggested a commission composed of the Vice President, the Secretaries of War, Navy, and State, and four public members."—Hewlett and Anderson, *op. cit.,* p. 488. Whichever is the correct version of Forrestal's testimony on the size and membership of the AEC, it is beyond dispute that he objected strenuously to a five-member Commission serving "at the pleasure of the President."

25. *The New York Times, ibid.* On March 12 the *Times* reported that Forrestal "is planning an amendment that would subordinate the AEC to a policy making advisory board consisting of the Secretaries of State, War and Navy, Speaker of the House, and chairman of the proposed commission."

Following his testimony to the Senate Special Committee on January 23, Forrestal was once again to complain bitterly about the difficulties involved in presenting the Navy's (and Army's) point of view. In certain sections of the press, in scientific quarters, in Congress and elsewhere, his emphasis on military participation in atomic-energy developments was interpreted as an attack upon the principle of civilian control.[26] Although several members of the Committee emphasized that military inclusion in atomic-energy decisions did not preclude civilian control, the general impression left by Forrestal was that he had little if any confidence in civilian management of atomic-weapons research and development. As a result, in part, of the impression he had created, Forrestal did not believe early in 1946 that the McMahon bill would be significantly changed in the direction that he desired.

Nevertheless, he thought it possible to salvage an important role for the military in atomic-energy applications, and he quickly initiated discussions toward that end with sympathetic senators, including Hart of Connecticut and Vandenberg of Michigan. Although McMahon himself, in an effort to compromise differences, suggested that his bill provide for the establishment of a military-applications advisory board,[27] neither Forrestal nor his supporters on the Committee were satisfied that a purely advisory role would adequately resolve the issue. Vandenberg, in March, there-

---

26. The interpretation was supported by a remark before the Senate Committee of President Robert M. Hutchins of the University of Chicago. Forrestal, Hutchins observed, "seemed to feel that complete military control of this new power would be highly desirable."—Quoted in Hewlett and Anderson, *ibid.*, p. 488.

27. The board proposed by McMahon would have consisted of an equal number of military officers and civilians. Authorized to "advise and consult with the Commission on all atomic energy matters relating to the national defense," the board was to be kept fully informed by the Commission, and it was empowered to make written reports to the Commission. McMahon also suggested that the Commission itself consist of four public members and the Secretaries of State, War, and Navy.—Hewlett and Anderson, *ibid.*, p. 505.

fore moved in committee that the Commission be required "to consult with the board, which could make written recommendations to the commission. The board's right of appeal to the President would be broadened to apply not only to 'military applications of atomic energy' but also 'to all atomic energy matters which the board deems to relate to the national defense.' "[28] The changes suggested by Vandenberg, incorporated in the so-called Vandenberg Amendment, were approved by the Committee, and ultimately were included in the Act.

As passed on August 1, 1946, the Atomic Energy Act, while something of a disappointment to Forrestal, represented a partial victory in terms of the criticisms he had advanced in January. The size of the Commission, for example, was fixed at five members, one of whom was to be designated as Chairman by the President, but they were to serve staggered terms of five years each, and they could be removed only "for inefficiency, neglect of duty, or malfeasance in office."[29] The administrative and executive functions of the AEC were to be exercised by a general manager whose term of office was not fixed. Although these provisions of the Act fell short of those originally favored by Forrestal, they were intended, as his own proposals were intended, to provide the Commission with a good deal of operating autonomy.

With respect to the role of the military, the Act had very little in common with the initial version of the McMahon Bill. Section 2, creating among other AEC divisions a Division of Military Application (DMA), declared that the Director of the DMA "shall be a member of the armed

---

28. Hewlett and Anderson, *ibid.*, p. 506. Vandenberg, while he believed that the military should not be excluded from the atomic-energy field, felt that the Commission itself should remain a civilian body. As a consequence he did not support proposals designed to add military representatives as ex officio members of the Commission.

29. Section 2(a)(2).

forces." Another portion of Section 2 established a "Military Liaison Committee consisting of representatives of the Departments of War and Navy . . . in such number as [the Secretaries of War and Navy] may determine." The Commission, Section 2 declared,

shall advise and consult with the Committee on all atomic energy matters which the Committee deems to relate to military applications, including the development, manufacture, use, and storage of bombs, the allocation of fissionable material for military research, and the control of information relating to the manufacture or utilization of atomic weapons.

After stating that the Commission and Committee shall keep each other fully informed, Section 2 further provided:

If the Committee at any time concludes that any action, proposed action, or failure to act of the Commission on such matters [military applications] is adverse to the responsibilities of the Departments of War or Navy . . . the Committee may refer such action, proposed action, or failure to act to the Secretaries of War and Navy. If either Secretary concurs, he may refer the matter to the President, whose decision shall be final.

Clearly the position taken by Forrestal and others on the question of military inclusion had more nearly carried the day than that represented by McMahon and his principal advisers.

Section 10 of the Act, entitled "Control of Information," was also closer to Forrestal's view than the equivalent section of the original McMahon bill. On September 21, 1945, Forrestal in a memorandum noted succinctly, "The answer of the military people on the question of the furnishing of information on atomic power to the world is 'no.' This of course is to be expected. This represents what you might call the civilian [*sic*] point of view." Differing from the McMahon bill, the 1946 Act surrounded the dissemination of atomic-energy information with a variety of restrictions and safeguards essentially consistent with what Forrestal had termed almost a year earlier the "answer of the military people." Of these restrictions, the most important provided:

That until Congress declares by joint resolution that effective and enforceable international safeguards against the use of atomic energy for destructive purposes have been established, there shall be no exchange of information with other nations with respect to the use of atomic energy for industrial purposes. . . .

Although Section 8 of the Act declared that any of its provisions in conflict with any international agreement "shall be deemed to be of no further force or effect," an international agreement was defined to mean "any treaty approved by the Senate or international agreement approved by the Congress. . . ." In other words, the President under the Act could not authorize, by Executive Agreement, an exchange of atomic-energy information with another nation.

Section 8 of the 1946 Act did not preclude a quest on the part of the United States for international control of atomic energy—a quest that is still underway more than seventeen years later—but on the other hand it did not make it easier for the President to negotiate atomic agreements. Whatever eventually was agreed upon in the United Nations or at Geneva or elsewhere, it was the clear intent of Section 8 that the final decision would be made not by the Executive Branch but by Congress. For better or worse, once more it was a case of "the President proposes, Congress disposes." And in the latter instance, if not both instances, the Act ensured that the opinions of the military would be taken into account.

As Forrestal viewed the world in 1946 and thereafter, this was as it should be.[30] Despite the pleas of Stimson in

---

30. On August 14, 1946, Forrestal wrote his friend Palmer Hoyt: "I would like to give you Forrestal's summation of the world in three words—'not so hot.'"

1945,[31] Forrestal then and later was determinedly opposed to sharing basic atomic information with the Russians or with anyone else. Whereas Stimson favored "a gamble on the good faith of Russia,"[32] Forrestal took the position that the Russians should not be trusted "until we have a longer record of experience with them on the validity of engagements." Reminding his colleagues that the Japanese had been our allies in World War I despite which they had not abided by subsequent naval agreements, Forrestal argued that "the Russians, like the Japanese, are essentially oriental in their thinking. . . ." It was therefore "doubtful that we should endeavor to buy their understanding and sympathy. We tried that once with Hitler. There are no returns on appeasement." Adding that "trust had to be more than a one-way street," Forrestal recommended that

just as certain nations were proposing to exercise trusteeship over certain areas of the globe on behalf of the United Nations,

---

31. At his last Cabinet meeting on September 21, 1945, Stimson in response to a request from Truman presented his views on the problem of atomic-energy control. Although he did not suggest that the bomb be given to the Soviet Union, he urged those present to bear in mind that "whether Russia obtained control of the necessary secrets of production in a minimum of four or a maximum of twenty years was not nearly as important to the world and civilization as it was to make sure that when the Russians did get the necessary knowledge they would be willing and cooperative partners among the peace-loving nations of the world. If . . . we failed to approach them directly now, if we merely continued to negotiate having this weapon ostentatiously on our hip, suspicion and distrust would grow with the years. . . ." Suggesting we propose to the Russians an arrangement that would control the use of the bomb and also facilitate the exchange of "benefits of future developments" involving the use of atomic energy for peaceful purposes, Stimson recommended that the United States "stop all work on military applications of the energy if England and Russia agreed to do likewise."—Elting Morison, *Turmoil and Tradition* (Boston: Houghton Mifflin, 1960), pp. 641–642. It was at this meeting, according to Forrestal, that Wallace was "completely, everlastingly and wholeheartedly in favor of giving it [the bomb] to the Russians."—*Diaries*, p. 95. Morison, however, describes Wallace as being completely, everlastingly and wholeheartedly in favor of Stimson's proposal, and as also believing that "Stimson was one of the wisest men ever to serve as a presidential advisor."—Morison, *op. cit.*, p. 642.

32. Morison, *ibid.*

so . . . we could exercise a trusteeship over the atomic bomb on behalf of the United Nations and agree that we would limit its manufacture for use on such missions as the United Nations should designate.[33]

Forrestal apparently failed to convince others in the Administration that the United States should offer to act as trustee for the bomb "on behalf of the United Nations." He was more successful, however, in urging that the United States retain control of certain Pacific Islands seized from the Japanese during the war. Despite opposition from advocates of United Nations trusteeship over these islands, Forrestal won support in the Senate and elsewhere for his view that "[u]ndivided control of certain strategic areas in the Pacific wrested from the Japanese by our armed forces . . . is essential to the security of the country."[34]

He also strongly supported continued American involvement in China. Despite a series of reports that were extremely critical of the Kuomintang regime, especially the extent to which it was characterized by inefficiency, corruption, and nepotism, Forrestal agreed with Byrnes, General Douglas MacArthur, and others that, in MacArthur's words in November, 1944, "[i]f Chiang Kai-shek is overthrown, China will be thrown into utter confusion."[35] He was therefore extremely critical of those who argued the necessity of a Kuomintang-Communist *rapprochement* and/or the withdrawal of American military forces from China. Against these views, which enjoyed some support in the Administration both before and after the failure of the Marshall mission to China,[36] Forrestal argued on numerous occasions that

---

33. *Diaries*, pp. 95–96.

34. Letter to Senator Tom Connally of the Senate Foreign Relations Committee, July 21, 1945.

35. Quoted from a report to Forrestal by Bert Andrews, Washington correspondent of the *New York Herald Tribune*, dated by Forrestal November 22, 1944. See *Diaries*, pp. 17–18.

36. The Marshall mission of 1945–46 was designed to lend the "good services" of the United States toward the establishment of a coalition govern-

if we came out of China, Russian influence would flow in and over the country; that whether we liked it or not, conditions of this order and of civil war in China could not be permanently acceptable to the United States because they were an invitation to some other power or group of powers to come in and dominate China; that . . . happened in the thirties, and it is precisely that which will happen in the forties except that Russia will be substituted for Japan.[37]

Opposed to those in the State Department and elsewhere who favored a "soft" policy toward the Chinese Communists, Forrestal was inclined in 1945–1946 to regard Marshall, in particular, as dangerously naïve in his approach to the problem of Communism in China. In November, 1945, he strenuously disapproved of the position reflected in a State Department cable to General Albert C. Wedemeyer, then United States Forces Commander in China, a cable stating, in part, that the United States "does not wish to support the Nationalist government directly against the Communists."[38] A few months later, following Wedemeyer's return to the United States, he requested Wedemeyer to submit to him a memorandum setting forth his criticisms of American policy in China, and these criticisms served to confirm Forrestal in his own suspicions of the China policy associated with Marshall and others.

American and free-world policy toward China, Wedemeyer wrote Forrestal, should base itself on the assumptions that China would be in difficulty for a long period of time, that Soviet Communism would move "into the vacuum created by the fall of the Nationalist Government," and that therefore the United States had no alternative "but to support Chiang Kai-shek and his government." Much of the

---

ment of Nationalists and Communists. The effort to promote a coalition was doomed to inevitable failure, but in 1945–46 it appeared to many that the only alternative to a coalition was a civil war that would end, in all probability, with a communist victory.

37. *Diaries*, p. 190.
38. *Ibid.*, p. 109.

Wedemeyer memorandum was given over to what Wedemeyer referred to as an "open challenge [to] General Marshall and the powerful political forces he represented at that time. . . ." There is a "question," he informed Forrestal,

whether Marshall realizes the delicate situation revolving around the peace conference in Paris and the necessity for keeping our political policies and relationships on a very even keel. . . .

There is a question that Secretary of State Marshall is fully aware of all the implications of the present world situation as it concerns the Soviet Union and the vital place China (good or bad) plays in maintaining some sort of world equilibrium. It is unfortunate that General Marshall does not have available the clear and forceful studies on the Russian situation which have been prepared at the request of President Truman.

In concluding his memorandum, Wedemeyer suggested that

[f]or the time being, the only useful action which can be taken is an indication to General Marshall that the suggestion by implication or otherwise of possible change in our Chinese policy (civil war or no civil war) is so serious that he should withhold comment on the U.S. position in any way at present. Further, he should not imply recognition of the Communists (which he has not done as yet in so many words). Finally, if General Marshall has not been briefed on the world and Russian situation, he should receive a message from the President, outlining the seriousness of the problem.[39]

---

39. General Albert C. Wedemeyer, *Wedemeyer Reports!* (New York: Henry Holt & Company, 1958), pp. 368–369. According to *Wedemeyer Reports!* Marshall's alleged gullibility did not relate to his motives, much less his association with "traitors" and "subversives" as later charged by Senator Joseph R. McCarthy. Rather, Marshall "had been subjected to . . . constant pounding by many and diverse people intent only on their own self-interest or that of the nations or ideologies they represented . . . had been constantly harassed by the British . . . had had neither time, inclination, nor opportunity to study the methods of Communism . . . had implicitly believed the reports of his old friend, General Stilwell, who ascribed all the ills of China to the government of Chiang Kai-shek . . . had also to contend with the vagaries of President Roosevelt who, even before his faculties failed during his fourth term, had been surrounded by intriguers and the soft-on communism eggheads who enjoyed his wife's patronage and were given formidable power by Harry Hopkins and others in the President's confidence" (p. 370).

Although Forrestal shared many if not all of Wedemeyer's reservations, he apparently made no effort to take "the only useful action" that Wedemeyer recommended.

The China problem was, of course, only one of many problems on many fronts. By the spring of 1947 the Soviet Union was in control of most of Eastern Europe, and Stalin was exerting pressure elsewhere in favor of Soviet objectives. The eastern Mediterranean and the oil kingdoms of the Middle East appeared to be directly threatened by Soviet expansionism. Taking advantage of the postwar poverty and unrest in Greece, communist forces in that country were engaged in a civil war with the existing government. The Russians were also insisting on joint control with the Turks over the straits connecting Soviet ports on the Black Sea with the Mediterranean. Simultaneously with these developments, reports began to reach Washington that communist agents were increasing their activities in a number of Middle East countries, including those upon whom the free world was dependent for oil. Traditionally these areas fell within the British sphere of influence, but when Prime Minister Attlee early in 1947 informed Truman that his government could no longer supply Greece and Turkey with significant economic assistance, it was clear, once again, that a dangerous power vacuum was being created.

Long before the Truman Doctrine was formally promulgated in 1947, Forrestal was strongly in favor of an American economic and, if need be, military commitment to the *status quo* in Greece, Turkey, and the Middle East. Although there were others who agreed with Eisenhower that "Greece and Turkey were not of strategic importance; that in the event of any trouble with Russia it would be impossible to hold either,"[40] Forrestal characteristically believed that a British

---

40. In a memorandum to Admiral Chester Nimitz of April 2, 1947, Forrestal reported "Congressman [Christian] Herter told me last night that Eisenhower had made a statement before 35 members of Congress at an

withdrawal *not* followed by American intervention would result in Soviet domination of both countries and, ultimately, the Arab world.

As early as February, 1946, Forrestal and Admirals Nimitz and Sherman had taken steps to ensure the gradual redeployment of naval units to the eastern Mediterranean. The movement of American warships began with the arrival of the USS *Missouri* at Istanbul, Turkey, in early April, 1946. Carrying the body of Turkish Ambassador to the United States Mehmed Münir Ertëgun who had died during World War II and had been temporarily interred at Arlington, the *Missouri* was in Turkish waters ostensibly on a courtesy visit. Under ordinary circumstances an Air Transport Command plane would have been used for the purpose, but Forrestal and other Navy officials did not regard the situation as in any sense ordinary. Thus when Admiral Sherman conceived the idea of using a warship for the return of the dead ambassador's body, Forrestal was enthusiastic. It was he, apparently, who chose the *Missouri* for the mission, and in view of the resistance to Sherman's proposal in certain Washington quarters, the choice of the *Missouri* was, as one of his aides put it, "a piece of calculated salesmanship."

Forrestal, however, was not permitted to send an accompanying Task Force with the *Missouri*. In lieu of such a force, other American naval units, each with a strong complement of Marines aboard, followed the *Missouri*'s lead in making courtesy calls at a variety of Mediterranean ports, including Istanbul, Piraeus (the port of Athens), Naples, Algiers, and Tangiers. Between February, 1946, and February, 1947, a total of two aircraft carriers, seven cruisers, eighteen destroyers, and four auxiliary vessels, in addition to the *Missouri,* had visited the Mediterranean area. The air-

---

informal meeting that Greece and Turkey were not of strategic importance; that in the event of any trouble with Russia it would be impossible to hold either. I can't imagine his having made such a statement but Herter was very specific."

craft carriers were the *Franklin D. Roosevelt,* at that time the world's largest and most powerful carrier, and the *Randolph,* while the cruisers comprised the *Providence, Fargo, Little Rock, Huntington, Houston, Portsmouth,* and *Dayton.*[41]

The enactment of the Truman Doctrine on May 15, 1947,[42] resolved, at least temporarily, the question of American involvement in the eastern Mediterranean. Policy problems in the Middle East, problems with which Forrestal became increasingly occupied after 1946, proved much more difficult and complex. On the one hand, there could be no doubt that the oil-producing Arab States were of vital strategic importance to the United States and her Western European allies. If, for whatever reasons, the Arab countries denied us access to their oil resources, the military and industrial capabilities of the entire free world would be significantly and perhaps decisively reduced. On the other hand, there was equally no question after the war that the United States and the United Kingdom were morally obligated to permit the emigration to Palestine of some portion of the surviving remnant of European Jewry. Indeed, many Jews and gentiles everywhere were strongly of the opinion that the moral obligation extended to support for the establishment of a Jewish national home in Palestine. But in the event that the United States committed itself to the creation of a Jewish state in the Middle East, it appeared certain to Forrestal and others that the Arab countries would retaliate by depriving us of their oil. He also believed that the Soviet Union would take the fullest advantage of the resulting discord, the end result of which might well be an economic and military alliance between the Arab and Communist blocs.

---

41. Much of this material is summarized from an unpublished article by Marx Leva. I am grateful to him for presenting me with a copy of this article.

42. The Truman Doctrine, in the form of An Act to Provide Assistance to Greece and Turkey, provided for an additional $400,000,000 of economic and military aid to Greece and Turkey.

Guided by this conviction, Forrestal for more than three years was bitterly opposed to a variety of American actions that were favorable to the Zionist cause. In fact, there can be no disputing the statement that his role in the Palestine issue was the most controversial of his entire career. Although there were others in the Administration—Marshall, Lovett, Acheson, the Middle East desk of the State Department, the Joint Chiefs of Staff—who shared Forrestal's views, they were less committed than Forrestal, perhaps less emotionally involved. It was Forrestal, for example, who "spoke to [Truman] repeatedly about the danger that hostile Arabs might deny us access to the petroleum treasures of their countries,"[43] and, again, Forrestal who repeatedly drew attention to Zionist influence in the United States. Whether as obsession or *idée fixe,* Forrestal's position on Palestine involved him in a continuing dispute with the President, some of Truman's closest advisers, including Clark Clifford and Robert E. Hannegan, and a large number of Democratic Party politicians. It also nurtured charges that Forrestal was essentially a "front man" for Wall Street banking firms and the oil interests. Finally, it encouraged suspicion in both gentile and Jewish circles that Forrestal personally was not merely anti-Zionist but anti-Semitic. Nor should it be overlooked that one consequence of these suspicions was that Forrestal, during his last months in office, harbored a conviction that he was under day-and-night surveillance by Zionist agents; and when he resigned as Secretary of Defense in March, 1949, he was convinced that his resignation was not unrelated to pressures brought to bear on the Administration by American Jewish organizations.[44]

---

43. Harry S Truman, *Memoirs,* II, *Years of Trial and Hope* (New York: Doubleday, 1946) , p. 162.

44. While these beliefs reflect the fact that Forrestal was a very ill man in March, 1949, it is entirely possible that he was "shadowed" by Zionist agents in 1947 and 1948. A close associate of his at the time recalls that at the height of the Palestine controversy, his (the associate's) official limousine

The events culminating in these mutual suspicions and misunderstandings began in August, 1945, when Truman urged the newly elected British Labour Government to permit the immediate emigration into Palestine of 100,000 Jewish displaced persons. When Foreign Minister Ernest Bevin and the Labour Cabinet rejected the proposal,[45] discussion between the two governments turned to the creation of an Anglo-American Joint Committee to study the entire Palestine issue. On April 30, 1946, the Committee issued a report recommending that 100,000 Jews be permitted to enter Palestine immediately. Instead of urging the partition of Palestine into Arab and Jewish states, the Committee suggested that Palestine be made a United Nations trusteeship or mandate. Both Jews and Arabs were unable to agree on these proposals, and neither the United States nor the United Kingdom took any action to implement the report.

Truman, nevertheless, again publicly supported the immediate admission of 100,000 Jews to Palestine. In June, 1946, he also appointed a special Cabinet committee, which significantly did not include Forrestal,[46] to study the entire problem; and in July, an American mission headed by Henry Grady initiated further talks with the British. Following receipt of the Grady Report in August, Truman issued a

---

was followed to and from his office by a blue sedan containing two men. When the police were notified and the sedan apprehended, it was discovered that the two men were photographers employed by a Zionist organization. They explained to the police that they had hoped to obtain photographs of the limousine's occupant entering or leaving an Arab embassy in order to demonstrate that the official involved was in close contact with Arab representatives.

45. The position of a number of leading Labourites, especially Ernest Bevin, was similar to that taken by Forrestal and other Truman Administration officials. They also resented the proffer of advice without the acceptance of responsibility, i.e., without an American commitment to send troops to Palestine to maintain peace between Arabs and Jews. Bevin himself, whose anti-Zionism was colored by anti-Semitism, always believed that Truman's espousal of the Zionist cause was dictated entirely by the electoral importance of the Jewish vote.

46. The Cabinet committee consisted of the Secretaries of War, State, and Treasury.

statement declaring that he had no plan for Palestine to present to the British and that no solution acceptable to all parties was possible. He added, however, that he was contemplating asking Congress for special legislation permitting the immigration to the United States of a fixed number of European displaced persons, including Jews.[47] On October 4, on the eve of Yom Kippur and not long before the 1946 elections, Truman published a message he had sent to Attlee recommending the immediate entry into Palestine of a substantial number of displaced Jews, and pledging American support for the formation of a separate Jewish state in part of the Holy Land.

Truman's statement, resented by the British and rejected by the Arabs,[48] resolved none of the issues involved, and subsequent American and British "compromise" proposals were no more successful. In February, 1947, with violence increasing in Palestine, Bevin referred the Palestine question to the United Nations. The report of the UN fact-finding commission on Palestine, submitted to the General Assembly on August 31, 1947, constituted, in effect, the last major attempt to find a solution acceptable to both Arabs and Jews. The principal recommendation of the commission, that Palestine be partitioned into Arab and Jewish states with Jerusalem under international supervision, was approved by the General Assembly on November 29, 1947, with the Soviet Union and the United States voting in the affirmative. Partitioning was to take effect by October 1, 1948.

Between November, 1947, and May, 1948, however, the Truman Administration reversed itself on the partition question, and made efforts in the UN and elsewhere to per-

47. Truman's statement was in response to British complaints that the United States, while urging that the British take some responsibility for the plight of European Jews, was itself not willing to permit them to settle in large numbers in the United States.

48. The British later claimed that Truman's message to Attlee undermined their own discussions with Arab and Zionist representatives.

suade the Arabs and Jews to accept the trusteeship plan. The reversal of the American position was due in large part to a belated recognition that the partition arrangement would require armed intervention by UN members, including the United States, for an indefinite period. At the time of the partition vote the American delegation to the UN had not proposed that a UN police force be created to keep peace in the Holy Land following the withdrawal of British troops. When it became clear that there would be civil war in Palestine without such a force, Truman capitulated to his military advisers, all of whom were opposed both to partition and to American military involvement.

But it was then too late to change direction. With the defeat in the General Assembly of the trusteeship plan and the end of the British mandate over Palestine on May 14, 1948, enmity between Arabs and Jews was transformed into open warfare. Although the independent state of Israel was proclaimed on May 14, and was formally recognized shortly after by the United States and the Soviet Union,[49] the Arab world neither then nor later was prepared to concede its existence. The great powers, for their part, while they had voted for partition, were not willing to enforce it.

Forrestal's anti-Zionist position was influenced by a variety of factors. In addition to fearing that American support of the Jews would alienate the entire Arab world and deprive us of oil, he believed that a war between Arabs and Jews might invite Russian intervention, especially if the Arabs appealed to the Soviet Union for military aid. And once the Russians were established in the Middle East, Forrestal was convinced, there would be no way short of war of getting

---

49. The United States, which accorded Israel *de facto* recognition on May 14th, would undoubtedly have recognized the new state sooner or later. The lack of any delay in recognition, however, owes less to State Department enthusiasm for the new country—there was practically none—than to the insistence of certain Administration officials that American recognition come before and not after Soviet recognition. The Russians accorded recognition on May 17.

them out. If, on the other hand, the United States militarily intervened on behalf of the Jews, the result might well be the same, that is, Soviet intervention on the Arab side. Moreover, he argued frequently, there were no American soldiers to spare for Palestine, whether to support Arabs or Jews, or merely to police the partition plan. He was also convinced, as were most military strategists, that the partition arrangement was doomed inasmuch as the Arabs, if there was an armed conflict, would be able to drive the Jews into the sea.

Those arguments appeared to him so compelling, almost so self-evident, that he became increasingly suspicious of the motivations of those on the opposite side of the issue. Early in the controversy he reached the conclusion that American policy toward Palestine was dominated by political considerations, and especially the fact that Jews "are injecting vigorous and active propaganda to force the President's hand. . . ."[50] In 1947–1948 he insisted repeatedly that neither Truman nor anyone else was justified in making pro-Zionist statements partly or mainly because such statements would have, in Hannegan's words, "a very great influence and great effect on the raising of funds for the Democratic National Committee."[51] Making his own inquiries of Bernard Baruch and other prominent American Jews, Forrestal discovered that not all Jews were Zionists, and he conveyed this information to those Democratic politicians who were most concerned with the problems of fund-raising and the "Jewish vote." In November, 1947, he made one of several attempts to persuade J. Howard McGrath, Senator from Rhode Island and Democratic National Committee chairman, that "no group in this country should be permitted to influence our policy to the point where it could endanger national security." Without conceding the point involved in Forrestal's statement, McGrath replied, according to Forrestal, "that

---

50. *Diaries*, p. 188.
51. *Ibid.*, p. 309.

there were two or three pivotal states which could not be carried without the support of people who were deeply interested in the Palestine question." Forrestal, far from won over, answered McGrath by saying, "I would rather lose those states in a national election than run the risks which I felt might develop in our handling of the Palestine question."[52] McGrath was not convinced, and in the end Forrestal was no more successful with Truman, Clifford, and a variety of politicians from both parties. The Palestine issue, rightly or wrongly, for better or worse, could not "be taken out of politics."

Whatever the merits of his position, Forrestal's persistence was extremely irritating to Truman and some of his close advisers. While it was legitimate to oppose a policy and seek to change it within the Administration, it was much less legitimate in their view to lobby actively against that policy in Congress and elsewhere. Unlike other critics of successive Palestine policy developments, Forrestal sought to bring pressure to bear on the Administration from circles outside it, circles in certain cases opposed in general to the Truman program. Thus, on January 19, 1948, testifying before a special subcommittee of the House Armed Services Committee, Forrestal was asked by Representative Dewey Short, Missouri Republican, whether the UN partition vote had weakened America's security. Forrestal's answer was to the effect that the Administration's decision to support partition was inimical to our security and interests. His reply to Short, in conjunction with other activities related to the Palestine issue, did not increase the number of his friends in the White House and the so-called liberal wing of the Democratic Party.

Because of his Wall Street background Forrestal had always been vulnerable to charges that his anti-Zionism was

---

52. *Ibid.*, p. 344.

related to his business connections, particularly to Dillon, Read's close ties to major oil companies. On March 10, 1948, Bartley C. Crum, California lawyer, Republican, member of the Anglo-American Joint Committee of 1946, and ardent Zionist, devoted most of a speech in Cleveland to these charges; and thereafter—Forrestal was to remain in office another year—they were never to lose their currency in any discussion critical of Forrestal's role in the Truman Administration. Although Crum did not suggest that Forrestal was anti-Semitic, he did not go out of his way to assert that anti-Semitism and anti-Zionism were two very different and distinct positions. Indeed, the tone of the speech, with its demagogic stress on an alleged conspiracy in the government of which Forrestal had been the central figure, implied that in opposing the creation of a Jewish state in Palestine, Forrestal was also opposed to the United Nations, peace, and the establishment of democracy in the Middle East.

Assailing the United States reversal on partition, Crum early in his speech asserted that "there is one man in Washington who has the power to decide [whether there is to be a Jewish state in Palestine] for all of us—in his own way—without reference to the honor and integrity of our nation, without reference to the peace or destruction of our world. That man is the Secretary of Defense, Mr. James Forrestal." Should anyone ask, Crum continued, " 'Upon what meat does this our Caesar feed, that he has grown so great?' [t]he answer is that Mr. Forrestal has found a new diet that even a Caesar might envy. It is oil—Arabian oil." Although Crum admitted that Forrestal "quite sincerely believes . . . that our oil supply should not be jeopardized," he insisted that in evaluating Forrestal's judgment "it is only fair to consider [his] background and training. For Mr. Forrestal has not, and cannot, in public office, rid himself of his past."

Forrestal's "past," according to Crum, included his personal participation, as partner and president of Dillon, Read, in floating large loans for the Standard Oil Company of California and the Texas Company. Both of these companies are heavily involved in oil operations in the Middle East—particularly in Saudi Arabia and Bahrein. . . . Dillon, Read also floated loans for the Royal Shell and its subsidiary, the Batavian Petroleum Company.

Forrestal's associates in the Defense Department, Crum continued, also have business backgrounds intimately related to the oil industry. Identifying these associates as Assistant Secretary of the Army William H. Draper, formerly with Dillon, Read, and Secretary for Air Stuart Symington, Crum observed,

when we look at the Defense Secretariat we find that all three branches—Army, Navy, and Air Force, as well as their central director—include men who have had close private interests in the oil industry.

"Does not justice require," Crum asked, "that the Secretary of Defense instantly and unhesitatingly remove himself from any connection with the Palestine issue, in which the oil companies of this country have an unconcealed interest?" Far from removing himself, Crum added, Forrestal "is in a position to determine whether my boy and your boy shall live or die."

Denying that he was making in any sense a personal attack on Forrestal, Crum concluded his speech with a variety of charges designed to prove that "Forrestal's power and influence in Washington are unmatched by any other person of Cabinet rank." The Secretary of Defense, Crum alleged,

controls the spending of nearly one-third of the national budget . . . has built up an impressive relationship with Congress . . . enjoys the unique position of having Congressmen bow to him . . . has access to the secret intelligence services and what they produce . . . is so powerful that he could, if he desired, raise a rumor to the status of an indubitable and frightening fact . . . is looked upon, in many quarters on Capitol Hill, not as a member of the Democratic Party primarily, but primarily as a great Wall

Street man . . . is able to get things done and to wield influence and to escape criticism . . . makes it almost a fetish not to be involved publicly in any controversial matter . . . [but] lets others do the fighting, the contending, in public . . . through his contacts with the press, has attempted to influence the very roots of public opinion in America . . . has even gone so far as to break down the time-honored distinction between private enterprise and government ownership in this country . . . [by] suggesting that the government should buy into the oil companies to preserve the national interest.

Bringing his speech to a close, Crum challenged Forrestal's right as a public official "to spearhead the oil lobby." Justifiably or not, he ended, Forrestal's role in the government "raises suspicion that these [oil] companies are being served by and from the most important single office in our government outside of the President's."

The exaggerations and distortions in Crum's speech of March 10, 1948, were obvious enough to those who knew the Washington scene, but they were not at all obvious to his listeners in Cleveland's Public Auditorium Music Hall and the circles that radiated from it. Forrestal, to be sure, held a good deal of power as Secretary of Defense, but neither before nor after Crum delivered his speech did he enjoy Truman's complete confidence or gain access to the inner circle of the President's advisers.[53] While his relations with Capitol Hill and the press were generally good, he had his critics in both places who shared Crum's views and, in certain instances, even went beyond them. For a variety of reasons, some of them relating to his personality, some to the political situation, and some to the complexities of decision-making processes in Washington, Forrestal did not become, and could not become, the *éminence grise* of the Truman Administration.

While it is probable that his Palestine position was in-

---

53. The relations between Truman and Forrestal are dealt with below, pp. 266–281.

fluenced to some degree by his Wall Street background—
certainly some of his friends were presidents and directors
of major oil companies—there is no evidence that Forrestal
consciously and deliberately used his power "to spearhead
the oil lobby." Both as Secretary of the Navy and Secretary
of Defense, he frequently endorsed policies to which all or
most of the business community was opposed, and there
were also occasions when he defended the Truman Administration's economic program against accusations of "Socialism" originating with some of his former colleagues at Dillon,
Read. Finally, his notes and papers make it abundantly clear
that he regarded our sporadic pro-Zionist proposals not
merely as politically motivated but as probably fatal to
American security in the Middle East. His intense and genuine conviction, however wrong it may have been, was that
in supporting, first, Jewish immigration to Palestine and,
later, the establishment of Israel, we were risking our oil
supply and also providing the Russians with an open door to
the entire Moslem world.

The question remains, however, whether Forrestal should
have permitted himself to become so convinced, and whether,
further, he was wise to go to such lengths in his opposition
to Zionism. In the light of post-1948 developments, there can
be no doubt that Forrestal was seriously misinformed by his
military advisers and oil-company friends. The former were
almost unanimously convinced that the Jews would be forcibly expelled by the Arabs from Palestine, and the latter
with very few exceptions were certain that American support
for Israel would deprive us of Middle East oil. Forrestal was
too easily persuaded by these views, and as a result he made
relatively little effort to obtain an outside assessment or
personally explore the situation that was developing between
1946 and 1948. It apparently did not occur to him, for example, that if the Arabs refused to sell their oil to the United
States and Western European countries, they would have
little or no opportunity to sell it elsewhere.

It also appears that Forrestal was generally unsympathetic to the Jewish cause as such. Although a generous and humane man in his personal relations, his attitude toward the Jewish survivors of Hitler's concentration camps was essentially one of indifference. The extent of his involvement or concern was reflected in the suggestion, put forward at various times, that the displaced Jews might be resettled in Peru or one of the other Latin American countries. He did not favor their immigration in more than token numbers to the United States.

Here, perhaps, his views were a direct reflection of his background. While Forrestal was not an anti-Semite, his attitude toward Jews was characterized by much ambivalence. Although he maintained good relations with his New York and Washington associates who were Jewish, notably Bernard Baruch,[54] his Defense Department legal aide Marx Leva, and Navy Captain Ellis M. Zacharias, he had difficulty accepting Jews as social equals. One of his Wall Street colleagues recalls that Forrestal

thought Jews were "different," and he could never really understand how a non-Jew and a Jew could be friends. I remember an

---

54. Forrestal had great respect for Baruch, although their personal relations were not close. In 1944, for example, he wrote Baruch that "without your patience . . . the beating at times might have been impossible." And on another occasion: "You have this curious effect upon men: your praise makes them search their souls to see whether they live up to it. I will have to work harder than ever now not to let you down." Forrestal was also aware, however, that Baruch "is very adept at the art of making his recommendation and advice so global that he can say, 'I told you so.' " Quoted from a telephone conversation with Brynes on April 28, 1948, in *Diaries*, p. 428. Baruch's admiration for Forrestal, however, was apparently unqualified. "Of all the men in wartime Washington," he wrote in 1960, "Bob Patterson and Jim Forrestal were among those I admired most. . . . Forrestal had much the same character as Patterson. [Patterson, according to Baruch, had demonstrated 'absolute concentration on the job of winning the war. He tolerated no compromises, no frills. . . .'] Perhaps more sensitive, and certainly a more tortured man, these very characteristics made him the highly conscientious, single-minded public servant he was."—*Baruch: The Public Years* (New York: Holt, Rinehart and Winston, 1960), pp. 310–311. See also Baruch, *Baruch: My Own Story* (Henry Holt, 1957); and Margaret L. Coit, *Mr. Baruch* (Boston: Houghton Mifflin, 1957).

occasion when I was involved in his presence in an argument with a Jewish friend. At one point I got over-heated and I said something like "you son-of-a-bitch." Jim was shocked that I could talk that way to someone who was Jewish. He himself was always very reserved with people who were Jews. I think there was something about them he couldn't understand, or maybe didn't like.

Whatever the significance of "maybe," it is worth noting that Forrestal lived most of his life in an anti-Semitic world. The early family circle was anti-Semitic, and many of his friends positively disliked Jews. During his Wall Street career a large number of prominent investment banking houses and law firms refused to employ Jews, and some of the New York and Washington clubs to which he belonged did not admit persons of Jewish origin. The Navy Department itself was notorious for its anti-Semitic promotion policy.

Before and during the Palestine crisis, Forrestal received from friends a large number of letters, generally anti-Semitic in tone, devoted to some of the issues involved. One letter of June 24, 1947, from a Wall Street associate who had recently traveled through Europe, Forrestal deemed important enough to have copied and sent to several Administration officials, including White House counsel Clark Clifford.[55] The letter began with a criticism of a bill then before Congress, the so-called Stratton bill, the purpose of which was to establish a special immigration quota for displaced persons. The Stratton bill, wrote Forrestal's friend, "will not enable any but the Jewish DP's to migrate to the United States." Noting that American Jews were busy raising money for Jewish displaced persons, the friend asked whether there were similar efforts underway in behalf of non-Jews. If not, he added, "we could very well end up by taking 75 percent of the quota in Jews . . . if this happens, I do not think the American public will be pleased."

---

55. Clifford returned the letter with the notation: "This fellow makes sense."

Recording certain impressions of his travels, Forrestal's informant declared:

I was amazed to find that Hitler had succeeded in one of his objectives. He has made it impossible for the Jews to live in Europe. Not only are they unwelcome in Germany. . . . This is true in Holland, Belgium, and France, as well, of course, as in Austria, Germany and Hungary. I do not know what the situation is in Italy.

The Jews do not like to admit that they are unpopular everywhere and unwanted by everybody, because this certainly would not help them, selling the idea to the American people that we ought to take them all into this country because nobody else wants them.

The anti-Semitic feeling in the group of men I was with was not lessened by this trip. We visited the DP camps and were much impressed by . . . the Balts and, to a lesser degree . . . the Poles. The Jewish camps were very unappetizing. The military people had great difficulty in getting them to keep their camps even reasonably clean. There seemed to be very little desire to create work for themselves.

The disposition of these people is really a terrific problem. From reports I received over there, nobody wants them and the commissions that are sent over by other countries are picking over the people chiefly in the non-Jewish groups, and we may well end up with those that no one else wants.[56]

Forrestal's indifference toward the fate of the European Jews, an indifference to which this and other letters similar in nature may have contributed, haunted him during his

---

56. The letter continued: "The Germans are using the whole denazification process for political purposes, and this power should be taken away from them and a general amnesty declared, except for a small number of the top Nazi officials who might just as well be lynched properly and end the whole business. The attempt to pin-point justice has resulted in such absurdities as the release of [Hjalmar] Schacht, who certainly is as guilty as any of the rest of them.

"American Military Government is doing a swell job under the severe handicaps placed upon them by a combination of fuddie-duddies who originally set policy and a group headed by Morgenthau who are only interested in vengeance and who apparently are willing to sacrifice the security of the United States in order to punish those who were responsible for the whole Jewish debacle."

last days in office. If, on the one hand, he felt that Jewish groups were determined to have him removed from office, he also had a sense of guilt about his role in the Administration during the years of the Palestine controversy. Following the establishment of Israel in May, 1948, he telephoned the Israeli Ambassador in Washington on several occasions to confess that he had been mistaken in his views.[57] In discussions at the time with certain newspapermen, he repeatedly drew their attention to the fact that he had made numerous efforts to improve the status of racial minorities in the Navy. He mentioned specifically a 1947 citation as one of seventeen Americans who had made "outstanding contributions last year to the improvement of race relations,"[58] and he reminded his listeners that he had promoted Zacharias from captain to rear admiral over the resistance of high-ranking admirals in the Navy Department.

In the spring of 1949 Forrestal also had evidence that he was not *persona non grata* to all Jews and Jewish organizations. Although he declined to be present, he was invited in February to attend a celebration at one of Washington's Reformed Jewish Temples. When his resignation was announced in March, he received a letter commending him for his past services and expressing regret from Myer Dorfman, National Commander of the Jewish War Veterans.[59] Many persons of Jewish extraction, during his stay at Bethesda, wired or wrote him expressing their hopes for an early recovery, and several added that his anti-Zionist position had by no means concealed or confused his great service to the country as our first Secretary of Defense.

---

57. Herbert Ellison in *The Atlantic*, November, 1951.

58. Forrestal was cited by the Schomberg Collection of Negro Literature of the New York Public Library for having abolished, by directive, racial segregation in the Navy. The citation was based on a national poll of one hundred prominent Negro leaders in the arts, sciences, education, journalism, the labor movement, and politics.

59. Forrestal replied by wire, thanking Dorfman for his "thoughtful comments and good wishes."

Forrestal, of course, never received these messages, and in any case it was then too late to relieve by ordinary means the guilts, fears, doubts, and anxieties that had precipitated his illness. However history may ultimately judge his opposition to the establishment of Israel, by 1949 it was clear that Forrestal was, in a sense, one of the casualties of the diplomatic warfare that had led to the creation of the Jewish state.

VI

☆ ☆ ☆ ☆ ☆

Soviet Expansionism and Defense Organization

FORRESTAL'S ATTITUDE toward Communism and the Soviet Union, like his attitude toward Zionism and the Palestine issue, was shaped by a variety of influences. As he had no friends who were pro-Zionist and pro-Israel, so he had none who were, by any labor of imagination, sympathetic to Soviet interests. Except for Hopkins, Stimson, and Leahy, his personal and professional associates were largely inclined to believe that peaceful coexistence was impossible and ultimate war inevitable; they differed only on the time, place, and circumstances of the future confrontation with the communist bloc. In addition, Forrestal's own analysis of Soviet ideology and policy confirmed him in the view that this unavoidable confrontation would occur sooner than later. Distrustful of any and all Soviet "peace" overtures,[1] Forrestal regarded each one as merely a tactical

---

1. In November, 1946, when there was talk at the United Nations, not for the first or last time, of disarmament, Forrestal obtained from John Hickerson, Acting Director of the State's Department's Office of European Affairs, a long quotation from the Comintern's explanation of Litvinov's proposal in 1927 for total disarmament." The "explanation," quoted from Chapter Four of the final report of the Comintern's Sixth Congress in Moscow (1928), declared that the "purpose" of all disarmament conferences and related

move in the Cold War designed to deceive those in the Western camp who were naïve, gullible or, worse, conscious apologists for Stalinism.[2] Finally, the reports that reached Forrestal's desk were rarely optimistic in their appraisals of Soviet intentions anywhere in the world, much less Soviet willingness to compromise outstanding differences with the United States and her allies. Although Forrestal was long since convinced that the Soviet Union after the war would exploit every Western weakness, every hesitation, every difference of opinion with respect to policy, it remains true that the information received by him from numerous sources was hardly conducive to a hopeful estimate of the situation.

Thus on April 2, 1945, Forrestal recorded in his notes of a meeting of the State, War and Navy Secretaries that the "Secretary of State [Edward R. Stettinius] advised of serious deterioration in our relations with Russia."[3] Two days later he began to include in his papers copies of cables from Averell Harriman, then in Moscow, urging that the United States and Britain "be guided . . . by the policy of taking care of our Western Allies and other areas under our responsibility first, allocating to Russia what may be left." By now we "have ample proof," Harriman cabled on April 4,

that the Soviet government views all matters from the standpoint of their own selfish interests. They have publicized to their own

---

efforts was to "camouflage" the imperialist intentions of the capitalist countries. Forrestal used this and other statements as evidence that the Russians were not seriously interested in disarmament.

2. Almost a year before the end of World War II, he wrote Palmer Hoyt that "whenever any American suggests that we act in accordance with the needs of our own security he is apt to be called a god-damned fascist or imperialist, while if Uncle Joe suggests that he needs the Baltic Provinces, half of Poland, all of Bessarabia and access to the Mediterranean, all hands agree that he is a fine, frank, candid and generally delightful fellow who is very easy to deal with because he is so explicit in what he wants."—Letter of September 2, 1944 (*Diaries*, p. 14).

3. *Diaries*, p. 38. One case of the "serious deterioration" was Soviet insistence that the communist or pro-communist Polish delegation, the so-called Lublin Poles, be invited to the United Nations organizing conference in San Francisco.

political advantage the difficult food situation in areas liberated by our troops . . . comparing it with the allegedly satisfactory conditions in areas which the Red Army has liberated . . . we should, through such economic aid as we can give to our Western Allies, including Greece as well as Italy, re-establish a reasonable life for the people of these countries who have the same general outlook as we have on life and the development of the world.

The Soviet Union and its satellite governments in Eastern Europe, he added,

have an entirely different objective. We must clearly realize that the Soviet program is the establishment of totalitarianism, ending personal liberty and democracy as we know and respect it. . . . The only hope of stopping Soviet penetration is the development of sound economic conditions. . . .[4]

On April 6 another Harriman cable made the point:

It may be difficult for us to believe, but it still may be true that Stalin and Molotov considered at Yalta that by our willingness to accept a general wording of the declaration on Poland and liberated Europe, by our recognition of the need of the Red Army for security behind its lines, and of the predominant interest of Russia in Poland as a friendly neighbor and as a corridor to Germany, we understood and were ready to accept Soviet policies already known to us.

Notwithstanding, it was a mistake to display to the Russians a "generous and considerate attitude," since this was interpreted by them as evidence of weakness. "I cannot list," he continued, "the almost daily affronts and total disregard which the Soviets evince in matters of interest to us." Per-

---

4. *Diaries*, pp. 39–40. Long before Marshall's speech at Harvard University on June 5, 1947, Forrestal, Harriman, and other top officials of the Truman Administration were in favor of what later became known as the Marshall Plan. Along Pennsylvania Avenue, as distinct from Capitol Hill, there was virtually no opposition to Marshall's proposal that the United States provide financial aid to any European country "willing to assist in the task of recovery." Although Forrestal believed, mistakenly, that the Russians would participate in the Plan because "they could no more afford to be out of it than they could have afforded not to join in the war against Japan . . ." (*Diaries*, p. 79), he did not, apparently, suggest that the Plan be drawn in such a way as to preclude communist participation.

haps, therefore, it would be wise to take a strong stand in "one or two cases where their actions are intolerable and make them realize that they cannot continue their present attitude except at great cost to themselves."[5]

In a conversation with Forrestal on April 20, Harriman again urged "much great firmness" in dealing with the Soviet Union,[6] and at a Cabinet meeting a few days later he supported Forrestal's (and Stettinius's) view that the Russians, in backing the Lublin Poles, had violated the understanding reached at Yalta on the future of Poland. Forrestal's position, identical with those he took on other occasions when the Russians were or appeared to be precipitating a crisis, was that the Russian stand on the Polish question

was not an isolated incident but was one of a pattern of unilateral action on the part of Russia . . . they had taken similar positions vis-à-vis Bulgaria, Rumania, Turkey and Greece, and . . . I thought we might as well meet the issue now as later on.[7]

On May 14 he entered in his notes the opinion of Harriman, with which he was in full accord, that Russian "conduct would be based upon the principal of power politics in its crudest and most primitive form." Diplomatic decisions "from here on," Harriman told Forrestal, must be faced

---

5. *Ibid.*, p. 40.

6. *Ibid.*, p. 47.

7. *Ibid.*, p. 49. Once again Stimson and Leahy saw the issue somewhat differently. According to Forrestal's notes, Stimson "hoped we would go slowly and avoid an open break. He said that the Russians had carried out their military engagements quite faithfully and was sorry to see this one incident project a breach between the two countries." Leahy "hoped the matter could be put to the Russians in such a way as not to close the door to subsequent accommodation."—*Diaries*, pp. 49–50. Bohlen, also present at the meeting, reported Stimson's "thought that the Russians perhaps were being more realistic than we were in regard to their own security." Leahy, in Bohlen's account, went even further than Stimson in stating that "he had left Yalta with the impression that the Soviet government had no intention of permitting a free government to operate in Poland, and that he would have been surprised had the Soviet government behaved any differently than it had." *Diaries*, pp. 50–51. Forrestal did not express his violent disagreement with these views, possibly because the President had already intimated that he would adopt a "tough" position on the Polish issue.

"with the consciousness that half and maybe all of Europe might be communistic by the end of next winter. . . ."[8]

Late in March, 1946, Forrestal received a copy of a lengthy and rather detailed report to the Secretary of State from George F. Kennan, American chargé d'affaires in Moscow. Kennan, whom Forrestal respected as perhaps our foremost analyst of Soviet behavior, began his dispatch with a statement that Forrestal found especially perceptive. "In recent days," Kennan prefaced his remarks,

we have noted a number of statements made either editorially in American papers or individually by prominent Americans reflecting the view that Soviet "suspicions" could be assuaged if we on our part would make great effort, by means of direct contacts, persuasion or assurances, to convince Russians of good faith of our aims and policies.

I have in mind particularly numerous calls for a new three-power meeting, *Philadelphia Record*'s proposal that U.S. give "assurances" to assuage Russia's fears, Lippmann's appeal for closer "diplomatic contact" and, above all, Henry Wallace's expressed belief (if BBC has quoted him correctly) that there is something our government could and should do to persuade Stalin that we are not trying to form an anti-Soviet bloc. . . .

I am sending this message in order to tell Department [of State] of the concern and alarm with which we view line of thought behind these statements. Belief that Soviet "suspicions" are of such a nature that they could be altered or assuaged by personal contacts, rational arguments or official assurances, reflects a serious misunderstanding about Soviet realities and constitutes, in our opinion, the most insidious and dangerous single error which Americans can make in their thinking about this country.

Any long-term understanding of Russian affairs, he continued, must proceed from a recognition of

this very simple and basic fact: official Soviet thesis that outside world is hostile and menacing to Soviet peoples is not a conclusion at which Soviet leaders have reluctantly arrived after honest

---

8. *Ibid.*, p. 57.

and objective appraisal of facts available to them but as an *a priori* tactical position deliberately taken and hotly advanced by dominant elements in Soviet political system for impelling selfish reasons of a domestic political nature. A hostile international environment is the breath of life for prevailing internal system in this country. Without it there would be no justification for that tremendous and crushing bureaucracy of party, police and army which now lives off the labor and idealism of Russian people.

Admitting that he did not know "whether Stalin himself is an author or victim" of the "psychosis" that "Russia is a country walking a dangerous path among implacable enemies," Kennan observed

there is strong evidence that he does not by any means always receive objective and helpful information about international situation . . . the entire apparatus of diplomacy and propaganda under him works not on basis of any objective analysis of world situation but squarely on basis of the pre-conceived party line which we see reflected in official propaganda.

Although "useful things" had been accomplished in the past and could be accomplished in the future by direct contact with Stalin, Kennan emphasized that the "cards are stacked against us." Ambassadors, he pointed out,

see Stalin only relatively rarely . . . Meanwhile Stalin is presumably constantly at the disposal of a set of inside advisors of whom we know little or nothing. As far as I am aware, there is no limit or extent to which these people can fill his mind with misinformation and misinterpretations about us and our policies, and all this without our knowledge. Isolation of foreigners and (this is important to note) of high Soviet figures as well, both from each other and from rank and file of Soviet population, makes it practically impossible for foreign representatives to trace and combat the flow of deliberate misinformation and misinterpretation to which their countries are victims.

To all this, Kennan continued, there should be added the

fact that suspicion is basic in Soviet Government. It affects everything and everyone. It is not confined to us. Foreign Communists in Moscow are subject to isolation and supervision more extreme, if anything, than those surrounding foreign diplomats. They enjoy no more than we do any individual confidence on part of Kremlin. Even Soviet internal figures move in a world of elaborate security checks and balances based on lack of confidence in their individual integrity. Moscow does not believe in such things as good will or individual human virtue.

When confidence is unknown even at home, how can it logically be sought by outsiders?

Under these circumstances, he concluded his dispatch,

there can be no more dangerous tendency in American public opinion than one which places on our government an obligation to accomplish the impossible by gestures of good will and conciliation. . . . On the other hand, there is no tendency more agreeable to purposes of Moscow diplomacy. Kremlin has no reason to discourage a delusion so useful to its purposes; and we may expect Moscow propaganda apparatus to cultivate it assiduously.

For these reasons, I wish to register the earnest hope that we will find means to bring about a better understanding on this particular point, particularly among people who bear public responsibility and influence public opinion in our country.

These final paragraphs of Kennan's communiqué of March 20 to the State Department could well have been written by Forrestal himself. Forrestal also regarded good will and conciliatory gestures as the expression of a "dangerous tendency," and he, too, had been advocating and would continue to advocate the need for a much greater effort by the government to promote "better understanding on this particular point." Indeed, he was so impressed by Kennan's analyses of Soviet conduct[9] that he requested Kennan to write a special paper on the subject to which he could refer in his discussions with congressmen and senators. Forrestal was not satisfied with Kennan's first draft, but eventually he received a paper that he approved in its entirety. He distributed unsigned copies to a large number of

9. Portions of another Kennan dispatch, also concerned with Soviet behavior, appear in *Diaries*, pp. 135–140.

influential persons in Washington, especially in Congress, and was gratified to find that most of them thought that it should be published with or without the author's name attached. Because of his State Department responsibilities Kennan insisted that the paper not be published over his name, and as a result the paper appeared anonymously in the July, 1947, issue of *Foreign Affairs*. It was there titled "The Sources of Soviet Conduct,"[10] with the author listed as a "Mr. X."[11]

---

10. Kennan's article, perhaps the most significant and best-known article ever published by *Foreign Affairs*, had an immediate impact here and abroad. Its authoritative character, coupled with the fact that Kennan's name was very quickly substituted for "Mr. X," caused it to be regarded by many as an official or quasi-official policy statement. The article began with an analysis of Soviet ideology, and went on to argue the case for a response to the Russian threat that was later styled "the policy of containment." It is clear, Kennan wrote, "that the main element of any United States policy toward the Soviet Union must be that of a long-term, patient but firm and vigilant containment of Russian expansive tendencies. Soviet pressure against the free institutions of the Western world is something that can be contained by the adroit and vigilant application of counter-force at a series of constantly shifting geographical and political points, corresponding to the shifts and maneuvers of Soviet policy, but which cannot be charmed or talked out of existence." Kennan also maintained that it was "entirely possible for the United States to influence by its actions the internal developments, both within Russia and throughout the international Communist movement. This is not only a question of the modest measure of informational activity which this government can conduct in the Soviet Union and elsewhere, although that, too, is important. It is rather a question of the degree to which the United States can create among the peoples of the world generally the impression of a country which knows what it wants, which is coping successfully with the problems of its internal life and with the responsibilities of a World Power, and which has a spiritual vitality capable of holding its own among the major ideological currents of the time. To the extent that such an impression can be created and maintained, the aims of Russian Communism must appear sterile and quixotic, the hopes and enthusiasm of Moscow's supporters must wane, and added strain must be imposed on the Kremlin's foreign policies."

11. Kennan, apparently, failed to anticipate that the identity of "Mr. X" would not long be kept secret. In May, 1960, he confided to one of Forrestal's former aides at the time his article appeared that "if it hadn't been for Secretary Forrestal's prodding, he undoubtedly would not have written such a document, and perhaps wouldn't have been pulled into the political arena to the extent that he soon thereafter was, an experience he found rather distasteful, on the whole, because of his retiring nature and scholarly background."—Letter to the writer, June 13, 1960.

The reports, memoranda, letters, and documents read by Forrestal—from Naval Intelligence,[12] from Ankara,[13] from Moscow, Warsaw, Prague, and Bucharest,[14] and from other free-world and iron-curtain capitals—served only to strengthen his conviction that "policy could not be founded on the assumption that a peaceful solution of the Russian problem would be possible."[15] In conversations with Marshall, Nimitz, and others in the spring of 1947, Forrestal repeatedly tried to focus discussion on "what steps this government was prepared to take in the event of a Russian *démarche* in Europe,"[16] and on June 23, at the conclusion of a Cabinet luncheon, he posed the question directly to Truman. "What does this country do," he asked,

politically or militarily, if it is confronted during this summer with a Russian *démarche* accompanied by simultaneous coups in France and Italy?

The President's reply, as summarized by Forrestal, was that

we would have to face that situation when it arose. . . . He said that he was afraid the answer would have to be found in history —of the struggle between the Romans and Carthage, between Athens and Sparta, between Alexander the Great and the Persians, between France and England, between England and Germany. He *hoped* that the present situation would not have to be answered the same way . . .[17]

In late 1947 and early 1948, however, it appeared there would not be time to search "in history" for an answer to

---

12. *Diaries*, p. 58.
13. *Ibid.*, p. 97.
14. *Ibid.*, pp. 97–98.
15. Millis in *Diaries*, p. 134. Millis implies that this conviction became "increasingly" strong after Stalin's speech of February 9, 1946, but it is extremely doubtful that Forrestal ever had much confidence in "a peaceful solution." Stalin's speech, which William O. Douglas, according to Forrestal, referred to as "The Declaration of World War III," committed the Soviet Union to a major expansion of its industrial and military capabilities. His speech, like most of the Soviet dictator's pronouncements, alleged "capitalist encirclement," and described the new economic program as a "guarantee . . . against any eventuality."
16. *Diaries*, p. 280.
17. *Ibid.*, p. 281.

Forrestal's question. On May 30, 1947, the Hungarian government led by Ferenc Nagy was overthrown by Communists and replaced with a regime subservient to Moscow. The Russians, contrary to Forrestal's expectations, rejected the Marshall Plan, and by so doing dealt a heavy blow to the hopes of some individuals in the Administration, including Marshall himself, for a "peaceful solution." In December, the abdication of King Michael of Romania was followed by the establishment of a so-called People's Republic under communist auspices. The latter months of 1947 also witnessed a communist-led maritime strike in France that crippled not only French shipping but also key industrial sectors dependent on coal and other imports. On February 10, 1948, Czech President Benes, forced to capitulate to communist pressure, appointed a pro-Soviet Cabinet.[18]

Less than a month later, on March 5, 1948, the United States Commander in Germany, General Lucius Clay, cabled to Washington his "feeling that [war] may come with dramatic suddenness,"[19] and on March 16th Forrestal made a note of the fact that the newspapers that morning were "full of rumors and portents of war." Observing that "[n]othing could be sillier" than a recent Wallace statement declaring that the Czech communist coup had been "an act of desperation" in response to a threat from the Right, Forrestal recorded his belief

that this country and its government are desperately anxious to avoid war. It is simply a question of how best to do it. If all Eur-

18. Benes resigned on June 7, and died on September 3. Jan Masaryk, Foreign Minister under Benes and son of Thomas Masaryk, founder of the Czech Republic, fell or jumped to his death from his office on March 10.

19. "For many months," the cable read, "based on logical analysis, I have felt and held that war was unlikely for at least ten years. Within the last few weeks, I have felt a subtle change in Soviet attitude which I cannot define but which now gives me a feeling that it may come with dramatic suddenness. I cannot support this change in my own thinking with any data or outward evidence in relationships other than to describe it as a feeling of a new tenseness in every Soviet individual with whom we have official relations. I am unable to submit any official report in the absence of supporting data but my feeling is real. . . ."—*Diaries*, p. 387.

ope lies flat while the Russian mob tramps over it, we will then be faced with a war under difficult circumstances, and with a very good chance of losing it.

It is inconceivable that even the gang who runs Russia would be willing to take on war, but one always has to remember that there seemed to be no reason in 1939 for Hitler to start war, and yet he did, and he started it with a world practically unprepared. Our effort now is to try to make the Russians see the folly of continuing an aggression which will lead to war, or, if it is impossible to restore them to sanity, that we at least have a start which will enable us to prevent our being caught flat-footed as we were in 1941.[20]

Yet one day later, on March 17, despite the "rumors and portents of war," Forrestal was able to write Kenneth G. Roberts "I feel better about the world situation than I have for 2½ years." Forrestal did not elaborate, but quite possibly his mood reflected in part his belief that the Selective Service bill, then before Congress, would be quickly enacted into law.[21] It was not until June 19, however, that the bill was sent to the President, and by that time Forrestal was no longer feeling "better about the world situation. . . ." He did not regard the Selective Service Act as a wholly satisfactory substitute for a Universal Military Training (UMT) measure of which he had been a determined advocate since 1943, and he was still not satisfied that the United States was either psychologically or militarily prepared for a possible war with the Soviet Union. With the successive international crises of the spring and summer of 1948, his pessimism increased;[22] meanwhile, he was unable to obtain from Truman definitive answers to his repeated questions about American

---

20. *Diaries*, pp. 394–395.

21. At a White House meeting on May 21, Forrestal commented that "[o]n March 17 we could have had Selective Service through both Houses in three days. Today there is serious question about the passage of such a bill. . . ."—*Ibid.*, p. 444.

22. The Berlin Blockade was initiated by the Soviet military commander on April 1, although it was not until midsummer that land corridors to

objectives and policies, including the question whether we would use the atomic bomb in the event of war.[23]

Nevertheless, Forrestal's insistence on a strong military posture did not incline him, while in office, to favor preventive war.[24] Although he believed that the United States—to use a later phrase—should "go to the brink" if Russian soldiers were preparing to move into western Germany, France, Italy, and other European countries, he did not agree with those who argued that the United States should initiate a war unprovoked by Soviet aggression. Even when it became clear that the Soviet Union would become an atomic power sooner than first had been expected,[25] Forrestal held to his

---

West Berlin were totally closed to the movement of food and supplies. On June 28 the Communist Information Bureau, or Cominform, denounced Tito and other Yugoslav communist leaders as betrayers of Marxism-Leninism.

23. Although it was not publicized at the time, the Berlin crisis found the United States inadequately prepared to wage war against the Soviet Union itself. A member of Forrestal's staff recalls that the "airplanes of the day—B 29's—had insufficient range to reach the interior of Russia and return. I went to my airforce friends and begged them to resurrect an air-to-air refueling study I had made during the war based on wartime British experience. Almost immediately the Air Force gave the Secretary [Forrestal] a presentation on their capabilities which had greatly increased! He said nothing at the time but after the presentation said . . . 'Find out why their "strings" (meaning radius of action) are nearly twice as long as they were last time.' (The Air Force reply was) 'that's our new air to air refueling method.' 'Is it installed?' 'No, but we've ordered it from England.' (*Sic*) *Next year* there was a news note: 'Seattle, Washington—Full wartime security has been thrown around the Boeing plant where B 29's are being converted to tankers.' "—Letter to the writer, August 22, 1960.

24. Nor did he favor retrospectively a policy in 1939–40 that would have appeased Hitler at the expense of the Soviet Union, a policy supported by, among others, former American Ambassador to Great Britain Joseph P. Kennedy. Reflecting on a conversation with Kennedy of December 27, 1945, Forrestal commented that while "there is undoubtedly foundation for Kennedy's belief that Hitler's attack could have been deflected to Russia . . . I think he fails to take into account what would have happened after Hitler had conquered Russia. Would he have been content to stop? Nothing in his record indicates that that would have been the case, but rather that having removed the threat to his eastern frontiers he would then have exercised the options open to him to construct a European German-dominated system to which he later gave expression after overrunning France."—*Diaries*, pp. 121–122.

25. Almost no one in Washington, including Forrestal, expected the Russians successfully to conduct an atomic-bomb test as early as September,

position that "anyone who thinks in terms of the concept of preventive war ought to have his head examined."[26] Unable to accept the thesis in 1948–1949, that the United States should strike before the Russians gained possession of the bomb, Forrestal recommended to his friends and associates, a recent paper on the subject, subsequently published in *The Atlantic Monthly*, by Harvard President James B. Conant. Conant's paper, regarded by Forrestal as "possibly the best presentation of the way any thoughtful person must react toward such an idea,"[27] declared that those

who have been flirting with the idea of preventative war have failed to see the implications of their position. Their argument says in effect, "In the next decade the Russians will have perfected their instruments of mass destruction; let's smash 'em now before they are ready." This reasoning of those who wish to force Russia to fight now might seem attractive at first sight to all who pride themselves on being hardheaded. I suggest that it is vulnerable, however, on realistic grounds. . . . I think it extremely probable that the men who rule Russia do not dream of a military victory over the United States . . . but rather a revolution in this country which would result in a totalitarian socialistic state with native American rulers. . . . If my assumption about the nature of the thinking in the Kremlin be admitted, it follows that the overall strategy of the United States must be aimed primarily at preserving the type of free society we have inherited from the past and now enjoy. Our open society rests on a fundamental moral basis; once we destroy this basis, we have destroyed the essence of this nation.

Arguing that any acceptance of the doctrine that the end justifies the means "would be the moral equivalent of drop-

---

1949. On September 23 Truman's announcement of an atomic explosion within the Soviet Union signaled, in effect, the end of the American nuclear-power monopoly.

26. Letter to William R. Mathews, March 3, 1949.

27. *Ibid.* Requesting Conant's permission to use part of his paper in a forthcoming speech, Forrestal wrote that he detected "a growth, more among the civilians than the military, of this [preventive war] thesis, and it seems to me it needs to be dealt with."—Letter to Conant, October 16, 1948.

ping atomic bombs on a dozen of our own cities," Conant insisted that

> a Machiavellian foreign policy which would culminate in our launching a surprise attack on the Soviet Union . . . would negate the very premises on which our culture rests.[28]

But while agreeing that preventive war was, in effect, unthinkable, Forrestal, like Conant, was by no means persuaded that Soviet expansionism would be contained short of war. And if war was forced upon us—in Western Europe or the Middle East or Asia—what combination of political, economic, psychological, and military capabilities would enable us to win it? Although he had strong views about the nonmilitary components of victory if war should come, his convictions regarding the purely military requirements were hardly less forceful or intense. As Under Secretary of the Navy in World War II, Forrestal had played a major role in the reorganization of the Navy Department, and thereafter, as Navy Secretary and, later, Secretary of Defense, he devoted an increasing amount of his time to postwar problems of military organization. Long before the enactment of the National Security Act of 1947, which created, at least in theory, a unified National Military Establishment, Forrestal was an active participant in discussions of various Armed Services unification proposals, and the complex questions raised by unification were far from resolved by his own appointment as the Nation's first Secretary of Defense. Nor were these questions resolved by his successors in that post, and indeed they remain unresolved today.[29]

---

28. *The Atlantic Monthly*, January, 1949. Conant added: "Let me make it plain, I am not advocating any policy of appeasement in regard to the present. The whole problem of our strategy for the months immediately ahead is another matter. If the Soviets force us into war by their own actions, that is another story. What I am opposing is the notion that we should precipitate a war a few years hence in order to beat the enemy to the punch in this matter of weapons for mass destruction."

29. On January 3, 1962, a front-page story in *The New York Times* announced that "President Kennedy started reviewing plans today [January 2]

It is tempting to argue, with respect to Forrestal, certain parallels between the Palestine and unification controversies. In the unification dispute he was, once again, a deeply committed man. While the outcome in 1947 was hardly a personal defeat, the early stages of battle over unification, like his opposition to Palestine, were a contributing factor, although for different reasons, in his later illness. In 1948, when he appealed for legislation that would strengthen his position as Defense Secretary, his motives were widely misunderstood. To the rumors and accusations of anti-Semitism and Wall Street favoritism was added the further charge that Forrestal, in supporting amendments to the National Security Act that would have increased his authority, was seeking "dictatorial powers" for himself, and also "conspiring with the administration to throw the country into war without even notifying the Congress.[30] Finally, Forrestal ultimately became convinced that he had been mistaken, but by then it was once more too late to correct what had been said and done. Perhaps the final irony of Forrestal's career was that the administrative difficulties he experienced as Secretary of Defense were due in no small measure to his own influence in shaping the 1947 legislation creating the position.

That influence was first exerted officially in the spring of 1944. Testifying in April and May before a House Select Committee on Postwar Military Policy,[31] Forrestal dealt at

---

for a major reorganization of the Army. One of the plans would give the Secretary of Defense a firmer grip on the Defense Department and cut deeply into the traditional authority and power of the chiefs of most of the technical services. . . ." One can imagine that Forrestal, were he alive, would have read the *Times* story with a wry smile.

30. In a speech to the Senate on January 13, 1949, Senator Harry P. Cain of Washington, referring to "an avalanche of mail" received from his constituents, declared that this "thought was expressed by most of the writers. . . ." Forrestal defended himself against these charges in a lengthy letter to Cain, described by the latter as a "prompt and thorough response [that] speaks for itself." For Cain's remarks and Forrestal's letter see *Congressional Record*, Appendix, January 13, 1949, 118–119.

31. The Select Committee was composed of members of the Committees on Military Affairs and Naval Affairs.

length with a War Department unification plan presented
to the Committee by General Joseph T. McNarney. The
McNarney plan, the first of several proposed by the War
Department, envisaged a single Department of Armed Forces
presided over by a Secretary. The Armed Forces Secretary
was to serve as principal adviser to the President and Congress on political and administrative matters relating to
defense, while the Joint Chiefs of Staff were to function as
advisers to the President with respect to the military budget
and allocation of funds. Under the McNarney proposal each
of the Services—Army, Navy, and Air Force—was to be
headed by an Under Secretary, and there was also to be a
Director of Common Supply Services.

Appearing for ailing Secretary Knox, Forrestal on April
28 declared that the Navy was in complete accord with the
desirability of a close and thorough examination of the
Military Establishment, both as regards military operations
and the procurement of matériel. The present study, however, should be undertaken with special reference to the
problems peculiar to the United States as a consequence of
its geographical position. Other countries with unified military organizations, he noted, such as Germany and the Soviet
Union, did not require a great navy, and there were other
differences as well between the American situation and that
of other countries. These differences and special circumstances, he informed the Committee, made him think there
were "no easy solutions to a problem with so many facets
as this."

Striking an analogy with business operations, Forrestal
observed that some mergers were successful and some were
not. While economies resulting from mergers could and did
produce great savings, the probability of savings was not easy
to transform into reality. There was also the problem of size,
and in this connection he was reminded of a statement by
railroad magnate James J. Hill that "no one man could run

more than 10,000 miles of railroad." Size, moreover, was no guarantee of efficiency. He had learned from experience that the important thing in an organization was to maintain contact with those who really do the work. Business executives of large corporations have difficulty in maintaining such contact, and also in preserving their own vitality and initiative. There is always a danger that they will be swallowed up in the amorphous mass of a vast organization, and hamstrung by the sheer inertia of size.

The Navy, he concluded in his statement, was opposed not only to the creation of a separate Air Service as advocated by the Army but was also opposed to legislation creating a single department of military services. The war year of 1944, he suggested, was not a propitious time for reorganization. Any move in that direction would require the services of Admirals Nimitz, Halsey, Turner, Stark, and Ingersoll, all of whom it would be extremely unwise to call back from their duties. Forrestal, however, hastened to inform the Committee that Naval officers of all grades had been instructed to state their personal views freely and frankly. His own impression, he commented frankly, was that the Committee was not impartial in the matter, since it was conducting hearings as if the case for merger were already established. In any event, he added, the Navy itself had no merger study or plan to propose at that time.

The questions and answers that followed Forrestal's statement mainly illuminated certain points he had made in arguing the case against unification. In reply to a comment stressing similarities in the work performed by the Army and Navy Secretaries, Forrestal emphasized the fact that a unified command would not and should not resolve all problems of duplication. Although he was aware of the possibility, as he told the Committee, that his reply might disturb his relations with Under Secretary of War Patterson, and promote acrimony, he cited two instances to prove his contention that duplication was sometimes very desirable. Friendly competition with the Army, he reminded the Committee, had given the Navy dive bombers, and it was also competition that had produced for the Navy, and later the Army, the air-cooled engine.

In response to a question asking him whether he would create "what we have today" for a "brand new nation with no military establishment," Forrestal declared that he would first want to study what other nations had done, but not with the intention of copying them. A possible result of centralization could be the centralization of errors. Essentially, he reiterated, the job of presiding over a unified military establishment was too big for any one man. The "business of the Navy" in 1944, he continued,

is 28 billion. The business of the Army is in the order of 70 billion. There is no human being capable, in my judgment, of sitting on top of all that and assuring that you have the fine integration and efficiency which it is presumed would result from . . . consolidation.

Three themes were paramount in Forrestal's testimony before the House Select Committee, and two were to remain paramount in his future appearances before congressional committees. The first, the least important and shortest-lived, was that while an examination of the entire military apparatus was justified, such an examination in wartime could only be disruptive. The second was that unification of the Armed Services was neither necessary nor desirable as a means of solving outstanding problems, especially problems of efficiency and economy. The third theme, simply stated, was that unification, if attempted, would not work because there was no one capable "of sitting on top of all that . . ."

The arguments supporting these themes, however, were not entirely those that Forrestal presented to the 1944 House Committee and subsequent committees. As he and other Navy Department officials viewed the early unification proposals, unification was designed less to streamline Pentagon organization than to relegate the Navy to junior status in the military establishment. Under various Army plans, the Navy would cease to be an autonomous Department, and also cease to be represented in the Cabinet. In addition, it would relinquish to the Air Force all its aircraft except seaplanes and carrier-based planes; the Navy would no longer hold basic responsibility for sea reconnaissance, antisubmarine operations, and protection of shipping. Finally, Forrestal anticipated that the choice of Armed Forces Defense Secretary would be influenced far more by the Army than by the Navy, and he therefore concluded that there was little chance that he or any other naval official would be appointed to the position. Doubtful that the Army properly appreciated the importance of the Navy and the role of sea power in modern warfare, he also was convinced that no unification law would be enacted that "would clearly leave the Secretary of the Navy free to run his own Department without kibitzing from above and (at the same time) give the Secretary of National Defense the global authority to make decisions on broad issues."[32]

Yet he knew as early as September, 1944, that he was fighting a delaying action, that in the end there would be some form of unification undertaken, in all probability, at the expense of the Navy. "Incidentally," Forrestal wrote Palmer Hoyt on September 2, 1944, "I would . . . like your views on what you think the public drift is on the single department of defense. I have been telling King, Nimitz and Company it is my judgment that as of today the Navy has lost its case and that, either in Congress or in a public poll the Army's point of view would prevail." Four days later, on September 6, Forrestal in a letter to Nimitz observed that as a result of the skilled use of public relations by the Army and Air Force, public opinion appeared to favor uni-

32. *Diaries*, p. 169.

fication. The Navy's role in the war, he added, was not being emphasized, and he urged on Nimitz the importance of cultivating good relations with newspapermen. Stressing the necessity of the Navy's using all media of communication to present its point of view, he commented that while the Navy was fortunate in having in the White House someone who understands sea power, there was a possibility that he would be replaced by someone who lacked such understanding. But "I may be overestimating the danger." And, "much to my surprise, I receive a good many letters from intelligent people conveying the gentle hint that I have become temporarily at least bereft of my senses in advocating maintenance after the war of a big sea and air power."

Whatever else he may have felt when the news of Roosevelt's death reached Washington, Forrestal was aware that the new President was on record in favor of unification,[33] and during the following months it became clear that almost all of Truman's close advisers shared his view. Generals Marshall, Eisenhower, and MacArthur, among others, endorsed the concept of a unified Defense Establishment, and there were even a few high-ranking naval officers who were not opposed in principle to unification. In an article published in the August, 1943, issue of the *United States Naval Institute Proceedings,* Admiral H. E. Yarnell argued that unity of command in a single Department of War headed by a civilian would be a necessary feature of postwar military organization. To eliminate confusion and waste due to overlapping of planning and procedures, and to rectify the unsatisfactory position of aviation in the policy-making sector, Yarnell proposed the establishment of Army, Navy, and Air branches. The final test of war, he observed, had failed to support the contention that these branches should remain independent. On May 18, 1944, testifying before the House

33. See, for example, Senator Harry S Truman, "Our Armed Forces Must Be Unified," *Collier's,* August 26, 1944.

Select Committee, Yarnell again stated that the one outstanding requirement of the military situation was a greater degree of unification. On that occasion, however, he suggested that the air Service be reorganized as a Strategic Air Force under the Army and Navy.

Despite Forrestal's charge that the position of the Select Committee was not impartial with respect to unification, the June 15, 1944, report of the Committee mainly confined itself to a recommendation that the Joint Chiefs of Staff, established under the emergency war powers of the President, be placed on a statutory, that is, permanent, basis. The report declared that the time was not propitious for any large-scale reorganization of the military structure.

By the end of 1945, four separate unification plans had been proposed, including a plan, based on the so-called Eberstadt Report, introduced by Forrestal himself. One proposal made by a committee of the Joint Chiefs of Staff called for a single Department of Armed Forces under a civilian Secretary. A member of the Joint Chiefs of Staff, the Secretary of the Armed Forces, was to advise the President on the political, economic, and industrial aspects of military problems. Each of the three military Services was to be headed by a military officer who would have autonomy in military operations. There was also to be a Commander of Armed Forces who would serve as Chief of Staff to the President.[34]

Discussion of the Joint Chiefs of Staff unification study produced a second War Department plan, the so-called Collins plan, which was rather similar in nature to its predecessors. Again, there was to be a single Department of Armed Forces under a civilian Secretary, and separate Army, Navy, and Air branches. Of the two chiefs of staff proposed, one was to be responsible for personnel, intelligence, joint train-

---

34. According to a survey made by the Joint Chiefs of Staff Committee, most Army officers and almost half of the Navy officers favored unification.— Senate Committee on Military Affairs, 79th Congress, First Session, *Hearings,* pp. 411ff.

ing, and logistics, and he was to report to the Secretary. The other was to serve as chief of staff to the President, and it was specified that the two chiefs were not to be appointed from the same military service.

Testifying in late 1945 before the Senate Committee on Military Affairs, Forrestal returned to the two themes he had advanced almost eighteen months earlier. The War Department's unification plan, he argued, involved a concentration of power "which I believe is beyond the capacity of any one man to use, and [it is] certainly beyond his capacity to obtain and digest the knowledge [upon which] its use could be based." Holding that a single Defense Secretary would be unable to master his job and, therefore, much of his authority would necessarily fall into the hands of his military advisers, Forrestal stated that the individual chosen for the position "would have authority without knowledge, and authority without knowledge must inevitably become impotent." As a consequence, unification would almost certainly weaken civilian control over the military. He also declared himself opposed to coequal status for the Air Force. Although he was in agreement, he indicated, with General H. H. "Hap" Arnold that the Air Force should not revert to its prewar position, he was not in favor of any proposal that was adverse to the continuation of the Navy's air arm. "You say," he addressed certain members of the Committee, "the preservation of the use of air to the Navy can be guaranteed. You cannot guarantee areas of responsibility to ambitious men when they are assailed by men who quite properly want to exploit their weapons."

The Eberstadt plan, introduced during the course of the hearings, was based on the lengthy report of a committee appointed by Forrestal under the chairmanship of his long-time friend and adviser Ferdinand Eberstadt. The report itself dealt in detail with the War Department proposals, and Forrestal regarded it as a compromise between his own views and those advanced by the Joint Chiefs of Staff. The plan based on the Eberstadt study accepted the case for three coordinate Departments, each presided over by a civilian Secretary aided by an Under Secretary and Assistant Secretary. There was also to be a National Security Council, the chief function of which was to link military and foreign policies. The President was to serve as Chairman of the Council, and its members were to include the Secretaries of State, Army, Navy, and Air, the Chairmen of the National Security Resources Board and Joint Chiefs of Staff, and the Director of the Central Intelligence Agency. The Joint Chiefs of Staff, established on a statutory basis, were to serve as the principal coordinating agency for the three military Departments, and, in addition, they were to advise on problems related to strategy, logistics, and budget. Of the other agencies created or continued under the Eberstadt plan, the most important were the Central Research and Development Agency, the Military Munitions Board, and the Military Education and Training Board.

In Forrestal's view, the Eberstadt plan, reflecting the principle of coordination rather than unification, satisfied all the major requirements of an adequate national security establishment. It provided the organizational means, he testified, for integrating foreign and domestic policies, mobilizing resources, translating strategic requirements into matériel and personnel requirements, coordinating budgets, eliminating waste and duplication, centralizing intelligence services, and fostering scientific research and development. The plan also provided full opportunity for each service to engage in its own specialized task, but not to become so autonomous that it could disregard, for all practical purposes, the requirements and problems of the other Departments concerned with military and foreign policies.

Much of Forrestal's testimony in favor of the Eberstadt plan dealt with the details of organization and especially the specific differences between the Eberstadt or Navy plan and War Department proposals, but in his final statement before the Senate Committee he again set forth the broad principles upon which the Navy had based its case against a single Defense Department. In addition to the fact that unification would be neither necessary nor helpful but, in fact, detrimental to the solution of problems, it was also true, he reminded the Committee, that

one of the most cherished principles of our democracy is that civilian authority shall control military authority. The continuance of separate departments as proposed by the Navy maintains civilian control, by providing each service with a civilian head of Cabinet rank, and by co-ordinating over-all policy making through new civilian organizations. Our democratic government is built on a system of checks and balances. The balance of national security must not be jeopardized by the elimination of a Cabinet officer.

Not long after his final statement Forrestal became the target of certain criticisms alleging misconduct in his role as the chief antiunification spokesman within the Administration. Although he repeatedly declared that naval officers were free to present their personal opinions of unification to congressional committees, there were recurring rumors between 1945 and 1947 that he had "muzzled" certain high-ranking officers, that is, had instructed them not to testify in favor of unification. Those who believed in the rumors cited as supporting evidence statements made in 1944 by Admirals Nimitz and Halsey. On December 8, 1944, testifying before the Joint Chiefs of Staff Committee, Nimitz had declared that he favored

the single department organization . . . I favor a single civilian Secretary of the Armed Forces with a complete elimination of civilian secretaries for Army, Navy and Air Force, with the idea of reducing any tendency to separation . . . it will be better to have a single Commander of Armed Forces who has all the authority and responsibility for issuing a directive.

In support of his position Nimitz stated that he

would like to prevent having a very eloquent, smooth talker for the Navy, for instance, go before a committee, appropriation committee, and persuade them that they should vote more money for this agency or that agency. In other words, continue separatism. I think that we would have a case there of a man who would have responsibility for conducting military operations having too much to say about getting funds.

But on November 7, 1945, appearing before the Senate Military Affairs Committee, Nimitz expressed his opposition to immediate unification. His earlier testimony, he apologized, had not been based on "adequate study." The passage of time and more experience (approximately one year) had convinced him that the proposed merger of the military Services would not achieve more than could be achieved under the existing system. His opinion now was that the establishment of a third, or Air Force, Department would promote "triplication," and he also voiced a fear that the unity of the services might hinder seapower.[35]

Admiral William F. Halsey, like Nimitz, also evidenced a change of attitude when he testified before the Senate Committee, thus increasing suspicions that at the very least strong pressures had been exerted within the Navy Department against those who differed with Forrestal. To the accusations of "muzzling" witnesses[36] was added the further

---

35. In May, 1946, appearing before the Senate Naval Affairs Committee, Nimitz presented still another view of unification. Testifying with reference to the Thomas-May-Austin unification bill, Nimitz declared: "I still believe that there must be established under the President a single civilian official to coordinate the War and Navy Departments and also a Department for the Air Forces established. However, the effectiveness of such an official will be greater if he is free from routinizing administrative responsibilities and is able to devote his attention to the coordination of policy and to resolving major questions and matters on which agreement has not been reached on lower levels." Senate Naval Affairs Committee, 79th Congress, Second Session, *Hearings*, p. 91. But it should be added that by May, 1946, Forrestal's views had also changed to some extent.

36. The "muzzling" allegations were not directed entirely at the Navy. Those in the Navy and elsewhere who opposed unification supplied news-

charge, in November, 1945, that the Navy's presentation of its case had been characterized by dishonesty. In a strong statement to the Senate Committee on November 9, General James Doolittle suggested that there was a good deal of hypocrisy in the Navy's position on the Air Force and on the merger of the Services under a single Secretary of National Defense. In its own interests, he alleged, the Navy wanted to retard the development of air power. The argument that no man could function effectively as Secretary neglected the roles played in the war by General Eisenhower and MacArthur in effecting the large-scale coordination of military activities, not to mention the functions of the President in this regard.

Five months later, following the submission to Congress of a unification measure supported by the Administration, Truman at a press conference issued a statement that was widely interpreted as a scathing criticism of the Navy in general and Forrestal in particular. Attacking opposition to the measure originating within the military Services, Truman on November 11 left the impression with correspondents present that he regarded as closed further discussion of the principle as contrasted with the form of unification. Disturbed by the tone of Truman's remarks, Forrestal arranged a conference with the President on November 17 designed both to communicate to Truman his own position on unification and to explore further the President's thinking on the subject.

In the notes he carefully prepared in advance for the conference, Forrestal emphasized that the points of conflict between the Army and Navy had less to do with the future of naval aviation and the Marine Corps than with differing

---

paper columnists with a number of stories alleging that the War Department was also engaged in "muzzling" activities. In effect, such stories and rumors constituted a type of psychological guerrilla warfare in which both sides freely indulged.

conceptions of the job to be performed by a single Secretary of Defense. The Army, he wrote,

feels that everything will flow once the bill creating a single Secretary and Chief of Staff is passed. We believe it has to be thought through more carefully than that. Navy sees need for continuation in peace of the functions of Byrnes, Vinson and Nelson, an alter ego for the President. The difference is that the Common Secretary under Navy conception would have a small but highly competent staff; that he would not run a department. Army feels that putting him at the head of a department gets the answer.

The Navy's fears quite frankly are: that the Navy's very real fear is that once this bill is passed in its present form, the Navy is merely another arm, and that is the Army intent.[37]

Although Truman neither affirmed nor denied Forrestal's view of the "differences" between the Army and Navy, Forrestal regarded his interview with the President as "most satisfactory." He was in accord, he wrote after the conference, with "the President's wishes that discussion of unification be confined, henceforth, to appearances before congressional committees." According to Forrestal,

The President is not taking sides either for or against the Army or Navy. He simply wishes to get the best organization possible for the national security. I share that wish as, I am sure, do all thinking citizens.

Speaking personally, I am for unification. The form it takes is for the President and Congress to decide, and the Navy is not foreclosed from presenting its view.[38]

Despite his statement that he personally was "for unification," Forrestal did not favor the Administration's own unification proposals of 1945–1946, and his continued opposition to these measures did not rest well with Truman and his immediate entourage. Although the "form" of unification was open to debate, Forrestal's critics did not concede

37. *Diaries*, pp. 151–152.
38. *Ibid.*, p. 152.

that he was able or willing to make a clear distinction between form and substance; many of them were convinced that in supporting a "weak" form of unification, Forrestal was ensuring that there would be no effective unification whatever. Meanwhile, too, the Navy, like the Army, continued to propagandize for its views, and representatives of both Services remained active on Capitol Hill and elsewhere organizing support for their respective positions. What was crucial in the political context, however, was that the Army enjoyed support from the Administration, and from the point of view of both Army and Administration Forrestal was engaged in lobby activities that verged on insubordination.[39]

Well aware of the personal risks involved, Forrestal on several occasions in 1945–1946 expected an imminent White House request for his resignation as Secretary of the Navy. Nevertheless, he continued to insist that coordination rather than unification should be the objective of any major reorganization of the Military Establishment. Testifying with reference to the Administration-supported Thomas-May-Austin unification bill during the spring of 1946, Forrestal once again objected to provisions that would strengthen the positions of a single Secretary of Defense and a single Chief of Staff at the expense of the military departments. The bill under consideration, he told the Senate Naval Affairs Committee, fails to distinguish between the necessity of unified command in a combat area and the very different requirements of planning functions at the seat of government. While planning functions must be coordinated, it was desirable that many minds rather than just one or a few participate in planning decisions. Furthermore, the bill reduced the

---

39. Critics of Forrestal's role in the unification controversy were hardly reassured by newspaper reporting of his position that tended to distort and exaggerate his opposition. Thus, on one occasion, the *New York Herald Tribune* informed its readers that Forrestal "served notice today that the Navy will use every means in its power to defeat a pending merger bill which is backed by the Army and has received a tentative nod of approval from President Truman. . . ." *Diaries*, p. 159.

War and Navy Departments to the status of mere agencies; they are denied Cabinet status and also membership in the proposed Council of Common Defense, the major coordinating organization for foreign and military policies. Forrestal also found that the duties of the new Secretaries of the Army, Navy, and Air Force were, "to put it mildly, somewhat obscure." For example, the jobs of the Navy Secretary and the Assistant Secretary of Defense would apparently overlap, thus creating a confusion of authority.

At one point in his testimony, Forrestal's obvious concern about the role of the Navy Secretary in the new defense organization led to a revealing exchange with Senator Harry Byrd of Virginia. Senator Elbert D. Thomas of Utah, one of the sponsors of the bill, "seemed to think," Byrd remarked,

> that [the service Secretaries] could go direct to the President.
> FORRESTAL: I cannot conceive if the man who was Secretary of Defense were a strong individual—and I would certainly, for the sake of the country, hope he would be—I cannot conceive that he would extend that—.
> BYRD (*interposing*): It would be an act of insubordination, I should think, if he did it.
> FORRESTAL: It would seem so to me.[40]

Forrestal's other major objection to the bill concerned the powers and responsibilities assigned to the Chief of Staff who was to serve as principal adviser on military affairs to the Defense Secretary and President. Stressing the dangers involved in concentrating such authority in the hands of one military man, Forrestal remarked that he mistrusted "the principle of relying on a single genius to make all basic decisions." Although the Chief of Staff would be under the nominal control of the Secretary of Defense, he would be difficult to control because the Secretary would lack the information needed to exercise effective control. "Decisions," he continued,

---

40. Senate Committee of Naval Affairs, 79th Congress, Second Session, *Hearings*, pp. 38ff.

which determine the success or failure of the strategic direction of global war have to be determined by the meeting of a number of minds, each of which contributes its own specialized knowledge, while also serving as a balance and check on the others. This is the system which has worked so well under the Joint Chiefs of Staff. It is a safeguard against the mistakes which can be made by one man acting unilaterally . . . to emasculate and destroy that instrument—the Joint Chiefs of Staff—which has worked in this war, is something we ought to think about very, very carefully before we substitute, as I say, this single mind of a single genius to take its place.

In concluding his testimony on the Thomas-May-Austin bill, Forrestal urged that the "Director of Common Defense" —or Secretary of Defense, if that was more desirable—should perform duties mainly of a coordinating and staff character. In addition to his authority to determine procurement and budget policies, he should be able to insist on coordination and cooperation but not be able to function, in any sense, as a military overlord. The military Services, he reiterated, should retain their Cabinet status, and also be given membership in the Council of Common Defense.

Even before the hearings on the Thomas-May-Austin bill, it was clear that no form of unification could succeed unless the outstanding points of difference between the Army and Navy were somehow compromised. Since January both Patterson and Forrestal had been under heavy pressure from a variety of sources to achieve some consensus of views upon which legislation could be based.[41] Truman had instructed the two Secretaries to meet to resolve their differences, and

----

41. In addition to pressure emanating from the Administration and Congress, friends of both men, disturbed by the possible effects of the controversy upon their personal relationship, urged them to make every effort to reach an agreement. On January 17 Forrestal received the first of several telephone calls from Mrs. Robert Patterson pleading with him to support her husband's position on unification. Disturbed on that occasion by a David Lawrence column in the Washington *Star* calling for the reorganization of the War Department, Mrs. Patterson complained that there was altogether too much bickering between the Army and Navy. With this Forrestal agreed, but he did not commit himself to the support of Patterson's point of view.

between January and May there were a number of Patterson-
Forrestal conferences devoted entirely to discussions of uni-
fication. Little progress toward agreement had been made,
however, and on May 13 Truman convened a White House
meeting of all those concerned, including in addition to
Patterson and Forrestal, Generals Leahy, Spaatz, Handy,
Norstad, and Vaughan, Admirals Nimitz and Sherman,
Captain Frank C. Nash (Forrestal's special assistant), and
Attorney General Clark. In the course of the discussion
Patterson, according to Forrestal's notes, said that

he and I had tried to get together several months previously but
had been unable to do so, partly, at least, because he had felt so
strongly on some of the points at issue. Patterson added that he
still felt the greatest efficiency would be obtained by the formation of a single Department, with a single Secretary and a single
Chief of Staff. As to the latter, however, he said he was not prepared to "jump into the ditch and die for the idea."[42]

In response to a request from Truman, Patterson and Forrestal expressed a willingness to make another effort, and to
submit a report on that effort by May 31.

Their report of that date to the President suggested that
Forrestal, "when it was necessary, *was* ready to 'jump into
the ditch'" to defend principles he regarded as of crucial
importance.[43] The major areas of agreement specified in the
report revealed that Patterson had made at least two significant concessions to Forrestal's position. Both Secretaries, for

---

42. *Diaries*, p. 161.
43. Millis in *Diaries*, p. 162. In Millis's view, Forrestal "*was* ready to
'jump into the ditch,' as subsequent events were to prove, because he knew
that he stood on principles that were firmly based in study and analysis.
If in the end Forrestal was largely the winner in the unification fight, it was
because he had thought more deeply, because he had enlisted Eberstadt and
others to think for him, because he had looked at the real and central
problems involved rather than accepted quick solutions which under the test
of time and events could not stand." Insofar as this interpretation implies
that the Army's proposals were not "firmly based in study and analysis," and
also implies that Forrestal's solution stood "the test of time and events,"
it is rather difficult to sustain in the light of later developments.

example, were now agreed that the Council of Common Defense, which was to integrate foreign and military policies, should include the civilian heads of the services as well as the Defense Secretary. Patterson also joined Forrestal in opposing the appointment of a single military Chief of Staff—the "single genius" to whom Forrestal had referred earlier.

They were still unable to agree, however, on the organization and functions of the proposed Department of Common Defense. Patterson, while conceding that the three Service heads should have access to the President, remained opposed to giving them Cabinet rank, whereas Forrestal continued to insist that each military Department should be represented in the Cabinet. There were also differences with respect to air organization, both Army and Navy, and the functions to be performed by the Marine Corps.

In a letter to Patterson and Forrestal on June 15, Truman took note of the progress that had been made toward agreement, and indicated his acceptance of their most important joint recommendations. The three Services, he emphasized, would have equal status in the Defense Establishment, and be represented on the Common Defense Council, but they would not hold Cabinet rank. The Air Force would have major responsibility for military air operations with the exception of ship, carrier, and water-based aircraft essential to the Navy and Marines, land-based aircraft necessary for the Navy's internal administration and for patrolling routes of sole interest to the Navy, and land-based aircraft employed in training; Air Force personnel, however, would be used in conjunction with Naval reconnaissance and antisubmarine missions.

Forrestal's reply to Truman on June 24 reflected his feeling that the President had been won over to the Navy's conception of the role of Defense Secretary. "Your principal objectives," Forrestal wrote, "are . . . creation of a single department of national defense under a civilian head with broad powers of overall supervision and control, while leaving full administration of respective services to Secretaries of War, Navy and Air." Referring to the "preservation of [the Navy's] integrity, autonomy . . . [and] morale," Forrestal stated that he regarded the "obtainable and recognized difficulties" involved in unification as "surmountable."

Although the exchange of letters between Truman, Patterson, and Forrestal resulted in an amended Thomas-May-Austin bill, Forrestal, still dissatisfied with the measure, insisted in July that an entirely new approach was required. The amended bill, he wrote Navy Under Secretary W. John Kenney on July 5, does not rectify "numerous basic defects of organization," and he added that it seemed to him "utterly impossible to incorporate directives of the President's plan into the framework of the Thomas bill." Whether or not he was correct in this view, his opposition to the bill, combined with opposition in both the Senate and House, ensured that no unification measure would be enacted in 1946 despite the urgent need, in terms of the international situation, to resolve the controversy.

On January 15, 1947, Patterson and Forrestal addressed a second joint letter to the President enclosing a draft of a proposed Executive order defining the functions of each military Service. Noting that "the necessity for agreement between the military Services is now even greater than at the time of our earlier letter," the two Secretaries announced that they had "agreed on the following points and will support legislation in which they are incorporated. . . ." The points specified included the establishment of a "Council of National Defense, a National Security Resources Board and a Central Intelligence Agency (which already exists) . . ." The Armed Forces, the letter continued,

shall be organized under a Secretary of National Defense so as to place the Army, the Navy (to include the Marine Corps and Naval Aviation), and the Air Force, each with a military chief, under the Departments of the Army, the Navy, and the Air Force respectively. Each shall be under a Secretary and, under the overall direction of the Secretary of National Defense, shall be administered as an individual unit. The Secretary of any of the three departments may, at any time, present to the President, after first informing the Secretary of National Defense, any report or recommendation relating to his department which he may deem necessary or desirable.

Urging, in addition, the creation of a War Council and a Joint Chiefs of Staff, the latter to be aided by a staff consisting "initially of not over 100 officers" provided in equal numbers by the three Services, Patterson and Forrestal devoted one paragraph of their letter to the functions of the Secretary of National Defense. The Defense Secretary, they agreed,

shall head the armed forces establishment, shall be vested with authority, under the President, to establish common policies and common programs for the integrated operation of the three departments and shall exercise control over and direct their common efforts to discharge their responsibility for national security.

With the Patterson-Forrestal letter of January 15 the unification controversy entered upon its last phase. Despite some efforts to revive earlier Army proposals,[44] the Senate and House committees that met in the spring and early summer of 1947 had before them in Senate bill 758 a measure of which Patterson and Forrestal approved. In Forrestal's view, S. 758 provided not only for the "coordination of the three armed services, but what is to me even more important

---

44. In April, 1947, testifying before the Senate Armed Services Committee, Army Under Secretary Royall and General Eisenhower expressed certain reservations regarding the roles assigned to the Navy Air Corps and Marine Corps in the proposed unification plan. Royall also recommended that the new Defense Secretary be given power to alter the duties and functions of the three Services, and Eisenhower expressed regret that there was not to be a single Chief of Staff. Forrestal was extremely irked by their statements, but he was even more disturbed when the Navy's budget requests were sharply revised downward, first by Truman in accordance with Budget Bureau advice, and second by Representative John Taber of the House Appropriations Committee.

than that, it provides for the integration of foreign policy
with national policy, of our civilian economy with military
requirements . . . continuing review of our raw material
needs and . . . continued advance in the field of research and
applied science." The bill under consideration, he commented to the Senate Committee,

makes it quite definite that each department shall be administered as an individual unit by a Secretary who shall have the
right of appeal to the President. We have the assurance of uniform policy for all services with the Secretary of National Defense
supervising and controlling while each individual service under
its Secretary remains autonomous with respect to internal administration. This is a matter upon which the Navy Department
has had a strong conviction and which I have come to share
through experience.

Reiterating his frequently stated opinion that "there is a
definite limit to the size of an administrative unit which can
be successfully directed by any one man," he observed that

[f]or a single man actively to administer an organization of much
greater size than the Navy itself would require a period of years
during which he would be, in effect, a novice. In fact, there is
some doubt in my mind that any man—and bear in mind that the
tenure of office of the average Secretary of the Army or Navy has
been on the order of 2½ years, and I think the average of the
Navy is somewhat less than that—in any reasonable length of
time would be capable of learning enough of the details necessary
to efficient administration of an organization on the scale of a
single department of war.

The new Secretaryship, Forrestal thought, combined "a
melange of functions having many different kinds of businesses," and in a statement even more revealing of his concept of the Defense Secretary as an essentially coordinating
official he expressed the view that the creation of the National Security Council "is perhaps the most important
feature of the bill now under consideration."

In response to questions from Committee members,

Forrestal made it clear that, in his judgment, the Defense Secretary would lack power, as Senator Bridges put it, to "destroy the autonomy or independence of the Navy or its component parts." Denying that the Secretary could "virtually put out of business . . . the Naval Air Force or the Marine Corps," Forrestal drew attention to

the checks and balances [that] still exist in Congress and in the right of the Secretary of this particular Department to appeal to the President, a fact which I think would not be unknown to the Congress, even assuming that he was a man who did not indulge in the habit or practice of letting it leak out that he had certain reservations.

"But," asked Senator Byrd, "you are depending upon the Congress in the future then? The protection is not in this bill?" Answering Byrd, Forrestal again emphasized that the "protection" was "dependent on all those checks and balances, such as the right to appeal to the President, from which I assume would flow the right of discussion in the Cabinet."[45]

Appearing in behalf of the House version of S. 758, or H.R. 2319, Forrestal again stressed the "checks and balances" operating in relation to the powers of the Secretary of Defense. In the first place, he reminded the House Committee on Expenditures in the Executive Departments, the essential power of the Defense Secretary was delegated to him by the President. Second, the three Service Secretaries enjoyed the right of appeal to the President. Third, Congress could call on any Secretary to appear before it. Noting that the new defense organization would depend upon the "closest harmony and confidence" between the four Secretaries, Forrestal added in a moment of prescience, "There will be no room for friction and, if it occurs, disaster could be the result."[46]

---

45. Senate Committee on Armed Services, 80th Congress, 1st Session, *Hearings*, pp. 2ff.
46. House Committee on Expenditures in the Executive Departments, 80th Congress, 1st Session, *Hearings*, pp. 93ff. There was much discussion

The future was to demonstrate, of course, that there was ample "room for friction" in the new Defense Establishment, but on July 26, 1947, when S. 758 was signed into law, Forrestal was entitled to feel that he had won a significant victory. The National Security Act of 1947, in accordance with his recommendations, established a National Security Council composed of the President, the Secretary of State, the Secretary of Defense, and the three Service Secretaries, among others. There were also created or continued under the Act a Central Intelligence Agency, a National Security Resources Board, a War Council, a Joint Chiefs of Staff Organization, a Munitions Board, and a Research and Development Board. The Act further provided that the Secretary of Defense, who was to head the new National Military Establishment, "shall perform" the following duties:

(1) Establish general policies and programs for the National Military Establishment and for all of the departments and agencies therein;

(2) Exercise general direction, authority, and control over such departments and agencies;

(3) Take appropriate steps to eliminate unnecessary duplication or overlapping in the fields of procurement, supply, transportation, storage, health, and research;

(4) Supervise and coordinate the preparation of the budget estimates of the departments and agencies comprising the National Military Establishment; formulate and determine the budget estimates for submittal to the Bureau of the Budget; and

---

during these hearings of the alleged "muzzling" engaged in by both the War and Navy Departments. In response to questions, Patterson and Forrestal denied such allegations. When Representative Porter Hardy of the Committee stated that a Navy officer whom he had asked to testify had refused to do so for fear of reprisals, Forrestal questioned the motives of the unnamed officer in making such a remark. He also expressed doubt that some 80 percent of Navy officers were opposed to the bill, thus taking issue with a statement attributed by Hardy to a high-ranking naval officer. In an effort to relieve the suspicions of Hardy and other Committee members, Forrestal on June 27 officially waived two naval regulations requiring officers to clear with the Department all communications to Congress.

supervise the budget programs of such departments and agencies under the applicable appropriation Act.

In addition to giving each Service Secretary the right to appeal to the President, the Act specified that each Service Department

shall be administered as individual executive departments by their respective Secretaries and all powers and duties relating to such departments not specifically conferred upon the Secretary of Defense by this Act shall be retained by each of their repective Secretaries.

Although a Department of the Air Force was established, naval aviation, assigned to the Department of the Navy, was as broadly defined as Forrestal insisted it be, and the Marine Corps was formally included within the Navy Department. Truly, as Hanson W. Baldwin later commented in *The New York Times*, the position of Secretary of Defense was "fashioned in [Forrestal's] own image,"[47] and it is hardly an exaggeration to add that the national Military Establishment was created, almost in its entirety, in accordance with Forrestal's views.

It was also on July 26 that Forrestal was nominated to be the nation's first Secretary of Defense. Yet Forrestal, rarely by nature self-congratulatory, was in no mood to celebrate when news reached him early in the morning of July 27 that his appointment had been confirmed by the Senate. Having played a major part in the creation of the new Defense Establishment, he was now entrusted with the job of running it, the job, he had frequently stated, "that was too big for any one man." Perhaps he intuitively felt on the morning of July 27 not so much that the job was "too big" but that it combined too much coordination with too little control, and too much responsibility with too little power.

---

47. "Big Boss of the Pentagon," *The New York Times Magazine*, August 29, 1948, p. 9.

The post of Defense Secretary *had* been created in his own image, and perhaps he sensed on the day of his appointment it was an image that would return, again and again, to mock him in his efforts to formulate policy for the National Military Establishment.

VII

☆ ☆ ☆ ☆ ☆

"Victim of the Washington Scene"

FORRESTAL'S APPOINTMENT as Secretary of Defense, like his earlier promotion to Secretary of the Navy, won general approval even from those who had no special reason to think well of the Truman Administration. Although it was known in some quarters that Patterson and not Forrestal had been Truman's first choice,[1] Republican and Democratic newspapers agreed that Forrestal was the obvious candidate for the job of implementing the National Security Act. With the exception of criticisms emanating from certain liberal and left-wing circles, a small number of columnists, and such magazines as *The Nation* and *The New Republic,* the articulated opinion of most Americans was that Forrestal's elevation to Defense Secretary was, as one of his admirers wrote him, "a fine thing for the country and for the Armed Services."[2] *Newsweek* quoted with ap-

---

1. Patterson, who declined the position "for personal and business reasons," resigned as Secretary of War in July, 1947.

2. "It is most important," the letter continued, "that the original program and policies be correctly planned, because they will inevitably set the pattern for the future. It was wonderful that you were willing to undertake this job and a grand thing for the Navy, because I fear that too many people have forgotten the tremendous importance of a first-class Navy for our defense." In his reply Forrestal noted, "I took this job largely for the reasons which you indicate. . . ."

proval an admiral's comment that Forrestal was "the toughest, smartest, finest guy we've got in government today,"[3]
and *U.S. News & World Report,* looking even further than
the Defense Department, suggested that

> Mr. Forrestal may have a political future ahead of him. Re-
> portedly, President Truman would like his new Secretary of
> Defense to run with him as vice-presidential candidate on next
> year's Democratic ticket.[4]

The New York Times of July 27, hailing the appointment,
declared that the selection of anyone else would have im-
peded the progress of unification. Forrestal enjoyed the confidence, according to the *Times,* of all military services.

The congratulatory letters, notes, and phone calls that
Forrestal received during the summer of 1947 struck a variety of chords,[5] but all of them found him in a cautious
mood regarding his new responsibilities. "This office," he
wrote playwright Robert Sherwood on August 27, "will
probably be the greatest cemetery for dead cats in history,"[6]
and in a letter to another acquaintance early in August,
thanking him for his "note and good wishes," Forrestal included the somewhat prophetic comment, "I shall certainly
need the latter—and probably the combined attention of
Fulton Sheen and the entire psychiatric profession by the
end of another year."[7] To his attorney Walter Dunnington

---

3. July 28, 1947.

4. September 5, 1947. The future was to demonstrate, of course, that this
prediction was no more accurate than an earlier *U.S. News* forecast of December 28, 1945, that Forrestal would resign as Navy Secretary because Truman
had rejected his ideas about unification. In its column "Washington
Whispers," the magazine reported that Edwin L. Pauley would probably
succeed Forrestal.

5. The only message that he included in his private papers as distinct from
office files was from Myron C. Taylor, the President's personal representative at the Vatican. "Congratulations on another great honor," it read, ". . .
stepping stones in a great career. May this one lead to world peace. If that
is impossible, then to effective war and enduring peace in timely sequence."—
Diaries, p. 299.

6. *Ibid.*

7. *Diaries,* p. 300.

he expressed the "hope" in late July that "it is patriotism and not egoism that makes me continue in this life—one never can be sure. Of one thing I am sure, however, and that is that this is my final contribution. At the end of the year both the Army and the country will be grateful for that."[8]

The reference to "my final contribution" was a familiar one, and because it was familiar neither his friends nor his associates were inclined to take it very seriously. As early as September 12, 1944, Forrestal had forthrightly declared to a friend, "[t]here isn't the slightest chance of my becoming a permanent public ham—I am going to be out of this joint as soon as my conscience lets me."[9]

Following the 1944 election Forrestal, in accordance with custom, handed Roosevelt an undated resignation statement "in the event it was wanted," and on April 13, 1945, when Truman succeeded Roosevelt, he again submitted an undated resignation. Asked by newspapermen in September, 1945, how much longer he expected to remain as Navy Secretary, Forrestal told them, "You can say so long as the President wishes me to stay, up to a limit of six months." In Miami, Florida, on January 2, 1946, Forrestal informed press representatives that he planned to resign "some time this year . . . the President knows that I want to get out. I'm no believer in the indispensability of one man."[10] When in February, 1947, Palmer Hoyt informed Forrestal that his newspaper, the *Denver Post,* would back him for the Defense Secretaryship, Forrestal advised Hoyt to "[l]ay off that idea of keeping me as a bureaucrat. If I don't get out of here I will

---

8. *Ibid.*
9. Letter to William S. Charnley, *Diaries,* p. 15.
10. *The New York Times* and *Washington Evening Star,* January 3, 1946. "President Truman," the *Times* story continued, "reported at a December press conference that the Secretary [of the Navy] had been trying to resign ever since his administration went into office, but he hoped that Mr. Forrestal would not resign at an early date . . . that the Secretary would continue in the job for some time to come."

become one, God forbid, and I will have ulcers both of the stomach and of the balance sheet."

By August, 1948, Forrestal was coming to the end of his first year as Secretary of Defense, and in numerous conversations and letters to friends he stressed that "by next January I will have finished 8½ years in this town and that will have been enough."[11] To Edward H. Little, President of the Colgate-Palmolive-Peet Company, he wrote on August 7 that he accepted and appreciated "the compliment implied in your hope that I'll continue beyond the end of this year—but both for the sake of the country and for myself I assure you that would not be wise and, under no circumstances, could I be induced to continue." In reply to an invitation to visit from Robert Matter, Forrestal declined owing to pressure of work but "[w]hen I wind up this 8½ year sentence," he added, "I will certainly be out to see you."[12] Writing to another friend on August 26, Forrestal observed, "I see at last the end of a long road as far as I am concerned but it looks, however, as if the closing months are going to be the toughest."[13] On September 13 Forrestal confided to Sidney C. Crawford, "I appreciate what you say about remaining on here, but by the end of this year I think I will have come to the end of the reservoirs of energy which you talk about." Not long after the November, 1948, election Forrestal, again in accordance with custom, submitted his resignation, and this time he believed that it would be accepted.

He was delighted to discover, however, that Truman wanted him to continue as Secretary of Defense. Although his "reservoirs of energy" were exhausted and he was already manifesting signs of serious illness, Forrestal, always an ambitious man, was too involved in his job and too absorbed by

---

11. Letter to Samuel A. Perkins, August 2, 1948.
12. Letter to Matter, August 18, 1948.
13. Letter to Edward J. Bermingham, August 26, 1948.

the Washington atmosphere to contemplate retirement seriously. Asked by reporters on January 11 whether he wanted to continue, and expected to continue, as Secretary of Defense, Forrestal replied succinctly, "Yes. I am a victim of the Washington scene."[14]

He was, in fact, "a victim of the Washington scene" almost from the beginning of his governmental career.[15] Despite the repeated denials to friends that he was temperamentally or in any other way qualified to be either a bureaucrat or a politician, Forrestal, like many another "reluctant candidate" for office, savored the rewards that come with power and prestige. A deeply committed man in the global struggle that was being waged, and still is being waged, against Communism, he consistently sought opportunities decisively to shape foreign, military, and domestic policies in the direction he regarded as essential to national security. The three major promotions he received in seven years afforded him ever larger scope for the play of ambition and influence, and when he became Secretary of Defense he was well aware that he held formal power that was second only to that of the President and Secretary of State. He also knew that if he was an outstanding success as Defense Secretary, there was the possibility of a still higher office in the government, namely, the White House itself.

Forrestal's political ambitions, including presidential ambitions, did not develop suddenly in 1947, or even in 1945 when he succeeded Knox as Secretary of the Navy. Late in 1944, Forrestal in a conversation with a friend deplored the tendency of businessmen to take little or no interest in political careers, and to assume that government and politics can

---

14. *Diaries*, p. 544.
15. His Washington colleagues were always conscious of the fact that, in the words of one: "Jim always said he wanted to get out of the government, but basically he didn't at all. He loved the government and he loved politics, although he wouldn't admit to being a politician. He loved every minute of it, and I never took him seriously when he said he wanted to leave."

somehow be kept separate and distinct.[16] When the friend inquired whether Forrestal's own plans included seeking the Presidency at a later date, Forrestal took the position that as a "renegade" Catholic he could hardly regard himself as a serious candidate for any high political office. But on March 4, 1945, Forrestal included in his private papers the following memorandum:

Specifications for a Presidential Candidate
1. Looks.
2. Height.
3. Legal or political background.
4. Desire for the job.
5. Political experience.

Although it is not clear what prompted the note, or "of whom or of what he was thinking,"[17] Forrestal significantly did not include religion among his "Specifications."

In the spring of 1945, Forrestal, a close associate recalls,

started taking an interest in activities outside the [Navy] Department, which is always fatal. He became close to a number of Senators and was increasingly politically inclined. When we had lunch together, which was often, there were always two or three political characters hanging around.

There was talk during the summer that Forrestal might be available for the Democratic gubernatorial nomination in New York, and in September, Forrestal was asked directly whether he was willing to become a candidate. On September 12 he wrote Frank A. Hart that he was "grateful" for Hart's interest

---

16. "My answer," he wrote William Gaston on October 4, 1948, "which has now become a bromide with me, is that you can no more divorce government from politics than you can separate sex from creation."—*Diaries*, p. 495. A "willingness to take the rap of running for office," he observed, "is, after all, the acid test of whether many of us mean what we say when we talk about 'taking an interest in government.' "

17. Millis in *Diaries*, pp. 32–33.

in what is supposedly to be my candidacy for the Governorship of New York State. The only difficulty is that I am not a candidate; I am not thinking beyond the period of my service in the Navy.

His letter to Hart, however, did not rule out the possibility, and on September 14 a *New York Times* story reported that New York State Democratic Chairman Paul Fitzpatrick had named Forrestal along with James M. Mead, Robert H. Jackson, and Oscar R. Ewing as potential candidates for the nomination.

In his *Times* column of October 28, 1945, Forrestal's long-time friend Arthur Krock discussed at some length Forrestal's qualifications for political office. Krock, who always enjoyed Forrestal's confidence and whose relationship with Forrestal stretched all the way back to their Cottage Club days at Princeton, authoritatively commented that Forrestal's name was being mentioned with increasing frequency in political circles. Democratic Party leaders, he noted, were thinking of Forrestal as someone who could block Henry Wallace's presidential aspirations in 1948. Should Truman not be a contender, it was probable that the CIO would attempt to nominate Wallace, or, if Truman became the candidate, push Wallace for the Vice-Presidency. Those who defeated Wallace in 1944, Krock continued, were searching for an alternative nominee, and they were more and more glancing in Forrestal's direction.

Krock made it clear, at least indirectly, that Forrestal's personal and political qualifications were substantial. Arguing that Forrestal had rid himself of the "Wall Street man" stigma, Krock maintained that he had impressed almost everyone with his "forceful" manner and conspicuous abilities. Forrestal had not only won the respect of officials, newspapermen, and national leaders; he had also impressed the Navy with his personality, athletic good looks, and personal courage; when Forrestal had "hit the beaches" with the Marines at Iwo Jima, Krock recalled, he had been motivated by a desire to understand better the Navy's problems and also to satisfy a conscience that was burdened by the responsibility of sending millions of men to possible death. Intellectuals were attracted by the depth and scope of his reading and his thoughtful, cultivated mind. Even radicals, inclined to denounce his Wall Street background, admired his intelligence. Finally, Krock observed, movie audiences were giving him more applause than almost any other public figure when his "diffident" image appeared on the screen. As a result, politicians, anticipating his early retirement as Navy Secretary, were talking of Senate as well as gubernatorial prospects, both of which would mature before the 1948 presidential election. Forrestal himself, Krock conceded, puts little stock in such talk, but a good many others take a serious interest in his political future.

Three days later, on October 31, the *Times* again referred to Forrestal as a possible candidate for the New York governorship, and on January 21, 1946, Justice Douglas suggested to Forrestal that he

have a definite stand on either the New York State governor or Senate nomination next autumn. He said he felt confident that I could get either. I told him that I had concluded to get out of public life and stay out when I had quit as Secretary of the Navy. He strongly urged that I reconsider, which I said I would, but added that I felt that my conclusion would be the same.

Douglas, according to Forrestal, believed that he "could undoubtedly get the nomination for the Senate, and with reasonable chances of success," if he declined to be a candidate for governor.[18] In a letter to Thomas P. Durell of January 24, Forrestal indicated that he was giving active consideration to his candidacy in the coming New York gubernatorial contest.

When it became clear, during the following months, that the Democratic Party in New York was far from united on a

---

18. *Diaries*, p. 130.

candidate for either the governorship or the Senate, Forrestal declined to place himself in the running. Following the party's choice of Herbert H. Lehman as its nominee for the Senate, Forrestal agreed to serve as one of the twelve honorary chairmen of the Independent Citizens Committee organized in Lehman's behalf.[19] Meanwhile, there were recurrent rumors that Forrestal was being considered for a variety of other posts, political and nonpolitical. On May 26, 1946, the *Times* reported that he might accept the position of first president of the International Bank of Reconstruction and Development,[20] and another story of February 7, 1947, mentioned Forrestal as one of several possible successors to the deceased Ambassador to Great Britain, O. Max Gardner.

In 1947 there was again talk of Forrestal as Truman's running mate the following year, and for some months Forrestal did little to discourage such speculation. During March and April he met frequently with Democratic Party politicians, and in May he attended a New York State Democratic Committee dinner honoring William O'Dwyer, Mayor of New York City. His address to the gathering at the Commodore Hotel on May 26 afforded him an opportunity to identify himself with the principles and traditions of the Democratic Party, and to express his own views about government and the political process. He was also eager to remove from the minds of his audience any lurking suspicion that he was a conservative businessman who distrusted politicians, and in his speech he invoked the names of a large number of political leaders, living and dead, whose names were familiar to his listeners. The life of Mayor O'Dwyer, with its "progress from deck-hand to policeman . . . to Mayor

---

19. The Democratic gubernatorial candidate in 1946, James M. Mead, was defeated by Thomas E. Dewey.

20. Forrestal, the *Times* noted, was the candidate supported by Edward E. Brown, president of Chicago's First National Bank and a member of the American delegation to the 1944 Bretton Woods Conference. Brown himself had been put forward for the position by Treasury Secretary Fred Vinson, but had declined for reasons of health.

and Chief Magistrate" testified not only to the "vitality of
American democracy," but reminded him of that other "great
New Yorker and great American, Alfred E. Smith." Stressing
that there were "Bill O'Dwyers in every city and town and
county of the United States" of which America could be
proud, Forrestal also made favorable references to several
Tammany Hall chieftains of the past and present, including
Bourke Cochran, Thomas Grady, and James Farley. His
"own inherited Democratic membership," he informed his
listeners,

was cemented by my admiration for two of its greatest leaders—
Woodrow Wilson and Alfred E. Smith, for whom I know Franklin Roosevelt had the same admiration and respect. Their names,
with those of Jefferson, Monroe, Madison, Grover Cleveland and
Newton Baker illustrate the diversity of appeal and the variety of
thought which have attracted me to the [Democratic] Party.

Noting that the Democratic Party was home to a variety
of social and economic philosophies, Forrestal praised the
diversity of views represented. Although it was not true that
"all Southern Democrats are reactionary and all Northern
urban Democrats are radicals," the differences that did exist
constituted an asset rather than a liability. "The essence of
democratic government," he suggested, "is to provide every
group in our system a fair chance for expression," and it
was the "genius" of President Truman that

By voice and deed he has demonstrated his deep belief in the
right of every man to express his opinions. It is a distinguishing
feature of his relations with his Cabinet and with the present
majority party in the House and Senate. There is no political
subtlety or smartness in the President's effort to cooperate with
the Republican Congress. He knows that the problems of the
world are too deep and too serious to be dealt with on the level
of domestic partisan politics.

Turning to his own political convictions, Forrestal declared that he believed "deeply and strongly" in

what we may call democratic capitalism . . . a system dedicated to the idea that the welfare of the country is better secured through the exercise of individual initiative and effort than it could be by a state-owned economy administered through a vast and complex bureaucracy.

Such a system entailed cooperation rather than conflict between capital and labor, and Forrestal indicated that he had considerable sympathy for the labor movement. "No group in our community," he insisted,

has a greater share in meeting and overcoming the great difficulties of the post-war world than American labor. At the moment the tide of popular sentiment seems to be running against labor and particularly against the leaders of labor. I would like to recall to businessmen that a little over a decade ago the tide was running sharply against business and its leaders.

His own knowledge of labor and labor leaders enabled him to testify that

most leaders of labor are neither Communists nor Socialists. Many of them realize the need of adjustments to rectify existing imbalances in labor laws. Bitterness against all labor and all labor leaders as a group is just as dangerous, just as unfair as the tendency fifteen years ago to smear all business and all management. Indicting fellow Americans by groups is the negation of democracy, for ours is a classless society in fact, not by empty boast.

In the final analysis, Forrestal added,

We are all workers. We are all consumers. We are all investors, not merely in real estate and securities but in the future of America.

While the success of American democratic capitalism was the ultimate guarantee of its continuance, there was also need to

send the spiritual message which is our real and greatest answer to the preachers of the doctrine of the economic and soulless man.

I know of no better expression of such a faith than a quotation which I read last week from a hitherto unpublished essay of Woodrow Wilson: "There is one thing I have a great enthusiasm about, I might almost say a reckless enthusiasm, and that is human liberty. The individual is indispensably the original, the first fact, of liberty. *There is no such thing as corporate liberty.* Liberty belongs to the individual or it does not exist."

Forrestal's speech of May 26, designed to appeal to a broad section of the Democratic Party, was widely interpreted as evidence of his political availability for the 1948 election. *Time* magazine of August 25 reported that Forrestal, on the assumption that Democratic victory prospects in 1948 were improving, had been requesting relatives to send him snapshots and clippings with which to bring the family album up to date. By November, 1947, however, Forrestal concluded, as did many others, that barring a miracle Truman would be defeated in 1948 either by Senator Taft or Governor Dewey. He was also convinced by that time that the reorganization of the Democratic Party following Truman's defeat would strengthen his own position with respect to the party's presidential nomination in 1952.[21] The ascendancy of the conservative wing of the party, he and some of his friends believed, would inevitably accompany that reorganization, and in that event he would become a leading contender for the nomination. He therefore told Truman on November 12 that he would like to make a statement saying that "under no circumstances" would he accept the vice-presidential nomination,[22] and early in December he de-

---

21. According to Lewis L. Strauss, Forrestal had decided even before the end of World War II "not to go back to Wall Street. Politics began to attract him. . . . Had Forrestal lived, there is the possibility that he might have been General Eisenhower's opponent in 1952. He denied ambition for the presidency . . . [but] I am convinced that the same considerations which persuaded him to accept appointment as the first Secretary of Defense would have led him to the nomination. . . ."—*Men and Decisions* (Garden City, N.Y.: Doubleday and Company, 1962), pp. 156–157.

22. *Diaries,* p. 343.

clared at a press conference that he was unable to "combine the executive functions" of his office "with political by-products or thinking." For that reason, he told reporters, "I will never become involved in political matters, and, therefore, I can never be considered a candidate for a political office."

Those who knew Forrestal were not inclined to take this and similar statements very seriously, and well into 1948 there was continuing talk in Washington and elsewhere of Forrestal's political availability. Such discussion was largely inspired, of course, by Forrestal's outstanding performance in the several posts he had held since 1940. Clearly, he worked at his jobs harder and longer and with more dedication than almost anyone else in the government service. He had long been associated with a "tough" policy toward the Soviet Union and international Communism, and this association won him the respect of that numerous circle of critics who regarded both Roosevelt and Truman as, in one respect or another, "soft on Communism." In addition, Forrestal's personality had about it something of a charismatic quality. His impressive knowledge of world affairs, his seeming certainty about issues that other men found complex and even confusing, his sense of humor and personal charm—these qualities drew many to him. And there was something more. Forrestal's physical presence exerted an almost magnetic attraction to which most men and women he met found it difficult not to respond. Although not a tall man, he appeared tall, and although not particularly robust he struck others as strong and powerful. The way he carried himself, together with the broken nose, tight mouth, and piercing eyes produced an impression, as Jonathan Daniels once observed, of "a quiet, animal quality about his apparent physical perfection." His "carriage," Daniels wrote when Forrestal was still Navy Secretary, was that "which the movies give dramatically to better gangsters," and in addition to its being "swift" and "easy," there was "the suggestion of the possibility of violence and the surface of perfectly contained restraint."[23]

The word most often chosen by friends and associates to describe Forrestal's appearance is the word "tough," and certainly there was about Forrestal, at least on the surface, a good deal that was "tough." With certain exceptions to be noted, his sense of humor, reflected in the jokes and stories he enjoyed most, was dry, sardonic, often cynical and ironic. The anecdotes especially were usually intended to make a point that related either to the inherent limitations of human nature, including his own, or the capriciousness of fate, history, or events. He would often preface his speeches, for example, with a story about his son, Peter, on the occasion of the latter's sixth birthday. Asked how he felt on reaching six, Peter replied, according to Forrestal, that "the older you get, the stupider you get." Another story of which he was fond involved one Orland S Greene who was captain of the Princeton baseball team during Forrestal's undergraduate days. In the ninth inning of a Princeton-Yale game, Forrestal recalled, Greene had hit a home run with the bases loaded, thereby winning the game. That night he was toasted by everyone as a great hero, but Greene refused to be taken in by the applause. "Yeah, I know," he remarked at one point during the evening, "a hero today, a shit tomorrow." Forrestal liked both stories less because they were intrinsically amusing than because the remarks quoted struck a responsive chord in his own ironic sensibilities.

In discussions of military preparedness and Cold War problems, he was frequently reminded of an anecdote involving Joseph Stalin, and like his other favorite anecdotes, the Stalin story was almost always told in a purposeful context. According to Forrestal, Stalin was once asked by an

---

23. Jonathan Daniels, *Frontier on the Potomac* (New York: The Macmillan Company, 1946) , p. 223.

American official[24] whether the Soviet Union during the war
had lost any significant number of men to combat duty as a
result of malingering, combat fatigue, psychoneurotic breakdown, desertion, and so on. The American had informed
Stalin that behavior problems of one kind or another had
deprived the United States Armed Forces of the equivalent
of many divisions of soldiers. Stalin had replied, in Forrestal's
account of the incident, that the Soviet Union had not had a
similar experience, and he then added, "It would take a
brave man to be a coward in the Soviet Army." Forrestal
after telling the story would often observe that the United
States, if it was to gain victory in the Cold War, would also
require an army in which cowardice was more hazardous
than combat duty.

But while Forrestal, so to speak, was inclined to take his
humor seriously, he could appreciate jokes and stories that
were merely funny or amusing. In one of his private notebooks, for example, he entered the following, presumably
apocryphal, "telegrams" without comment:

WESTERN UNION

SALT LAKE CITY, UTAH

FAST   JULY 12, 1941
                                               6:00 P.M.

DOCTOR M. GOODHUE
CURATOR MUSEUM NATURAL HISTORY
NEW YORK NY

JUST SHOT A STRANGE AND CURIOUS SPECIMEN IN KAIBAB MOUNTAIN
FOREST NEAR SALT LAKE STOP DESCRIPTION AS FOLLOWS SIX FEET
SEVEN INCHES TALL GORILLA-LIKE HEAD LONG STRAGGLING BEARD TO
KNEES BARREL-LIKE CHEST ARMS DANGLING BELOW KNEES TUSKLIKE
TEETH STOP WHEN ERECT TESTICLES DRAG ON THE GROUND STOP CAN
YOU TELL US WHAT THIS IS? REGARDS

J. BROWN, FIELD DIRECTOR

---

24. On one occasion Forrestal identified the American involved as former
Ambassador to the Soviet Union Edward R. Stettinius, but on another occasion he attributed the story to General Eisenhower.

NEW YORK NY

FAST   JULY 13, 1941
                                                                                                   9:30 A.M.

DR. J. BROWN
EXPLORATION FIELD DIRECTOR
SALT LAKE CITY, UTAH

GET THE HELL OUT OF UTAH QUICKLY STOP YOU HAVE JUST SHOT A
MORMON BISHOP. REGARDS

GOODHUE

Another of his favorite stories, a friend recollects,

concerned a gentleman who, already struggling under a pretty
fair load, entered a bar. He ordered a drink, whereupon the bartender politely told him he already had enough. The gentleman
squinted his eyes and pointing to a cat in the doorway said: "If I
was drunk I would say that cat coming in the door over there had
four eyes, but I can see just as plain he's got only two." The
bartender leaned over the bar and in a low voice said: "I still say
you've had enough. That cat ain't coming in, he's going out."

Forrestal's literary interests, like his humor and wit, took
a variety of forms. In addition to reading each day the major
Washington and New York newspapers, he was actively interested in patterns of newspaper ownership and control. On
several occasions he asked friends to inform him when any
important newspaper was available for purchase, and in
1946, when the New York *Sun* was in financial difficulties, he
seriously considered acquiring it. "Krock thinks," he wrote
C. Douglas Dillon, on January 27, 1946,

if [the *Sun*] were turned into a really good tabloid—an intelligent
compression of the real news—that it would have a field of influence as well as profit. My chief interest in it would be to get a
place for Palmer Hoyt, who I believe has the three qualities of
being a good editor, a good businessman, and a liberal (without
being a screwball) point of view. He would be a healthy breath of
air in the New York atmosphere. I am writing to Lewis Strauss to
this effect and adding that I would not be interested in going in
any group, or, for that matter, leading it on the assumption of

controlling policy of the paper. I am a firm believer in the philosophy that newspapers should reflect the opinions and beliefs of the man who runs the individual paper. In other words, I don't like opinions created on a mass basis, nor do I believe in reflecting the views of an owner, unless he also is actually running the operation.

Eventually he decided against making a bid for the *Sun,* but he never entirely lost his desire to become the owner or part-owner of a newspaper that had already achieved, or could achieve, national significance.

It was also in 1946 that Forrestal gave serious thought to the preparation of a book about his wartime and postwar experiences. Cass Canfield of the publishing firm of Harper & Brothers offered him a contract for such a book, and Forrestal instructed his aide, Eugene Duffield, to draft a detailed outline of a book that would feature, in Duffield's words, a "recital of opinions and final impressions, using factual incidents as supporting or illustrative material." Duffield's suggested outline envisaged a four-part book devoted to "World Coalition and the Men Who Built It" (Part I), "Mobilizing Industrial America" (Part II), "Sea Power and Victory" (Part III), and "Future Problems of National Defense" (Part IV). After some talk with Duffield and others, Forrestal supplemented the outline with a five-page memorandum specifying some of the points with which he particularly wanted to deal in the proposed book. Forrestal thought it desirable that the book begin by emphasizing that the "business of government" was "the maintenance of a free society." It would then compare "Government in a small village (Matteawan), middle-sized city, Mount Vernon (Poughkeepsie), and government of a state (Washington)." Other topics to be discussed included, in the order listed by Forrestal:

> Coming to Washington in July 1940, the introduction to anonymity. My meetings with the President and Harry Hopkins.

My first meeting with Frank Knox.
The building of the Navy. Navy organization.
What was available to do the procurement job.
Our relations with the Army.
The need for an over-all and global plan for mobilization,
allocation of material, manpower, food, and so forth.
The job was done piecemeal in spite of Baruch's report and
the Industrial Mobilization Plan. (Very few ever read the
first and the latter was practically unread until Eberstadt
dug it out in 1941 after he became Chairman of the Munitions Board.)

The word "failure" occurred frequently in Forrestal's
memorandum, and reflected his feeling that the conduct of
the war had been faulty in the extreme. There had been, to
begin with, our "failure to profit by the lessons of 1917 and
1918," and "our failure to create small craft" able to "com-
pete with the sub." There was also the "British Navy's failure
to develop planes because of their lack of a naval air arm,"
and the "failure to recognize the fact that raw materials,
manpower, food, were all part of the same pattern." According to Forrestal, "[Donald] Nelson was given full powers but
he failed to use them partly due to FDR's inability to keep
hands off." The memo also referred to the "British failure
and ours fully to appreciate the possibilities of submarines,"
the "Army's failure to understand and appreciate sea power,"
and the "failure of FDR to (possibly largely due to Hull's
inertia) foresee the Russian objectives. Russia could have
been dealt with in 1943 before the landing in Normandy."
Forrestal did not further comment on Roosevelt's "failure"
to anticipate Soviet objectives, nor did he indicate in what
fashion "Russia could have been dealt with in 1943 . . ."
Toward the end of his memo he simply noted:

> Russia, the exemplar of the other way of life. Full develop-
> ment of the Hegelian derivative in communism. The Marx-
> ian thesis of revolution. Ferrero's book on the Reconstruction
> of Europe.

What we're faced with: Communism grows in the soil of anarchism, chaos and despair. Therefore, Russia is not particularly concerned whether or not Europe recovers fast. We are, and they know it.

While the book was never written, Forrestal did not entirely abandon the project, and he frequently drew upon his memo for speech and article subjects. He also indicated to friends and inquiring editors that when his government career finally ended, he intended to spend some part of his time writing his memoirs. These memoirs would include, he emphasized, a comprehensive statement of the factors that made the American system of capitalist democracy superior to any other system that had ever been developed.

His intention ultimately to publish his memoirs had much to do with shaping his own literary interests during the Washington years. In addition to reading or at least perusing a large number of books, Forrestal or his aides made detailed notes on certain books that Forrestal thought important, and his notebooks contain numerous magazine articles, newspaper columns, and transcripts of speeches photostated or typed in their entirety. These materials, of which the following index, quoted from "Scrap Book No. 1," is a representative listing, were designed not only to be of use in the preparation of articles, speeches, and books but also to aid Forrestal in organizing his thoughts and reflections on a variety of subjects:

SCRAP BOOK NO. 1—POLITICAL

FILE I

INDEX

SCRAP BOOK NO. 1—POLITICAL

FILE I

INDEX

The "scrap books" also contained bibliographies of books
that Forrestal had already read or intended to read. Arranged
according to author, the bibliographies dealt with the works
of Joseph Conrad, Edith Wharton, William Dean Howells,
Arthur Koestler, William Wymark Jacobs, Anthony Trol-
lope, Raymond Chandler, and Washington Irving. There
were numerous references to the books and writings of Forrestal's favorite political commentator, Walter Bagehot, and
in November, 1947, Forrestal expressed an interest in acquiring books by Lord Acton, Henry Thomas Buckle, James
Anthony Froude, Edward Gibbon, and G. M. Trevelyan.[25]
In 1947 he borrowed from the Navy Department library a
biography of William Pitt, several books on diplomacy, including Maurice Hankey's *Diplomacy by Conference* (which
he later bought), two books concerned with the American
Revolution and its aftermath, and H. G. Wells's *The Outline
of History*. Early in 1948 he withdrew from the Library of
Congress Budd Schulberg's *The Harder They Fall,* and
Cleveland Amory's *The Proper Bostonians*. On January 16
he ordered a book about banking, and not long after he purchased F. S. C. Northrup's *The Meeting of East and West* and
Arnold Toynbee's *A Study of History*.

By November, 1948, Forrestal's literary eclecticism and
catholic tastes were reflected in a personal library of several
hundred volumes almost equally divided between "heavy"
and "light" literature. On the one hand, there were books
by Woodrow Wilson, Ruth Benedict, Walter Lippmann,
Harold Nicolson, Henry Adams, James P. Warburg, Lecomte
de Noüy, and Winston Churchill, in addition to those au-

---

25. On November 11 he received from an aide a list of their books available
from Brentano's and Scribner's bookstores which included the price of each
book.

thors already mentioned. There were, of course, a large number of books about the war, including naval histories by Samuel Eliot Morison and Fletcher Pratt. Biographies and related books were represented by H. R. Trevor-Roper's *The Last Days of Hitler,* G. Lynn Sumner's *Meet Abraham Lincoln,* Henry L. Stimson's and McGeorge Bundy's *On Active Service in Peace and War,* James F. Byrnes's *Speaking Frankly,* Robert Sherwood's *Roosevelt and Hopkins,* Gordon Carpenter O'Gara's *Theodore Roosevelt and the Modern Navy,* Cyril Clemens's *The Man From Missouri,* and Merriman Smith's *A President Is Many Men.* The Forrestal library also contained Nick Kenny's *Day Unto Day,* P. G. Wodehouse's *Full Moon,* Thornton Wilder's *The Ides of March,* Norman Mailer's *The Naked and the Dead,* Louis Sobol's *Some Days Were Happy,* Kathleen Winsor's *Forever Amber,* and several books by John O'Hara. Some of the older books were Book-of-the-Month Club selections prior to November 18, 1941, when Forrestal canceled his club membership.

Forrestal made a habit of sending books, photostats of magazine articles, and magazine subscriptions to friends and associates. His choice of such reading matter was so varied as to be almost indiscriminate, but in a large number of cases the selections made were designed to "educate" or otherwise instruct the recipients. Thus an article by C. Hartley Grattan, "What British Socialism is Up Against," in the July, 1946, *Harper's* was sent to James F. Byrnes, John W. Snyder, Robert Patterson, Tom C. Clark, Robert E. Hannegan, Harold L. Ickes, Clinton P. Anderson, Lewis B. Schwellenbach, and Henry Wallace. Photostats of *Harper's* profiles of Senators Taft and Vandenberg were also sent to various people. In 1948 Senators Pepper and Knowland received gift copies of Gugliermo Ferrero's *The Reconstruction of Europe,* for which Forrestal had a high regard, and Lord Hankey's *Diplomacy by Conference;* the latter book was also sent to General Marshall. C. Douglas Dillon, Clark Clifford, and Senator Fulbright were presented with Bagehot's *The English Constitution,* and Representative John Taber received Russell Hill's *The Struggle for Germany.* Among other books bestowed as presents on various people were Evelyn Waugh's *The Loved Ones,* Dwight Macdonald's *Henry Wallace,* Robert Benchley's *Benchley or Else,* John Steinbeck's *The Wayward Bus,* Arnold Toynbee's *A Study of History,* Thomas Heggen's *Mister Roberts,* John O'Hara's *Hellbox* and *Short Stories,* James Byrnes's *Speaking Frankly,* William Bullitt's *The Great Globe Itself,* and Bessie Breuer's *Memory of Love.*

While Secretary of the Navy, Forrestal presented a number of Naval Officers' Clubs with gift subscriptions to *Esquire, Cosmopolitan, Red Book Magazine, Time, Life,* and *Look.* Subscriptions to the *New Yorker* were sent to various European friends and acquaintances, including Madame Guido Branca of Rome, Italy. Forrestal himself subscribed to many of these magazines, and, in addition, to *The Atlantic, Harper's, Collier's, Editor and Publisher, Fortune, Newsweek,* and *The Saturday Evening Post.* He also read the (London) *Economist* and *The (London) Times,* and received a number of newsletters such as the "Kiplinger Letter" and the "Whaley-Eaton Letter."

Forrestal typically read for a purpose, and the purpose was usually to enlighten himself with respect to history and current events. When he read for amusement or entertainment, he would often turn to the novels and short stories of John O'Hara and to humorous books, especially those of Robert Benchley. According to friends, Forrestal was particularly fond of O'Hara because O'Hara, too, was a "Mick" (a word Forrestal used frequently in referring to himself) and was, like Forrestal, "someone who had come a long way," as one friend expresses it, "but was never entirely taken in by the society crowd of which he became a part." Forrestal also appears to have admired O'Hara's relative freedom from

258	*James Forrestal*

inhibition and "devil may care" attitude toward life, although neither of these personality traits was characteristic of Forrestal himself. But whatever the reasons that led him to prefer O'Hara's fiction to that of any other contemporary novelist, he became something of an amateur authority on O'Hara's works. He had no interest, apparently, in the books and stories of another "Mick" writer who "had come a long way" during the twenties and thirties, namely, F. Scott Fitzgerald. Despite their similarities of background, similarities that included Princeton, there is no evidence that Forrestal and Fitzgerald were acquainted or that Forrestal ever read a Fitzgerald book.

Evidence is also inconclusive that Forrestal read widely or thoroughly among the books he owned and borrowed. During the Washington years, a close associate of his recalls:

Jim would usually walk around with a book under his arm, or a newspaper. For the same reason that some people carry swagger sticks, Forrestal carried books. If he were alive today, I'm sure he'd be walking around with *Exodus* or *Advise and Consent* under his arm, or perhaps Toynbee, but you'd know damn well Jim would never get through Toynbee.

He always liked to feel that he read through a broad spectrum, but he didn't absorb nearly as much as he nibbled. He felt it served a useful purpose to be thought of as an intellectual.

Although he was regarded as an intellectual by many of his Washington friends and colleagues, it remains true that Forrestal's personal tastes in books, music, and poetry did not advance very far beyond levels associated with mass or "pop" culture. The counterparts in music of O'Hara and Benchley were Handel and Rimsky-Korsakov; the former's "Largo" and the latter's "Hymn to the Sun" were, apparently, his favorite musical works. Rudyard Kipling's numerous poems in praise of the military virtues, selfless bravery, and the innate heroism of the common soldier led Forrestal to admire Kipling's poetry and to quote him more frequently than any other literary figure, Kipling, in effect, served Forrestal as the Cold War's foremost muse, articulating in his poems moods and themes for which Forrestal sought, in his speeches and writings, the prose equivalents.[26]

These tastes and preferences, however, did not preclude a certain amount of serious reading which ensured Forrestal a somewhat higher intellectual ranking than that enjoyed by most of his Cabinet colleagues. Apart from Forrestal there were few, if any, members of the Truman Cabinet who had read or even skimmed Walter Bagehot, and fewer still who could expound, even superficially, on dialectical materialism,

---

26. Forrestal owned the Sussex Edition of *The Complete Works in Prose and Verse of Rudyard Kipling*, and transcribed into his private notebooks a large number of Kipling's poems. During the war he established some kind of association with the Kipling Society of London, and from it he received from time to time copies of Kipling's poems that had been published in British newspapers at the time of the Boer War. He was especially fond of the poem "Dane-Geld (A.D. 980–1016)," and had copies made for distribution to friends and colleagues. The text of "Dane-Geld" is as follows:

> "It is always a temptation to an armed and agile nation,
>   To call upon a neighbour and to say:—
> 'We invaded you last night—we are quite prepared to fight,
>   Unless you pay us cash to go away.'
> "And that is called asking for Dane-geld,
>   And the people who ask it explain
> That you've only to pay 'em the Dane-geld
>   And then you'll get rid of the Dane!
> "It is always a temptation to a rich and lazy nation
>   To puff and look important and to say:—
> 'Though we know we should defeat you, we have not the time
>   to meet you.
>   We will therefore pay you cash to go away.'
> "And that is called paying the Dane-geld;
>   But we've proved it again and again,
> That if once you have paid him the Dane-geld
>   You never get rid of the Dane.
> "It is wrong to put temptation in the path of any nation,
>   For fear they should succumb and go astray;
> So when you are requested to pay up or be molested,
>   You will find it better policy to say:—
> " 'We never pay *any*-one Dane-geld,
>   No matter how trifling the cost;
> For the end of the game is oppression and shame,
>   And the nation that plays it is lost!' "

geopolitics, or the Congress of Vienna. The number of those who could positively identify Fichte, Kant, and Hegel, much less connect these individuals with Karl Marx, was extremely small, and there was a significant number of policy makers, Forrestal discovered to his dismay, who rarely read anything except memoranda and official papers. While Forrestal, it is clear, "didn't absorb nearly as much as he nibbled," the "nibbling" of other high officials in the government had seemingly ceased on or before graduation from a college, university, or military academy. By comparison with them, Forrestal could appear to be a man of intellectual stature, and while this stature was exaggerated by friends, it was not entirely without some basis in fact.

The impression of intellectual breadth if not depth was strengthened by Forrestal's wide-ranging interests. Willett, Duffield, and several other Washington aides were kept busy preparing memoranda not only on diplomatic affairs, history, Marxism and Communism, and current events but also on topics as far removed from each other as the Liberian economy and religious occultism in Southern California.[27] Several of these memoranda dealt with the economic analyses of the Swedish economist Gunnar Myrdal, and in October, 1944, Forrestal distributed to friends and government associates copies of a Myrdal speech titled "The Economic Development in the United States and the Business Cycle Trends." Forrestal regarded the speech as a cogent analysis of the problems that would face the American economy after the war, including above all the problem of averting a depression. On April 3, 1946, he received from Willett a paper concerned with Jean-Paul Sartre and existentialism, and a

27. In August, 1948, Forrestal, at the request of a friend, promised to "look into" the case of a certain naval officer who had resigned his commission in order to accept a position with an obscure religious movement in the Los Angeles area. Since the former officer, he wrote Navy Secretary John L. Sullivan on August 25, "seems to have come to his senses with reference to the facts of life and the state of the world, perhaps he should be considered for reinstatement."

year later Forrestal entered in one of his notebooks an excerpt from the book *My Boyhood in Siam* by Kamut Chandruang.[28] The book, which had been brought to his attention by Mrs. Chase Donaldson, dealt in part with certain of the author's impressions of America, among which was the impression that Americans worked too hard to enjoy themselves or make maximum use of the freedom and liberties that were available. But one excerpted section of particular interest to Forrestal was a comment on love and family relations. "It is sad, I think," the author observed,

that they [Americans] have so little time for love. Their men have no time with their wives and children. The father goes to work, the children go to school and they reunite only in those hours when exhaustion forces them to sleep. Their vacations are for rest—not for love. For love they go to the movies, where professional Romeos and Juliets will do their love-making for them.

Forrestal did not indicate why he thought this excerpt important enough to include in his notebook, and it is almost the only reference to love and family life that his notebooks contain.

On August 1, 1948, Forrestal queried one of his aides, "What are the four estates—I remember three, church, landed proprietors and the press but I forget the fourth," and, again, it is not clear why or for what purpose he thought the question important. Although he had always taken an interest in the state of the national economy, in 1948 he began to compile rather elaborate data on production, consumption, distribution, capital investment, wage and profit rates, and related matters. In a memo to an aide of July 5, Forrestal requested information related to the gross national product, net national production, national income in 1932, 1933, 1937, 1939, 1941, and 1947, consumer credit, and installment sales.

Early in his Washington career Forrestal became con-

---

28. New York: John Day & Company, 1940.

vinced that the federal government, and especially the executive branch, was characterized by archaic and obsolete principles of administration, and thereafter he was a firm believer in the need for thorough reorganization. His wartime trips to London, in the course of which he met a large number of ministers and senior civil servants, persuaded him that the British system of Cabinet government was more effective and efficient than our own form of executive organization, and after the war he was without question the foremost exponent within the government of administrative reforms modeled after the British experience. He also strongly believed that businessmen should serve in the government during some period in their careers, and he therefore favored tax changes and other measures that would reduce the financial sacrifices involved. On numerous occasions he expressed concern that younger businessmen, because of taxes, were unable to make enough money to consider government employment at sharply reduced salaries, no matter how vital their services, and on other occasions he lamented the fact that government salaries were too low to attract most men of demonstrated ability and competence. To friends he confided in 1947 that he was spending approximately $60,000 each year in Washington and that most businessmen were in no position "to pay the high cost of government service." He had come to Washington in 1940, he told an associate not altogether facetiously, as a member of the upper-middle class, and unless he left soon he would depart from Washington with lower-middle-class or working-class status.

During and after the war, much of the research done for Forrestal by his staff was directed to detailed studies of government organization and recruitment here and in Britain. It was in this connection that Forrestal was engrossed by Bagehot's writings on the British constitution, but he also acquired some familiarity with later treatments of British government, including Don K. Price's "Civil Service in Britain," and, despite his bias against the author, Harold J. Laski's "The British Civil Service."[29] One memo submitted by an aide in 1945 or 1946 was an eight-page "Note on the British Civil Service and Departmental Procedure" which summarized policy-making procedures at the Cabinet level, the concept of ministerial responsibility, civil-service recruitment and promotion, and ministerial methods of dealing with correspondence and questions raised in Parliament.

In November, 1945, a *Washington Evening Star* editorial quoted Forrestal as feeling that there was "some imbalance in the predominance of statisticians, lawyers and economists in our Government, as contrasted to the number of men drawn from a more general experience." By "general experience" Forrestal usually meant business experience, and he was often critical of the relative absence in government of men who, as he once put it, "knew how to survive the tyranny of the balance sheet." Without such "tyranny," he frequently observed, it was difficult to think of a way by which efficiency and ability could be measured. "One of the great difficulties of anyone who goes to work in Washington," he observed to Hanson W. Baldwin in 1945,

is that in any place in which there is even a normal flow of work it is quite easy for him to have his day fully occupied and go home at night with the sense of at least having been busy. . . . Reverting again to the analogy of business, there is the pragmatic axe of the income account and the balance sheet to make executives in that field go through a constant examination of their productivity. In government the criteria are not always so visible, and in fact they are apt to be negative in character. The bad administration only shows up when you are made an ass of by some committee in Congress.[30]

---

29. Price's article was first published in several issues of the *Washington Post* in the mid-thirties. The Laski piece appeared in the Winter, 1937, *Yale Review*.

30. *The New York Times Magazine,* December 9, 1945.

While he could think of no government equivalent of the "income account" as a measure of job performance, he consistently took the position that the public service would benefit from a generous infusion of able businessmen and skilled managerial personnel. This was his theme in a speech delivered to the Princeton bicentennial conference on university education in November, 1946, and there he also stressed the need to increase the rewards of public service by raising government salaries and enhancing the prestige of government employment. In July, 1947, he was appointed to the Commission on Organization of the Executive Branch (Hoover Commission), and it appeared to his many friends and admirers that he was the best possible choice for Commission membership. "No administrator," wrote Arthur Krock in *The New York Times,* "has made a closer or more intelligent study of the government [than] Secretary Forrestal."[31]

The Hoover Commission and Cabinet meetings in 1948 provided Forrestal with additional opportunities to expound his views relating to civil-service recruitment and administrative reorganization. In January he drew the attention of the Cabinet to "the real need" of appointing ambassadors "with some business experience and background as well as negotiating skill, who would vigorously and continuously push the interests of American business." Citing Mexican problems in exploiting oil resources "and the deficiencies of an amiable but untrained personnel," Forrestal implied that there was some relationship between these problems and the business experience or inexperience of American diplomatic officials in Mexico. He apparently believed that the Mexican

---

31. Of all Cabinet members, Krock continued, Forrestal "was the natural choice of the President because of his preoccupation throughout his Washington career with the problems the group will attempt to solve." Noting that Forrestal might become Defense Secretary—"the high hope of the departments themselves and many in Congress and outside it"—Krock commented that "even in a brief service, or through a deputy thereafter, his contribution will be great."

oil industry would be more successful in increasing production if the American embassy staff included persons with oil-business backgrounds. In any event, he repeatedly insisted, if government salaries are not increased significantly, the public service must necessarily rely on "either incompetence or retired millionaires and sometimes they are not entirely disassociated."[32]

It was also in 1948 that Forrestal began to give even stronger emphasis to the importance of major administrative reforms at the highest policy-making levels. As early as 1945 he had declared to Hanson W. Baldwin that in government administration "there will always be need for these two things: (1) doing the job and (2) exposition of how it is done." Doubting that "you can wrap up the two in the same person," Forrestal offered as his "solution" the creation of "a staff of permanent civil servants who will do continuous and possibly interchangeable duty in the departments." Although there were "a lot of arguments pro and con—the corrosion that is apt to accompany long continued public service, the quality of men that you will get, etc.," he was nevertheless persuaded that his suggestion "should be tried."[33]

In a diary entry of August 18, Forrestal recorded as one of his "deep impressions" the contrast between the Canadian and American governments with respect to policy continuity. Meeting with the Defense Committee of the Canadian Cabinet, Forrestal noted that the meeting included certain Cabinet members who were shortly to be replaced in office by ministers attached to the newly elected Liberal Party headed by L. S. St. Laurent. Furthermore, he noted,

32. Letter to James N. Rowe, Jr., August 6, 1948. Rowe had recently rejected a federal position because of its pay scale.

33. *The New York Times Magazine,* December 9, 1945. In a conversation with John McCone in September, 1948, Forrestal observed that in government "the constant job is to have someone with enough imagination to be sure that the links between different interests are brought together." The "imagination" required, he believed, would be facilitated by permanence and interchangeability of top civil-service personnel.

the ministers involved represented not only the Cabinet but "the control of the Canadian Parliament. . . . Therefore expressions of policy at this meeting are the statements of a responsible government."[34]

Applying these impressions and convictions to the American scene, Forrestal made a number of efforts to transform such organizations as the National Security Council and the Cabinet itself into agencies that resembled closely their British and Canadian counterparts. The Executive Secretary of the National Security Council, for example, was to function as an overseer of other agencies, and he was also to be responsible for the implementation of decisions reached by the Council. Forrestal also advocated a Cabinet secretariat which would have charge of Cabinet meetings' agenda and to which a good deal of detailed policy formulation and execution could be delegated. The chief of the secretariat would play a role, in effect, rather similar to that of the Secretary of the British Cabinet, while the Executive Secretary of the National Security Council would possess certain powers, at least, that in Britain are associated with the Permanent Secretary of the Treasury.

These proposals of Forrestal were hardly popular with other members of the Truman Administration, and least of all with the President himself. Forrestal, in the latter's view, was attempting to transform the National Security Council "into an operating super-cabinet on the British model," and, in general, "advocating our using the British Cabinet system as a model in the operation of the government."[35] Others in the Truman Administration saw in Forrestal's proposals an effort to transfer key powers and responsibilities from the

34. *Diaries*, p. 474.

35. Harry S Truman, *Memoirs*, II, *Years of Trial and Hope* (New York: Doubleday and Company, 1956), p. 60. While there "is much to this idea," Truman wrote, under the American system "responsibility rests on one man— the President. To change it, we would have to change the Constitution, and I think we have been doing very well under our Constitution. We will do well to stay with it."

President to other officials who would be more in sympathy than Truman with Forrestal's own position. In the view of some members of the Truman entourage, Forrestal's "super-cabinet" recommendations reflected not only a personal disloyalty to the Chief Executive but a desire to render the President a mere figurehead and largely ceremonial head of state. They imagined, rightly or wrongly, that Forrestal in late 1947 and 1948 was engaged in a "grab for power," and there were several who believed rumors circulating at that time that Forrestal was holding secret meetings at his home devoted to discussions of means and methods of implementing his proposals regarding Cabinet and National Security Council reorganization.

Whatever the truth or falsity of these suspicions, there can be no doubt that Forrestal's own political philosophy—that is, the central ideas, attitudes, and convictions that characterized his political thinking—was at variance with that espoused by the President, and, more often than not, sharply at variance. Although he thought of himself as a liberal, and was in fact more liberal than many of his Wall Street friends, he usually defined a liberal as someone who believed that government should intrude as little as possible on private enterprise and private initiative, especially business initiative. "The basis of our society," he once wrote his son Michael,

is a balance between State Socialism, Communism, call it what you will, and individual anarchy—between the people who want to get all reforms accomplished by explosion by next Monday, and the liberal who wants to keep constantly pushing in the direction of liberal thought and action, but who is well aware that the Bantu pygmies are not all eligible for Porcellian by next week.[36]

---

36. Letter of January 10, 1948. "By way of corrective for reactionary tendencies in the Old Man," he sent Michael a copy of a recent speech by Justice Douglas and recommended to him a *Political Science Quarterly* article of December, 1946, by Frank Tannenbaum titled "The Balance of Power in Society." He also sent a copy of the letter to Justice Douglas.

By "State Socialism" Forrestal meant not the totalitarian system of the Soviet Union but the type of mixed economy that
was associated with the postwar British Labour Government.
Convinced that such Labour Party leaders as Cripps, Dalton,
Bevan, and Morrison had been too much influenced by Kant,
Fichte, Hegel, Marx, and, needless to say, the ubiquitous
Harold Laski, he was not inclined to regard the British combination of private enterprise, economic planning and controls as constituting, in essence, another kind of democratic
capitalism. "I am not much concerned," he wrote Paul C.
Smith on March 10, 1947,

about the handing on of great fortunes, but I *am* very much
concerned about the ability of a lad without a stake to make one
within his own lifetime. Unless we can keep that we will go into
state socialism backwards which, God forbid, if the results produced by the thinkers in Great Britain is [*sic*] any criterion. . . .

In his speeches and writings 1940–1949, Forrestal dealt
with a variety of economic and political issues generally from
a conservative point of view. While he approved of high
taxes for military purposes, he was opposed in principle to
taxation for welfare ends. He was a critic of a number of
antitrust suits instituted during the Truman years, especially
those involving the oil industry, and on at least one occasion
strongly advocated that the government promote industrial
mergers rather than prevent them.[37] He supported govern-
ment-financed medical care for the indigent, but did not
favor plans and proposals popularly referred to as initiating
"socialized medicine." The "danger" with such plans, he
wrote a medical friend early in January, 1947,

is that in recognizing the need for moderate government help,
the translation of this into action is apt to attract all the crackpots who think that Government can do everything and that they

---

37. On May 21, 1947, Forrestal wrote Clark Clifford that the aircraft
industry would "come on serious days" unless some consolidations were
effected.

will get control into their hands. If there is one thing I have learned in the last six years, it is that you cannot run the United States 100 percent from Washington, but there are a lot of people who believe you can.

"Crackpots," Forrestal believed, had infiltrated too many areas of government and education,[38] and he frequently commented on the tendency of professors and others to be influenced, as he once put it, "by European isms and philosophies."[39] In remarks at Princeton in 1947, Forrestal stressed that education "without practical experience" is of no great value. "There can be over-emphasis on Phi Beta Kappa keys," he added, "as well as on athletics." There could also be too much emphasis, he thought, on ideas as such, and in 1946, when he was still a financial contributor to *The Nation,* he was often privately contemptuous of the magazine for its failure, in his view, to realize that no government based on democracy "can compel human action into a blueprint." In December, 1947, commending its "tough realism," he sent various friends subscriptions to the ultraconservative magazine *Plain Talk*. He was particularly impressed, he wrote some of these friends, by the articles of Ayn Rand.

---

38. In January, 1948, Forrestal commended columnist David Lawrence for a column that was bitterly critical of Eugene V. Rostow's book *A National Policy for the Oil Industry*. Noting that Rostow's study had been financed by a foundation, Lawrence wrote that the book was "an ironic example of how the philanthropic funds of men who earned their surplus in life through individual initiative are subsequently utilized, not in objective studies of a factual nature but in economic partisanship and class-conscious crusades."— *Washington Star,* January 27, 1948.

39. "In general," Forrestal told a Williams College audience in June, 1946 (he was there to receive a Doctor of Laws degree) , "Americans have been susceptible to imported philosophies and to an admiration for the things of other times and other continents. It is quite proper that we should draw upon the wisdom and culture of the past. . . . But self-depreciation can be as overdone as self-esteem. It has been my view that the over-precise rationalism of Kant, Fichte, and Hegel pervaded much of the university thinking in this country from 1840 to 1910. The admiration for those admittedly great German philosophers of the 19th Century is too often duplicated today in the admiration for another philosophy deriving to a considerable extent from the same origins and equally inapplicable to American life."

Men in government, he observed on other occasions, fail to realize "how vital business and trade are to the state." Arguing that business can and does accomplish "what governments are too big and clumsy to do— releases initiative and enterprise and gets the wheels of commerce spinning," Forrestal frequently stressed in his speeches that the American system of democratic capitalism was very largely created by "promoters and salesmen." Most liberal politicians, he thought,

have a vague notion that you can get production by simply having engineers to produce. They completely overlook the fact that management, as has been pointed out by [James] Burnham in his book, is a curious, almost instinctive quality with certain men. . . .

Liberals also fail to appreciate the role of the salesman, but

as a matter of fact, it is the salesman who created the wants of the average American, the satisfaction of which necessitated the building of the vast industrial machinery which is now America. Without the salesman there would have been no General Motors, United States Steel, or General Electric. What Russia actually needs is some good American promoters and a whole lot of American salesmen and above all, of course, American management.

Although he was careful in his speeches not to overlook labor contributions to economic expansion, Forrestal was always convinced there were "inequities" in the statutes affecting labor, and these "inequities" worked in favor of irresponsible union power, corruption, and costly strikes and work stoppages. In 1946 he sent copies of several articles written about union "bosses" to friends and associates,[40] and in 1947 he unsuccessfully urged Truman on several occasions to approve the Taft-Hartley bill which was subsequently

---

40. In January, 1946, Forrestal distributed to friends and associates copies of a *Portland Oregonian* article of December 27, 1945, entitled "The Power of Petrillo." Petrillo at the time was the so-called Czar of the American Federation of Musicians, and the article, Forrestal wrote RCA Victor vice-president Frank M. Folsom and others, was "of possible interest."

enacted into law over the President's veto. In a lengthy memo to Truman of June 20, 1947, which, apparently, was never sent, Forrestal took the position that the bill would improve labor relations, and therefore should be signed by the President. That action, however,

should be accompanied by a strong and clear statement pointing out the respects in which the bill should be improved through the amendment process. . . . I would recommend your adding a request that the Joint Committee [on Labor-Management Relations] recommend such legislation in this regard on or before 15 March 1948.

While he was "fully aware," Forrestal's memo continued, that the bill "goes too far" with respect to the government's power to secure injunctions, the unions' liability in damage suits, and so on, nevertheless the bill would become law and its undesirable features "will be on the statute books regardless of what you may do." The President, in Forrestal's view, by signing the bill would be in a much better position to secure changes, but in addition to that, Forrestal insisted, there were good features as well as bad ones in the bill. Among the former were

the right of free speech which is restored to employers, and the great provision for honest elections. In this connection I carry in my mind the recollection of a strike at Allis-Chalmers in 1941 which was called as a result of an election in which there were several thousand admittedly illegal ballots cast. The strike lasted from January to April. It cost the Navy turbines for 37 destroyers, ships. . . .

There was, finally, another advantage in signing the bill, and that related, Forrestal wrote, to his "strong belief that Republicans do not have a mortgage on the entire business community." Reminding Truman that there were businessmen Democrats in Wall Street who had "fought for" the Securities Exchange Act and other measures, Forrestal commented:

Particularly among persons representing businesses of moderate size, there has been a growing conviction since last Autumn that you are motivated by only one consideration: Do whatever is best for the country. I believe your signature to this bill will augment your position with these people.

The Taft-Hartley bill was, in the end, one more issue upon which Forrestal differed with the President, and it illustrates, albeit in a limited way, the extent to which Forrestal's conception of liberal politics diverged from that represented in the White House. In truth, Forrestal was one of the more conservative members of the Truman Administration, and while there were others who frequently thought as he did, they were more inclined than he was to moderate their positions, give ground when necessary, and retreat altogether when it was strategic to do so. They also were more disposed than Forrestal to confine their policy recommendations to their own areas of responsibility. Forrestal, by contrast, was a Cabinet Francis Bacon who took the whole political world for his province.

Since a part of that world included territory within the jurisdictions of other executive departments, Forrestal's relations with his Cabinet colleagues were not always easy, and his relations with Truman himself were, at various times, rather strained. While the Truman-Forrestal association had never been close, by late 1948 it had reached the stage of acute deterioration. Both of them self-made men, although Forrestal much less one than Truman, their personalities tended to conflict, and in such a setting the frequent policy differences could function only as a further irritant. Truman, while still a senator, had learned to respect Forrestal's abilities, but he distrusted his views on foreign and domestic policy issues, views Forrestal rarely hesitated to articulate. Forrestal, it frequently appeared, was determined to intrude upon policy areas that not only were outside the scope of his office but also often fell within the compass of presidential responsibility. With interests that touched on almost all aspects of government operations, foreign and domestic, Forrestal inevitably came to be thought of as someone who, a former Truman aide remarks,

wasn't satisfied to be *just* Secretary of the Navy, and *just* Secretary of Defense. Sometimes he tried to be Secretary of State, Treasury Secretary, and Attorney General—and there was more than one occasion when he tried to be President.

While Forrestal's public references to Truman were invariably respectful, he privately was often critical of the President's tendency, in his view, to sacrifice foreign-policy and military-security needs in behalf of domestic political considerations. Roosevelt, he once observed to a friend, was unable to say "No" to Stalin no matter what the dictator demanded; Truman could and did say "No" but was often incapable of following through with the necessary action, or, in certain cases, did not see the military and foreign-policy implications of "No." Forrestal in the early forties had also taken a strong dislike to a number of Roosevelt's intimates, and he was no more comfortable with those who were close to Truman. Although he made several valiant efforts to reduce the social distance between the President and himself—such as playing poker more or less regularly with Truman, Vinson, Clifford, and others, a game which he disliked and at which he usually lost large sums of money—he was never one of those in whom Truman confided or with whom the President preferred to relax. Despite Forrestal's efforts, those closest to Truman were well aware that Forrestal had no great taste for the back-slapping camaraderie and smoking-car atmosphere that often prevailed at the White House on stag social occasions.[41]

41. Observing that Truman and Forrestal were never close friends, "probably because of their quite different backgrounds and interests," one of Forrestal's former aides comments that Forrestal "seemed to have almost a schoolboyish devotion to the *position* of President, and that probably helped him gloss over in his thinking any deficiencies he might observe in the man

From their point of view, Forrestal's "meddling" in policy areas for which he had no responsibility began within weeks of Truman's being sworn in as President in April, 1945. Certainly it is true that Forrestal's relations with Truman were not helped when Forrestal arrived, uninvited, at the Potsdam Conference of July–August, 1945. His exclusion from the official delegation was deeply resented by him, and while he could do nothing about it, he could and did arrange a European trip that would bring him to Berlin while the conference was in session. While the President was cordial, even having Forrestal to breakfast, it is doubtful that Truman welcomed the reprimand that was implicit in Forrestal's unexpected appearance at the conference.

Sending the President numerous memoranda from 1945–1949, Forrestal's suggestions and comments dealt with policies, appointments, elections, and reading material which he thought Truman would find of special interest. In August, 1945, he recommended that a place be found on the Supreme Court for Robert Patterson. In November he called the President's attention to the fact that the Secretary of the Treasury was selling Victory Bonds on the slogan "Make it home for the boys overseas," whereas he (Forrestal) was stressing in his speeches that the United States would continue to need substantial forces overseas. "Obviously," Forrestal wrote to Truman, "the two statements are in contradiction," and he suggested a Cabinet meeting to assure uniform policy.

On July 25, 1946, Forrestal dispatched a memo concerned with Walter Bagehot, and in September he recommended that Truman appoint John Sonnett as Solicitor General. From time to time he suggested others for various positions,

---

who held the position. . . . President Truman was not by any means an admirable character as an individual, and he seemed to enjoy the companionship of some of his old cronies who were by no means up to the levels of character and ability that most Americans would expect. I'm sure that Forrestal was aware of these imperfections. . . ."—Letter to the writer, July 5, 1960.

adding in one note of December 18, 1947, recommending Edmond Hanrahan for chairman of the Securities and Exchange Commission, "I hope you will forgive me for making recommendations outside of my own field." On October 31, 1946, Forrestal commented in a memo to Truman that the appointment of David E. Lilienthal as AEC chairman was "a very wise selection." Late in 1947 or early in 1948, Forrestal strongly protested to the President and Attorney General Clark a criminal antitrust suit then pending against a number of investment banking firms. According to one source, Forrestal at a Cabinet meeting told Clark: "You can't do that. They're honest men." When Clark responded that such suits "were good for businessmen. It keeps them on their toes," Forrestal asked the Attorney General how he would feel if he were sued by the government on criminal charges. Although he was not successful in urging first Clark and then Truman to withdraw the suit, he was satisfied that he had done everything possible to have the suit dropped.

In addition to his numerous personality and policy conflicts with Truman, Forrestal's increasing political involvement did not increase his popularity in White House circles. To begin with, he was not always discreet in his choice of persons with whom he discussed his policy and political differences with Truman. Thus, following the election of a Republican Congress in 1946, later castigated by Truman as a "do-nothing Congress," Forrestal wrote a friend that the

over-turn of last Autumn in many respects was a healthy thing. The new Senators and Congressmen are, on the whole, an extraordinarily good lot. . . . Congressman John Rankin of Mississippi made the remark that the Democrats were not defeated last November but were de-loused.[42]

It appears probable that this and similar comments between 1946 and 1949 were reported if not to the President at least to some members of his staff.

---

42. Letter of March 1, 1947.

In 1948 Forrestal also let it be known that *when* Governor
Dewey was elected—there were very few who believed there
was any *if* about it—he was willing to remain in the govern-
ment as either Defense Secretary or Secretary of State. On
July 26 he paid particular interest to a *Portland* (Maine)
Press-Herald editorial that was inserted in the *Congressional
Record* by Congresswoman Margaret Chase Smith. "When,"
ran the editorial,

—it is hardly necessary to put in an "if"—Governor Dewey is
elected President next fall, he will have about 10 weeks in which
to select a Cabinet . . . there is one man in the Truman Cabinet
who richly deserves to be retained. That is James Forrestal. . . .

Although he wrote the newspaper's publisher, Guy P. Gan-
nett, on July 30 that no matter what the outcome in November, "the end of this year will also be the end of my
bureaucratic career," he added that his approaching retirement "does not make me any less appreciative of your
support." Apart from the fact that Forrestal had been anticipating the end of his "bureaucratic career" for a good many
years, an anticipation which his friends had long since ceased
to take seriously, Forrestal himself and some of his close
associates were already involved in discussions with Governor
Dewey related to the Defense Department and Forrestal's
position in it. "I am informed," one of these associates wrote
him on October 12, "that Dewey would be delighted to
have you as his Secretary of Defense. . . ." Whatever the basis
for this statement, it is true, according to Mr. Dewey, that
Forrestal

came to see me at least two or three times during the latter half
of 1948. He was disturbed about the condition of our defense and
we discussed it at considerable length. I had been nominated for
President but not elected and it would have been presumptuous
for me to discuss with him the possibility of his remaining in the
Cabinet although I confess I had given it some consideration.[43]

43. Letter to the writer, June 25, 1959.

Forrestal subsequently denied to National Press Club members that he had been "in communication with Governor Dewey during the campaign,"[44] but it is doubtful that he was believed by anyone in the audience or, for that matter, by anyone in Washington.

Forrestal's statement to the National Press Club did not settle the controversy that raged at the time not only about his alleged dealings with Governor Dewey but also about his relationship to the Truman-Barkley Democratic ticket in 1948. Those who were involved in the controversy differ on a number of facts, and it is therefore impossible, even fifteen years later, to determine the extent to which Forrestal was financially involved in the Democratic campaign. There can be no doubt at all, however, that rumors of his partisanship for Dewey or, at best, his election "neutrality" angered a number of influential Democrats, and after the election some of these individuals began to press very hard for Forrestal's resignation.

The controversy relates, in part, to a substantial contribution that Forrestal did or did not make to the Truman-Barkley Committee *before* the election. The contribution, if made, came from a fund that Forrestal established in 1940 just before his departure for Washington. Depositing $16,-000 with his friend and attorney Walter Dunnington, Forrestal informed Dunnington in June, 1940, that the money was to be spent as Forrestal directed but at no time, unless instructed otherwise, was Dunnington to reveal that the money belonged to Forrestal. The purpose of the fund, Forrestal explained, was to enable him to make certain expenditures to which his name would not be attached, such

---

44. On February 1, 1949, Forrestal in an address to the Club also denied that he had contributed money to the Dewey campaign. "I have not been active in politics," he told the newspapermen. "I voted, obviously, for President Truman. . . . I have been a Democrat—whether rightly or wrongly—I have been a Democrat since the inheritance of my vote, and I must confess I split my ticket now and then for the last 25 years."

as campaign contributions and gifts of money to friends, organizations, and "causes."

Between 1940 and 1948 several withdrawals from the fund went into Senate and House campaigns, local elections in Dutchess County, New York, and charitable undertakings. Among the senators whose campaigns were aided during that time were Lyndon B. Johnson and Burnet R. Maybank, and in 1947 Forrestal contributed $100 to John J. Gartland, Jr., who was running on the Democratic ticket for district attorney in Dutchess County. A number of deserving and needy Princeton students benefited from the fund, and occasionally one of Forrestal's old classmates or Wall Street friends who had fallen on hard times received a cash present through the mail with no indication of from whom it had come.

In August, 1948, according to Dunnington, Forrestal instructed him to send a check for $2,500 to Louis Johnson, then chief fund-raiser for the Truman-Barkley Committee and later Forrestal's successor as Defense Secretary. Dunnington did so, and not long after the election received an acknowledgment of his [Dunnington's] contribution from Truman. By that time, certain Washington columnists were freely speculating that Forrestal had privately been a Dewey supporter, and it was also true that Dunnington did not wish his own name to be attached to any campaign contribution. In an effort to correct the record, Dunnington wrote Truman that the $2,500 check, while written by Dunnington, represented Forrestal's money and the acknowledgment should therefore be sent to Forrestal. Failing to receive a reply to his letter, Dunnington subsequently spoke to Democratic Committee Chairman J. Howard McGrath about Forrestal's contribution, and McGrath indicated that Dunnington's explanation of the $2,500 check would be communicated to Truman.

More than ten years later, in July, 1959, Louis Johnson, when asked about the check, knew "nothing about any fund

sent in on behalf of Mr. Forrestal from anyone." Although
he did recall "[t]here was quite a row, according to the public
records, as to Forrestal's contribution to the Truman campaign," he was "not involved therein, and do not now propose to become a party thereto."[45] Unfortunately for the
determination of the historical record, the canceled check
written by Dunnington and the letters from and to Truman
no longer exist, and there is no reference to the matter in
Forrestal's papers.

It is clear, however, that on September 27, 1948, Forrestal
was asked by Paul F. Fitzpatrick of the New York State
Democratic Committee for a campaign contribution and for
a list of friends who could be approached in behalf of campaign finance. He apparently sent such a list but it is not
known whether the list was accompanied by a check. On
October 15, less than three weeks before the election, Democratic fund-raiser George E. Allen wrote Forrestal:

I know that recently you have been asked many times to contribute to the Democratic Campaign, but this is, as far as I am
concerned, the final request. . . . Would you join me in making a
donation?

Allen's note implies that he, at least, was unaware of any
previous contribution by Forrestal, and the latter did not
inform him that a "donation" had already been made
through Dunnington. Instead, on October 18 Forrestal sent
Marine Sergeant William M. Russ to Truman-Barkley Club
headquarters in Washington with an envelope containing
$100 in cash. Sergeant Russ received a receipt which read:

Received of William M. Russ, T/Sgt., USMC, Agent for the Hon.
James Forrestal—the amount of $100 in currency as his con-
tribution to the National Truman-Barkley Club.

On November 1, one day *before* the election, Allen solicited
Forrestal on the telephone, and Forrestal agreed to make a

45. Letter to the writer, July 29, 1959.

contribution to the Democrats' congressional campaign fund. But it was not until November 9, one week *after* the election, that he sent a check for $250 to the Democratic National Congressional Committee, and in January the timing of his contribution received some attention in the Washington *Times-Herald.* "Defense Secretary Forrestal," ran a *Times-Herald* story of January 12,

and White House military aide Harry H. Vaughan led a list of prominent persons who poured money into the Democratic campaign after President Truman's surprise victory. . . . Forrestal contributed $250. His check was dated November 9, a week after the election.

By that time Forrestal, already a very ill man, had been hurt and depressed by a number of newspaper stories circulating about him, stories which, as noted earlier, reflected adversely on his personal courage, integrity, and loyalty to Truman. Aware that his continuance in office depended upon Truman's good will, Forrestal was particularly upset by the *Times-Herald* story of January 12, and he had one of his aides obtain from George E. Allen assurances that the newspaper had distorted the facts of the case. The point Forrestal wished to establish was that while his check had been dated November 9, his promise to contribute the money had been made on November 1. In due course the aide reported back Allen's verification that "it was the day *before* the election that he talked to you on the telephone and you gave the $250 then." Moreover, the aide added, Allen

said there is no question about it—and he has told everyone he knows. He will be a witness anywhere, anytime, he said. And not to mind those pip-squeaks; he knows how great the President thinks you are.

Forrestal was grateful for Allen's statement, which he communicated to some of his newspapermen friends, but he attached little importance to Allen's reference to his standing with Truman. There was no doubt in Forrestal's mind that the charges of personal and political disloyalty, in addition to their long-standing policy differences, had steadily worsened his relations with the President. His seeming ambivalence toward the election results, his failure to campaign for Truman or even, so far as anyone knew, to make any substantial financial contribution to the Democratic Party which, at the time, was heavily in debt, had added to the already large number of his enemies in the Administration and in liberal Democratic circles. Although Forrestal justified his inactivity by arguing that it was "inappropriate" for any Secretary of Defense in a crisis period to become embroiled in partisan politics, there were those who believed he had other reasons for his refusal to involve himself. And one of these reasons, some of his critics alleged, was that he had made some sort of "deal" with the Republicans, that, had Dewey won, would have enabled him to remain in office.

It was also true in January, 1949, that Forrestal was far from satisfied with the functioning of the national Military Establishment and with his own performance as Defense Secretary. By that time he had devoted sixteen months to a grueling and demanding job, and he had achieved, he thought, even less unification of the Services than he himself had originally desired. Regarding himself as something of a failure, he was aware, as were his closest associates, that he had reached a physical and psychological state of almost total exhaustion. Yet he could not bring himself to resign, although he was urged to do so by certain friends who were extremely disturbed by his appearance and behavior. By January, 1949, he was too much a "victim of the Washington scene" to leave it willingly, but it is just possible that when he used that expression on January 11 he was thinking of himself as a "victim" in more than one sense of the word.

VIII

☆ ☆ ☆ ☆ ☆

Secretary of Defense

ON SEPTEMBER 24, 1947, exactly one week after taking the oath of office as Defense Secretary, Forrestal registered a Smith & Wesson revolver with the Metropolitan Police Department of Washington. While no one can say with precision what was in his mind on that occasion, the action was at least symbolic of Forrestal's deepening apprehension at the state of the world and the nation's security. Three years earlier, when he was awaiting congressional action on his appointment as Navy Secretary, Forrestal had been amused by a telegram from some of his Princeton classmates that read: "Stop worrying. Princeton Class of 1915 ratified your appointment." Apparently the Class of 1915 did not send a similar wire in 1947, and had it done so it is doubtful that Forrestal would have found it as amusing as the earlier communiqué.

Although the nation was at war in 1944, it was a war that Forrestal and everyone else in Washington were confident we were winning. The nation was not precisely at war in September, 1947, when Forrestal was sworn in as Defense Secretary, but it was engaged in a worldwide struggle with Communism, and he was by no means convinced it was a struggle that would be won. The struggle, in any case, would be a costly one, and Forrestal took office as Defense Secretary with the firm conviction that as there was no ultimate weapon in any war, there was no absolute or cheap guarantee of the national security. "It has long been one of my strongly held beliefs," he wrote Hanson W. Baldwin on January 2, 1948,

that the word "security" ought to be stricken from the language and the word "risk" substituted. I came to that conclusion out of my own business experience. Al Wiggin once defined a speculation as an investment that has gone sour.
The great danger in any country is for people to believe that there is anything absolute about security. Air power, atomic bombs, wealth—by itself none of these can give any security.

The phrase "by itself" in Forrestal's letter to Baldwin was an oblique reference to those who were arguing in January, 1948, that a seventy-group Air Force was indispensable to the preservation of peace and security, and during the months that followed much of Forrestal's time was occupied in efforts to strike a balance between air power and other components of the national defense. But there were other problems as well, and Forrestal quickly found that his authority as Defense Secretary would depend less on the National Security Act of 1947 than on his relations with the President and Cabinet colleagues, the three Service Secretaries, the Joint Chiefs of Staff, and key members of Congress. The 1947 legislation, which had been loosely written largely as a consequence of Forrestal's position on unification, was not designed to enable Forrestal or any other Defense Secretary to administer the Pentagon as, in Navy parlance, "a tight ship," and yet Forrestal early recognized that integration of the Pentagon departments, not to mention unification, would be extremely difficult to achieve. Perhaps, however, something could be achieved through force of personality, and Forrestal again and again tried to demonstrate that, as he once put it, vis-à-vis the three Service

Secretaries, "his was not the dummy hand." A few days after taking office on September 17, 1947, according to one story, Forrestal convened a War Council meeting of the Service Secretaries and the three Chiefs of Staff. "I expect each of you gentlemen," Forrestal began, "to attend every meeting of this body." Following General Eisenhower's remark, "I presume if we are out of town we can send our deputies," there was a moment's silence while all present waited for Forrestal's reaction. Forrestal repeated his previous statement, to which Eisenhower's rejoinder was, "I had to break a very important engagement to get here this morning." There was another silence, and then Forrestal delivered his earlier statement for the third time. Eisenhower did not comment further, and the meeting proceeded to other business. On another occasion, to be discussed later, Forrestal demanded an explanation of certain remarks made in a Los Angeles speech by Air Secretary Symington, and for a time he contemplated asking for Symington's resignation. These incidents, and others as well, failed to convince those involved, including Forrestal himself, that "his was not the dummy hand," and long before the end of 1948 the force of personality was very largely spent. The political and policy battles in which Forrestal had engaged for more than eight years, in addition to his internal struggles and conflicts, were moving toward a final tragic moment of truth.

The turmoil of Forrestal's last eighteen months in office was occasioned in part by controversies within the government related to defense requirements. There was, to begin with, the question of how much defense the country could afford without abandoning its free-enterprise economy in favor of production, prices, profits, and wages controls. Related to this was a budget controversy that found Forrestal on one side and the President and Budget Bureau on the other. Despite the Cold War crises of 1947–1948, Truman insisted on defense-budget limits that Forrestal did not feel were adequate for military security. As Defense Secretary, however, he was forced to defend the Truman budget in his public speeches and testimony before congressional committees. The Joint Chiefs and Service Secretaries, on the other hand, were less reconciled to the successive "ceilings" on defense expenditures, less inclined to defend them, and on the whole reluctant to reduce their estimates of what was required.

There was also a continuing argument, reminiscent of the unification hearings, about the functions and missions of the Services. Notwithstanding an earlier Executive order dealing with the problem, the Navy and the Air Force engaged in bitter wrangling over their roles in strategic bombing operations. If the Air Force was insistent upon seventy groups, the Navy was hardly less insistent that it, too, required expansion, and, as part of that expansion, an 80,000-ton supercarrier program. The Army, supported by the President, was advocating universal military training and an increase in the number of its combat units. Forrestal was not only involved in all these controversies; by virtue of his position he was also compelled to seek compromises between the President's views, his own views, and those of the Service Secretaries and Chiefs.

His efforts to achieve such compromises began with budget discussions in the summer and fall of 1947. Despite some reservations, Forrestal agreed to support Truman in urging Congress to appropriate for defense in fiscal 1949 (that is, the fiscal year ending June 30, 1949) an amount slightly in excess of $11 billion. The Truman budget provided for fifty-five air groups instead of the seventy favored by the Air Force, and in January, 1948, the issue was joined when the seventy-group proposal was endorsed by the President's Air Policy Commission headed by Thomas K. Finletter (hereafter referred to as the Finletter Commission), and the Congressional Aviation Policy Board (hereafter referred to as the Brewster-Hinshaw Board). The latter relied heavily upon testimony before the Finletter Commission, and there can be no doubt that the Commission's report was largely responsible for the later House and Senate decision to increase Air Force strength to seventy groups.

The Commission and Board also urged that the Joint Chiefs of Staff adopt an integrated military strategy and reach some agreement with respect to the functions of the respective Services. The Brewster-Hinshaw Board noted that the Navy and the Air Force, in particular, differed in interpretation of certain sections of the National Security Act and Executive Order 9877, the order defining the functions and missions of the Services. According to the Navy, the Act and the order were in conflict, and since the Act took precedence, the order could be ignored. The Air Force held that there was no conflict, and its spokesmen made it clear they would not be bound by the Navy's concept of Air Force missions.

One consequence of the conflicting testimony before the Finletter Commission and Brewster-Hinshaw Board was a Joint Chiefs of Staff Conference at Key West, Florida, in March, 1948. At a press conference on March 10, Forrestal announced that he was convening the meeting to resolve the controversy over missions and to decide "who will do what with what." If the Joint Chiefs were unable to reach agreement, he told reporters, "I shall have to make my own decisions." He did not indicate what these decisions would be, but he made it clear that all concerned—the President, the Service Chiefs and Secretaries, and Forrestal—were convinced that the only alternative to UMT was a revival of the draft.[1]

Events were to demonstrate that the Key West conference resolved few if any of the major problems, and the decisions that were reached did not sharply reduce the acrimony

---

1. Summarized from the *New York Herald Tribune* of March 11, 1948, in *Diaries*, p. 390.

already existing in the Defense Department. In a press release of March 28, however, Forrestal implied that almost all crucial issues had been settled at Key West, including the issue of "who will do what with what." Under a new Executive Order (9950) replacing Order 9877, he announced that

each service is assigned specific functions in which that service has a clear-cut responsibility. Such functions are defined as primary functions. In addition, each service is charged with collateral functions, wherein its forces are to be employed to support and supplement the other services. . . . As an illustration of this principle, strategic air warfare has been assigned as a primary function of the Air Force, and the Navy is assigned as a primary function the conduct of air operations necessary for the accomplishment of objectives in a naval campaign . . . the Navy will not be prohibited from attacking any targets, inland or otherwise, which are necessary for the accomplishment of its mission.

The references to naval air missions could mean a great deal or very little. The Air Force chose to think that, in the words of one of its high-ranking officers, it had been "done in" by the Navy and Forrestal at Key West. Although strategic air warfare remained one of its primary functions, Air Force officials were deeply resentful of decisions that permitted the Navy to acquire high-altitude bombers capable of delivering atomic bombs, and to initiate construction of an 80,000-ton supercarrier. The Navy, for its part, resented the fact that it was deprived of its own strategic air force. It was also noted that the Key West conference, largely because of opposition from the Army, Navy, and Forrestal, did not declare itself in favor of a seventy-group Air Force. The Marine Corps was not happy with the decision to limit its strength to four divisions, especially in view of the declared need to increase the size of the Army.

Even the decisions that were reached with some degree of unanimity proved in the end controversial. The Joint Chiefs agreement, for example, that a draft law be reenacted in lieu of the politically explosive and therefore improbable

UMT proposal never received more than lukewarm support from Air Force spokesmen. Another Key West recommendation, that the Military Establishment be given custody of atomic weapons, drew fire from Congress, the Atomic Energy Commission, the Cabinet, and the President himself. Although it is doubtful that this issue "may have been a turning point in Forrestal's relations with the President"[2]—that point had been turned earlier—Forrestal's insistence on military authority over the Bomb did not improve his relations with Truman and some key members of Congress, especially those senators and representatives who sat on the Joint Atomic Energy Committee.[3]

The issues that divided the Joint Chiefs were those in which House and Senate committees were most interested, and during the spring of 1948 Forrestal made several appearances before a variety of legislative committees. In his first appearance before the Senate Armed Services Committee a few days after the Key West conference, Forrestal emphasized the need for a "balanced" military force that would take into account overall budget and manpower requirements. Well aware that congressional opinion strongly favored a seventy-group Air Force, Forrestal was careful to indicate his support in principle for a strong air arm in accordance with the recommendations of the Finletter Commission and the Brewster-Hinshaw Board. But he pointed out that such an air arm would cost a good deal of money and that, in general,

---

2. Lewis L. Strauss, *Men and Decisions* (Garden City: Doubleday & Co., 1962), p. 160. Admiral Strauss, who was a member of the AEC at the time, advised Forrestal not to press the issue on the grounds that Truman would decide against him. Forrestal's response, according to Strauss, was that "he was entirely prepared to resign if the President overruled him on a matter in his area." He did not resign, of course, and Strauss suggests "in looking back, Forrestal's difficulty with the decision [*sic*] may have been an early indication of his failing health."—*Ibid*.

3. Forrestal's efforts to transfer custody of the Bomb began shortly after the Key West Conference and culminated in a White House meeting on July 21, 1948. For Forrestal's own account of this meeting, which was attended by the entire AEC, see *Diaries*, pp. 460–461.

provision for any one of the Services must be made in the light of budgetary limitations affecting all of the Services. While he endorsed the Joint Chiefs' recommendation that all three Services be strengthened, he would not commit himself to "exact figures," he told the Committee, until "a more exact study" could be made of the problems involved. Such a study, he indicated, would shortly be available.[4]

Questioned about a newspaper report that the Navy was opposed to UMT, Forrestal admitted that the Navy had first been opposed but had "come to the realization" that its reserve training program would not provide it with the needed manpower. Implications that the Navy and Air Force were coerced into supporting UMT were denied by John L. Sullivan and Symington, the respective Secretaries. UMT, they agreed, was essential to national security. They also were in accord with Forrestal that the disagreements among the Joint Chiefs had been exaggerated, or at least misunderstood. For example, the Joint Chiefs had always been capable of planning operations for the entire Military Establishment. The problem was with procurement, and also with what Forrestal preferred to call the "functions" of the Services as distinct from their "roles and missions." He was not altogether explicit about the differences between "functions" and "roles and missions," and he did not prove to the satisfaction of those present that the latter expression was "somewhat misleading language."

In a second appearance, on March 25, Forrestal dealt with the "exact figures" to which he had earlier referred. A "balanced force" would be created, he proposed, if the Army were increased by 240,000 men (from 542,000 to 782,000), the Navy by 63,000 (from 397,000 to 460,000), the Marines by 11,000 (from 81,000 to 92,000), and the Air Force by 35,500 (from 364,500 to 400,000). The Air Force figure, it

---

4. *Hearings*, Senate Committee on Armed Services, 80th Congress, Second Session, p. 34.

was quickly brought out, would sustain the Air Force at fifty-five groups rather than at the seventy recommended by the Finletter and Brewster-Hinshaw study groups.

Much of the testimony that followed Forrestal's statements was concerned with the problem of how much defense the economy could afford. Forrestal's proposals were within limits set by the Truman budget; the question was whether budget estimates were sufficient to maintain our fighting forces at adequate strength. Forrestal's own position, in which he was supported by Navy Secretary Sullivan and Army Secretary Kenneth C. Royall, was that not much more could be spent on defense unless the nation was willing to tolerate a partly planned and regimented economy. Unlike Truman and most other members of the Administration, Forrestal was willing to resort to emergency economic measures, although he recognized and lamented the fact that the nation as a whole was unprepared and unwilling to make the sacrifices involved. Nor would it be prepared or willing, he believed, until it was acquainted with the harsh facts of the world situation, and it would not become acquainted with those facts, he had long since concluded pessimistically, until Truman was replaced in office. Only then could there be generated a sense of alarm and an awareness of the very real dangers confronting the United States.

In March and April, 1948, there was little doubt in Forrestal's mind that Truman's political future could be measured in months, but meanwhile there was a very real possibility that Congress would "buy" a seventy-group Air Force at the expense of the other two Services, UMT *and* Selective Service. In that event, Forrestal was convinced, we would be inadequately prepared for war and severely handicapped in keeping the peace. Again and again he emphasized that a strong Air Force by itself could not ensure peace or gain victory in war. In peace and in war, he stressed, a strong Army and Navy were also needed to guard sea lanes and to hold vital ground that might otherwise be occupied by communist forces.

Although the Service Secretaries and Joint Chiefs were instructed to support the Truman military budget and Forrestal's rationale for a "balanced" military capability, they refused to commit themselves to the position that the Truman budget was adequate for national security. Air Secretary Symington, in particular, refused to retract his testimony to the Finletter and Brewster-Hinshaw committees in favor of a seventy-group Air Force. The expansion to seventy groups, he told members of the Senate Armed Services Committee in late March, 1948, had been his recommendation for several years, and he did not propose to change it. Why then, asked Senator Lodge, has the Air Force been restricted to fifty-five groups? Denying that the Air Force had any problem recruiting personnel, Symington indicated that the major problem was money, that the Air Force could not afford seventy groups. This answer did not satisfy Lodge. "I want to know," he continued the pursuit,

> why the minimum has dropped from 70 to 55; that is all I want to know. There is probably some good reason. I would like to know what the reason is.
>
> SYMINGTON: Well, Senator, I think you are probably with your experience in government able to know a lot more about the reason than I do.
>
> LODGE: I do not know anything about it at all. It seems to me a fair question. If it is not, I withdraw it.

Fair or not, he did not withdraw the question, and again Symington was asked about the reduction from seventy to fifty-five groups. "My answer," he replied,

> is that we have not got the men because we have not got money and we have not got the airplanes because we have not got money.

Lodge, who earlier had claimed, "I do not know anything about it at all," then suggested that the money should be

requested from Congress. He correctly forecast that if the
money were requested, Congress would oblige, and the public, too, "will support the money to get the seventy air
groups." Encouraged by this, Symington under direct questioning admitted that, in his opinion, a seventy-group Air
Force was essential to the nation's security. Air Force Chief
of Staff General Carl Spaatz added his view that the seventy-
group force was a "minimum air defense" that would require
502,000 men rather than the 400,000 contemplated in the
Truman estimates.

Forrestal, extremely disturbed although not surprised
that Symington and Spaatz had contradicted his own earlier
testimony, again declared to Committee members that the
seventy-group Air Force represented a "unilateral" rather
than a joint Defense Department proposal and that such a
force was unrelated to the requirements of the other Services.
If, assuming the seventy groups, the "balance" with the other
services was maintained, he estimated that the budget would
have to be increased by approximately $18 billion. Cost
studies that had been done in the Defense Department at the
time of the Finletter report, he revealed, had produced "sums
[that] were so staggering as to be unrealistic."

Testimony by Forrestal and the three Service Secretaries
before other committees proceeded in much the same vein.
Forrestal continued to emphasize the need for "balance,"
and insisted that there was a close relationship between
defense spending levels and the state of the national economy. Symington, usually under questioning but occasionally
independently of it, reiterated the case for seventy groups; in
connection with the Air Force proposal he was apt to use
such words as "minimal," "essential," and "basic." The Army
and Navy Secretaries also made it clear that the proposals
submitted by Forrestal were not those they had favored in
discussions within the Defense Department, but unlike
Symington they expressed an awareness, albeit reluctantly,

that the nation's economy and taxpayers could not or would not pay for a gigantic defense "package" in peacetime. As Secretary Royall put it, the Army had requested more men and money that it was allocated in the Truman budget, but it was willing to abide by Forrestal's decision allocating funds between the three Services. "We recognized the need," Royall testified,

for a financial limit for defense expenditures even at the time. We further recognized that unification and its great benefit to national defense would be endangered by unilateral action of any department at this time.

While the amount requested for the Army "cuts the cloth very close," the Army, Royall implied, could probably manage on it.

In appearances before the House Armed Services Committee, Forrestal was closely questioned about his opposition to a seventy-group Air Force. "I think it is very dangerous," he indicated on one occasion,

to select any part of our national military power without being sure that elements necessary to go with it are present in sufficient power and force to make it usable. In other words, to shorten the speech, I mean simply this: You cannot separate in modern war any one segment from the other two. They march together.

Asked whether the proposals before Congress would give the United States an Air Force capable of carrying atomic bombs to the Soviet heartland, Forrestal distinguished between airpower requirements in peace and war. The Air Force proposed would not be capable of fighting a war for the reason that in wartime the air strength required "would go very far beyond the amount you are speaking about, and which we can never sustain and should never try to sustain because the economy could not stand it." He warned the Committee that "[w]e must not bust ourselves into the loss of a war before it occurs." The fifty-five-group Air Force, he observed, would provide the "foundation" for a wartime Air Force when and if required.

Although the issue of the seventy-group Air Force was already foreclosed—both Senate and House Armed Services Committees had voted in favor of the expansion—the House Committee, in addition to questioning Forrestal, heard further testimony from Symington and Spaatz. Once again they argued the case for the seventy groups, but in his appearance on April 13 Symington revealed that he was not in accord with other recommendations submitted by Forrestal and the Joint Chiefs. Previously he had supported Selective Service legislation, but on April 13 he informed the Committee that the Air Force did not require the draft in order to increase its personnel strength to 502,000 men. "We are completely in support of selective service," he testified, "because the Army wants it and needs it. We feel the Army is essential to the efficient operation of the Air Force." To avoid possible misunderstanding, several Committee members queried him closely about this statement, and Symington made it clear beyond dispute that he did not assign the highest priority to either Selective Service or UMT. "If you had to make a choice," he was asked,

> of methods of insuring the security of this nation, do you think we are more likely to insure the security of this nation with a strong effective seventy-group Air Force or with UMT?
>
> SYMINGTON: Well, if my two boys have to go back again into the Army and the Marines, I would rather see them have a minimum Air Force [seventy groups] than I would a group of younger boys trained for six months or a year.

"And, incidentally," he added gratuitously but for good measure,

> I am in complete agreement—and the Air Force is—with the Compton Report. The Compton Report said that if UMT had to be at the expense of the military services they not only would not be for it, they would be against it. That is our position.

It was not Forrestal's position, however, and in the company of his friends and associates he made no secret of the fact that Symington's testimony had been insubordinate and disloyal. Symington, he felt, had the right under the Unification Act to appeal over his head to the President but not to Congress. He also disagreed with Symington's interpretation of a conference they had had before the hearings began. According to Symington, who was asked by a Committee member whether "there has been any pressure put on the Air Corps [*sic*] to back down from the [seventy-group] position," Forrestal had given him and other Air Force officials permission to "come before these committees and . . . to tell what we thought was right." In reply to another question, Symington was positive that the President would not veto a measure providing for a seventy-group Air Force, despite rumors to that effect current in Washington.

It is entirely possible that Symington had cleared his testimony with Truman, and was therefore appearing before the House Committee with Truman's tacit approval. In Forrestal's judgment, however, Symington's statements before the Committee were deliberately designed not only to disrupt the military "balance" but to discredit his own judgment and that of his military advisers. He also felt, in April, that Symington merited a strong reprimand from the President for his attitude toward Selective Service and UMT. Indeed, had Forrestal received any encouragement from Truman he would have requested Symington's resignation. But there was neither reprimand nor encouragement, and Forrestal began to suspect that Truman was far more influenced by his Air Secretary than by his Secretary of Defense. He also became convinced that Symington very much wanted to be Defense Secretary, and would lose no opportunity to turn the President against him. He had never entirely liked Symington or entirely trusted him, and after April, 1948, he positively disliked and distrusted him.

More than a year earlier, when Forrestal and Patterson were negotiating their unification disagreements, Forrestal had become aware that Symington's ambition had charted a course from the Pentagon to the White House. Symington, then an assistant to Patterson, was involved in much of the bargaining, and Forrestal quickly perceived that Symington had a distinct personal interest in the success of the negotiations. Thus on one occasion Symington in behalf of the Army accepted Forrestal's position on three of the five remaining issues in controversy. One of Forrestal's aides, pleased with developments, commented to Forrestal that since the Navy could give in to Symington on at least one of the remaining two issues, an agreement or "deal" was very close at hand. Forrestal remarked, the aide recalls, that it would not be necessary to compromise on either of the two issues because Symington would not insist that the Navy defer to the Army's position. "I know Stu from way back," he told the aide, "and I know that he wants to be Secretary of Defense so badly that he'll be willing to compromise the Army position to any extent needed to get our agreement on a bill." According to the aide, Forrestal's prediction "proved to be quite correct because in short order Symington did accept the Navy's position on the two remaining issues. . . ."

Forrestal as Defense Secretary did not want Symington as Air Secretary, but he was unable to persuade the President to appoint someone else. He was also unable to persuade Truman in 1948, when it became clear that Symington was campaigning in and out of Congress for an Air Force that had little relationship to the size and strength of the other Services, that it was appropriate to request his resignation. Forrestal's alternative, which was not successful, was to send Symington occasional memoranda scolding him for his air-power propaganda activities, and to request an "explanation" on at least one occasion when it was reported in the press that Symington had attacked Forrestal indirectly as an "ax-grinder dedicated to obsolete methods" of warfare.

The public occasion on which Symington was most critical of Forrestal, at least by implication, was witnessed by more than five hundred aviation engineers in Los Angeles on July 17, 1948. According to *The New York Times* of the following day, Symington upon his arrival

was handed a prepared speech—presumably as approved by higher quarters in the Department of Defense—which had been wired here and laboriously manifolded for distribution. Considering it as too inconsequential to deliver, it was stated, he summarily rejected it and spoke "off the cuff" with frequent undisguised tinges of acerbity.

Assailing "ax-grinders dedicated to obsolete methods" of warfare, who contended that large Air appropriations might "unbalance" the three Services, Mr. Symington declared that air power should be put in balance not with the Army or the Navy, but with the power of potential enemies, and that "the American people have put their money on air power. . . ."[5]

Provoked by the *Times*'s account of Symington's "off the cuff" remarks, Forrestal sent the Air Secretary a message referring to these remarks as, if accurately reported, "an act of official disobedience and personal disloyalty." While awaiting a reply he had another conference with Truman about Symington, and again he was discouraged from taking any action.[6]

On July 23 Forrestal informed Truman in Symington's presence that, in effect, he was satisfied with Symington's explanation of the Los Angeles incident. Symington, he told Truman, had explained that the written speech approved in Forrestal's office had arrived in "nonusable form," had given Forrestal a "copy of his original remarks," and had also "denied having made any impromptu remarks." So far as is known, that meeting with the President marked the official end of the affair that had begun almost a week earlier in Los Angeles, but Forrestal was to ponder its implications for

5. *Diaries*, pp. 462–463.
6. *Ibid.*, pp. 463–465.

many months to come. He did not believe Symington's disclaimers of disobedience and disloyalty in Los Angeles. Symington's feelings, if not his actual remarks, Forrestal knew, had been reported accurately, and yet it was clear that despite this and other acts of insubordination the President did not favor disciplinary action. Relative to the Air Secretary, Forrestal felt, "his was the dummy hand," and he would continue to play "dummy" until there was a change of Administration and/or a revision of the National Security Act that would increase the authority of the Secretary of Defense. In the meantime, he concluded, it was essential that he avoid an open break with Symington, and despite a good deal of provocation after July, Forrestal managed to avoid an ugly and dramatic confrontation. Even when he became convinced late in 1948 that Symington was gathering information about his personal and professional life—was, in so many words, spying on him—he abided by his earlier resolve.

To whatever degree Symington was loyal or disloyal to his nominal superior in the Pentagon, his attitude toward military requirements was supported by most legislators and by the public at large. The essence of his position, that air power should be in "balance" not with the other Services but with the Soviet Air Force, had also been a major theme in the Finletter and Brewster-Hinshaw reports. A seventy-group force, moreover, would require fewer sacrifices by citizens than a vastly expanded Army and Navy. The seventy groups would cost money, of course, but they would not require manpower draft levies of any substantial size. If, as Symington suggested, such an Air Force was an alternative to UMT, and if, further, as most air-power proponents insisted, the next war would be won or lost in the air, there could be no question where most Americans stood. Polls showed that a majority of citizens were in favor of seventy groups and even more, and Congress responded accordingly. The vote in favor of the seventy-group force, in the form of a vote on a supplementary appropriations bill, was 343 for and 3 against in the House, and 74 for and 2 against in the Senate.

Although the Air Force received the lion's share of the additional money for defense, the bill provided for some expansion of the other Services. In an effort to preserve the principle if not the actuality of "balance," and also because the other Service Secretaries and Chiefs had followed Symington's unilateral lead in expressing their own dissatisfaction with the original estimates, Congress voted additional funds for the Army and Navy. The seventy-group decision was, to some extent, compromised by a provision that money appropriated for aircraft procurement could not be spent without the President's approval. Despite successive appeals from Truman, Forrestal, and others, Congress refused to endorse UMT, but the draft was reenacted on June 19.

Forrestal regarded the final outcome of the 1948 defense debate as both a personal defeat and conclusive evidence that the nation lacked the leadership and stamina necessary for victory in the Cold War. The personal defeat, he felt, had been administered less by Congress than by Truman, Symington and, to a lesser extent, the other Service Secretaries and Chiefs. Truman had insisted, and would continue to insist, that defense spending not exceed a total of $15 billion, and Forrestal was unable to persuade him that much more was needed if the nation was to preserve its own security and that of other free nations. Nineteen forty-eight was an election year, and Forrestal came to embrace the suspicion, not for the first time, that Truman was guided less by the national interest than by political considerations. Truman, he believed, was too much a prisoner of the ancient political rule that taxes and spending should never be increased during any period immediately preceding voting day. Nevertheless, he reluctantly agreed to support the budget proposals, only to find that he could not depend on the loyalty of his own subordinates in the Defense Department.

Although each Service Secretary and Chief of Staff who testified paid his respects to Forrestal, none of them concealed the fact that he was disappointed with the estimates for his own Service. And Symington, who went a good deal further than the others in putting the principle of "balance" in jeopardy, could not even be properly disciplined, it appeared to Forrestal, because he had some sort of understanding with the President.

Concluding that his judgment had been questioned and his authority undermined by the defense-budget controversy in March and April, 1948, Forrestal anticipated that he would encounter even more opposition in the preparation of the defense budget for fiscal 1950. Nor was he disappointed in this expectation. Despite the Cold War crises of the spring and summer of 1948, Truman continued to insist on the $15 billion "ceiling" for defense, a figure that included $600 million for stockpiling strategic raw materials. The remaining $14.4 billion, Forrestal frequently reminded Truman, fell short of the amount necessary to maintain all our bases and overseas lines of communication. The proposed ceiling, he told Truman on October 5, 1948, would "probably" give us the means of air reprisal against any enemy "using England as a base," but the "Mediterranean would be ruled out." To provide for the Mediterranean sector Forrestal wanted to proceed with another budget of approximately $18.5 billion, but the President, in effect, vetoed his effort to lift the "ceiling." Truman, according to Forrestal,

said he wished it [the $18.5 billion budget] to be held in reserve, that the fact of its presentation would be interpreted as a step toward preparation for war and that additional estimates could be kept in the form of supplementals, to be presented if and when the situation became more dangerous.[7]

This statement and other Truman statements struck Forrestal as fanciful in the extreme. The situation, from

7. *Ibid.*, p. 498.

Forrestal's vantage point, *was* dangerous and was steadily becoming more dangerous. Furthermore, if there was not enough money to maintain our ships and bases in the Mediterranean, what was the sense of proclaiming the Truman Doctrine in March, 1947? To Forrestal it seemed, once again, that the President was unable or unwilling to confront the military implications of his foreign-policy convictions. Such obtuseness, Forrestal conceded, was also to be found in Congress and in the public at large, but he remained convinced that, no matter what the difficulties, it was the President's job not merely to follow but to lead. While Forrestal was aware of the political risks involved in such leadership, he was certain that graver risks would be the consequence of a weakened defense capability. The Cold War, he remarked to a friend at the time, "would not take a recess until the election."

When it became clear that Truman would not consider a budget increase at least before the 1948 election, Forrestal was faced with the problem of defending a "ceiling" over military expenditures that he himself regarded as inadequate. On October 6, 1948, he notified the Joint Chiefs that he was expecting from them "a definitive recommendation" respecting the division among the Services of the $14.4 billion. The Joint Chiefs had supplied him with a recommendation, although they did not wholeheartedly support it, in the earlier budget wrangle largely concerned with the seventy-group Air Force. But in October that cooperation appeared to be at an end. In a message to Forrestal on October 7, transmitted to him by Admiral Leahy, they took the position that there was no agreement possible on a defense budget not to exceed the Truman figure. In effect, they were notifying Forrestal that they would take no responsibility for "a definitive recommendation;" if one was made to the President and Congress, it would be made by Forrestal and not his military advisers.[8]

---

8. *Ibid.,* p. 499.

On October 15 Forrestal attempted to overcome the intransigence of the Joint Chiefs by encouraging them to submit an "intermediate" budget, that is, a budget that was
more than the Truman "ceiling" but less than the total
requested by the three Services. A board of three high-
ranking officers, one from each Service, appointed by Forrestal in June and thereafter referred to as the McNarney
Board,[9] had recommended a military budget of $23.6 billion.
This figure, Forrestal indicated, was wholly unrealistic, but
it was not unrealistic to think in terms of $17.5 or $18 billion
provided the Joint Chiefs could agree on an estimate in this
range. Whether they could come to any agreement in the
following weeks Forrestal did not know, but he expressed a
desire to participate in the discussions that would take place.
"I want to say to you men also," he declared,

that I am going to try to be in on this as much as I can myself, so
I would appreciate attending any meetings. I am not there as a
spy. My job is going to have to be to convince the President and
his successor, if there is one, that we have taken every drop of
water out of this thing that we could find—we can't catch it all—
but I have got to be able to say that we have gone into this thing
from the ground up and prefer to go at it from the top down. . . .

The two "realistic objectives," he continued, were the $14.4
billion "minimum" and the "intermediate" $17.5 or $18
billion, and the "intermediate" budget "is what I want really
to get to ceiling." The "maximum," or McNarney, budget,
he observed, would enable the United States "to make an
effective and immediate reprisal if the Russians move," while
the "intermediate one will enable us to make reprisals and
at the same time have the tables of organization and the
cadres to fill out promptly."[10]

---

9. The McNarney Board of so-called "budget deputies" drawn from the
Services consisted of Lieutenant General W. H. Haislip from the Army,
Admiral W. H. P. Blandy and Captain Arleigh A. Burke from the Navy, and
General Joseph T. McNarney from the Air Force.
10. *Diaries*, pp. 504–505.

The meeting with the Joint Chiefs led Forrestal to believe he would have their cooperation in preparing a budget that would total less than the McNarney "maximum," and meanwhile he sought to build support elsewhere in the government for the "intermediate" figure. In a note to Secretary of State Marshall on October 31, Forrestal stated that the Truman "ceiling" "will not be adequate to maintain the level of forces which we are scheduled to attain at the end of the current fiscal year [June 30, 1949]." Requesting from Marshall some indication of whether, in Marshall's view, the world situation had improved or worsened since the spring of 1948, Forrestal indicated that he would submit to the President a budget within the $14.4 billion "ceiling." In addition, he wrote Marshall, he felt

an obligation to inform him [Truman] of the weakening of our strength which this budget entails, in the opinion of the Joint Chiefs of Staff, and I am also considering sending the President, as my own recommendation, a proposal that he lift the ceiling to approximately $17.5 billion—which, in my opinion, while involving some risks, would provide us with forces capable of taking effective action in the event of trouble.[11]

Marshall and others approached by Forrestal did not commit themselves to the "intermediate" figure, despite a world situation which Marshall regarded as no better than it had been the previous spring. Forrestal, therefore, was without support except from the Joint Chiefs of Staff when he urged the President to lift the "ceiling" to the "intermediate" $17.5 billion finally requested by the Joint Chiefs. Although Forrestal regarded the "intermediate" budget as a substantial concession by the Joint Chiefs to the President's point of view, Truman was neither grateful nor in a mood to compromise. The $14.4 billion ceiling remained intact, and when the total federal budget was submitted to Congress on January 10, 1949, it provided $14.2 billion, exclusive of

---

11. *Ibid.*, pp. 509–510.

stockpiling, for the Military Establishment. Instead of the fifty-nine air groups requested by Forrestal, there were to be forty-eight, and the 1,980,000 men called for in Forrestal's "intermediate" preparedness program had been reduced to 1,617,830. By an ironic coincidence, which Forrestal did not live to witness, the end of fiscal 1950 coincided almost exactly with the beginning of the Korean War, and at that time the armed strength of the United States was even less than the Truman "minimum." While there were forty-eight air groups on June 25, 1950, there were only 1,465,000 men in the three Services.

Apart from their military and foreign-policy implications, the controversies over Service missions or functions, budgetary requirements and other matters were convincing evidence that the Defense Department was in need of administrative reform. Forrestal had been aware of this need almost from the day he was sworn in as Defense Secretary, and much of his time during the final months was given over to questions of Pentagon reorganization. In his first and only annual report as head of the Military Establishment, Forrestal recommended a number of important changes in the National Security Act of 1947. Provision should be made, he suggested, for "an Under Secretary of Defense . . . [to serve] as the alter ego of the Secretary. . . ." The latter's position should also be strengthened

by making it clear that the Secretary of Defense has the responsibility of exercising "direction, authority, and control" over the departments and agencies of the National Military Establishment.

Noting that the 1947 Act gave the Secretary "general direction, authority, and control," and authorized him to establish "general policies and programs," Forrestal urged that "the word 'general' should be deleted . . . and the authority of the Secretary should be broadened in other related respects." Once these changes were made, and the Defense

Secretary's authority "clearly set out in the act," there would be no need "to change the titles of the departmental Secretaries, who would serve as heads of the respective departments under the Secretary of Defense." He also favored certain changes in the organization of the Joint Chiefs, and the exclusion of the Service Secretaries from statutory membership on the National Security Council.[12]

Almost all of Forrestal's recommendations were enacted into law with the passage of the National Security Act Amendments of 1949. The word "general" was stricken from the 1947 statute, and the Defense Secretary was provided with additional staff assistance in the form of a Deputy Secretary and three Assistant Secretaries. The position of Joint Chiefs of Staff Chairman was established, and the Joint Chiefs staff was increased from 100 to 210 officers. The Army, Navy, and Air Force lost their status as Executive Departments and became military departments without Cabinet representation or statutory membership on the National Security Council. Primary budget responsibility was entrusted to the Comptroller of the Defense Department, a new position that was to be filled by one of the Assistant Secretaries. A comptroller was also to be appointed in each of the military departments. Title IV of the 1949 Amendments left no doubt that with respect to budget matters the Secretary of Defense could henceforth deal himself something more than a "dummy hand."

Forrestal did not live to see the Amendments enacted on August 10, 1949, but it was abundantly clear in late 1948 that the Amendments, like the original National Security Act, would owe much to his influence. His role in revising the 1947 Act, together with his outstanding achievements as a devoted public servant, led many of his friends to assume that he would continue as Defense Secretary no matter what

---

12. National Military Establishment, *First Report of the Secretary of Defense* (Washington: Government Printing Office, 1948), pp. 3–4.

the election results. Although many of these friends were depressed by the prospect of another four-year term for Truman, they felt strongly that Forrestal was almost alone in the Truman Cabinet in his concern for the national security, and they urged him to continue in office. They also assumed, despite the many differences between the President and Forrestal, that Truman would want him to remain.

But a few friends and associates were aware as early as the spring of 1948 that Forrestal was not a well man, and by these friends he was advised to resign or, at the very least, take a long vacation from his Pentagon duties. While they did not know the precise nature of his illness, they were conscious that his behavior was becoming more and more symptomatic of deep mental distress.

Physical signs included a loss of appetite and weight, digestive disturbances, insomnia, and chronic fatigue. In March of 1948, some of his aides began to notice that Forrestal was developing a variety of nervous habits; one of these consisted of dipping his fingers into a water glass or finger bowl and moistening his lips with them. They also were aware that Forrestal picked or scratched almost continually at a certain portion of his scalp which, as a consequence, became irritated. During meetings his mind had a tendency to wander away from the subject under discussion, and he was inclined to postpone decisions, even trivial ones, as long as possible. Once decisions were made, he was prone to worry and fret about them. One of the speeches he gave at this time, which was of no great consequence in terms of its subject, went through eight drafts, although the changes made from draft to draft were of an extremely minor nature. There were also mistakes of identity and memory slips.

Much of this became known to the President late in 1948, but White House circles did not immediately conclude that Forrestal's behavior required medical attention. Thus when Truman learned of Forrestal's belief that he was being followed and that his phone was tapped, he quietly ordered an investigation by Secret Service Chief U. E. Baughman. Baughman's "first assumption," which was probably shared by the President, was "that if Mr. Forrestal thought he was being followed he probably *was* being."[13] Instead, Baughman learned from Forrestal's butler that in addition to memory lapses and nervousness

Mr. Forrestal had become so overly suspicious that whenever the front door was opened or the bell rang, he would go to the area and peer out secretly to see who was there. And only the week before, Mr. Forrestal had come into the kitchen while he, the butler, was there. The Defense Secretary was wearing his hat around the house, apparently forgetting that he had it on, or that he had decided to go out. On this occasion he looked right at the butler and asked: "Where's my butler?" When the butler said, "I'm here, Sir," Mr. Forrestal looked confused and could not remember what he wanted.[14]

Baughman's "final discovery" was that Forrestal had made out his last will and testament, and had also acquired a large number of sleeping tablets. Although Baughman does not assign a specific date to his investigation of Forrestal's suspicions, it is probable that it took place late in 1948 or early in 1949. Whatever the date, his inquiry convinced him that Forrestal was suffering "a total psychotic breakdown . . . characterized by suicidal features," and he communicated this conclusion to the President.

Despite the mounting evidence that Forrestal was seriously ill, most of his government colleagues tended to assume that he was exhausted and nothing more. Forrestal himself was willing to admit that he needed a rest, and he told one friend during the summer of 1948 that he intended to "take a long rest away from Washington at the end of the year."[15]

---

13. U. E. Baughman with Leonard Wallace Robinson, *Secret Service Chief* (New York: Harper & Brothers, 1961), p. 94.
14. *Ibid.*, p. 95.
15. Letter to the writer, July 5, 1960.

But he was eager to remain in office, and only a few close friends were aware of his physical and mental distress. In an effort to keep up appearances he attended a number of cocktail parties between Christmas and New Year's, 1948, and, as was his habit, spent very little time at any one of them; he had always been proud of the fact that he could arrive at a cocktail party, greet the hostess and host, drink a martini, and leave—all in a period of eight minutes. He also played golf at the Chevy Chase Country Club, and, as was his habit, covered the eighteen holes in a shorter time than any other club member; Forrestal, a golfing companion recalls,

played golf as if his life depended on it. He rarely talked or wasted any time going from one green to another. He would hit the ball, practically run after it, and hit it again. For him golf was never a relaxing game. It was just exercise.

He sent Christmas flowers, as usual, to the wives of a number of friends and associates, including Mrs. Harry S Truman, Mrs. Thomas G. Corcoran, Mrs. Marx Leva, Mrs. Omar N. Bradley, Mrs. Hoyt S. Vandenberg, and Mrs. John L. Sullivan. Lord Halifax received a bottle of bourbon and Lady Halifax a box of food; bottles of bourbon were also dispatched to several congressmen, Leslie Biffle, and Charles Messina, Forrestal's favorite barber at the Racquet Club. For Arthur Krock, Congressman John McCormack, John R. Steelman, and General Hoyt S. Vandenberg there were boxes of cigars. Marx Leva received four white shirts. Each of the White House telephone operators—there were ten in all—was given a box of hors d'oeuvres, and the household servants and Pentagon mess boys received cash gifts ranging from five to twenty-five dollars.

Incoming presents ranged from a case of Scotch (from Walter G. Dunnington) to a box of Life Savers (from Robert H. Hinckley). Amon G. Carter sent six bottles of Ambassador Scotch, and bottles of bourbon arrived from Senators Estes Kefauver and Kenneth McKellar. Two bottles of King's Ransom Scotch and one of chartreuse liqueur were received at the house but there were no cards and no indication of from whom they had come. Senator Lyndon B. Johnson gave Forrestal a turkey, and Mr. and Mrs. John McCone's Chrismas gift was a box of candy. Other presents included phonograph records, a case of Squirt, a box of grapefruit, and several boxes of nuts. Turkish Ambassador and Madame Erkin bestowed on Forrestal twelve boxes of Turkish cigarettes, one bottle of cherry liqueur, one of Curaçao rum, and two bottles of a beverage known as Teldel Idaresi. Attorney General Clark sent a book titled *Highlights from Addresses by Tom Clark*, and the President's gift was a plaque with the presidential seal, made from the original wood that was used in constructing the White House.

Truman's gift did not compensate Forrestal for the President's failure to indicate, either publicly or privately, that he wanted him to remain in the Cabinet as Defense Secretary. Ten days after the November election Forrestal had flown to Truman's vacation retreat at Key West, Florida, "with the intention of settling the whole question of his continued tenure in office. . . ."[16] He did not raise the question, however, and the President did not volunteer the assurance that Forrestal had gone to Florida to obtain. The Key West meeting was followed by a spate of newspaper stories alleging, in the words of a Washington *Evening Star* report of November 19, that "President Truman was in the market for a new Secretary of Defense. . . ." There were also rumors that Forrestal's job had already been promised to Louis A. Johnson in return for the latter's campaign services. According to these rumors, Forrestal's resignation was being delayed by Truman resentment of the "advice" he was receiving from Drew Pearson and others who disliked Forrestal. "No S.O.B.," he declared on one occasion, "could tell him what changes to make in his cabinet. . . ."[17]

---

16. Millis, in *Diaries*, p. 529.
17. Quoted by David Lawrence in his Washington *Evening Star* column of March 4, 1949.

By January there was a veritable torrent of "advice" reaching the White House. In favor of Forrestal's retention as Defense Secretary were most Capitol Hill Republicans and a significant number of Democrats, the major Washington and New York newspapers, almost all the mass-circulation news magazines, and such influential Washington columnists as Arthur Krock and David Lawrence. As early as August 27, anticipating a change in White House occupancy after November, Lawrence had urged in his Washington *Evening Star* column that "it would be a mistake to appoint a new Secretary of Defense next January." Forrestal, he argued, should remain in office at least another year in order to make a further contribution to the cause of unification. Noting that Roosevelt in 1940 had appointed Republicans Stimson and Knox to head the Army and Navy Departments, Lawrence concluded that the "next President, if he be a Republican, could continue the precedent of retaining a Democrat in the post of Secretary of Defense."

While there were many who agreed with Lawrence, there were others who felt strongly that Forrestal's resignation was long overdue. Arrayed against him were, in the order listed by *Time* magazine,[18] "Communists, Zionists, Wallaceites, liberals, deserving Democrats who coveted his job . . . gossip columnists," the *Daily Worker*, the New York *Post*, *The Nation*, Walter Winchell, Drew Pearson, and Robert Allen. On January 3 James G. Patton, president of the National Farmers Union, demanded that Forrestal quit the government on the grounds that his first report as Defense Secretary "regards the United States as practically already at war . . . [Forrestal] wants to be able to strike out wherever and whenever he desires to use the military power. . . ."[19] Several columns by Walter Lippmann late in 1948, alleging that Washington policy-makers were relying too heavily on purely

---

18. January 24, 1949.
19. Washington *Evening Star*, January 3, 1949.

military solutions to world problems, were read by many as criticisms of Forrestal.

Forrestal's mental and physical condition was hardly improved by the rumors and accusations that flooded Washington during the two months between the election and the inaugural. Many of them dealt with his personal life, and by these especially he was deeply hurt. As a consequence he was only too ready to believe in January that, as *Time* put it, "he had been marked as the victim of one of the biggest headhunts in the history of Washington politics."[20] He was also prepared to believe that the "headhunters" included persons high in the Truman Administration, a belief that became more plausible when Secretary of State Marshall and Under Secretary Lovett were replaced in January by Dean Acheson and James E. Webb. While Marshall and Forrestal had often held different and occasionally directly opposed views about foreign-policy questions, their relations were cordial partly owing to Lovett efforts to mediate between them. Lovett himself was perhaps Forrestal's most trusted friend in Washington, and his departure from the government was particularly grievous for Forrestal. In addition to their shared Wall Street backgrounds, the two men were in agreement on a variety of issues, and they had also established a warm personal relationship. Lovett, whose home was not far from the Forrestal residence, had long since told Forrestal that whenever he saw a light burning in Lovett's study late at night, he was to feel free to stop in for a chat. With Lovett's replacement by Webb on January 20, these opportunities ceased to exist, and indeed there was almost no one else in Washington to whom Forrestal could unburden himself.

The incoming Secretary of State, whose respect for the President approached veneration, was not one of Forrestal's admirers. Although their views were rather similar, Acheson,

---

20. *Time,* January 24, 1949.

like Forrestal, tending to favor a "tough" foreign policy, there
was a personality conflict between the two that agreement
on issues was never able to bridge. Forrestal was inclined to
regard Acheson as arrogant and intellectually pretentious,
and he was conscious that Acheson thought of him as insubordinate and disloyal to the President. Acheson's second-in-
command, Under Secretary James E. Webb, had been Budget
Bureau Director, and as such, an opponent of Forrestal's
efforts to raise the military "ceiling." The combination in
the State Department of Acheson and Webb, Forrestal knew,
would greatly reduce his own remaining influence in the
formulation and execution of foreign policy.

Yet he intended to remain in office for an indefinite
period. Despite the rumors and gossip, the departure of
Marshall and Lovett, the advice of some friends that he
resign, and his private awareness that his health was deteriorating, Forrestal refused to believe in January that his *pro
forma* resignation would be or should be accepted. On January 11, following a talk with Truman, Forrestal informed
the press that he expected to continue as Secretary of Defense. Although his resignation would be submitted "as a
matter of course," he indicated he did not expect it to be
accepted.[21] In late January he told a number of friends that
he would continue to serve for at least another ninety days,
that is, until May 1 or later. Some of these friends took him
seriously, and others remembered that he had been "resign-
ing" from the government once or twice each year for a good
many years. The few who were aware of his health problems
or who believed that Truman had already chosen Forrestal's
replacement hoped he would resign before there was any
White House request for his resignation.

The events culminating in Forrestal's formal letter of
resignation, dated March 2, 1949, are clouded by controversy
and contradiction. In a brief speech to Washington's Post

---

21. Washington *Evening Star*, January 11, 1949. It was on this occasion that
he declared himself to be "a victim of the Washington scene."

Mortem Club on May 17, 1949, Louis A. Johnson, Forrestal's successor, declared that "in the latter days of January" Forrestal had asked him to become Secretary of Defense. It was at that time, according to Johnson, that Forrestal was told

a story had been printed saying I had been undercutting him—seeking his job. Mr. Forrestal replied that he had double-checked the story and was satisfied that there was not and had never been a word of truth in it.

I found to my continuing satisfaction that Mr. Forrestal disclaimed having anything to do with the attacks which had been aimed at me by some [friends] of his who did not understand the situation.

The President "insisted" that he accept the position, Johnson recalls; Generals Marshall and Eisenhower had previously stated to Truman that Johnson was Forrestal's "logical successor."[22]

Ten years later Johnson's view of the circumstances surrounding his appointment was unchanged. "Forrestal himself," he reiterated,

asked me to be Secretary of Defense to succeed him. It was his choice. I did not seek or want the job, and Forrestal knew this. I have had so many inquiries about this that it is disgusting. . . .[23]

Former President Truman, in support of Johnson, recalls that

Forrestal wanted to resign long before he did, and I kept him from it, although I realized later that I should have let him quit when he wanted.

He left because of failing health, and that's all there was to it. He, himself, recommended Louis Johnson as his successor.[24]

Those individuals who were close to Forrestal during the four months that elapsed between the election and his resignation do not agree with these statements. Forrestal, they report, was shocked and disturbed by the reelection of

22. Copy of speech entitled "As Told by Secretary Johnson to the Post Mortem Club, Tuesday, May 17 (1949)."
23. Letter to the writer, July 29, 1959.
24. Letter to the writer, July 16, 1959.

Truman, not least because he suspected that his position had
already been promised to Johnson. He had never been fond
of Johnson and had never regarded him as qualified for the
difficult post of Defense Secretary. He would gladly have
resigned to make way for either Marshall or Lovett, but he
was not willing to resign in order to provide a Cabinet job
for a political appointment.

In January, however, Forrestal was informed that Johnson would succeed him as Defense Secretary on or about
May 1. He had several meetings with Johnson during February, essentially of a briefing nature, and had his aides
prepare a variety of background papers for Johnson's perusal.
On Tuesday, March 1, Forrestal was summoned to the White
House shortly after noon. He spent almost two hours with
Truman, in the course of which the President asked him to
submit an immediate letter of resignation. Forrestal, stunned
by the suddenness of the request, spent a good part of the
afternoon by himself in his office.

Returning home at seven that evening, he requested
Marx Leva to come to the house and help him draft the letter
of resignation. Leva was unable to do so, and Forrestal made
at least two calls during the night to a close friend in New
York requesting his advice in the preparation of the letter.[25]
Forrestal apparently slept little if at all, and he arrived at his
office the following morning haggard, depressed, and exhausted. After several hours of work by Forrestal and his
assistants, the letter, which was revised a number of times,
was sent to the White House. In it Forrestal referred to his
eight and one-half years of government service as a "privilege." The progress that had been made under the 1947
National Security Act enabled him, he wrote Truman,

for the first time to take into account those urgent personal considerations about which I have spoken to you and submit my
resignation in the hope that you may accept it, effective on or

_____
25. *Diaries*, p. 552.

about March 31. . . . I am mindful of the wish that this will not
mark the end of our association, and repeat that if at any time in
the future you desire to call upon me for service, I shall be at
your command. . . .[26]

In his letter accepting Forrestal's resignation that began
"Dear Jim," Truman placed Forrestal's retirement from
office in the context of their "many previous conversations
and discussions." He was therefore "fully cognizant of the
considerations which prompt your desire to relinquish your
duties as the Secretary of Defense," and he recalled that it
was because of his "personal urging" that Forrestal had
remained in Washington "far beyond the time when you had
expressed a hope of leaving government service." Following
a tribute to Forrestal's services in the three major positions
he had occupied, there was again a reference to "urgent
personal considerations. . . ." Because of these "considerations" the resignation was accepted effective March 31, 1949,
although accepted "reluctantly."

Both letters, which were dated March 2, were released
the next day accompanied by an announcement of Johnson's
appointment. Press reactions were sharp, varied, and for the
most part predictable. In the Washington *Evening Star* of
March 4, Doris Fleeson headed her column, "Johnson Loyalty Pays Off: Nobody 'Got' Forrestal; President Soured on
Him in His Own Time." According to Miss Fleeson, Forrestal, who was "no yes-man," had angered the President
with his position on the three issues of unification, oil, and
Palestine. Forrestal, she noted,

did a lot of talking for the military view that the oil came first
and he did not confine it to Cabinet meetings. In the whispering
galleries of Washington, his outcries were at least indiscreet if
they did not actually reach the point of a deliberate attempt to
build a backfire against what the Secretary kept saying the politicians were making the President do.

---

26. Quoted in *ibid.*, p. 553.

[The Palestine issue] marked the end of the Forrestal-Truman cordiality. . . .

David Lawrence, in a bitter news article that appeared on March 4, argued that in "firing" Forrestal, Truman had vindicated the predictions of a certain "radio commentator who has been consistently hammering away at Mr. Forrestal. All of which means merely that Mr. Truman made up his mind to fire Secretary Forrestal about the time of his election and almost everybody hereabouts has known about it."[27]

Writing in the *Christian Science Monitor* of March 8, Joseph C. Harsch noted that Forrestal had been " 'released' in favor of Louis Johnson" for reasons that were numerous and complex. "One of the first" reasons, Harsch alleged, was that Johnson

raised the money for the Truman campaign, and did it well, while Mr. Forrestal took the attitude of Secretary of State Marshall that their positions of public trust were too important in a difficult period of history to permit mixing with politics. . . . Thus when Mr. Johnson wanted the job at the Defense Department, he had both powerful arguments and powerful friends, whereas Mr. Forrestal actually did desire to retire from his period of public service.

A further reason, continued Harsch, was that Forrestal was regarded by some as carrying

a prominent "anti-Russian" label on his shoulder. He had become "persona non grata" to that group within the administration which thinks that "Old Joe [Stalin] isn't such a bad guy," and that there might be merit in sending a chief justice [Fred Vinson] to Moscow to talk with him. Mr. Forrestal was one of those who stamped hard on the Vinson-to-Moscow idea.

Observing that Forrestal was "anything but the 'warmonger' which Moscow propaganda had painted him," Harsch wrote cryptically, "When it comes to rattling sabers, Mr. Johnson is far more practiced than Mr. Forrestal."

---

27. Washington *Evening Star*, March 4, 1949.

Time magazine of March 14, in a column headed "Paid in Full," attributed Forrestal's retirement to pressure from Zionists, the urging of Democrats who objected to his Wall Street background, and his refusal "to politick" for Truman in the 1948 election. *Time* doubted that Johnson, whose name was preceded by "beefy," "flamboyant," "glad-handing," and "hulking," had the "stature to fill little Jim Forrestal's shoes. . . ."

While most comment in the press and elsewhere paid fulsome tribute to Forrestal's abilities and expressed regret at his departure, the reactions of his critics ranged from mild to enthusiastic approval. "Many Washington observers," *The Nation* editorially commented on March 12,

> believe that James Forrestal would have been dropped from the cabinet immediately after the election if he had not been the target of extensive criticism . . . we can only hope that [Truman] will not rehire Mr. Forrestal if we express our pleasure at his going.

With the international situation what it is, the *Nation* editorial continued, it was hardly wise to entrust any responsibility for foreign policy "to a man on leave from Dillon, Read and Company." Forrestal, whose "background was a compound of cartels and oil," was charged by the *Nation*, together with Lovett, with having conducted a "running rebellion against the President's policy on Palestine." Although Forrestal was widely regarded as an able administrator, the results, according to *The Nation*, "are hardly visible . . . last week the Hoover Commission found the military establishment 'perilously close to the weakest type of department.'" Returning to the Wall Street theme, *The Nation* concluded:

> it is good to know that with Lovett, Forrestal, and William H. Draper [also a Dillon, Read graduate] all happily retired, the President has gone far to rid his official family of the kind of

Wall Street influence he denounced so vehemently during the election campaign.

It is doubtful that this comment, and most others both pro and con, ever reached Forrestal during his final month in office. He had long since told at least one friend that he found it a "torture" to read newspapers and magazines, a "torture" presumably because he was very likely to read something about himself or the Military Establishment that would provoke anxiety. But he could not avoid encounters with newspapermen, friendly or otherwise, many of whom were eager to obtain the "inside story" of his resignation and replacement by Johnson. To these reporters he had nothing to say that had not been said officially before; if they persisted in their questions he was apt to leave the room, or take some other action that indicated the interview was over. About his future plans he was inclined to be vague. Early in March he denied rumors that he was to be Harold Dodds's successor as president of Princeton, and he also indicated that he had "no immediate plans" to write a book about his experiences in government. On March 15 Washington newspapers reported that the Forrestals would travel to England in May for an extended vacation, and it appears that reservations were in fact made on the *Queen Mary*.

Only his closest associates were aware of his rapid physical and mental deterioration during those last weeks. As his appointments calendar shows (see Appendix I), Forrestal made a desperate effort to keep up official appearances. From March 1, the day his immediate resignation was requested, to March 28, when his successor took the oath of office, Forrestal made a number of appearances before House and Senate committees, attended several meetings of the National Security Council and War Council, saw the President on various occasions, and participated in a variety of ceremonies honoring individuals and organizations. But he was a spent man, and there was one notation on his appointments calendar in March that symbolically could only have served to increase Forrestal's pain, anguish, and sense of failure. Following every meeting of the Joint Chiefs of Staff, there was the entry on Forrestal's appointments calendar " (you are not expected)."

IX

☆ ☆ ☆ ☆ ☆

James Forrestal: An Appraisal and a Memorial

"WHO WAS JAMES FORRESTAL?"
was the question asked many pages ago, with the expectation
that the following chapters would attempt to provide a
tentative answer. Of course, those who insist on simplicity
and certainly in biography will not like the word *tentative*,
and those who liked or admired Forrestal, and those who
hated him, will be reluctant to accept the answer that has
emerged. Everyone agrees that Forrestal was complex, even
enigmatic; beyond that there is no agreement about the man
who was James Forrestal, and there may never be agreement.

Perhaps the nub of the problem is that "man" should be
written "men," for Forrestal was, to vary an old expression,
all men to all men. Consider the matter of his politics. He
considered himself an enlightened conservative, or a "liberal
conservative," as he once termed himself. To Forrestal these
labels—a word he disliked—referred to something more than
the fact that he placed himself somewhere between New Deal
Democrats and Hoover Republicans. Once, in reading a review of a book about William Hazlitt, Forrestal was struck
by Hazlitt's statement, "I believe in the theoretical benevolence and the practical malignity of man." Forrestal under-

lined the sentence and pasted the review, which was entitled
"William Hazlitt, a Man Not Made for Love," in one of his
scrapbooks.[1] The application to governmental problems of
man's "theoretical benevolence" and "practical malignity"
was, for Forrestal, the foremost task of "liberal conservatives"
like himself.

"Moderate" and "middle-roader" are terms Forrestal also
found acceptable as self-references, but they are not terms
that everyone would regard as accurate. To many liberals
Forrestal was and is a symbol of reaction—the word "Fascist"
is occasionally used—and by them he is remembered as a
dangerous man who might have become, had he lived, a
malevolent man of destiny. But Walter Millis, also a liberal,
has described Forrestal's career as "great and singularly selfless," and he has praised Forrestal's "courage, insight . . .
firmness of his counsel . . . high abilities . . . unswerving
integrity of purpose."[2]

Many conservatives, while using similar language in paying tribute to Forrestal, are inclined to emphasize Forrestal's
role in alerting the nation to the threat of Communism. "He
clearly saw," writes James F. Byrnes, "the menace of communism before his colleagues recognized it. Frequently he
warned of their plans for world domination and the dangers
of relying upon promises made by them."[3] According to General Albert C. Wedemeyer, Forrestal was one of the few men
after the war who "understood the full implications of communism. . . ." As a "reward for his prescience and honesty,"
Wedemeyer alleges, "Forrestal was actually hounded into
suicide."[4] Former Major General Edwin A. Walker, the sub-

---

1. The Hazlitt biography was Catherine Macdonald Maclean's *Born Under Saturn: A Biography of William Hazlitt* (New York: The Macmillan Company, 1944). It was reviewed by Clara G. Stillman in the *New York Herald Tribune* of April 16, 1944.
2. *Diaries*, p. 555.
3. Letter to the writer, March 12, 1962.
4. General Albert C. Wedemeyer, *Wedemeyer Reports!* (New York: Henry Holt & Company, 1958), p. 430.

ject of considerable controversy in 1962 with reference to military education and propaganda activities, has gone even further than Wedemeyer in associating Forrestal with other distinguished opponents of a "no-win" policy toward the communist world. Walker, a member of the John Birch Society, testifying in April, 1962, before a subcommittee of the Senate Armed Services Committee, declared that

General MacArthur, Senator Joseph McCarthy, Secretary James Forrestal, Syngman Rhee, Chiang Kai-shek, Tshombe, myself, and others, with more to come, as well as untold thousands who have not made the headlines, have all been framed by this hidden policy.[5]

Forrestal has also been eulogized in at least one novel, the hero of which is charged with mental incompetence because of his efforts to combat communist subversion.[6]

Although it is doubtful that Forrestal would have been sympathetic to either former Major General Walker or the John Birch Society, his evident appeal to the extreme or radical right in America merits analysis, and we shall return to the phenomenon shortly. It is already clear, however, that Forrestal the political man is someone who defies the simple and conventional political labels. Forrestal the human being is also someone to whom the usual categories do not apply. Many of his associates, for example, think of him as a cold individual who was sparing of his emotions—as a man, in short, "not made for love." But one friend who knew him better than most puts the point somewhat differently. Forrestal, he recalls,

was gregarious and yet frightened of people. He had a quality which inspired people to treat him with great loyalty and want to know him, and yet he always kept them and everyone else at arm's length.

---

5. *Hearings Before the Special Preparedness Subcommittee of the Committee on Armed Services,* United States Senate, 87th Congress, Second Session, Part 4, April 5, 1962, p. 1524.

6. Colonel Victor J. Fox, *The Pentagon Case* (New York: Freedom Press, 1958).

He never had many close friends. I had a great many friends, and once I had a large number of them over for a party. He asked me if they were *really* all friends, and when I said I wouldn't have asked them if they weren't friends, he seemed somewhat surprised. His own experience, he said, was that you only had a few close friends, and that he himself only had three or four. He felt that every man only has a certain amount of himself to give to others and it should not be squandered.

Certainly he did not squander what *he* had to give, and as is often the case with those who hoard or repress their emotions, he was in many respects a lonely man. His aides recall a number of Christmas eves and New Year's days when Forrestal worked in his office, and he sometimes appeared oblivious of the fact these were occasions most men spent with their families or friends. "I recall one Christmas morning," a colleague reports,

when Forrestal telephoned to ask me to play golf with him around noon at the Chevy Chase club. I risked a serious argument with my wife when I accepted, but after some discussion she agreed that I should do so if Forrestal felt the need for that kind of activity and companionship on Christmas day when most of us would think only in terms of being at home with the family. After the game, as I remember it, he went to the office, and I went home.

There is a pathetic quality about this story, but it is important to keep in mind the many occasions when Forrestal did not want companionship and was tactless in rejecting it. More than one Washington hostess can remember a dinner party that Forrestal promised to attend but at which he never appeared. And there was one abortive yacht cruise on the Potomac that did not endear him to a number of his government colleagues and their wives. Forrestal preferred to entertain guests on the yacht available to the Secretary of Defense partly because, as he once put it, a yacht party did not require him to "wait around" until the guests were ready to depart. "When the boat docks," he confided to a friend, "the party's over." On the occasion referred to, however, the yacht never sailed. Although the guests were aboard at the time scheduled—there were several Supreme Court Justices and Cabinet members among them—Forrestal himself was absent. When an aide was finally able to locate him, Forrestal declared flatly that he would not join his guests and that the yacht should sail without him. "Tell them I'm tied up at the office and can't get away," he instructed the aide. The aide did so, and the guests walked off the yacht, some of them making no secret of their displeasure with Forrestal's behavior.

Yet he could also be charming, thoughtful, and capable of inspiring loyalty and affection. The wife of a distinguished newspaper correspondent recalls that she was prepared to dislike Forrestal; she had heard that he was cold, ruthless, and reactionary. But when she met him she found him one of the most attractive men she had ever met. Other friends, belying his reputation for parsimony, remember his usually anonymous gifts of money to friends and college classmates whose luck had turned bad, and it is beyond question that he gave financial assistance, also anonymously, to a number of deserving Princeton students. A former butler in the Forrestal household testifies to his generosity in dealing with the servants; they were paid well, and there was at least one occasion when Forrestal offered to lend a valet the money required for a business venture. During the war he made it a point to write consoling letters to old Beacon and Wall Street friends whose sons or husbands had become casualties, and when he himself was abroad he took pains to visit a medical ward where someone from Beacon was receiving treatment.

Parsimony and generosity, rudeness and thoughtfulness, above all keeping people "at arm's length" and reaching out to them—Forrestal's personality was peculiarly dichotomous; it is almost as if he never was able to decide what sort of man he wanted to be. As a result, any given characterological statement or interpretation can be contradicted, whether the statement pertains to a large or small detail of his life. One would expect, for example, that those who saw him regularly would be in agreement about the manner of his dress, a small detail and because small, a detail that should provoke minimal controversy. But while some friends and associates remember him as a man who dressed in perfect taste, others argue, with some photographic evidence to support them, that Forrestal preferred "flashy" combinations that frequently succeeded in being garish. Forrestal, one colleague recalls,

went in for loud, pin-striped suits, striped shirts, and two-tone shoes. The shoulders were usually overpadded, and the pin-stripes a bit too conspicuous. It was expensive stuff, all right, but not really in good taste. I think it was his way of rebelling against the dull blues and grays of bureaucratic clothing in Washington, but later his taste also became more conservative. When he was Defense Secretary he usually went in for flannel suits, sports jackets, button-down collars, and so forth.

This comment and many others suggest the essential truth in the statement of one business friend that Forrestal

was a strange mixture. I never met anybody exactly like Forrestal or even remotely like him. But everybody who knew him at all respected and admired him, and the comparative few who were close to him had real affection for him. In business some people might have called him a slavedriver, but I don't think they would have done so if they realized that he drove himself much harder than he did other people. All through the time that I knew him he worked at least sixteen hours a day. I don't think he ever quite understood why everybody else didn't do the same. . . .

Did Forrestal understand why *he* worked sixteen hours a day? Putting the question in a larger frame, Did Forrestal know he was "a strange mixture," and if so did he know why? Probably no one now living can answer this question with any certainty, but one friend of almost thirty years' standing is convinced that Forrestal was caught in a variety of conflicts into some of which he had a good deal of insight. "The story of James Forrestal," he comments, is is many ways an American tragedy; the stuff of a Dos Passos or Dreiser novel. It contains much that need be said about the social and moral structure of America. . . .

It is not just the Irish Catholic boy who never stopped thinking of himself as a "Mick." It is the man who thought Princeton and Wall Street spelled grace, charm, success and strength; the man who embraced the American dream and found it wanting.

The fault does not lie just with a deeply religious mother who wanted her son to join the priesthood, which he rejected. It is the society in which he lived which saw the Racquet Club as a social nirvana. The tragedy was that Forrestal was aware of it all. He lived his life as a conflicted man, walking a tightrope held taut by a concept of original sin at one end, the American dream of success and recognition at the other.

There is still another tragedy. Forrestal came close to being a caricature. Deeply sensitive, uncertain, afraid of intrusions upon his soul, he solved his dilemma by becoming a caricature of the Rational Man. Functioning almost entirely on a rational level, he could never allow himself to enter the world of childhood, for to do so would have meant shedding the self-woven cocoon by which he protected his vulnerability. Above all else, Forrestal was vulnerable. He smothered himself in his own highly developed art of self-protection as few men have.

The "rational face" Forrestal chose to present to the world, continues the friend, was also "that of the physical man." To Forrestal

strength of character and body were synonymous. He was the man with the broken nose who exercised daily, stressed independence, and allowed no contact with his interior.

He was a character Hemingway would have loved, but not understood.

"He lived his life as a conflicted man"—a perceptive comment. But to speak of the "original sin at one end" of the tightrope and the "American dream of success" at the other is to speak of only one strand of the "tightrope." There were the other strands—Forrestal's lifelong struggle to appear stronger and tougher than he actually was, and his efforts during the Washington years to impress others as the very

model of a philosopher-king. For a good part of his life Forrestal was also the agnostic who was never able to free himself
entirely from the moral strictures of Catholicism, and in
Princeton and New York he was the Irish Catholic or "Mick"
who was never completely at ease in an Anglo-Saxon Protestant environment. The Wall Street Forrestal never quite
overcame a suspicion of the rich and well-born although he
envied and emulated them, and the Washington Forrestal
distrusted liberals although he served in the administrations
of two of the most liberal Presidents in history. Indeed, it is
one of the major paradoxes of his life that he was appointed
to the highest position he achieved in government by a
President for whose personality and principles he felt an
active dislike.

It would be plausible but not very profound to suggest
it was ambition that brought a conservative investment
banker to a liberal Washington, and that it was ambition
that had earlier transported the Irish Catholic to Protestant
Princeton, and the smalltown Democrat to Republican Wall
Street. It would be equally plausible but not very profound
to attribute Forrestal's work habits—the sixteen-hour days
and seven-day weeks—to ambition. But what is meant by
ambition, and why was Forrestal, apparently, more ambitious than most of his contemporaries in Wall Street and
Washington?

In answer to the latter question, many of his friends
believe that the unhappy marriage played a large role in
Forrestal's striving for success. As one of them puts it:

Everyone who knew Forrestal was aware that his family life was
unhappy, and I always thought this was the main reason he
worked so hard. He found in work some of the satisfactions that
other men find in their family relations. If he had been a happier
man I doubt that he would have driven himself—and others—as
hard as he did. There really wasn't much for him to go home to
at the end of the day, so why not stay at the office and get a
headstart on the next day's business?

This interpretation is not without merit, but it neglects the point that Forrestal worked long hours, and was inclined to expect subordinates to work long hours, before his marriage in 1926. No one who knew him, in fact, including the surviving Beacon friends of his youth, can remember a time when Forrestal was without ambition and a stubborn resolve to succeed. While still an adolescent, he concluded that sheer determination and hard work were the twin keys to success in life, always provided that one possessed a modicum of intelligence. Those activities that were simply relaxing or playful or merely fun he was rarely able to enjoy; instead he converted them into purposeful enterprises that, to some degree, functioned as outlets for determination and work. Thus golf, tennis, handball, and other sports were approached, not as forms of relaxation, but as body-building exercises, and most of the books, jokes, and anecdotes he enjoyed were appreciated less for their entertainment value than for their capacity to instruct and enlighten. Forrestal, in other words, was too driven a man to enjoy, much less indulge in, those aspects of the human experience that are purely frivolous.

This fatal flaw in his personality undoubtedly owes much to his childhood and adolescence. In general, these years provide support for the thesis that in Forrestal's case, as in the case of many another political man, the quest for fame and power was a response to early psychic deprivation.[7] The early home life did not nurture a personality that was self-confident and outgoing, but one that was insecure and withdrawn. Forrestal's father, the more permissive of his parents, was less important than his mother in his own and his brothers' upbringing, and it is clear that Mary Toohey Forrestal did not welcome open demonstrations of affection,

---

7. The relationship between power-seeking and personality development has been most fruitfully explored in the works of Harold D. Lasswell. See especially his *Power and Personality* (New York: W. W. Norton and Company, 1948).

assertions of independence, and violations of rather strict household rules. Ultimately her youngest son rebelled, but by that time the essential form of his personality had been cast, and it was a form that was not broken until the last months of his life. The Forrestal who, as a child, had been deprived of love and understanding would not, as an adult, be able to give much love and understanding to others. The Forrestal who, in his youth, was uncertain of his abilities and lacking in confidence would, in his mature years, work harder and longer than most men, and would also attempt to prove himself by becoming first richer, and then more powerful than most men. The young Forrestal who was often ill, ashamed of his physique, and perhaps uncertain of his masculinity, would, all his life, exercise strenuously, emphasize body-contact sports, and try to appear "tough."

The early home life may also have been reflected in his personal and professional relations. To what extent, for example, was his decision to marry Josephine influenced by conscious or unconscious feelings about his mother? If we assume, as do all his friends, that Josephine was never really "his type," the reasons for the marriage must have involved something more than mutual attraction or even simple convenience. Certainly it can be argued that Forrestal should never have married in the first place; it is still more certain that he should never have married Josephine, and that the marriage had tragic consequences for both of them.

Forrestal's father, it appears, was less significant than his mother during the childhood years, and partly for that reason we know little about his relations with his youngest son. Those in Beacon who remember him suggest that most of his energies went into his business activities, local politics, church affairs, the militia, and related areas. If, as one Beaconite indicates, it was his wife who "wore the pants" in the family, we can infer that to Forrestal his father must have appeared weaker than his mother, perhaps even less

masculine. How did he feel about this father who cast a
somewhat flickering male image or manly model for his sons
to imitate? One can imagine that Forrestal may have felt a
good deal of ambivalence toward a father who marched in
parades at the head of the column but who walked very
softly around the house. If the accounts of old family friends
can be trusted, Mary Forrestal's bark was much more to be
feared than James Forrestal's bite.

Mary Forrestal may also have helped define her son's
later concepts of strength and masculinity. While Forrestal
came to reject much that his mother represented, his dependence upon her during childhood undoubtedly contributed to a certain passivity in his own nature of which he
became increasingly aware in the adolescent and early adult
years. Regarding such passivity as a feminine attribute,
Forrestal may have felt, consciously or unconsciously, that
he would have to struggle more than most men to establish
his essential masculinity. If the quest for a male identity
frequently led him to a gym or other sports arena, it more
significantly influenced his attitude toward a variety of Cold
War issues. In Forrestal's world of foreign policy and military
problems involving the Soviet bloc, to be militant was to be
masculine.

It is possible that Harry Truman, many years later, acti-
vated some of the ambivalence that Forrestal felt toward his
father. Both Truman and the senior Forrestal had been
small-town businessmen, and there were other similarities
between the former AEF artillery captain and the one-time
major in the New York National Guard. Truman could
bluster, swagger, and swear on public occasions, but it
seemed to Forrestal that he was weak and even timid in
dealing with party politicians, Zionists, air-power lobbyists,
and others who placed narrow interest above national interest. From Forrestal's point of view Truman as President and
free-world leader left something to be desired, but it is fair

to remark that all his life Forrestal had difficulty relating to and accepting authority. For those in authority whom he regarded as weak he generally had contempt; those who were strong he tended to dislike and resent. The former category may have included his father; there can be no doubt it included certain business associates and a large number of politicians, chief among them Truman. In the latter group were one or two professors at Princeton, various employers after he left Princeton, including some of his superiors at Dillon, Read, Admiral King, and Franklin D. Roosevelt. Priding himself on his own independence, he regarded dependence upon others as a form of weakness, and he was also inclined to avoid people who were or would become dependent on him.

Forrestal's personality, in other words, was one that never fully matured, if maturity be defined as the ability to emerge from a bleak childhood with a minimum of emotional scar tissue. But paradoxically, it was a personality that could and did function with great success much of the time Forrestal held office. Whatever its roots, the compulsion to work, to be grim, to flex the muscles and jut the jaw suited the national temper during World War II. A taut personality could be understood to reflect the conviction that the defeat of the Axis would be followed by Soviet efforts to exploit the victory over Germany and Japan. In May, 1944, when the Allied invasion of France was still a month away, Forrestal exclaimed to George Earle, "My God, George, you and I and Bill Bullitt are the only ones around the President who know the Russian leaders for what they are."[8] When one considers that those "around the President" included Stimson, Patterson, McCloy, Admirals Leahy and King, and General Marshall, considers further that Harriman was serving as ambassador in Moscow and Hurley as our emissary to China, the statement can be viewed as evidence that Forrestal was

---

8. Wedemeyer, *op. cit.,* p. 417.

almost obsessed by the idea that he was indispensable in the prosecution of the Cold War. Knowing "what they are" and strongly inclined to believe that the Second World War would surely be followed by a third, Forrestal did not have to justify to his associates the seven-day weeks and sixteen-hour days. If the nation was to win *both* wars, all citizens, and not merely the Secretary of the Navy, would need a continuing dedication to preparedness no matter what the personal sacrifice.

Unfortunately for Forrestal, his mood of tense toughness was less suitable after 1945, when the nation, despite his warnings, sought to relax and return to "normalcy." The mothers, wives, and children wanted the men back, and the men, despite the lures—and there were many—dangled before them by the Services, wanted to get out of uniform and into civilian clothes. A soldiery determined to return to the college, the office, the factory, and the farm as soon as possible, and a citizenry eager to splurge on consumer goods, could not be easily persuaded that Stalin was not only another Hitler but also far more dangerous. The attitude favoring business-as-usual gradually changed, but it did not change either fast enough or far enough to suit Forrestal and those who saw the world as he did. He especially lamented the fact that there were almost as many in the Truman Administration as there had been in the Roosevelt Administration who were, not to put too fine a point on it, naïve with regard to Soviet intentions and tactics. At various times he expressed reservations about Truman, Byrnes, Harriman, Marshall, Leahy, Stimson, in addition, of course, to his particular *bête noir*, Henry A. Wallace.

In the context of postwar affluence and "togetherness," Forrestal could be and was made to appear a warmonger by those who disliked him or who disagreed, for whatever reason, with his views. In certain respects, he was an easy target for all those who favored "peaceful coexistence"—and it would be foolish to pretend that Stalinist sympathizers were not among them. Insights and understandings based on psychology are not common in political discourse, and hence it was relatively simple for fellow travelers, liberals, and pacifists to attribute Forrestal's Cold War militancy to his Dillon, Read background. In the simplest expression of this formula, Forrestal was *against* the Soviet Union and Communism because he was *for* Wall Street and capitalism. Few if any of his critics suggested that his position may have been much more a reflection of his Matteawan background than of his years as an investment banker.

His friends and admirers, on the other hand, dismiss both Matteawan and Wall Street in their assessment of his role in the Cold War. Forrestal, in their view, was guided solely by objective considerations, namely, the true and factual nature of the threat posed to the free world by Soviet Communism. In the simplest expression of their formula, Forrestal was one of the great heroes and patriots in American history; indeed, some of them believe that he was the only hero and patriot of high rank in postwar Washington. For those on the far Right, like former Major General Walker, the number of patriots during the Truman era was exceedingly small, including, in addition to Forrestal, only General MacArthur and Senator Joseph R. McCarthy.

It is doubtful that either of these appraisals is correct. Forrestal would hardly have avoided being influenced by the twenty years spent on Wall Street, but that does not mean that he was purely and simply a "Wall Street imperialist." And while it is true that Forrestal was both conservative and a deeply committed man in the struggle against Soviet Communism, he was not a reactionary and not, until he became ill, a fanatic. In short, the man who functions as villain for many liberals and radicals is not the real Forrestal but a gross caricature. And the man who is hero-worshiped by the John Birch Society is not the well Forrestal but the sick one.

These conclusions emerge from any careful examination

of Forrestal's own prescriptions for American foreign and defense policy. To be sure, Forrestal was willing to "go to the brink" far more often than most other members of the Truman Administration. He also thought it essential to spend more on defense, even if such spending required some regimentation of the economy. He was even willing, in the name of national defense, to restrict certain freedoms that in peacetime had never before been curtailed. In 1945, for example, he proposed that all radio and cable services be merged into one privately owned corporation operating under limited government supervision. The merger, he thought, would facilitate the reliability and security of communications.[9] In February, 1949, he urged on newspaper, radio, and movie executives the necessity of their practicing "voluntary" censorship in all cases which directly or indirectly involved national security. Almost all those he approached, including publishers Arthur Hays Sulzberger of *The New York Times* and Roy Howard of the Scripps-Howard chain, were opposed to the proposal, and he did not pursue it further during the remaining weeks he held office.

Forrestal also believed that the United States could not afford to be scrupulous in the tactics employed to combat communist influence internally and externally. In addition to favoring the utmost extension of counterintelligence activities engaged in by the FBI, CIA, and other agencies, he was an early advocate of training in clandestine or guerrilla warfare of the type that has since become almost conventional in Southeast Asia. Thus in October, 1947, he endorsed a memo from William J. Donovan urging that magazine articles be written to inform the public of "the nature of irregular war and the manner in which the Soviet Union has employed it." Enclosing an article of his own, Donovan wrote Forrestal, "There is no one who can take the lead in this but you" and "Jim, we must not let this get away

9. *The New York Times*, March 20, 1945.

from us." Crossing out the first statement, Forrestal circulated copies of Donovan's memo to others in the government, including Lovett, with the notation ". . . there is plenty of obvious sense in what he says. . . ."[10]

But while Forrestal placed great stress on the nation's security and military capabilities, he was hardly unaware of the political and economic aspects of the Cold War. This awareness is particularly evident in a memorandum sent to the President via Clark Clifford on March 6, 1947. The day before Forrestal had discussed with Clifford the opportunity for the United States to exercise world economic leadership; indeed, he emphasized, if most of the world was to remain free, the United States could not escape "responsibility for leadership." The memo of the following day put in writing the points Forrestal had developed in his discussion with Clifford, and because it constitutes a fairly complete statement of what he meant by "responsibility for leadership," it is worth quoting in full. "For a long time now," Forrestal began,

it has been clear that there is a serious, immediate and extraordinarily grave threat to the continued existence of this country. These are the facts:
1. The present danger which this country faces is at least as great as the danger which we faced during the war with Germany and Japan. Briefly stated, it is the very real danger that this country, as we know it, may cease to exist.
2. From 1941 to 1945 we won a war by enlisting the wholehearted support of all our people and all our resources. Today we are losing a comparable struggle without ever having enlisted the strength of our people and our resources—and the consequences of our loss will be the same consequences that would have followed if we had lost the war of 1941–45.
3. Of the strategic battlegrounds of the present struggle, we have already lost Poland, Yugoslavia, Romania, Bulgaria, and a number of others; Greece is in imminent peril; after Greece,

---

10. Memo to Lovett, October 9, 1947. "But what [Donovan] forgets," he added, "is the wide gap between the genial attitude of Congress toward his activities during the war and the present short rations."

France and Italy may follow; and after France and Italy,
Great Britain, South America, and ourselves.

4. We lost strategic battlegrounds in the war of 1941–1945,
also—but even while we were losing some battlegrounds, we
were planning the offensives by which we were to win the ultimate victory. And we won the victory by pressing home our
attacks—by landing our troops at Guadalcanal, North Africa,
Guam, Iwo Jima, Normandy, the Philippines, and a host of
other places.

5. This country cannot afford the deceptive luxury of waging
defensive warfare. As in the war of 1941–45, our victory and
our survival depend on how and where we attack.

6. By providing outstanding economic leadership, this country
can wage its attack successfully—and can thereby build the
foundations of a peaceful world. For the only way in which a
durable peace can be created is by world-wide restoration of
economic activity and international trade.

7. In order to be successful, our product—our economic
leadership—will have to prove its superiority to the com-
modity which Russia has lately been so successful in peddling.
Russia has a product which is skillfully tailored to appeal to
people who are in despair—and thanks to German and
Japanese aggression, Russia has had a wealth of customers
who are sufficiently desperate to turn to anything. Moreover,
the accomplishment of Russia's aims has been greatly simpli-
fied by the fact that we have heretofore offered the world no
practical antidote for the Russian poison.

8. What we must do is create the conditions under which a
free world society can live. With that as our object, a group of
our most competent citizens should be called together in order
to enlist the full support of all elements of our economy in
the accomplishment of this basic American task. For only by
an all-out effort on a world-wide basis can we pass over from
the defense to the attack. In making our all-out effort, we will
be forwarding not only world stability but also our national
interest—which includes, of course, business interest, labor
interest, and public interest.

9. As specific examples of the sort of thing which we must do,
the following may be enumerated:

(*a*) Japanese assets amounting to some $137,000,000 are
presently impounded. If these assets were set up as a revolv-

ing fund with which Japan could import raw materials for its industries, Japanese exports could again enter the channels of world trade—and Japanese workers would have employment and something to eat.

(*b*) A similar revolving fund could be set up for Germany, for a durable peace can rest only upon a Germany that, while militarily impotent, is industrially active.

(*c*) Financial support should be provided for local enterprises in those countries where a struggling economy needs a helping hand—but the furnishing of such support should in every case be handled by competent American personnel, in order to assure that the money goes into *productive* enterprises that are of direct use both to the country in-involved and to world trade. (Wherever possible, *private capital* in this country should render the necessary financial assistance—for this is essentially a business task, in which government's greatest contribution is the creation of favorable conditions under which business can work.)

10. The group referred to above should be called together promptly. It should consist of our best brains—from management, from labor, from both the executive and the legislative side of the government, from any source that has a contribution to make—for the issues to be faced are crucial, and we must attack if we are to survive.

The actions taken during 1947 and 1948 did not convince Forrestal that Truman fully understood the relationship between foreign policy and defense needs, and in his speeches and writings he sought to persuade the public, if not the President, that our "responsibility for leadership" required a stronger military establishment. With many friends in the newspaper and magazine world, Forrestal could always be certain that his own point of view, with or without his name attached, would be accorded a hearing. The Luce publications, especially *Fortune* magazine, had occasionally devoted space to Forrestal's views, and in October, 1948, he was given another opportunity to build support for an increase in military spending beyond the amount fixed by the President. Asking Forrestal to talk with Robert Elson and

Roy Alexander of the *Fortune* staff, publisher Henry Luce
requested Forrestal to give them his "prescription" for

how much defense we need in order to carry out foreign policy.
Of course, for what we say there we will take entire responsibility
. . . what we'd like to have is—confidentially or what not—your
prescription, which in all probability we would adopt.

In its December, 1948, issue *Fortune* published an article
titled "The Arms We Need" that was almost entirely based
on Forrestal's "prescription." While most people knew Communism could not be contained without military force, the
article commented, "only a tiny fraction" was able to judge
how much military strength was required. "For two months,"
continued the article,

FORTUNE has gone to school on this problem, both with responsible military experts and with leading foreign policy strategists.
As a result of this study, FORTUNE has come to the unpleasant conclusion that if the US intends to continue its present foreign
policy, it will in all probability need greater military force than
it now possesses . . . (costing) $18 billion for fiscal 1950.

The $18 billion, *Fortune* suggested, would not buy a "war
force" but a

force strong enough to:
1. Convince the Politburo that we mean business.
2. Make us a desirable, reliable partner in alliances.
3. Provide a shield behind which our allies can recover their
   morale, rebuild their governments and rally their forces.

Such a "barebone outline" of a military program was worth-
less, however, unless it related to both American foreign
policy and Soviet military strength. There were, of course,
no absolute guarantees of security, but the United States
"must and can be prepared to secure and maintain certain
geographical footholds from which we can operate to check
the advance of Communism." *Fortune* did not identify these
"footholds," but it implied that Truman's $14.4 billion ceil-
ing on military expenditures would have an adverse effect

on their maintenance. To illustrate its point that the budget ceiling was "politically expedient but strategically unwise," the article noted that the ceiling had been imposed

at the moment when the US had challenged the Soviet power in Europe by inaugurating the air lift. In effect, the gesture was to raise the Soviet bid and, at the same time, by limiting the military budget, give the tip-off that we were betting only a few white chips. It is conceivable that these contradictory actions may have undermined all efforts to settle the Berlin crisis on favorable terms.

Strength in foreign and military policies, *Fortune* indicated, would be achieved only if appropriations for their support took precedence over programs "of political interest." Increased spending on arms was possible without rationing and higher taxes provided the Administration limited spending "on social objectives." Conceding that such restraint would require "remarkable self-denial," *Fortune* nevertheless emphasized that

Mr. Truman, confirmed in his own right and in his own power as President, has never been in a better position to put the national interest ahead of partisan politics. . . . He, more than any other American, should now understand that the only way to avoid having American foreign policy dominated by crisis is to live in crisis—prepared for war.

The necessity "to live in crisis—prepared for war" was, for Forrestal, so far beyond dispute that he was inclined to question the intelligence and motivations of those who disagreed with him. It may well be that future historians will endorse his approach to crisis and preparedness and that some of them will even entertain similar suspicions of certain officials who made policy in the United States between 1940 and 1950. But whatever the judgment of history, it is difficult to avoid the conclusion that Forrestal's personality needs and policy recommendations were closely related. The Cold War, no matter how inevitable, provided him with an arena for the play of transference and projection. Anxieties and insecurities, regardless of personal source, could become focused on Soviet behavior and be partially appeased by a stubborn insistence on a "tough" foreign and military policy. Suspicions of all sorts readily attached themselves to real or alleged communist conspiracies at home and abroad, and fears directed at the Soviet Union could appear wholly sane and rational. Until the last few months of his life, Forrestal could impress almost everyone as a "reasonable" man because it was "reasonable," in the context of the Cold War, to feel anxious, insecure, suspicious, and fearful. Above all, it was "reasonable" to appear "tough," to warn against compromises and concessions, and to talk of "forcing the issue" and the necessity of "showdowns."

The reality of Forrestal's personality, however, whether or not it was also the reality of our foreign policy, was not essential toughness but essential weakness. A stronger man, it is plausible to suppose, would have been less oriented toward power and more able to accept rebuffs and ultimate rejection. A more confident man would have been more flexible in his attitude toward foreign and domestic issues, and a more self-sufficient man would have retired from office, as others have done, perhaps a trifle bloody and bowed, but unbeaten. Unfortunately and tragically, Forrestal was none of these men, and when he found his power sapped and his ambition thwarted, he could not command their resources.

It needs also to be said that even at the height of his career Forrestal was never quite able to resolve contradictions in his professional life, some of which partook of the nature of "double-binds," that is, splittings of personality caused by a pulling and tugging in opposite directions. To the conflicts of his personal life, which were numerous, were added the sharp and frequently bitter policy conflicts between warring factions in both the Roosevelt and Truman Administrations. More often than not, Forrestal found himself on the conservative side, but there were occasions when he thought of himself as a man-in-the-middle who was caught not between friends and enemies but between friends.

This was especially the case after the war in certain economic policy areas. As a Cabinet officer Forrestal was in the position of having to embrace the Truman economic program, or at least maintain a public silence on issues where he was in disagreement. Many of his Wall Street and business associates, however, called upon him again and again to intervene in policy areas involving business regulation, antitrust suits, and labor legislation. On several occasions Forrestal was strongly urged to exert influence on behalf of the oil industry, some sections of which, during and after the war, thought themselves threatened by nationalization. Forrestal, although sympathetic, was sometimes reluctant to interfere in policy areas that were not his concern, and he also knew that such intervention risked the displeasure of other Administration officials and invited charges that he was a Wall Street "front man." Yet he usually resolved the conflict of loyalties in favor of his friends. It was generally true, as one oil executive put it many years later, that "I could always count on Jim when Ickes or some other damn fool was trying to make trouble. All I had to do was pick up the phone." It is doubtful that this friend and others similarly placed ever realized what price in torn loyalty and career tension Forrestal paid for their assurance that they "could always count on Jim . . ."

In the end, of course, Forrestal paid with psychosis and suicide, in effect paid with his life for an accumulation of guilts, tensions, frustrations, and conflicts that finally became overwhelming. But is it possible to say that this price need not have been paid, that Forrestal on March 1, 1949, might have been enabled to bear the burden of what amounted to "a dismissal under fire"?[11] These questions raise a variety

---

11. Millis in *Diaries*, p. 553.

of difficulties, not the least of which is a difficulty, perhaps inherent, in psychiatric biography. And that difficulty, in brief, is that such study is more productive of hindsights than foresights. Many personality and situational characteristics that contributed to Forrestal's illness and suicide developed during the early years of his life history, and it is therefore possible to "account" for the terminal tragedy, at least in part. But at what points in his life could that tragedy have been predicted, assuming that Forrestal made no effort to exploit the resources of psychiatry? When he left Matteawan for Hanover and Princeton? When he ceased to regard himself as a believing Catholic? When he was married and far advanced on his Wall Street career? When he went to Washington in 1940, or when he became Defense Secretary, or when his immediate resignation was requested?

No certain answers are possible, but it is certain that no one close to Forrestal advanced such predictions, even as late as March, 1949. Although some friends and associates suspected he was ill late in 1948, it does not appear that they urged him to consult a psychiatrist, much less enter a "rest home" or private sanitarium. And when the President became aware that his Defense Secretary was experiencing a breakdown, it did not occur to him to recommend anything more than a lengthy vacation followed by a fact-finding trip around the world that would include visits to our defense installations. Even on March 29, when there could hardly be any doubt that Forrestal was suffering from a psychosis, the official recommendation involved nothing more than an extended visit to Hobe Sound, Florida. His ailment, it was believed, would quickly succumb to a therapy of golf, swimming, sunshine, and rest.

Had his friends and associates been more sensitive to his condition during the last months of 1948, Forrestal might have been restored by measures less drastic than confinement at Bethesda. But they were not sensitive, despite a variety of cues provided by the sick man. The apparent suicide of Czechoslovak Foreign Minister Jan Masaryk on March 10, 1948, made a deep impression on Forrestal, and he referred to it often, both in public and private, as a key turning point in the Cold War. The frequency of reference, however, suggests that Masaryk's death may have had for him a more personal meaning. It was also in 1948 that Forrestal began to make numerous allusions to the physical and mental health of other officials. Thus on one occasion, in September, 1948, discussing with John McCone a certain episode involving Vannevar Bush, Forrestal suggested that Bush's behavior "reflects a certain amount of nervous and physical instability. I mean—not his mind but just he's drawn pretty fine, I think."[12] Forrestal, no doubt, would not have welcomed suggestions that he, too, was revealing "a certain amount of nervous and physical instability," for the relief of which psychiatric counseling was imperative. Indeed, it is probable that he would have regarded such counseling as, on his part, a confession of weakness. In any event, there is no evidence that he was advised by anyone to see a psychiatrist until early in April at Hobe Sound. It also appears that apart from William Menninger, he was not acquainted with any psychiatrist in Washington or elsewhere; he was also inclined to minimize the importance of psychiatry as both theory and therapy.[13]

---

12. Forrestal, who himself was always "drawn pretty fine," had long been aware of this quality in others, but his sensitivity to it sharply increased during 1948. Two years before the discussion with McCone, Forrestal had visited General Clay in Berlin and had concluded that Clay was beginning to show the strains of the tense USA-USSR confrontation in Germany. In a memo to Patterson in July, 1946, Forrestal wrote, "I think you should order General Clay to take a ten-day or two-week holiday—nothing else will make him do it—and if he doesn't get some break he runs the risk of blowing up entirely. . . ."—*Diaries*, p. 183.

13. Many years before, when Forrestal was still with Dillon, Read, someone close to him had gone to a psychiatrist to seek a cure for alcoholism. The alcohol problem remained unsolved, and it is possible that Forrestal's distrust of psychiatry and psychiatrists owed something to this experience.

If, in the special sense suggested, Forrestal was failed by his friends, his associates, and himself, he was also failed by the peculiar mythology of official Washington, a mythology which then and now reaches not only into the Pentagon but into all departments and agencies of government. The essence of this mythology, as Albert Deutsch observed following Forrestal's death, is the denial that any Very Important Person can become mentally ill while in office. Thus it follows that while ordinary people holding ordinary jobs can and do become psychotic, VIP's do not. It also follows that ordinary people who can afford it visit psychiatrists, but not VIP's. Finally, it follows that ordinary people may spend some time in mental hospitals, but never VIP's. These and other themes constitute the mental-health mythology of official Washington—despite the fact that Washington has more psychiatrists in proportion to population than most other cities in the world.

This mythology, to which Washington psychiatrists themselves are forced to subscribe, is not always conducive to proper treatment when the psychosis of a VIP can no longer be concealed, denied, or defined as mere fatigue or exhaustion. Because Forrestal was not only a VIP but someone who was identified with crucial foreign and military policies, the mental-health mythology as it applied to him was extremely stubborn and resistant to modification. The nature of his illness was not revealed until after his death, and even now, more than fourteen years later, certain details have not been made public. Forrestal's VIP status was also responsible for his being assigned a room on the sixteenth floor of the Bethesda Naval Hospital despite the protests of Raines, the psychiatrist in charge; it is clear that Raines recognized the risks involved in moving a depressed and suicidal patient from a closely watched ward on a lower floor to a room on one of the top floors that was never designed for someone mentally ill. On at least one occasion Raines was overruled with reference to a particular treatment he wished to employ, and on other occasions he had limited authority over Forrestal's contacts with the external world. He was able to shut off the telephone, mail, newspapers, and radio, but there was little he could do about those visitors to Forrestal's room who were also VIP's. For reasons already discussed at some length, perhaps the last persons who should have been permitted to see Forrestal at Bethesda were President Truman and Defense Secretary Johnson.

Official Washington's sensitivity to the implications of Forrestal's illness—its fear that the Russians would make the maximum propaganda use of it—is, of course, understandable. Moscow radio *did* assert that Forrestal had been "insane" for a very long time and that our foreign policy reflected his "insanity." In the UN Soviet spokesmen wondered out loud whether the "sanity" of other Truman Administration officials could any longer be taken for granted. Nevertheless, it is doubtful that official Washington's response to the situation was the most rational possible. Washington gossip and the combinations of fact and rumor that found their way into certain newspaper columns supplied the Russians with all the "evidence" they required. However much the Pentagon tried to undermine the gossip and dispel the rumors, it was common knowledge in the foreign embassies and at the Cosmos Club that Forrestal was suffering from a severe depression complicated by paranoia and suicidal tendencies. Certainly it can be argued that there would have been fewer rumors, fewer distortions, fewer half-truths and outright falsehoods, had the official mythology yielded for once to reality.

Despite their propaganda, the Russians were undoubtedly aware that Forrestal well or ill had not made policy single-handedly; certainly they knew of his differences with Truman over Palestine, unification, military spending, and other issues. Whether or not it was true that Forrestal's militant anti-Communism during and after the war had overtones of paranoia, there can be no disputing the fact that his extreme concern was not shared by everyone in Washington, and his intense alarm did not extend to all White House circles. Forrestal, in other words, influenced policy but he did not determine it. These was, therefore, much less need than Washington imagined to pretend until the very last that Forrestal was at Bethesda simply "for a rest." Inasmuch as almost everyone, including the Russians, knew better, it is difficult to believe that adherence to the official mythology served any useful purpose.

Indeed, it is possible to argue that such a mythology is not only misleading but dangerous, dangerous because it denies certain implications of the Forrestal case. Forrestal, to be sure, did not make policy single-handedly, but that does not mean that mental illness in high office is without risk to the national security or without consequence for the issues of world war or peace. Suppose, for example, that Forrestal had not been Defense Secretary but President? Suppose, further, that the nation's military capability had been based on missiles rather than on manned aircraft? Suppose, finally, that push-button warfare had reached the development stage then that it has since achieved?

Clearly no nation *now* can afford the breakdown in office of high officials in a world where the difference between a first strike and second strike, between a nuclear initiative and a nuclear response, is a matter not of days or hours, but of minutes and seconds. The policy process in such a world, the need to take far-reaching decisions in a fraction of the time formerly available, is difficult enough even assuming the sanity and rationality of those involved. Assuming that sometime, somewhere, a decision will be made by one or more persons suffering from certain types of mental illness, eventual annihilation is assured.

Thus the problem in part is one of prevention and detection of illness in high office, but before it can be real-

istically approached statesmen and politicians will have to
abandon their considerable personal and professional stake
in the official mythology. They must be willing to make available evidence that mental and physical illness has played a
significant role in decision making, and this requires that
they be *un*willing to regard as secret and confidential information pertaining to illness. Furthermore, only by detailed study of the Forrestal case and other cases will future
breakdowns and suicides in office be prevented. Until the
relevant medical records are accessible, there will be instances, again and again, of the dead burying the dead. Forrestal, after all, was not the first public official to commit
suicide, and given the official mythology, he will not be the
last.

It is also necessary to dispel the belief, popular in Washington but not only there, that mental illness even in mild
form is disreputable and per se renders one unfit to hold a
responsible position. Such a belief ensures that every effort
will be made to conceal the fact of illness and to delay treatment, thus sustaining the illness itself. Forrestal's suicide, for
example, owed something to his conviction that whether or
not he made a full recovery, his political career was over. No
one in a position to do so made any serious effort to dispel
this conviction, although it is possible that such an effort
would have had far more therapeutic value than any treatment Raines prescribed.

If more is to be known about the mental and physical
health of our political leaders, physicians and especially
psychiatrists may have to reassess their traditional attitude
toward the privacy of the doctor-patient relationship. At
present, that attitude makes it difficult if not impossible to
investigate in a systematic fashion the extent to which medical resources are involved in the complex interplay of politics,
personality, and policy. As a consequence, we do not know
what proportion of Cabinet officers, senators and representatives, generals and admirals, avail themselves of psychiatric

services, and for what purposes. We do not know how many suffer from ulcers and other ailments of a psychosomatic nature. The number of those who consume tranquilizers has never been totaled, and we know even less about the significance of alcohol and marijuana in the relief of tensions arising from everyday Washington life. In the absence of reliable information rumors abound that one President suffered several strokes prior to his attendance at an important international conference, that another took Miltown in a rather impressive dosage, that a third was placed on a drug regimen for a physical ailment, the side effects of which drug include mental states not conducive to rational thinking. The point is not that alcohol, narcotics, tranquilizers, and other drugs have played a role in this or that policy or decision. The point is: *We do not know.*

The prevention and detection of mental illness in high office raises equally difficult questions. In Washington and elsewhere, however, the annual or semiannual physical checkup has become almost a commonplace, and it is appropriate to inquire whether a regular mental checkup would not be at least as desirable. To be sure, the mental-health examination would be less easy to construct, and hence less easy to administer and interpret. Psychiatry being less a science than other branches of medicine, psychiatrists lack exact equivalents for blood-pressure tests and measures of sugar in the urine. It follows that in the practice of psychiatry, more depends on the state of the psychiatrist than on the state of the discipline.

Nevertheless, a variety of tests have been developed for the identification and treatment of personality disorders, and some of them are widely used by the Armed Forces and space agencies where, for obvious reasons, certain personality disorders cannot be tolerated.[14] The battery of psychological

---

14. It is pertinent to mention that the mental health of employees has become a matter of increasing importance to corporations. Certain firms, such as United States Steel and Kodak, employ psychiatrists as consultants,

tests "to determine personality and motivation" given to the Mercury Astronauts included

interviews; Rorschach (ink blot); apperception (tell stories suggested by pictures); draw-a-person; sentence completion; self-inventory based on 566-item questionnaire; officer effectiveness inventory; personal preference schedule based on 225 pairs of self-descriptive statements; personal inventory based on 20 pairs of self-descriptive statements; preference evaluation based on 52 statements; determination of authoritarian attitudes and interpretation of the question, "Who am I?"[15]

The Astronauts were also tested for their capacity to withstand stress and fatigue, and they were given the most complete physical examination that modern medicine has been able to devise.

If, toward the close of 1948, Forrestal had been given even a few of the tests that were taken by the Astronauts, it is probable that symptoms of illness would have been detected. Had he been examined at that time by a psychiatrist or clinical psychologist, it is almost certain that the examiner would have referred him to an appropriate medical authority for immediate treatment. Perhaps a more thorough physical examination than the one he received at Walter Reed on February 8, 1949,[16] would have produced the same result; by that date Forrestal's physical condition had visibly deteriorated, and the state of his physical health might have alerted a sensitive general practitioner or internist to the possibility of mental illness. So far as is known, however, no

and others avail themselves of the services of psychiatric clinics and hospitals. I am indebted to Dr. William Menninger of the Menninger Foundation and Dr. Milton R. Sapirstein of the Division of Organization Psychiatry, Mount Sinai Hospital in New York, for information pertaining to mental health programs sponsored by their respective institutions.

15. National Aeronautics and Space Administration, *Mercury Astronaut Selection Fact Sheet*, April 9, 1959, Appendix IV.

16. See Appendix I. According to Forrestal's appointments calendar, he paid a second visit to Walter Reed on February 10. On March 23 he saw a dentist at Bethesda. There is no record of any other medical appointment between January 3 and the appearance of Menninger and Raines at Hobe Sound, Florida.

Astronaut-type physical or psychological examinations were administered, and no referrals were made.

As Forrestal's behavior became more and more tense, he was consulted less by his associates and involved less in decisions. The apparent intention was, on the one hand, to reduce the strains of office in the hope that he would recover on-the-job, and on the other to expedite decisions with which Forrestal was having a great deal of difficulty. In certain Pentagon circles there was also a desire to protect the Military Establishment from possible later charges that policy had been made by someone who was seriously ill. Bureaucracies, whether governmental, corporate, or academic, do not welcome in their ranks those who are odd, deviant, or excessively nonconformist in behavior, and the military bureaucracy was no exception.

There is something to be said for such exclusion insofar as it penalizes those whose neuroses or psychoses might endanger the nation's security and world peace. But if exclusion succeeds in one area, it fails in another, albeit an area of much less significance. In Forrestal's case, the effect of exclusion was to increase his anxiety and sense of failure, and the more manifest these feelings became, the more his aides and associates, for a complex of reasons, refrained from seeking his advice. The final exclusion was the request for his immediate resignation. Whatever may be said about the necessity, form, and timing of that request, it came at a moment when Forrestal very badly needed to be needed. From that moment until he committed suicide the night of May 21–22, Forrestal could only regard himself as

> Worn by the waste of time—
> Comfortless, nameless, hopeless . . .

Sophocles's "Chorus from Ajax," which he was reading minutes or seconds before his death, must have seemed to him less poetry than obituary.

Beacon, Princeton, and Washington are not without their

memorials to James Forrestal. And in whatever harbor, on whatever seas, can be found the USS *Forrestal,* there too can be found a tribute to the nation's first Secretary of Defense. But it may be doubted that these memorials are homage enough to a man whose death was both tragic and unnecessary. The school in Beacon does not quite compensate for the unhappy years that Forrestal spent in the house on Fishkill Avenue, and the research center at Princeton does not quite erase Forrestal's failure to graduate with other members of the Class of 1915. The bust at the entrance to the Pentagon is as much a symbol of failure as of success, and the USS *Forrestal,* like other defense components that reflect his inspiration, has long since been overtaken by newer military tactics and technologies.

Perhaps the most lasting tribute to James Forrestal would be a massive effort to reduce the incidence of physical and mental breakdown in political life. Much remains to be known about the conditions that produce ulcers, heart disease, and mental illness, and we still know relatively little about the relationship between these ailments and the decision-making process. Although a good deal of progress has been made, the techniques of prevention, detection, and treatment are rather primitive in development and haphazard in application. If there are not to be other Wilsons and Roosevelts, other Forrestals and Winants, above all if there are not to be sick men in high office or at military command posts, the effects of illness on politics and policy must be systematically explored. Until such a research area is no longer treated as both secretive and gossipy, until the official mythology that died with Forrestal is also interred with him, there can be no certainty that mental and physical illness is of little consequence for the resolution of fateful issues. In choosing its heroes and leaders, in selecting those who will decide man's fate for all time, society is entitled to something more than a choice between the sick and the dead.

APPENDIX I

☆ ☆ ☆ ☆ ☆

Forrestal's Appointments Calendar
January 3, 1949, to March 28, 1949

Jan. 3, Monday	10:30 A.M. Cabinet meeting 1:00 P.M. lunch with Truman (off record) 6:15 Miss Billie*
Jan. 4, Tuesday	12:00 Mr. J. R. McLean 12:45 Lunch: Lovett, Hiffman, Carpenter, Gruenther, Lemnitzer, Lutes 2.30 Dr. Kimball 10:30 "Try to drop in: Mrs. Sloane—2101 Conn. Ave., Apt. 1"
Jan. 5, Wednesday	9:30 Shields and Jordan 12:15 Joint Chiefs of Staff lunch White House 1:00 Truman addresses Congress
Jan. 6, Thursday	9:00 Munitions Board Meeting 9:15 Senator McKellar 12:45 Lunch: Clifford, Elsey, Leva, Stauffacher 2:30 National Security Council 5:00–7:00 Hoover Commission 5:30 Reception: Attorney General for Speaker Rayburn 7:00 President and Mrs. Truman, etc.

---

* According to one of his close associates, "Miss Billie" refers to a hairdresser who shampooed Forrestal's hair almost every Monday he was in Washington. Forrestal, the aide reports, did not like the shampoo administered by his barber.

Jan. 7, Friday	8:15 Breakfast at home: Mr. Weeks
	9:00 Candid camera shots
	9:30 General Persons
	9:30 Hoover Commission
	12:45 Mr. Clifford Folger
	3:30 Dr. Morgan, Leva, Larkin, Gray, Kenney, Zuckert: re Military Justice
	5:00 Hoover Commission
Jan. 8, Saturday	10:00 Hoover Commission
	5:00–7:00 Hoover Commission (tentative)
	7:45 Mr. Gates and Mrs. Lovett for dinner. Also Admiral Radford
Jan. 10, Monday	9:30 Hoover Commission
	1:00 Lunch with Truman—Blair House
	4:30 Hoover Commission
	5:30–7:30 Cocktails, Mrs. Lord, Mayflower Hotel
	6:15 Miss Billie
Jan. 11, Tuesday	10:00 War Council
	11:45 White House off the record (East Entrance)
	3:30 Hoover Commission
Jan. 12, Wednesday	9:15 Frank, Hennessy
	9:30 Hoover Commission
	10:00 Mr. Tel Berna and Machine Tool Builders
	11:45 Mr. Cooper
	12:00 Meet with the President and Committee on Equality of Treatment and Opportunity—President's Office, White House
	12:45 Lunch: Generals Persons, Russell, Ruffner, White
	2:00 Admiral Gingrich
	3:00 War Council
	3:30 Hoover Commission
	7:45 Senator Robertson
	Go in after dinner: McCloys
Jan. 13, Thursday	8:15 Dr. Elliott for breakfast
	9:00 Munitions Board
	9:30 Hoover Commission meeting
	10:00 Research and Development Board
	12:45 Mr. Vinson for lunch here
	4:30 Hoover Commission
Jan. 14, Friday	9:30 Hoover Commission
	10:00 Cabinet

| | 12:45 | Lunch: Senators Hunt, Chapman, O'Mahoney, General Paul |

12:45 Lunch: Senators Hunt, Chapman,
      O'Mahoney, General Paul
5:00–6:00 Cocktails for Dr. Morgan
6:00 Reception at New Zealand Embassy
8:20 Dinner: Mr. Baruch

Jan. 15, Saturday 10:00 Your car will meet Mrs. Forrestal at Union Station at 10:15
12:45 Lunch: Senator Pepper
2:30 Golf—Admiral Glover
8:00 Dinner: Cowles, etc.
10:30 Sulgrave—white tie

Jan. 17, Monday 9:15 Mr. Franges
9:30 Staff meeting
5:45 Members of class of 1915 at Duquesne Club
6:30 Reception, Chamber of Commerce, Wm. Penn
7:00 Dinner, Wm. Penn Hotel, black tie

Jan. 18, Tuesday 9:15 Messrs. Blum, Ohly, Halaby re Security
10:00 Four Secretaries Meeting
12:00 Generals Gruenther, Persons, Leva. Messrs. Halaby, etc.
1:00 Lunch, Mr. Niles
2:15 Mr. John A. Kennedy
4:00 Generals Bradley, Vandenberg, Adm. Denfield
7:00 Truman-Barkley Club Dinner—Mayflower Hotel—Main Ballroom—Dress optional

Jan. 19, Wednesday 9:30 Mr. John Lord O'Brian, Paul Fitzpatrick
12:30 Joint Chiefs—lunch
12:45 Lunch—Mr. John Kennedy
      Senator Kilgore (?)
4:00–6:00 Receptions. Chapmans—Westchester Apts.
4:00–6:00 Governors Reception Davies
4:30–10:00 Cocktail party: Judge Townsend
5:00–7:30 Reception in honor of Stevensons and Douglas'
6:15 Reception in honor of President and Vice President
6:30 Inaugural Dinner, Main Ballroom Mayflower, white tie
8:30 Inaugural Gala national guard armory

Jan. 20, Thursday 8:15 Mr. Dunnington for breakfast
10:00 Prayer service—St. Johns

	12:00 Inaugural ceremonies for President
	1:00 Inaugural parade to start
	5:00 The President's reception (National Gallery of Art)
	6:30 Cocktails, Buffet, at Biddle's
	10:00 Inaugural Ball—white tie

Jan. 21, Friday
    8:15 Mr. Westbrook Pegler for breakfast
   10:00 Stag breakfast, New York State Democratic Comm.
   11:00 Oath of Office, Mr. Acheson (President's office)
    5:00 Reception in honor of President and Mrs. Truman, Miss Truman (Secretary Snyder)
    6:30 Reception, Shoreham Hotel, to meet members of Democratic National Comm. (Senator and Mrs. McGrath)

Jan. 22, Saturday
    9:00 The Artist (it is hoped you will sit this one out) *
 5:00–7:00 Cocktails: Assistant Secretary of Navy and Mrs. Andrews
    7:30 Mr. McNeil's daughter's wedding. Reception following

Jan. 24, Monday
    8:15 Mr. Eliahu Epstein for breakfast, house
    9:30 Staff meeting
    9:30 Hoover Commission
   10:30 Public relations council
   12:30 Joint Chiefs of Staff lunch—with General Eisenhower
    2:30 Hoover Commission
    6:15 Miss Billie

Jan. 25, Tuesday
    9:15 Messrs. Havanner, Welch, Miller (re San Francisco Bay Bridge location)
   10:00 War Council (Mr. Harriman to address)
   12:45 Lunch, Mr. Arthur Fleming
    2:00 Hoover Commission
 5:00–7:30 Cocktails: Congressman Melvin Price for new Congressmen

Jan. 26, Wednesday
   10:00 House Armed Services Committee
   12:30 Buffet lunch for Committee here
    2:00 Hoover Commission

---

* This is in reference to Forrestal's impatience with a portrait artist who was painting his picture.

Jan. 27, Thursday	9:30 Hoover Commission
	10:00 House Appropriations Committee
	12:45 Buffet lunch for Committee here
	1:45 Mr. McNeil at American Legion Meeting
	2:30 Munitions Board Meeting
	3:00 National Security Council Meeting at White House
Jan. 28, Friday	9:00 White House—re Committee on Germany
	10:00 Cabinet
	11:00 The President (off-the-record)
	7:45 Dinner—Ambassador Douglas
Jan. 31, Monday	9:30 Staff meeting
	10:00 House appropriations hearings
	10:30 Public relations council
	1:00 Lunch—the President—off-the-record—Blair House
	2:00 Hoover Commission
	2:30 House Appropriations Committee hearings
	6:15 Miss Billie
	After dinner: Mr. McCloy's, with Mr. Hinton
Feb. 1, Tuesday	9:30 Messrs. Ohly, Hinton, Dr. Rusk
	9:45 Mr. Sherman
	10:00 Four Secretaries meeting
	11:00 Swearing in: Messrs. Pace, Lawton
	11:30 Barber
	12:15 —Address Press Club luncheon
	1:15 Your address starts
	2:00 Hoover Commission
	2:30 Messrs. Blum, Ohly, Halaby
	4:15 Attorney General, Mr. Hoover, Mr. Souers (re Internal Security)
	7:45 Dinner: Connallys, Mr. Finletter, Mrs. Shevlin, Mr. Merry del Val
Feb. 2, Wednesday	9:00 Mr. Frank Weil
	10:00 Senate Armed Services Committee
	12:30 Buffet lunch for Senate Armed Services Committee
	2:00 Hoover Commission
	6:00 Jefferson-Jackson Victory Dinner Comm., Mayflower
Feb. 3, Thursday	9:00 Munitions Board meeting
	11:30 Mr. William E. Levis
	12:45 Cabinet lunch here

	2:30	National Security Council meeting— White House
	3:30	Messrs. Clifford, Pace, Leva, Stauffacher (Mr. Clifford's office, White House)
	5:00	Memorial service for Woodrow Wilson
Feb. 4, Friday	10:00	Cabinet
	12:00	Messrs. Durning, Coleman, Foley
	8:00	Dinner: Parkers, 3314 "O" Street (black tie)
Feb. 5, Saturday	9:30	The Artist
	10:30	Generals Lemnitzer and Gruenther
	12:30	Col. Solberg
	1:00	Lunch—Mr. Symington
	3:00	Cabinet Room, White House: Messrs. Draper, Kenny, Symington, Clifford, Leva, Pace, Stauffacher
	8:00	Dinner: Radio correpondents—Statler
Feb. 7, Monday	9:30	Staff meeting
	10:30	Public relations council
	11:30	Admiral Conolly
	1:00	Lunch—The President (Blair House—off the record)
	2:00	Hoover Commission meeting
	4:30	Mr. Clauson Roop
	5:00	Secretary Acheson's office—Messrs. Harriman, Hoffman, re Economic Cooperation Adm. testimony
	6:15	Miss Billie
Feb. 8, Tuesday	9:45	Mr. Sherman
	10:00	War council
	2:00	Hoover Commission
	3:00	Walter Reed—for check up
	5:30	Cocktails: General and Mrs. Hill, for Thomases
Feb. 9, Wednesday	9:30	Mr. Charles S. Thomas
	12:00	Generals Kuter, Nowland, Olds, Haynes, Admirals Whitney, Tomlinson
	12:45	Lunch: Generals Eisenhower and Gruenther
	2:30	Hoover Commission
	3:00	The President
	Between 4:00 and 5:00	Boy Scouts of America on tour of Pentagon will come to office: **You to greet if available**

	5:30 Cocktails: Advertising Council at home of Mr. Philip Graham
	7:00 Attorney General and Mrs. Clark, Snyders, Andersons, Symingtons, etc.
	9:00 Congressional Club reception for President and Mrs. Truman
Feb. 10, Thursday	9:00 Munitions Board meeting
	10:00 Photos: with General Eisenhower
	10:30 Mr. Folsom will call
	12:00 French Ambassador Mr. Bonnet
	12:45 Cabinet lunch at Justice Department
	2:30 Mr. Clifford, Mr. Pace
	8:30 Walter Reed
Feb. 11, Friday	10:00 Cabinet
Feb. 14, Monday	9:30 Staff conference
	10:00 (Grover Loening due in Washington today)
	10:30 Public relations council
	1:00 Lunch—The President (Blair House—off the record)
	2:00 Hoover Commission
	6:15 Appointment at House
	7:45 Stop by for a drink: Alibi Club, Mr. Coffin
Feb. 15, Tuesday	9:45 Mr. Sherman
	10:00 Four Secretaries meeting
	12:30 Mr. Charles S. Thomas—lunch
	2:15 Depart for Andrews Air Force Base
	5:30 Mr. Eberstadt
Feb. 16, Wednesday	10:00 Testify before House Armed Services Committee re under secretary bill
	10:00 Orientation conference opens for American Ordnance Association
	1:00 Luncheon for Conferees
	2:00 Hoover Commission
	4:00 White House—Cabinet Room The President, Mr. Leva, Clifford, Elsey, Pace, Stauffacher, re changes in Security Act. *Use East Entrance—Off-the-record*
	5:00 Reception for Conferees
	8:00 The President—Blair House
Feb. 17, Thursday	9:00 Munitions Board meeting
	9:30 Mr. Blum

	10:00	Joint Chiefs meeting
	12:45	Cabinet lunch here
	2:30	National Security Council meeting
Feb. 18, Friday	8:15	Breakfast, Mr. McGraw
	9:15	Army Day Recording, Dining Room
	10:00	Cabinet
	12:45	Lunch: Senator Humphrey
	5:40	Meet General Bradley in his office
	6:00	Reception in honor of General Bradley
Feb. 19, Saturday	10:00	Intelligence briefing
	11:30	Mr. Tack (1028 Conn. Ave., Apt. 1107)
	1:30	Meet Generals Eisenhower, Bradley, etc.
	7:45	Dinner at house
Feb. 21, Monday	9:30	Staff meeting
	10:00	House Armed Services Committee hearings
	10:30	Public relations council meeting
	12:00	Mr. Donald Douglas
	1:00	Lunch: The President—Blair House—off the record
	2:00	Hoover Commission
	6:15	Appointment at House
Feb. 22, Tuesday	9:30	Mr. Royall—CCC
	12:30	Lunch
		The Artist
	2:00	Hoover Commission
	6:30	Stag supper for Mr. Bill Boyle, Mayflower
Feb. 23, Wednesday	9:00	Air meeting (Mr. Symington)
	9:45	Mr. Sherman
	10:00	War Council
		Research and Development Board
		Hoover Commission
	1:15	Lunch—Dr. Menninger
	2:00	Hoover Commission
	6:00	Mrs. Fowler—for Munsons, 35th Street
	7:00	Cocktails—Dr. Compton—Research and Development Board, Wardman Park Hotel
Feb. 24, Thursday	9:00	Munitions Board meeting
	11:30	Mr. K. Reynolds
	6:00	Mr. Maple Harl (Room 260, Mayflower Hotel)
	6:45	Dinner—Jefferson-Jackson Day, Statler
Feb. 25, Friday	9:15	Accept citation of distinguished merit for armed forces radio services

	10:00	The President
		Off-the-record, use East Entrance
	11:30	Press conference (Cooper Comm.)
	12:30	Buffet lunch: radio correspondents
	1:50	Mr. Webster
	2:00	Messrs. Webster, Compton, Gerstell
	2:30	General Richard J. Marshall (Supt. Virginia Military Institute)
	3:00	Mr. Holliday and Scientists in Dr. Compton's office
		After dinner: Wigglesworths', 3257 "N" St., NW
	9:00–1:00	Office Secretary of Defense dancing party—National Press Club

Feb. 26, Saturday
    9:15 Colonel Fuller at CCC
    1:30 The Artist

Feb. 28, Monday
    9:30 Staff conference
   10:30 Public relations council
    1:00 Lunch—The President
       (Blair House: Off the record)
    2:30 General Hull, Mr. Morse
    6:15 Appointment at House
    7:00 Dinner: Mr. Mead, Metropolitan Club for Hoover Commission

March 1, Tuesday
    8:15 Mr. Lester Markel for breakfast at home
    9:15 War Council special meeting
   10:00 Hoover Commission
   12:30 East Entrance (Off-Record)

March 2, Wednesday
   [crossed out] 10:45 The President—Off-Record. (Use East Entrance)
   12:00 Secretary Acheson, Mr. Pike, Mr. Souers
    3:00 Ladies of the 78th Congress to view office
  5:00–7:00 Reception for Mr. Frank Folsom

March 3, Thursday
    9:00 Munitions Board meeting
   10:00 82nd Airborne Division of Fort Bragg, N.C. (Col. Wood handling)
   10:30 Hearings on US Bill before Senate Armed Services Committee (Mr. Leva handling)
   12:30 Go in after lunch: Cabinet lunch at Interior (Krug's office)
    2:30 National Security Council meeting

March 4, Friday
   10:00 Cabinet
   12:00 Navy Industrial Association (Capt. Berry handling)

	12:45	Lunch for Conferees of Navy Industrial Association
	2:00	Generals Morgan, Eisenhower, Gruenther
	3:15	The President, Pace, Royall, Sullivan, Symington re Armed Services budget off-record—use east entrance
	4:00	Conference follows re changes in Security Act (Mr. Leva will join)
March 5, Saturday	10:00	Armed Forces Medical Advisory Comm.— with General Eisenhower
	3:00	CCC
	7:30	White House Correspondents Association dinner, Statler, head table guests to assemble between 6:30 and 7:00
March 7, Monday	9:30	Staff conference
	10:00	Testify before House Armed Service Committee re military justice code
	10:30	Public relations council
	6:15	Appointment at House
March 8, Tuesday	8:15	Mr. Jim Shepley
	12:45	Lunch; Mr. Strauss
	2:30	War Council
	6:15	Mr. Perry Brown at House for cocktails
March 9, Wednesday	12:00	Swearing in of Mr. Dan A. Kimball
	7:30	Dinner: go in after: Business Advisory Council
March 10, Thursday	9:00	Munitions Board meeting
	10:30	Mr. Nash
	11:00	Senate Armed Services Committee: Testify re under secretary bill
	3:00	President's office to discuss provisions of National Security Act
March 11, Friday	12:00	Certificate of appreciation to Mr. Hinton
	2:00	Estimated Time Departure, Mats Terminal
	4:30	Estimated Time Arrival
March 14, Monday	10:00	to 4:30 Joint Chiefs of Staff (You are not expected)
	10:30	Public relations council
	3:30	Secretary Acheson—Attorney General Clark, State Department
	6:15	Miss Billie
March 15, Tuesday	9:30	War Council
	10:00	to 4:30 Joint Chiefs of Staff (You are not expected)

	2:00 Film on first 4 chapters Eisenhower book
March 16, Wednesday	9:30–12:00 Joint Chiefs of Staff meeting (not expected)
	10:00 Mr. Reid and General Lanham
	8:00 Dinner—Swiss Legation
March 17, Thursday	9:00 Munitions Board
	10:00 House Appropriations Committee
	10:00 to 4:30 Joint Chiefs of Staff meeting (not expected)
	3:45 Leave office for airport (New York)
	6:45 Reception—Friendly Sons of St. Patrick, Astor Hotel
	7:30 Dinner
	10:00 Address (to be televised)
March 18, Friday	No calendar [Forrestal presumably was in New York]
March 19, Saturday	9:00 CCC
	10:00 Joint Intelligence Committee Presentation
	12:45 Lunch—Service Academy Board
	7:30 White House News Photographers Association dinner, Statler
March 21, Monday	9:30 Staff conference
	1:00 Lunch—The President
	6:15 Miss Billie
	7:45 Dinner—Eisenhowers (Mrs. Forrestal) Statler Hotel
March 22, Tuesday	10:00 Committee of Four Secretaries
	12:00 Investiture ceremony for Dr. Bush (Knighthood of British Empire, British Embassy)
	1:15 Lunch, officers dining room
	2:30 National Security Council meeting (White House)
	4:00 Mr. Myer Dorfman (Col. Wood handled)
March 23, Wednesday	9:00 Dentist at Bethesda
	10:30 You told Mr. Myron Taylor you would call him
	11:00 Admiral Blandy (call first)
	12:00 Mr. Reid awards certificate of appreciation for advisory pay commission
	2:30 Atlantic Pact discussion (Col. Johnson, Lemnitzer, Halaby, Ohly, Blum)
	7:00 Cocktails—Mr. Royall—Mayflower
	8:00 Dinner—Mayflower

March 24, Thursday	8:45	Mr. McNeil to address war college on budget
	9:00	Munitions Board meeting
	10:30	Present National Military Establishment plaque to chairman of committee Senate Armed Services
	2:30	Admiral Hill
	3:00	General Revers, French Chief of Staff
	3:30	Mr. Reid, General Lanham
March 25, Friday	9:15	War Council photo
	10:00	Cabinet
	11:30	Mr. Mellinger (not firm)
	3:15	Distinguished Service Medal to Admiral Leahy—President's office White House
March 28, Monday	9:30	National Military Establishment insignia awards
	10:00	Captain Smedberg
	11:00	Swearing in of Col. Johnson
	1:00	Lunch—The President, Blair House, off record
	2:30	Secretaries Royall, Sullivan, Symington
	3:30	The President
	5:45	Appointment at House
	6:30	Cocktails—Col. Johnson for Secretary Johnson
	7:30	Dinner, Mayflower, black tie

APPENDIX II

☆ ☆ ☆ ☆ ☆

Forrestal's Travel Log as Secretary of Defense

ARRIVED		POINT	DEPARTED		REMARKS
		Washington, D.C.	1600	9–19–47	Personal—
1935	9–19–47	New York, N.Y.	2005		Ex-Secty Stimson's
2145	9–21–47	Washington, D.C.			80th Birthday
		Washington, D.C.	1630	9–24–47	Official Navy
1752	9–24–47	New York, N.Y.	1200	9–25–47	Industrial Assn.
1317	9–25–47	Washington, D.C.			Dinner
		Washington, D.C.	1650	9–26–47	Personal—
1852	9–26–47	Quonset Pt., R.I.	1612	9–28–47	Weekend at
1812	9–28–47	Washington, D.C.			Newport, R.I.
		Washington, D.C.	1609	10–1–47	Official—Army
1729	10–1–47	New York, N.Y.	1016	10–2–47	Ordnance Assn.
1139	10–2–47	Washington D.C.			Dinner
		Washington, D.C.	1654	10–4–47	Personal—
1852	10–4–47	Quonset Pt., R.I.	1645	10–5–47	Weekend at
1851	10–5–47	Washington, D.C.			Newport, R.I.
		Washington, D.C.	1150	10–11–47	Official—
1307	10–11–47	New York, N.Y.	1645	10–12–47	Army-Illinois
1745	10–12–47	Washington, D.C.			Football Game
		Washington, D.C.	1530	10–14–47	Official—
1650	10–14–47	New York, N.Y.	0908	10–15–47	Alfred E. Smith
1022	10–15–47	Washington, D.C.			Dinner

ARRIVED	POINT	DEPARTED	REMARKS
	Washington, D.C.	1720 10–15–47	Official—
1838 10–15–47	New York, N.Y.	1556 10–16–47	Dinner for Mrs.
1722 10–16–47	Washington, D.C.		Horton (Test.)
	Washington, D.C.	1613 10–20–47	Official—
1745 10–20–47	New York, N.Y.	0900 10–21–47	NY Herald-
1020 10–21–47	Washington, D.C.		Tribune Forum
	Washington, D.C.	1523 10–30–47	Official—Off the
1650 10–30–47	New York, N.Y.	0055 10–31–47	Record Speech at
0715 10–31–47	Washington, D.C.		Waldorf-Astoria
	Washington, D.C.	1555 11–21–47	Personal—
1655 11–21–47	Trenton, N.J.	1635 11–22–47	Princeton-Dart-
1815 11–22–47	Baltimore, Md.	1900 11–22–47	mouth Football
2030 11–22–47	Washington, D.C.		Game
	Washington, D.C.	1610 11–25–47	Personal
1724 11–25–47	New York, N.Y.	0943 11–26–47	
1107 11–26–47	Washington, D.C.		
	Washington, D.C.	0845 11–29–47	Offic'l—Army-Navy
1130 11–29–47	Philadelphia, Pa.	1630 11–29–47	Football Game but
1930 11–29–47	Washington, D.C.		expenses defrayed
			from private funds
	Washington, D.C.	1525 12–9–47	Personal
1700 12–9–47	New York, N.Y.	2210 12–9–47	
2335 12–9–47	Washington, D.C.		
	Washington, D.C.	1430 12–22–47	Official, except for
1900 12–22–47	Eglin Field, Fla.	1400 12–23–47	stay at Palm Beach.
1700 12–23–47	Palm Beach, Fla.	1600 12–30–47	Inspected at Eglin
1800 12–30–47	Maxwell Fld. Ala.	1400 12–31–47	Maxwell
1800 12–31–47	Washington, D.C.		
	Washington, D.C.	1330 1–22–48	Official—Address
1700 1–22–48	Chicago, Ill.	1000 1–23–48	at Commercial
1500 1–23–48	Washington, D.C.		Club Dinner
	Washington, D.C.	1515 1–26–48	Personal—
1615 1–26–48	New York, N.Y.	0055 1–27–48	Transportation de-
0715 1–27–48	Washington, D.C.		frayed w/ pvt. funds
	Washington, D.C.	1640 2–8–48	Official
1745 2–8–48	New York, N.Y.	1705 2–9–48	
1826 2–9–48	Washington, D.C.		

ARRIVED		POINT	DEPARTED		REMARKS
		Washington, D.C.	1400	2–12–48	Official
1800	2–12–48	New York, N.Y.	0055	2–13–48	
0715	2–13–48	Washington, D.C.			
		Washington, D.C.	1545	2–21–48	Official
1700	2–21–48	New York, N.Y.	1230	2–22–48	
1635	2–22–48	Washington, D.C.			
		Washington, D.C.	1600	2–28–48	Personal—Expen.
1935	2–28–48	New York, N.Y.	0055	2–29–48	paid from personal
0715	2–29–48	Washington, D.C.			funds
		Washington, D.C.	1300	3–10–48	Official—
1730	3–10–48	Stuart, Fla.	1700	3–11–48	Joint Chiefs of
1830	3–11–48	Key West, Fla.	1600	3–14–48	Staff Conference
1730	3–14–48	Stuart, Fla.	1200	3–15–48	
1630	3–15–48	Washington, D.C.			
		Washington, D.C.	1530	4–2–48	Official—Address
1700	4–2–48	New York, N.Y.	0845	4–3–48	Army & Navy
1000	4–3–48	Washington, D.C.			Alumni Dinner
		Washington, D.C.	1700	4–10–48	Official
1815	4–10–48	New York, N.Y.	2345	4–10–48	
0100	4–11–48	Washington, D.C.			
		Washington, D.C.	1600	4–14–48	
1935	4–14–48	New York, N.Y.	0900	4–15–48	
1000	4–15–48	Princeton, N.J.	1320	4–15–48	
1420	4–15–48	Washington, D.C.			
		Washington, D.C.	1615	4–22–48	Official—American
1740	4–22–48	New York, N.Y.	0055	4–23–48	Newspapers Pub.
0715	4–23–48	Washington, D.C.			Association Speech
		Washington, D.C.	1545	5–12–48	Official—Army &
1700	5–12–48	New York, N.Y.	0055	5–13–48	Navy Chaplains
0655	5–13–48	Washington, D.C.			Dinner Speech
		Washington, D.C.	1545	5–19–48	Official
1700	5–19–48	New York, N.Y.	2245	5–19–48	
2400	5–19–48	Washington, D.C.			
		Washington, D.C.	1500	6–7–48	Official—Address
1630	6–7–48	New York, N.Y.	0810	6–8–48	at U.S. Military
0945	6–8–48	West Point, N.Y.	1315	6–8–48	Academy, West
1335	6–8–48	Stewart Fld., N.Y.	1350	6–8–48	Point, N.Y.
1530	6–8–48	Washington, D.C.			

ARRIVED		POINT	DEPARTED		REMARKS
		Washington, D.C.	0930	6–14–48	
1030	6–14–48	Princeton, N.J.	1245	6–14–48	
1345	6–14–48	Washington, D.C.			
		Washington, D.C.	1540	6–28–48	
1700	6–28–48	New York, N.Y.	1000	6–29–48	
1130	6–29–48	Washington, D.C.			
		Washington, D.C.	1615	7–2–48	
1830	7–2–48	Newport, R.I.	1515	7–5–48	
1730	7–5–48	Washington, D.C.			
		Washington, D.C.	1230	7–12–48	
1400	7–12–48	New York, N.Y.	2220	7–12–48	
2357	7–12–48	Washington, D.C.			
		Washington, D.C.	1530	7–30–48	Official—Dedicat.
1645	7–30–48	New York, N.Y.	1635	7–31–48	of Idlewild Inter-
1805	7–31–48	Washington, D.C.			national Airport
		Washington, D.C.	0900	8–4–48	Official—Addressed
0940	8–4–48	Harrisburg, Pa.	1000	8–4–48	Armed Forces
1030	8–4–48	Carlisle Bar., Pa.	1340	8–4–48	Information School
1410	8–4–48	Harrisburg, Pa.	1415	8–4–48	
1610	8–4–48	Washington, D.C.			
		Washington, D.C.	1620	8–7–48	
1820	8–7–48	Newport, R.I.	1545	8–8–48	
1810	8–8–48	Washington, D.C.			
		Washington, D.C.	1710	8–13–48	Official—Visit to
1915	8–13–48	Newport, R.I.	1215	8–15–48	Canada and
1400	8–15–48	Ottawa, Ontario	1000	8–17–48	Ogdensburg
1130	8–17–48	Prescott, Ontario	1210	8–17–48	Bi-Centennial
1230	8–17–48	Ogdensburg, N.Y.	1440	8–17–48	
1545	8–17–48	Messena, N.Y.	1550	8–17–48	
1810	8–17–48	Washington, D.C.			
		Washington, D.C.	1500	8–20–48	Official—
1730	8–20–48	Newport, R.I.	2130	8–22–48	Meeting of Joint
2345	8–22–48	Washington, D.C.			Chiefs of Staff
		Washington, D.C.	1715	8–26–48	
1755	8–26–48	Wilmington, Del.	0933	8–27–48	
1009	8–27–48	Washington, D.C.			

ARRIVED		POINT	DEPARTED		REMARKS
		Washington, D.C.	1630	8–27–48	
1845	8–27–48	Newport, R.I.	1630	8–29–48	
1845	8–29–48	Washington, D.C.			
		Washington, D.C.	1415	9–4–48	Official—
1600	9–4–48	Chicago, Ill.	0900	9–5–48	American Veterans
1255	9–5–48	Washington, D.C.			Convention
		Washington, D.C.	1615	9–22–48	
1735	9–22–48	New York, N.Y.	2240	9–22–48	
2400	9–22–48	Washington, D.C.			
		Washington, D.C.	1620	10–15–48	
1730	10–15–48	New York, N.Y.	2225	10–15–48	
2345	10–15–48	Washington, D.C.			
		Washington, D.C.	1450	10–19–48	Official—
1735	10–19–48	Eglin Fld., Fla.	1310	10–20–48	Witness
1800	10–20–48	Washington, D.C.			Combine II
		Washington, D.C.	1630	10–24–48	
1815	10–24–48	New York, N.Y.	0055	10–25–48	
0700	10–25–48	Washington, D.C.			
		Washington, D.C.	1518	11–9–48	Official—
2200	11–9–48	Steph'ville, Nfld.	2335	11–9–48	Inspection and
1704	11–10–48	Paris, France	1237	11–12–48	Familiarization
1300	11–12–48	Lakenheath, Eng.	1435	11–12–48	Trip—Western
1540	11–12–48	London, England	1450	11–13–48	Europe
1900	11–13–48	Berlin, Germany	1220	11–14–48	
1408	11–14–48	Frankfurt, Ger.	0900	11–15–48	
1030	11–15–48	Heidelberg, Ger.	1300	11–15–48	
1410	11–15–48	Frankfurt, Ger.	1430	11–15–48	
2200	11–15–48	Gibraltar	2400	11–15–48	
0420	11–16–48	Lagens, Azores	0620	11–16–48	
1415	11–16–48	Steph'ville, Nfld.	1550	11–16–48	
1935	11–16–48	Washington, D.C.			
		Washington, D.C.	0715	11–18–48	Key West, official
1205	11–18–48	Key West, Fla.	1600	11–18–48	trip
2115	11–18–48	Washington, D.C.			
		Washington, D.C.	1615	12–1–48	Official—Address
1730	12–1–48	New York, N.Y.	2315	12–1–48	English Speaking
0030	12–2–48	Washington, D.C.			Union, NYC

ARRIVED		POINT	DEPARTED		REMARKS
		Washington, D.C.	1600	12–22–48	
1720	12–22–48	New York, N.Y.	2240	12–22–48	
2358	12–22–48	Washington, D.C.			
		Washington, D.C.	1226	12–24–48	
1730	12–24–48	Stuart Field, Fla.	1300	12–30–48	
1803	12–30–48	Washington, D.C.			
		Washington, D.C.	1530	1–17–49	Official—Address
1830	1–17–49	Pittsburgh, Pa.	2235	1–17–49	Pittsburgh C'mber
2335	1–17–49	Washington, D.C.			of Commerce
		Washington, D.C.	1400	3–11–49	Weekend trip
1650	3–11–49	Monk's Cor., S.C.			
		Charleston, S.C.	1630	3–13–49	
1906	3–13–49	Washington, D.C.			
		Washington, D.C.	1610	3–17–49	St. Patrick's
1730	3–17–49	New York, N.Y.	0055	3–18–49	Day Speech
0715	3–18–49	Washington, D.C.			

APPENDIX III

☆ ☆ ☆ ☆ ☆

Principal Officers of the War, State, and Defense Departments, 1940–1949

STATE DEPARTMENT

Secretary of State
Cordell Hull, 1933–1944
Edward R. Stettinius, 1944–1945
James F. Byrnes, 1945–1947
George C. Marshall, 1947–1949
Dean G. Acheson, 1949–

Under Secretary of State
Sumner Welles, 1937–1943
Edward R. Stettinius, 1943–1944
Joseph C. Grew, 1944–1945
Dean G. Acheson, 1945–1947
Robert A. Lovett, 1947–1949
James E. Webb, 1949–

WAR DEPARTMENT

Secretary of War
Henry L. Stimson, 1940–1945
Robert P. Patterson, 1945–1947
Kenneth C. Royall, 1947–

Under Secretary of War
Robert P. Patterson, 1940–1945
Kenneth C. Royall, 1945–1947
William H. Draper, Jr., 1947–

Assistant Secretary of War
Louis A. Johnson, 1937–1940
Robert P. Patterson, 1940–1941

John J. McCloy, 1941–1945
Howard C. Petersen, 1945–1947
Chief of Staff
General George C. Marshall, 1939–1945
General Dwight D. Eisenhower, 1945–1948
Chief of Staff to the Commander-in-Chief
Admiral William D. Leahy, 1942–1949
Chairman of the Joint Chiefs
General Omar N. Bradley, 1949
Chief of Staff of the Army
General Dwight D. Eisenhower, 1945–1948
General Omar N. Bradley, 1948–1949
General J. Lawton Collins, 1949–

NAVY DEPARTMENT
Secretary of the Navy
Frank Knox, 1940–1944
James Forrestal, 1944–1947
Under Secretary of the Navy
James Forrestal, 1940–1944
Ralph A. Bard, 1944–1945
Artemus L. Gates, July–December, 1945
John L. Sullivan, 1946–1947
Assistant Secretary of the Navy
Ralph A. Bard, 1941–1944
H. Struve Hensel, 1945–1946
W. John Kenney, 1946–1947
Assistant Secretary of the Navy for Air
Artemus L. Gates, 1941–1945
John L. Sullivan, 1945–1946
Chief of Naval Operations
Admiral Ernest J. King, 1942–1945
Admiral Chester W. Nimitz, 1945–1947
Admiral Louis E. Denfeld, 1947–1949
Admiral Forrest P. Sherman, 1949–

DEPARTMENT OF DEFENSE (set up in July, 1947)
Secretary of Defense
James Forrestal, 1947–1949
Louis A. Johnson, 1949–1950
Deputy Secretary of Defense
Robert A. Lovett, 1950–

DEPARTMENT OF THE ARMY
Secretary of the Army
Kenneth C. Royall, 1947–1950
Under Secretary of the Army
William H. Draper, 1947–1949
Archibald S. Alexander, 1949–

DEPARTMENT OF THE NAVY
  Secretary of the Navy
    John L. Sullivan, 1947–1949
    Frances P. Matthews, 1949–
  Under Secretary of the Navy
    W. John Kenney, 1947–1949
    Dan A. Kimball, 1949–
DEPARTMENT OF THE AIR FORCE
  Secretary of the Air Force
    W. Stuart Symington, 1947–1950
  Under Secretary of the Air Force
    Arthur S. Barrows, 1947–1950
  Chief of Staff of the Air Force
    General Carl Spaatz, 1947–1948
    General Hoyt S. Vandenberg, 1948–
OTHER CABINET MEMBERS
  Secretary of the Treasury
    Henry Morgenthau, Jr., 1934–1945
    Fred M. Vinson, 1945–1946
    John W. Snyder, 1946–1953
  Attorney General
    Robert H. Jackson, 1940–1941
    Francis Biddle, 1941–1945
    Tom C. Clark, 1945–1949
    J. Howard McGrath, 1949–1952
  Postmaster General
    Frank C. Walker, 1940–1945
    Robert E. Hannegan, 1945–1947
    Jesse M. Donaldson, 1947–1953
  Secretary of the Interior
    Harold L. Ickes, 1933–1946
    Julius A. Krug, 1946–1950
  Secretary of Agriculture
    Claude R. Wickard, 1940–1945
    Clinton P. Anderson, 1945–1948
    Charles F. Brannan, 1948–1953
  Secretary of Commerce
    Jesse Jones, 1940–1945
    Henry A. Wallace, 1945–1946
    W. Averell Harriman, 1946–1948
    Charles Sawyer, 1948–1953
  Secretary of Labor
    Frances Perkins, 1933–1945
    Louis B. Schwellenbach, 1945–1948
    Maurice J. Tobin, 1948–1953

BUREAU OF THE BUDGET
  Directors
    Harold D. Smith, 1939–1946
    James E. Webb, 1946–1949
    Frank Pace, 1949–1950
ATOMIC ENERGY COMMISSION
  Chairman
    David E. Lilienthal, 1947–1950*
    Sumner Pike, 1950†
    Gordon Dean, 1950–1953
    Lewis L. Strauss, 1953–
AMBASSADORS
  To Great Britain
    John G. Winant, 1941–1946
    W. Averell Harriman, 1946
    O. Max Gardner, 1946–1947
    Lewis W. Douglas, 1947–1950
  To the U.S.S.R.
    W. Averell Harriman, 1943–1946
    General Walter Bedell Smith, 1946–1949
  To China
    Patrick J. Hurley, 1944–1945
    General George C. Marshall, 1945–1946
    J. Leighton Stuart, 1946–
  To France
    Jefferson Caffrey, 1944–1949
  To Italy
    James C. Dunn, 1946–

* Dates are dates of confirmation and resignation, respectively.
† Served as acting chairman for a brief time.

☆ ☆ ☆ ☆ ☆

Acknowledgments

MANY PERSONS, living and dead, have contributed a great deal to this book, and in the doling out of praise or censure, as the case may be, their shares should not be overlooked. Equally not to be overlooked are those persons who could have contributed much but, instead, contributed nothing. For a variety of reasons, I was unable to interview or correspond with certain individuals who knew James Forrestal quite well. Some of these persons were motivated by a desire to protect the privacy of a dead friend, and I was unable to persuade them that Forrestal's privacy had long since been invaded by gossip, rumor, and hearsay. Perhaps, I suggested, there was something to be gained by substituting facts, which may be unpleasant but are not malicious, for gossip which is both unpleasant and malicious. I failed to convince them, and that of course was my loss; but it was also, I think, Forrestal's loss.

Fortunately, those of Forrestal's friends and associates who were helpful far outnumber those who were not, and I am glad to have a long list of persons to thank. To begin with, I owe a debt to his brother, Henry L. A. Forrestal. Without his cooperation the book would have been a much more difficult undertaking. I want also to thank Seymour Lawrence,

Director of the Atlantic Monthly Press, for making available to me the research notes and papers of John McClain. Much of this material broadened and deepened my own knowledge of Forrestal's life prior to his departure for Washington in 1940.

My gratitude to those who were willing to be interviewed, or who supplied letters and other documents by or about Forrestal—or who were otherwise cooperative—my gratitude, in short, to those who in a very real sense made the study possible is beyond measure. Not all of them can be listed here, and it is obvious that some contributed much more than others. But all those mentioned were helpful or tried to be helpful, and they therefore are listed in alphabetical order: Dean Acheson, Hanson W. Baldwin, Brandon Barringer, Philip E. Barringer, Admiral J. W. Boundy, Aileen Branca, Marie Briggs, James F. Byrnes, C. Lawton Campbell, Stanley Campbell, Dan Caulkins, Earle D. Chesney, Marquis Childs, David H. Clark, M.D.; Clark M. Clifford, John T. Connor, Mathias F. Correa, Charles F. Detmar, Jr.; Albert Deutsch, Thomas E. Dewey, Richardson Dilworth, Frederick Dodson, Eugene Duffield, Walter G. Dunnington, Clair Engle, United States Senator; Erik H. Erikson, Russell Forgan, Admiral John E. Gingrich, Jerry Greene, Brandon Grove, Jr.; Fowler V. Harper, H. Struve Hensel, Austin Hoyt, Palmer Hoyt, Don D. Jackson, M.D.; Louis Johnson, Arthur Krock, Admiral Paul F. Lee, Frank P. Leslie, Hugh L'Etang, M.D.; Marx Leva, Robert Lovett, Dean Mathey, William C. Menninger, M.D.; Walter Millis, Alfred Putnam, George N. Raines, M.D.; Sam Rayburn, Joseph E. Ridder, W. S. S. Rodgers, Admiral Murray L. Royar, Edgar Scott, Edward L. Shea, Kenneth R. Smith, Harry S Truman, Caleb Warner, Westmore Willcox, and Admiral William Brent Young.

I was fortunate to have the able research assistance of Sheilah Rosenhack, Dorothy Stern, and (through John McClain) Ellen A. Pryor and Beverly Gary. Ralph D.

Quinter, III, was also a research assistant, but he was much more than that. The book contains very few chapters that were not substantially improved by his comments and criticisms.

Finally, there are those who provided the money, the released time from other duties, and the places in which to work. For money, time, and facilities my thanks go to Haverford College, Stanford University, Princeton University, and the Center for Advanced Study in the Behavioral Sciences. Among the individuals involved—and it is of course individuals who sign checks, allocate space, and grant leaves-of-absence—I wish to mention particularly President Hugh Borton of Haverford College, Albert H. Bowker, former Dean of the Stanford Graduate Division, William S. Dix of the Princeton University Library, and Ralph W. Tyler and Preston Cutler of the Behavioral Sciences Center.

For encouragement I am indebted to Emile Capouya, former Senior Editor of The Macmillan Company, and James Oliver Brown of James Brown Associates. Permission to reproduce two portrait photographs of Forrestal was kindly granted by Philippe Halsman and Ollie Atkins. I wish to thank the *New York Herald Tribune* and Princeton University for permission to quote from *The Forrestal Diaries,* edited by Walter Millis and published by Viking in 1951; Time, Inc., for permission to quote from the *Memoirs of Harry S Truman,* Vol. I © 1955, Time, Inc., and Vol. II © 1956, Time, Inc.; and Mrs. George Bambridge and Doubleday & Company, Inc., for permission to reprint Rudyard Kipling's "Tommy" from *Rudyard Kipling's Verse: Definitive Edition,* and "Dane-geld," copyright 1911, by Rudyard Kipling and C. R. L. Fletcher. The manuscript was ably typed by Helen Aplin, Patricia Case, Viola Joyce, and Jacqueline Spencer.

I need hardly add that no one mentioned is responsible for any error of fact or interpretation; if errors there be, I alone am culpable. Nor should it be construed that those mentioned approve of or agree with my interpretation of the life and career of James Forrestal. Some approve or agree, and some do not; my gratitude, in any case, extends to them all.

ARNOLD A. ROGOW

STANFORD, CALIFORNIA
August 1, 1963

INDEX

Index

DATE DUE

DATE DUE			
MAY 5 '75			
GAYLORD			PRINTED IN U.S.A.

E
748
F 68
R6

23617

*Photograph of Forrestal taken by Philippe Halsman in August, 1947.
Copyright by Philippe Halsman, and used with permission.*

Forrestal on March 3, 1949. His resignation as Defense Secretary, effective on or about March 31, had just been announced.

...mes and Josephine Forrestal, with their son Peter, in 1942.

...rrestal shortly after taking the oath of office as Navy Secretary, May 19, 1944. Others in ...e official Navy photograph are (left to right): Senator John H. Overton, Assistant Navy ...cretary for Air Artemus Gates, Assistant Navy Secretary Ralph A. Bard, Representative ...rl Vinson, Senator David I. Walsh, Forrestal, Admiral Ernest J. King, Rear Admiral ...homas L. Gatch, Representative Melvin J. Maas, and Senator James J. Davis.

Josephine Forrestal
in late 1946 or early 1947.

JAMES
FORRESTAL

JAMES
FORRESTAL

A Study of

Personality, Politics, and Policy

ARNOLD A. ROGOW

The Macmillan Company, New York